Reviewing European Union Accession

Law in Eastern Europe

A SERIES PUBLISHED IN COOPERATION WITH LEIDEN UNIVERSITY
AND THE UNIVERSITIES OF TARTU AND GRAZ

General Editor

Joseph Marko

VOLUME 67

The titles published in this series are listed at *brill.com/laee*

Reviewing European Union Accession

Unexpected Results, Spillover Effects, and Externalities

Edited by

Tom Hashimoto
Michael Rhimes

BRILL

NIJHOFF

LEIDEN | BOSTON

Library of Congress Cataloging-in-Publication Data

Names: Hashimoto, Tom, editor. | Rhimes, Michael, editor.
Title: Reviewing European Union accession : unexpected results, spillover
   effects, and externalities / edited by Tom Hashimoto, Michael Rhimes.
Description: Leiden ; Boston : Brill/Nijhoff, 2017. | Series: Law in Eastern
   Europe ; volume 67 | Includes bibliographical references and index.
Identifiers: LCCN 2017034324 (print) | LCCN 2017035112 (ebook) | ISBN
   9789004352070 (E-book) | ISBN 9789004316478 (hardback : alk. paper)
Subjects: LCSH: International and municipal law--European Union countries. |
   Law--European Union countries--International unification. | European
   Union--Europe, Central. | European Union--Europe, Eastern. | European
   Union--Economic integration. | European Union countries--Politics and
   government.
Classification: LCC KJE969 (ebook) | LCC KJE969 .R48 2017 (print) | DDC
   341.242/24--dc23
LC record available at https://lccn.loc.gov/2017034324

Typeface for the Latin, Greek, and Cyrillic scripts: "Brill". See and download: brill.com/brill-typeface.

ISSN 0075-823X
ISBN 978-90-04-31647-8 (hardback)
ISBN 978-90-04-35207-0 (e-book)

Printed by Printforce, the Netherlands

Contents

List of Illustrations

Figures

Graphs

Tables

Notes on Contributors

Ana Bojinović Fenko
PhD (Ljubljana); Associate Professor and Head of the International Relations Chair, University of Ljubljana, Slovenia.

In her research, she focuses on issues such as "Small States and Parliamentary Diplomacy: Slovenia and the Mediterranean" (co-authored, *Mediterranean Quarterly*, 2016), "Compatibility of Regionalizing Actors' Activities in the Mediterranean Region: What Kind of Opportunity for the European Union?" (*Journal of Southeast European & Black Sea Studies*, 2012), and "From the Balkans to Central Europe and back: Foreign Policy of Slovenia" (co-authored, in *The Foreign policies of Post-Yugoslav States: From Yugoslavia to Europe*, Palgrave Macmillan, 2014). She is currently co-editor of *International Journal of Euro-Mediterranean Studies*.

Laura Chappell
PhD (Birmingham); Lecturer in European Politics, University of Surrey, UK.

Her research focuses on the Common Security and Defence Policy encompassing European strategic culture, the Battlegroup Concept, defence capability development, EU military operations, and civilian missions as well as Polish and German security and defence policies. She has published a number of articles and book chapters on these areas as well as co-editing a book on the EU, Strategy and Security Policy, published by Routledge in 2016. Her monograph on Germany, Poland and the Common Security and Defence Policy was published by Palgrave Macmillan in 2012. She is currently co-editor of *European Security*.

Sandra Fernandes
PhD (Sciences Po); Professor, University of Minho, Centre for Research in Political Science (CICP), Portugal.

She conducts research on the European Union, the relationship between the European Union and Russia, foreign policy analysis, and international security. She has been publishing on these issues, as for instance (*In*)*Secure Europe. European Union, Russia and the Atlantic Alliance: The Institutionalization of a Strategic Relationship* (Principia, Lisbon, 2005) which won the Jacques Delors Prize, and her latest publication, "EU-Russia Relations and Norms Diffusion: The Role of Non-State Actors", in R. Piet and L. Simão (eds.), *Security in Shared Neighbourhoods: Foreign Policy of Russia Turkey, and the EU* (Palgrave MacMillan, London, 2016).

Sergiu Gherghina

PhD (Leiden); Lecturer in Comparative Politics, University of Glasgow, UK.

His research focuses on party politics, political participation, legislative behavior, direct democracy, and Central and Eastern European politics. He published in a range of international peer-reviewed journals as well as authored and edited several books examining political parties, elections and democratization. He is the guest editor of two special issues on political participation (*East European Politics*) and appointed elites in Western Europe (*Acta Politica*), and is the author of a monograph on party organization and electoral volatility in Central and Eastern Europe.

Mariusz Jerzy Golecki

LL.M. (Cambridge), PhD (Łódź), LL.D./dr. hab. (Łódź); Professor and Director of Laboratory for Cognitive Research in Law, University of Łódź, Poland.

He expertizes in law and economics, jurisprudence, cognitive legal theory and comparative law. His research concentrates on contract law, tort law, corporate governance, and EU law, and served as Marie-Curie Fellow at the University of Hamburg, Visiting Scholar at the University of Cambridge, Visiting Professor at Keio University and ICU in Tokyo, and John von Neumann Senior Research Visiting Scholar at University of Debrecen. He also teaches within a framework of the European Master in Law and Economics Program coordinated by the Erasmus University in Rotterdam. He is a member of the Board of Directors of the Polish Association of Law and Economics, and the Editorial Board of the *Economic Analysis of Law in European Legal Scholarship* (Springer). Author of 5 books and about 60 articles.

Amelia Hadfield

PhD (Kent Brussels), SF HEA; Jean Monnet Chair in European Foreign Affairs and Director of the Centre for European Studies, Canterbury Christ Church University, UK.

She combines research, teaching, consultancy, and doctoral supervision on key aspects of European foreign affairs. Her areas of expertise include Common Security and Defence Policy, EU-Russia Energy Relations, EU Neighbourhood Policy, EU Development policy (with a focus on sub-Saharan Africa), the strategic role of the Arctic, and the role of energy security within the broader framework of EU foreign policy and energy governance. She is currently completing research monographs on the development and application of sovereignty, contemporary foreign policy analysis, the foreign policy of EU Member States, as well as articles on EU-Russian energy geopolitics and a retrospective of the EU's neighborhood policy.

Tom Hashimoto

LL.M. (EMLE), DPhil Candidate (Oxon), FHEA; Director of MSc in Financial Economics, ISM University of Management and Economics, Lithuania; Lecturer of International Relations and Economics, Vistula University, Poland.

He specializes in post-socialist financial center development and regulatory reforms. His foci are financial institutional reforms, collective political will, and socio-legal philosophy behind the economic transition. His commentaries can be found in CE *Financial Observer*, published by the National Bank of Poland. He is a recipient of Career Integration Fellowship from CERGE-EI, and teaches a summer course on H.L.A. Hart (jurisprudence) for pupils at Oxford.

Vratislav Havlík

PhD (Masaryk); Assistant Professor, Masaryk University, the Czech Republic.

His research focuses on Europeanization, multi-level governance, paradiplomacy and the role of cities in the EU, and further on Hungarian and German politics and Hungarian-Slovak relations. He is the author of the monograph *Města jako partner v procesu vládnutí* (*Cities as Partner in Governance Process*, 2013). He has also published various research articles mainly dealing with participation of sub-state actors in European governance and current Hungarian politics.

Balázs Horváthy

JD (dr jur, Eötvös Loránd), PhD (Eötvös Loránd); Research fellow, HAS Centre for Social Sciences, Hungary; Associate Professor, Széchenyi István University, Hungary.

His current research interests include Member States' policy leeway in EU law, integration of societal values in EU trade law, and "Trade and Environment" issues. He teaches courses in EU public law and EU Policies. He is a member of the Lendület-HPOPs Research Group on "The Policy Opportunities of Hungary in the EU" since 2013.

Hiroshi Kaneko

PhD Candidate (Kozminski); independent researcher, Poland.

He specializes in judicial control over administration in Poland and Japan, as well as reception of law in Asia and in Eastern Europe. His recent publications include "Ścieżka reform sądowej kontroli administracyjnych w Japonii i w Polsce (The Reform Path of Judicial Review of Administrative Acts in Japan and Poland)", *Państwo i Prawo* (2016) and "Dlaczego w Japonii sąd często odrzuca skargi w sprawach administracyjnych? (Why in Japan Courts Often Reject Complaints in Administrative Issues?)", *Państwo i Prawo* (forthcoming).

Alar Kilp
PhD (Tartu); Lecturer in Comparative Politics, University of Tartu, Estonia.

His research specializes in religion and politics as well as church-state relations in post-communist Europe. He has co-edited a special issue on "Religion, the Russian Nation and the State: Domestic and International Dimensions" (*Religion, State and Society*, 2013), published a paper on religious nation in a volume by Brille and several articles in *Religion, State and Society*, *Studies in Church History*, and *Proceedings of Estonian National Defence College*.

Olga Khrushcheva
PhD (Nottingham Trent); Lecturer in Politics at Manchester Metropolitan University, UK.

Her interests include Russian energy policy, EU energy policy, and EU-Russia energy relations. She also teaches security studies and European politics at the Manchester Metropolitan University. Her recent publications include "The Arctic in the Political Discourse of Russian Leaders: The National Pride and Economic Ambitions", *East European Politics* (with M. Poberezhskaya, 2016) and "The Future of EU-Russia Energy Relations in the Context of Decarbonisation", *Geopolitics* (with T. Maltby, 2016).

Simon Lightfoot
PhD (Nottingham Trent); Senior Lecturer in European Politics, University of Leeds, UK.

His research focuses on the politics of foreign aid, with an emphasis on foreign aid in Central and Eastern European donor countries and UK aid. He is author of *New Europe's New Development Aid* (with B. Szent-Iványi, Routledge, 2015) and editor of *Development Cooperation of the "New" EU Member States Beyond Europeanization* (with O. Horký-Hlucháň, Springer, 2015).

Katarína Lezová
PhD (Goldsmiths London); Goldsmiths, University of London, UK.

Her research has focused on examining the question of Slovakian foreign policy towards Kosovo's unilateral declaration of independence and exploring how governments manage foreign policy issues that bring the demands from the EU into conflict with domestic politics. Her latest contribution was to the Special Issue of *Europe-Asia Studies* dealing with self-determination after Kosovo.

Ondřej Mocek
PhD (Masaryk); Specialist, Masaryk University, the Czech Republic.

His research focuses on the European Union, especially the European Parliament and the behavior of MEPs, while he is also interested in local Czech politics. He mainly utilizes quantitative analysis, and his most resent articles are based on the research on roll call votes in the European Parliament e.g. "Roll Call Votes in the European Parliament: A Good Sample or a Poisoned Dead End?" and "Analysis of the Voting Behaviour of Czech Members of European Parliament in Areas of the Europe 2020 Strategy."

Marek Neuman

PhD (Groningen); Assistant Professor, University of Groningen, the Netherlands.

He works on three research strands. The first deals with the role Central and Eastern European countries play in the European Union's foreign policy. The second strand takes particular interest in uncovering the dynamics behind the EU's relations with the Russian Federation and other Eastern European countries. The third, and most recent one, ventures into the area of perception, trying to understand how the European Union's foreign policy is perceived in third countries.

Marianna Poberezhskaya

PhD (Nottingham), FHEA; Lecturer in International Relations, Nottingham Trent University, UK.

Her research interests include environmental communication, Russian climate politics, and the political economy of mass media. She has recently published a manuscript *Communicating Climate Change in Russia: State and Propaganda* (Routledge, 2016) as well as the following articles: "Media Coverage of Climate Change in Russia: Governmental Bias and Climate Silence", *Public Understanding of Science* (2015) and "Measuring and Modelling Russian Newspaper Coverage of Climate Change", *Global Environmental Change* (2016, with C. Boussalis and T. Coan).

Jure Požgan

PhD Candidate (Ljubljana); Teaching Assistant, University of Ljubljana, Slovenia.

His research focuses on the External Action of the EU (with a special emphasis on EU-ACP relations), Common Foreign and Security Policy, and the role of the EU in post-conflict reconstruction in Kosovo. He is currently completing his PhD on the normative power of the EU. He also teaches in International Relations and European Studies BA programs at the University of Ljubljana.

Michael Rhimes

LLB (Hons) (Lond), BCL (Oxon); Fourth référendaire to Judge Christopher Vajda, Court of Justice of the European Union, Luxembourg.

He has wide interests in the law, having previously published on trade defense measures and standing under EU law. He also has an interest in fundamental rights and constitutional matters, and writes regularly for online publications.

Boyka Stefanova

PhD (Delaware); Professor, University of Texas at San Antonio, USA.

Her research interests focus on political conflict, European governance, territoriality and politics in the context of European integration, and security issues in Europe. She has published three books: *The European Union beyond the Crisis* (editor, Lexington Books, 2014), *The Europeanization of Conflict Resolution* (Manchester University Press, 2011), and *The War on Terror in Comparative Perspective* (co-edited with Mark Miller, Palgrave Macmillan, 2007). Her new book, *The European Union and Europe's New Regionalism: The Challenge of Enlargement, Neighborhood, and Globalization* (Palgrave Macmillan) advances a new approach to studying the EU's regional and global relevance by bringing together its enlargement, neighborhood, Transatlantic, and key Eurasian policies into an integral project of regionalism.

Balázs Szent-Iványi

PhD (Corvinus); Lecturer in Politics and International Relations, Aston University, UK; Associate Professor in International Political Economy, Corvinus University Budapest, Hungary.

His research focuses on the political economy of foreign aid, with an emphasis on how foreign aid decisions are made in the emerging Central and Eastern European donor countries, as well as foreign direct investment in Central and Eastern Europe (especially in East Central Europe). His latest book, an edited volume entitled *Foreign Direct Investment in Central and Eastern Europe: Post-crisis Perspectives*, has been published with Palgrave in 2017.

Robert Summerby-Murray

PhD (Toronto); Professor of Geography and Environmental Studies, President and Vice-Chancellor, Saint Mary's University, Canada.

He has promoted international mobility and intercultural learning throughout his professorial and administrative career. His other research interests include environmental histories and industrial heritage in Atlantic Canada and global geopolitics in Europe and North America. Recent publications appear in the *London Journal of Canadian Studies* (2015, 2016), the *European Journal of Higher Education* (2015, with Amelia Hadfield), and *The Round Table: the Commonwealth Journal of International Affairs* (2017). He serves on committees of Universities Canada, the Atlantic School of Theology, and a national round table of the Canadian Bureau of International Education. He is a 3M National Teaching Fellow (2006) and an elected Fellow of the Royal Canadian Geographical Society.

Paweł Tokarski

PhD (Warsaw School of Economics); Senior Associate, the German Institute for International and Security Affairs (SWP).

He specializes in policy-oriented research concerning the stabilization and reform processes in the Euro area as well as the economic and political situation in France, Southern Europe, and Poland. He is a regular commentator on these topics in international media. His recent publications include, "Better off Without: What if the EU Had Never Created the Euro?", in "What if the EU ...?": An Exercise in Counterfactual Thinking to Address Current Dilemmas, *DGAP Analyse* (October 2014) No.19 and "Economic Reforms in France", *SWP Comments* 2014/C 39 (September 2014).

Anna Visvizi

PhD (Warwick); Head of Research, Institute of East-Central Europe (IESW), Poland; Associate Professor, Deree – The American College of Greece.

She is a political scientist and economist, editor, and research consultant with extensive experience in academia and the think-tank sector in Europe and the U.S. Her expertise spans four interrelated areas of research: the political economy of European integration, including the crisis in Greece; politics, economy, and security in Central Europe, especially the Visegrad (V4) countries; global safety and security, including Transatlantic relations, and theoretical dimensions of these processes.

Tamas Dezso Ziegler

JD (dr jur, *Pázmány Péter Catholic*), PhD (*Széchenyi István*); Research Fellow, Hungarian Academy of Sciences; Senior Lecturer, *Eötvös Loránd* University, Hungary.

He specializes in EU/comparative commercial law, justice and home affairs, and EU private international law. He has conducted various research projects at Free University Berlin, Max Planck Institute for Comparative and International Private Law in Hamburg, Swiss Institute of Comparative Law in Lausanne, Fordham University School of Law, Columbia University, and the University of Aberdeen. In practice, he has been working for OSCE, ODIHR, and Baker & McKenzie, among other major law firms.

Introduction: Reviewing 2014, Welcoming 2017, and Envisioning 2020

Tom Hashimoto and Michael Rhimes

While we happily celebrate the 10 year anniversary of Bulgarian and Romanian Accession to the European Union, the years ahead are likely to be overcast by the process of the United Kingdom's withdrawal from the Union, tensions in EU-Russia relations over Ukraine, and the rise of Eurosceptic populism. Yet, we must remember that politicians and officials in Central and Eastern Europe (CEE), too, are presented with clear challenges, as the CEE states presented a spectrum of novel issues for the Union in the two waves of accession in 2004 and 2007. Indeed, even after accession, Slovenia, for example, employed 245 graduate and undergraduate students to support diplomatic activities during its Presidency of the Council of the EU in 2008[1] – in other words, the Member States who have recently acceded to the Union do not necessarily have the luxury of extensive specialization in every of the many issues of European importance. This makes the scholarly discussion of such issues ever more critical. It is in this spirit that this book has been written, whose first aim is to, in a sense, accept the shared cognizance of being overwhelmed by divergent and yet pressing issues surrounding accession to the Union, and evaluate critically how the intra- and supra-national discussion has taken place and taken form.

To this extent, the book is divided into five sections, containing a total of seventeen chapters. The first section deals with legal aspects of the European Union beyond what is traditionally conceived of as the core diet of EU law. The second section touches on 'skepticism' as an overarching concern, while the third section focuses on education and values. The fourth section deals with EU foreign policy and various national initiatives within that framework, and the final section deals with EU-Russia relations.

A central theme running through these chapters, as indicated by the title, is the focus on *spillover effects, unexpected results, and externalities* in respect of the accession of the CEE states to what is now the European Union. As we see it, the European Union (and its two waves of Eastern Accession) is a highly complex regional project whose effects have spilled over to many areas of European polity in polycentric and multi-dimensional ways. The pooling

---

1 Sabina Kajnč, "Channels of Cooperation: A Case Study of Slovenia's Presidency of the EU", *EPIN Working Paper* (2009) No.21, 3.

of sovereignty, for example, has had implications not only from a political perspective, but from a constitutional one as well; issues that once were considered within the exclusive purview of a state now require supra-national and collective solutions. Many results were unexpected, and actors who were not in the initial process have been affected ('externalities'). For example, the creation of 'European' citizenship has led to not only economic ramifications on social security schemes but broader conceptual issues of multiculturalism and, perhaps, a search for a European identity that, certainly in some quarters, is lacking.

The stylistic choice for the book reflects our own editorial philosophies and epistemological traditions. Each chapter contains an abstract, keywords, and bibliography (unlike the other volumes published in this book series), so that readers are able to grasp the main arguments and share the scholarly works each chapter refers to. The bibliographies in this book exclude primary sources, news articles, and governmental reports as they are sufficiently treated in each analysis and cited in the footnotes. Thus, our bibliographies are the collections of analytical works from which our constructive discussion shall commence. To this end, works by the same author are listed in an anti-chronological manner (sometimes known as the OUP style) with an assumption that scholars reflect and develop their older works as time goes by.

This book is hardly the only project dedicated to the 10 year anniversaries of the 2004/2007 accessions, and certainly not the promptest. However, the lapse of time offers a certain advantage in being able to look back with greater maturity of thought, prompting more interesting reflections on the longer-term projections and consequences of CEE accession. We therefore *review* 2014, *welcome* 2017, *and envision* 2020, the year which many EU-level policies will be revisited within the 'Europe 2020' strategy framework. It is an apt moment to analyze and reflect upon a project that has seen an unprecedented investment of capital and will, both social and political, from so many different actors. This, of course, prompts critical insight into whether these efforts are worth it. On one hand, we can list numerous regulations and treaties within the scope of legal harmonization (or 'Europeanization' – the term which we would like to avoid due to ambiguous and multiple definitions). On the other hand, social, political, and economic observers are ready to question the efficiency and expediency of many of the projects and broader policies undertaken by the Union. Implementation is, thus, the ignition key for this collective work, and we pursue inter-disciplinary research as a strategy to facilitate constructive discussions for 2020.

Finally, this book is a result of endless effort and assuring commitment by our industrious editorial assistants, Danielle Buckett, Xhensila Gaba, Ewa

Lipińska, and Anna Lukina. They deserve our thanks and our respect for their unfailing commitment to this work. In that regard, we cannot fail to mention Ms. Ingeborg van der Laan whose unremitting and benign assistance from Brill has been fundamental to our endeavor, and Prof. William Simons, former editor of the *Law in Eastern Europe* series who first encouraged us to gather not only our brains, but also our passions to the presented work. So, we thank you.

Tom Hashimoto, LLM (EMLE), FHEA
Michael Rhimes, LLB (Hons) (Lond), BCL (Oxon)

PART 1

Law – Developing Norms

∴

CHAPTER 1

Towards Adverse Spillover Effect?
The Judicialization of the EU and the Changing
Nature of Judicial Governance after Enlargement

Mariusz Jerzy Golecki

Abstract

The enactment of the Treaty on Functioning of the European Union resulted in many national court judgments within the Union, in which the concept of "sovereignty" plays an important role. This chapter thus focuses on the legal discourse surrounding "sovereignty" presented by the Constitutional Courts in Poland, Germany, Hungary, and the Czech Republic, and analyzes how these courts applied the principle known as the "primacy of EU law" in relation to the supremacy of national constitutional law. The different doctrines adopted by these Courts do not necessarily lead to the inefficacy of EU law, as they function as a part of judicial dialogue between the new Member States and the EU (the Court of Justice in particular) towards further harmonization in judicial governance. While the judicial dialogue among the Member States may lead to their unified position against the principle of the primacy of EU law (i.e. adverse spillover effect), the judicialization of the EU provides an additional tool for judicial governance in Central and Eastern Europe.

Keywords

judicialization – judicial governance – primacy of EU law – Constitutional Courts

1 Introduction

Recent developments in the law of the European Union raised a question concerning the scope of application and the meaning of the principle of the "primacy of EU law" within the context of judicial rulings. The Constitutional Courts in Poland, Hungary and the Czech Republic adopted different doctrines regarding the principle of primacy (or the autonomy between EU law and the national constitutional law). In Poland, the doctrine of the constitutional supremacy of the Polish Constitution has been adopted, whereas the Czech Constitutional Court adopted the doctrine of the constitutional review of EU law. Finally the position adopted by the Hungarian Constitutional Court was based on the doctrine of absolute separation between the Hungarian Constitution and EU law. Later on, the doctrines of all three constitutional courts in Central and Eastern Europe (CEE) converged under the shadow of the judgments of the German Constitutional Court concerning the constitutionality of the enactment of the Treaty on Functioning of the European Union (TFEU). The enactment of the Treaty has thus resulted in judicial discussions on sovereignty, a discourse significant not only to national constitutionalism(s), but also for the development of the European legal order.

It seems that the judicial discourse in Europe has been split into two parallel yet not necessarily congruent relationships: between the judiciary in Member States and the Court of Justice of the EU (CJEU) on one hand (i.e. legal harmonization), and among Constitutional Courts plus the CJEU on the other. The former type of judicial dialogue traditionally plays an important if not crucial role in preserving efficacy of EU law and its applicability in Member States. The later *constitutional* dialogue seems to be split between the vertical and the horizontal dimension, namely the dialogue with the CJEU and the dialogue with other Constitutional Courts. Such a Neofunctionalist approach to European integration vividly addresses the concerns in CEE where the Courts find themselves in the midst of political struggle for power especially in Hungary.

2   The Construction of European Legal Order Trough Judicial Monologue

The autonomous character of EU law has been established due to the process based on judicial doctrine of the autonomy of the European Communities and later on the European Union as a separate legal order. The autonomy has been shaped by series of cases in which the European Court of Justice (ECJ, a predecessor of the CJEU) established the doctrine of primacy of EC law over the legal systems of the Member States. In two benchmark cases the ECJ introduced this concept, stating in Case 26/62 *Van Gend en Loos* [1963], that the EC law created "a new legal order" and reaffirming this in later Case 6/64 Costa v. ENEL [1964], where it has been emphasized that the Communities in reality are governed by their "own legal system." These developments gave rise to the assertion that EC law must be superior over any other legal system of any Member State. The content of this doctrine has albeit never been clear.

The question arises how to solve the potential conflict between EC law and the *constitution* of any Member State. One potential solution to this problem has been unsuccessfully offered by the authors of the Treaty establishing a Constitution for Europe. The art. I-6 of the Treaty contained the explicit statement concerning the primacy of the EU legal order:

> The Constitution and law adopted by the institutions of the Union in exercising competences conferred on it shall have primacy over the law of the Member States.

Additionally art. I-6 has been supported by the political declaration of the Member States, according to which the explicit statement on the primacy of EU law should have not been treated as constitutive in a sense that it was intended to create a new legal principle. According to the declaration the principle of primacy was rather to be found as declaratory and based on the long standing doctrine having been established by the European Courts, since Declaration 1 reads as follows:

> The Conference notes that Article I-6 reflects existing case-law of the Court of Justice of the European Communities and of the Court of First Instance.

The idea of inserting the primacy claim into the system of quasi constitutional rules on European level failed when the Constitution for Europe was rejected by voters in France in May 2005.[1] The other solution was to be found and has been founded indeed. The solution based on the political obligation rather than on the existence of the explicit rule is to be found in the Treaty on Functioning of the European Union (TFEU). The obvious primacy claim of article I-6 has been removed from Lisbon Treaty and eventually expressed in Declaration 17 annexed to its Final Act:

> The Conference recalls that, in accordance with well settled case law of the Court of Justice of the European Union, the Treaties and the law adopted by the Union on the basis of the Treaties have primacy over the law of Member States, under the conditions laid down by the said case law.

Most interestingly, the Conference has additionally decided to attach the Opinion of the Council Legal Service on the primacy of EC law as set out in 11197/07 (JUR 260). The opinion explicitly refers to the well-established judicial practice:

---

1   *Le Monde* (27 May 2005), available at <http://www.lemonde.fr/societe/infographie/2005/05/27/les-resultats-departement-par-departement_655042_3224.html>.

It results from the case-law of the Court of Justice that primacy of EC law
is a cornerstone principle of Community law. According to the Court, this
principle is inherent to the specific nature of the European Community.

This solution creates a very interesting puzzle, because in many legal systems
the concept of sovereignty sets out limits for the application of the principle of
"superiority." From the functional perspective, the concept (or a constitutional
principle) of sovereignty plays an important role, creating a ground for the institutionalized *Kompetenz-Kompetenz* dilemma:[2] the question arises whether
the interactive character of EU law and the EU as an intergovernmental and
multilevel structure leads to any deviation from the traditional doctrine of
sovereignty. According to the traditional meaning of sovereignty (*a la* J. Austin or C. Schmitt), sovereignty is to be based on the idea of autonomy, exclu-
sivity, and independence (external aspect), while it is also associated with
superiority and concentration of undivided power (internal aspect). Its jur-
isprudential interpretations range from H.L.A. Hart and H. Kelsen to different constitutional doctrines such as ultra vires in English law, or the principle
of constitutional sovereignty in Germany, France, Poland, and Spain. The question remains whether the development of the EU law in general and the content of the principle of superiority/primacy, formally constructed in judgments
of the ECJ/CJEU, has added anything to this traditional picture.

It is possible to refer to the competing concept of sovereignty based on the
notion of inclusion and influence upon other states rather than on autonomy
and exclusion. It is linked to the governance and the governability, associated
with such authors as U. Beck and G. Arigghi.[3] The concept of the inclusive sovereignty is based on the opposition between the center of political, economic
or legal affairs and the peripheries. According to this interpretation, inclusive

---

2   For the definition of sovereignty in *Kompetenz-Kompetenz* (i.e. competence of a court to
    rule comes from its competence on the case at hand), see Paul Laband, *Das Staatsrecht des
    Deutschen Reiches* (*The Constitutional Right of the German State*), vol.2 (Mohr, Tübingen,
    1901), 85–88. MacCormick emphasized the unresolved character of competing claims to
    superiority, observing that: "[t]he legal systems of member-states and their common legal
    system of EC law are distinct but interacting systems of law, and hierarchical relationships of
    validity within criteria of validity proper to distinct systems do not add up to any sort of all-
    purpose superiority of one system over another. It follows also that the interpretative power
    of the highest decision-making authorities of the different systems must be, as to each sys-
    tem, ultimate." Neil MacCormick, *Questioning Sovereignty* (Oxford University Press, Oxford,
    1999), 118.
3   Urlich Beck, *Risk Society: Towards a New Modernity* (SAGE, New Delhi, 1992); and Giovanni
    Arrighi, *The Long Twentieth Century: Money, Power and the Origin of Our Times* (Verso, Lon-
    don, 1994).

sovereignty is understood as an ability to maintain control over some pivotal parameters and at the same time to influence other agents (e.g. states) acting within a wider structure of governance or managerial framework such as global financial market, regional and international organizations. Inclusive sovereignty is understood not in negative but rather in positive way as an ability to play an important role in a wider international (or regional) system. The centers of such power do not necessarily coincide with traditional states, since states are understood as a nexus of different multilevel structures of governance. The concepts of inclusive sovereignty could thus successfully be integrated with legal discourse pertaining to the problem of the superiority principle and the very nature of EU law. In cases such as *Van Gend en Loos* [1963], *Costa v. ENEL* [1964], *Internationale Handelsgesellschaft* [1970], *Amministrazione delle Finanze dello Stato v. Simmenthal SpA* [1978] and in the more recent judgments e.g. *Kadi and Al Barakaat v. Council* [2008], the EU courts adopted the concept of *exclusive* sovereignty, whereas the jurisprudence of some constitutional courts, e.g. German, Polish, and Spanish adopted a more refined concept of sovereignty based on a multilevel and multi-centric (i.e. inclusive) character of law in Europe.

3   After Enlargement: Judicial Dialogue among Different Constitutional Doctrines

Over the years, the monologue of the Court of Justice has transformed into more refined and complex version of judicial discourse: judicial dialogue. Two types of judicial dialogue may be distinguished. Firstly, the vertical dialogue between the ECJ/CJEU and the supreme and other courts of Member States. The institutional framework for this kind of dialogue is based on the preliminary reference procedure based on art. 267 of the TFEU.[4] The other type of judicial dialogue is rather informal and based on observation, adjustment, and coordination of the judicial practice of different judicial institutions in the Member States. This kind of judicial dialogue may take different forms, varying form explicit references to other courts' decisions to implicit references to some concepts and doctrines applied by other courts in Member States.[5]

---

4 Adam Łazowski (ed.), *The Application of EU Law in the New Member States: Brave New World* (T.M.C. Asser Press, The Hague, 2010).

5 Mathias Kumm, "The Jurisprudence of Constitutional Conflict: Constitutional Supremacy in Europe before and after the Constitutional Treaty", 11(3) *European Law Journal* (2005), 262–307.

Poland – The Doctrine of (National) Constitutional Supremacy

In three judgments the Polish Constitutional Tribunal established a refined doctrine of (national) constitutional supremacy and its limits. It began when the Court found the European Arrest Warrant Framework Decision (EAW) unconstitutional as the Polish Constitution explicitly prohibited extradition of Polish citizens.[6] The Court suspended the annulment of the EAW for an 18-month adjustment, during which time the Polish Constitution was changed, enabling the operation of the EAW in Poland. A similar interaction took place in Germany, with the German Constitutional Court also finding the framework decision unconstitutional.[7] However, the immediate annulment of the European Arrest Warrant Framework Decision put Germany in a difficult situation.[8] The validity of EU law has been questioned and the EAW had not been operative for some period of time.

In another decision concerning the constitutionality of the Treaty of accession between Poland and the EU, the Polish Constitutional Tribunal emphasized the need for cooperation and political participation, criticizing the extension of the pro-European interpretation of legal acts in Polish law. Departing from relatively traditional concept of supremacy as control over the interpretation of the Constitution, the Court reached the conclusion that the Constitution was interpreted in a manner sympathetic to EU law, but "[i]n no event may it lead to results contradicting the explicit wording of constitutional norms."[9] Additionally, the court explicitly established its right to the control of constitutionality over EU law and its potential contradiction with the Polish Constitution. The Court found, that:

> [t]he supremacy of the Constitution finds its confirmation in the constitutionally regulated mechanism of control of constitutionality of the Accession Treaty and acts which form its integral parts. This mechanism is based on the same principles as those on a basis of which the [Tribunal] may adjudicate upon constitutionality of ratified international agreements. In such a situation other acts of primary law of the EC and EU being parts of the Accession Treaty, however indirectly, become subject to the control of constitutionality.[10]

---

6   Polish Constitutional Tribunal, P1/05, 27.042005.

7   The German Federal Constitutional Court, 2 BvR 2236/04 of 18.7.2005.

8   Jan Komárek, "European Constitutionalism and the European Arrest Warrant: In Search of the Limits of 'Contrapunctual Principles'", 44(1) *Common Market Law Review* (2007), 9–40.

9   Polish Constitutional Tribunal, K18/04, 11.05.2005.

10   *Ibid.*

At the same time the Court sketched the wider concept of a multi-centric legal order and inclusive sovereignty, stressing the need for cooperation and participation within the EU lawmaking process. This reasoning was based on the assumption that the application of EU law is based on "coexistence of different legal rules produced by different law-making bodies and applied by various courts' structures."[11]

Finally, the Polish Constitutional court established a doctrine of constitutional *identity*, constituting the claim for sovereignty in particular areas strictly limited to basic constitutional principles and the protection of human rights. Thus, the source of sovereignty is found in the sophisticated concept of rights protection rather than in political power and its monopoly over the territory. This problem loomed on the horizon together with the doubts concerning the constitutionality of the TFEU. In the judgment concerning the Treaty, the Polish Constitutional Tribunal clearly articulated the concept of constitutional identity as a source of sovereignty which enables the state to participate in the EU within the constitutional limits. The Tribunal observed that:

> Article 90 of the Constitution, being a normative anchor to the state's sovereignty, determines the limits of conferring competences on the Union. This limit is constituted by the following factors determining constitutional identity of the Republic of Poland: the respect for the principles of Polish sovereign statehood, democracy, the principle of a state ruled by law, the principle of social justice, the principles determining the bases of the economic system, protection of human dignity and the constitutional rights and freedoms.[12]

Similar reservations to the unlimited primacy of EU law have been raised by the German Federal Constitutional Court, the Czech Constitutional Court and the Hungarian Constitutional Court. It has been suggested that the doctrine of sovereignty has been used by the constitutional courts in Central Europe primarily for domestic, internal reasons. Wojciech Sadurski has pointed out that the constitutional courts in the EU often attempt to gain recognition and legitimacy through the process of the protection of the national system against exuberant, extensive application of the principle of the primacy of EU law while it was not the case in any post-socialist new Member States.[13] The courts in Poland, Hungary, and the Czech Republic simply adopted the skepticism

---

11   *Ibid.*

12   Polish Constitutional Tribunal K 32/09, 24.11.2010.

13   Wojciech Sadurski. "'Solange, Chapter 3': Constitutional Courts in Central Europe – Democracy – European Union", 14(1) *European Law Journal* (2008), 1–35; and *id.*,

concerning the superiority of EC/EU law, having been expressed many years earlier by the German Federal Constitutional Tribunal in two waves of the so called "Solange" cases in 1974 and 1986.[14]

Germany – Voicing the Concern

The German Federal Constitutional Court has emphasized the need for constitutional control and protection of constitutional rights, concentrating on the relationship between the German Constitution and the development of EC/EU law. The court cautiously avoided direct invalidation of EC law, at the same time setting out the potential limits of constitutionality in respect of the application of EU law.[15] The recent case concerning the constitutionality of the TFEU entails the complete doctrine of sovereignty based on the concept of *Staatenverbund* – the Sovereign Association of Sovereign States. The Court explicitly referred to the development of the primacy of EU law, taking into account three fundamental issues: the implicit and vague character of the principle of the primacy of EU law, the unlimited power vested upon the Constitutional Tribunal in order to control and guard the constitutional order, and the character of the EU as the purpose-oriented association of interdependent rather than independent, but sovereign states. The Tribunal expressed these three concepts in the following three lucid passages:

1. The primacy of Union and Community law over national law is still not explicitly regulated. (par. 33)
2. The obligation under European law to respect the constituent power of the Member States as the masters of the Treaties corresponds to the non-transferable identity of the constitution (Article 79.3 of the Basic Law), which is not open to integration in this respect. Within the boundaries of its competences, the Federal Constitutional Court must review, where necessary, whether these principles are adhered to. (par. 235)
3. Article 24.1 of the Basic Law underlines that the Federal Republic of Germany takes part in the development of a European Union designed as an association of sovereign states (*Staatenverbund*) to which sovereign

---

Constitutionalism and the Enlargement of Europe (Oxford University Press, Oxford, 2012), 99–104.

14   German Federal Constitutional Court, Judgment of 29 May 1974, 37 BVerfG 27 and Judgment of 22 October 1986, 73 BVerfG 339.

15   Mathias Kumm, "Who is the Final Arbiter of Constitutionality in Europe?: Three Conceptions of the Relationship Between the German Federal Constitutional Court and the European Court of Justice", 36(2) *Common Market Law Review* (1999), 351–386.

powers are transferred. The concept of *Verbund* covers a close long-term association of states which remain sovereign. (par. 230)[16]

In a sense, states remain sovereign, as possessing the control over the degree of participation, the content of participation or lack thereof, in a similar way in which the Constitutional Tribunal possesses the control over constitutionality of EU law in Germany. Although, the Court boasts a strong history of compliance with EU law and only very rarely decides against the validity of EU law or its applicability in Germany.

Furthermore, the Court has referred to the concept of constitutional control exercised by national constitutional courts, emphasizing the procedural aspects of constitutional sovereignty. The Court reinforced the doctrine and commented on the practice of different supreme and constitutional courts in other EU Member States, considering these judgments as reflecting common constitutional principles and practices of the EU Member States. The Court observed that:

> The above-mentioned principles concerning the protection of the constitutional identity and of the limits of the transfer of sovereign powers to the European Union can also be found, with modifications depending on the existence or non-existence of unamendable elements in the respective national constitutions, in the constitutional law of many other Member States of the European Union [...][17] This applies to all constitutional organs, authorities and courts. It results from the constitutional

---

16   German Federal Constitutional Court, Judgment of 30 June 2009, BVerfG, 2 BvE 2/08.

17   The German Federal Constitutional Court explicitly referred to the following judgments: the Kingdom of Denmark: Hojesteret, Judgment of 6 April 1998 – I 361/1997 –, para. 9.8.; for the Republic of Estonia: Riigikohus, Judgment of 12 July 2012 – 3-4-1-6-12 –, sec. no. 128, 223; for the French Republic: Conseil constitutionnel, Decision no. 2006–540 DC of 27 July 2006, 19th recital; Decision no. 2011–631 DC of 9 June 2011, 45th recital; for Ireland: Supreme Court of Ireland, Crotty v. An Taoiseach <1987>, I.R. 713 <783>; S.P.U.C. (Ireland) Ltd. v. Grogan, <1989>, I.R. 753 <765>; for the Italian Republic: Corte costituzionale, Decision no. 183/1973; Decision no. 168/1991; for the Republic of Latvia: Satversmes tiesa, Judgment of 7 April 2009 – 2008-35-01 –, sec. no. 17; for the Republic of Poland: Trybunal Konstytucyjny, Judgments of 11 May 2005 – K 18/04 –, n. 4.1., 10.2., of 24 November 2010 – K 32/09 –, n. 2.1. et seq.; of 16 November 2011 – SK 45/09 –, n. 2.4., 2.5., with further references; for the Kingdom of Sweden: Chapter 10 Art. 6 sentence 1, Form of government; for the Kingdom of Spain: Tribunal Constitucional, Declaration of 13 December 2004, DTC 1/2004; for the Czech Republic: Ústavni Soud, Judgment of 31 January 2012 – 2012/01/31 – Pl. ús 5/12 –, para. VII.).

principles of democracy (Art. 20 sec. 1 and sec. 2 GG) and the rule of law (Art. 20 sec. 3 GG), as well as from Art. 23 sec. 1 GG, and is safeguarded under European Union law by the principle of conferral (Art. 5 sec. 1 sentence 1 and sec. 2 TEU) and the obligation of the European Union to respect the national identities of the Member States (Art. 4 sec. 2 sentence 1 TEU, cf. BVerfGE 123, 267 <352>).

Besides the institutions of the European Union, German constitutional organs are also responsible to make sure that the programme of integration is observed.[18]

At the same time, the Court decided to suspend the case and to refer questions for a preliminary ruling on the interpretation of various provisions of EU law to the CJEU, in accordance with the Art. 267 sec. 1 b TFEU. Thus, the control over the decision and the content of the decision remain two separate issues.

Hungary – Controlling the Implemented EU Law

The same issue of controlling the application of EU law has been raised by the Hungarian Constitutional Court at the moment of accession. In May 2004, the Hungarian Parliament enacted a law "On Measures Concerning Agricultural Surplus Stocks" – implementation of Commission Regulations (EC) No. 1972/2003 of 10 November 2003 and (EC)No. 60/2004 of 14 January 2004. In Case 17/04 AB Hat from 25 May 2004, the Hungarian Court decided that the Act was unconstitutional for being contrary to the requirement of legal certainty, as it was retroactive.[19] In later decisions the Hungarian Constitutional Court reaffirmed the decision explaining, that the court limits the application of its power to control the constitutionality to domestic laws. The court expressed the view, that: "Under Article 2/A of the Constitution community law applicable in Hungarian law is just as valid as is law adopted by Hungarian legislation."[20]

This line of argument, reflecting the internal division between international law, which is not controlled in respect of its constitutionality, and the internal law, including the implemented EU law, which constitutes the subject of control on account of constitutionality, has also been reflected in the decision

---

18   German Federal Constitutional Court, Judgment of 14 January 2014, BVerfG, 2 BvR 2728/13.
19   András Sajo, "Learning Co-Operative Constitutionalism the Hard Way: The Hungarian Constitutional Court Shying Away from EU Supremacy", 3 *Zeitschrift für Staats- und Europawissenschaften* (2004), 351–371.
20   Hungarian Constitutional Court, Decision 61/B/2005. AB, Judgment of 29th September 2008, ABH [2008].

concerning the constitutionality of the TFEU within the Hungarian law.[21] In Decision 143/2010 of 12.07.2010 (the so-called "Lisbon Treaty Decision"), the Hungarian Constitutional Court adopted two views. The first view concerns the formal aspect of the constitutional control, enabling the Court to control the scope of transfer of sovereignty from the state to the institutions of the European Union. Interpreting art. 2/A of the Hungarian Constitution,[22] the court has thus observed, that: "Article 2/A had established a competence for the court to determine whether the transfer of further competences in amendments to the EU treaties is acceptable." This position should be maintained under the new Hungarian Constitution, since art E of the Fundamental Law of Hungary[23] essentially copied the so called "European Clause" contained in art. 2/A of the former Constitution. Secondly, the court pointed out that the doctrine of sovereignty should still be treated as the source of constitutional identity. The Court expressed the view that the Constitution cannot be interpreted in a way that would deprive the constitutional provisions on sovereignty and the rule of law of their substance, while the Court referred to the concept of sovereignty as the indirect albeit ultimate limitation of the principle of the primacy of EU law. Additionally the principle of the rule of law limits the operation of the principle of the primacy of EU law.[24]

The Czech Republic – The Doctrine of Constitutional Review

The participatory character of the sovereignty has also been emphasized by the Czech Constitutional Court. In the decision on the constitutionality of the aforementioned EAW, the Czech Court, unlike its counterparts in Germany and Poland, found that the requirement of cooperation was more important than the sole literal meaning of the legal act, and did not decide against the constitutionality. The doctrine having been elaborated by the Czech

---

21   László Blutman and Nora Chronowski, "Hungarian Constitutional Court: Keeping Aloof from European Union Law", 5(3) *Vienna Journal on International Constitutional Law* (2011), 329–348.

22   "In the interest of participating as a Member State of the European Union on the basis of international treaties – to the extent required to exercise rights and to perform obligations set forth in the basic treaties – Hungary may exercise some of its authorities stemming from the Constitution in conjunction with the other member states through the institutions of the European Union", The European clause, ex art. 2/A 1989 Constitution.

23   Adapted on 18 April 2011, in force since 1 January 2012. The Hungarian Constitutional Law has been a target of politically motivated amendments. See the relevant chapter in this volume.

24   The decision 143/2010. (VII. 14.) of the Constitutional Court of the Republic of Hungary on the constitutionality of the Act of promulgation of the Lisbon Treaty.

Constitutional Court in decision Pl ús 50/04 of 8 March 2006 was based on the assumption that the Court plays an essential role in deciding the scope of integration, since it preserves the constitutional doctrine of sovereignty. The court observed that:

> [t]he delegation of a part of the powers of national organs may persist only so long as these powers are exercised in a manner that is compatible with the preservation of the foundations of state sovereignty of the Czech Republic [...] [I]n such determination the Constitutional Court is called upon to protect constitutionalism.

Later on in the decision from 2009 the Czech Constitutional Court also found the Treaty of Lisbon constitutional, however at the same time, the Court set out the limits for the transfer of powers from the sovereign state to the EU institutions directly referring to the famous *Kompetenz-Kompetenz* expression:

> there would be a breach of the Czech Constitution if, on the basis of a transfer of powers, an international organization could continue to change its powers at will, and independently of its members, i.e. if a constitutional competence (competence-competence) were transferred to it.[25]

Thus it seems that in all relevant jurisdictions, namely, Poland, Germany, Hungary, and the Czech Republic, the judicial understanding of the sovereignty doctrine is based on two fundamental assumptions. Firstly, the European Union does not exert sovereign powers, and thus the principle of the primacy of EU law should be limited to those cases where the Member States transferred the power to the EU. Nevertheless, secondly, there are some "inalienable" powers, namely the powers to waive the power of transferring the power. Accordingly the whole process of transfer of powers should be controlled by constitutional courts, since the courts control constitutionality of the integration process understood as further log-term association of cooperating sovereign states.

---

25   The constitutionality of the Lisbon Treaty in the Czech Republic, Decision of the Constitutional Court of the Czech Republic 2009/11/03 – Pl. ús 29/09. For the more recent judgment of the Czech Constitutional Court which declared the ECJ judgment void, see Decision 2012/01/31 – Pl. ús 5/12.

4   In Search of Explanation: Neofunctionalist Understanding of European Integration

The phenomenon of judicialization of the EU plays an important role in the discourse pertaining to the theory of European integration. It seems that the integration through the judicial activism of the ECJ/CJEU and the so-called "constitutionalization" of European integration gives strong arguments in favor of Neofunctionalism as a theory which explains the integration as a process based on spillover effects. According to the classical definition proposed by Lindberg:

> "spill-over" refers to a situation in which a given action, related to a specific goal, creates a situation in which the original goal can be assured only by taking further actions, which in turn create a further condition and a need for more action, and so forth. [...] [T]he initial task and grant of power to the central institutions creates a situation or series of situations that can be dealt with only by further expanding the task and the grant of power. Spill-over implies that a situation has developed in which the ability of a Member State to achieve a policy goal may depend upon the attainment by another Member State of one of its policy goals.[26]

Applying this mechanism to EU law, it is not strange then that the unique position and role played by the ECJ/CJEU as an initiator of judicial multi-level dialogue led some theorists to the proposition of the CJEU-centric (i.e. judicialized) European integration, especially when the political discourse is blocked by the lack of unanimity or power of major players on both the EU and the national levels.[27] The construction of governance structure based on the judicial activism of the ECJ/CJEU has even been explained as "the judicial *coup d'état*", where the European Court created the doctrine of the primacy of European Communities law.[28] The spillover effect may, however, play an *adverse* role as an obstacle to integration, since the Member States, and especially

---

26   Leon N. Lindberg, *The Political Dynamics of European Economic Integration* (Stanford University Press, Stanford, 1963).

27   Joseph H.H Weiler, "The Transformation of Europe", 100(8) *Yale Law Journal*, (1991), 2403–2483; *id.* "A Quiet Revolution: The European Court of Justice and its Interlocutors", 26(4) *Comparative Political Studies* (1994), 510–534.

28   Alec Stone Sweet, "The Juridical Coup d'État and the Problem of Authority", 8 *German Law Journal* (2007), 915–926.

their courts, may adopt a similar set of doctrines, reasoning, concepts, and legal instruments, in order to diminish the effect and scope of the primacy of the EU law doctrine.[29] While the discretion enjoyed by the ECJ/CJEU has not been curbed by any successful strategies adopted by any Member States,[30] the Constitutional Courts in CEE have limited the application of EU law by rejecting the full application of the doctrine of the primacy of EU law.

Sadurski[31] explains the process in two ways. First, the constitutional doctrine of sovereignty has been emphasized in CEE as it preserves the control over the protection of rights by the national constitutional courts, while empowering these courts vis-à-vis other domestic actors, especially the elected lawmaker. Second, Sadurski refers to Euroskepticism by the CEE courts whereby the *Solange* style argumentation was repeated in different contexts.[32] Indeed, the Czech Constitutional Court, which declared the constitutionality of the EAW, strengthening its own position *vis-a-vis* the Czech Parliament and the Czech President. Later on, in the Lisbon Treaty case, the Czech Constitutional Court declared its competence to review constitutionality of the EU treaties. On the contrary, however, the Polish Constitutional Tribunal declared the need to shift some of its competences to the lawmaker in the aforementioned EAW case.[33] Meanwhile the Hungarian Constitutional Court has never declared its position concerning the primacy of EU law or of the Hungarian Constitution, observing the separation doctrine according to which the Court rules over EU law only when it is implemented within the domestic legal order. Even in case of the Lisbon Treaty, the Court declared the compatibility between the Hungarian constitution and the act of ratification of the Treaty and its incorporation into Hungarian legal order. Thus, Sadurski seems to have oversimplified the analysis.

At the same time, the references to EU law and the obligations resulting from the Hungarian membership in the EU became an additional protection for the Hungarian Constitutional Court against the lawmakers who seek to

---

29   Anthony Arnull, "Me and My Shadow: The European Court of Justice and the Disintegration of European Union Law", 31(5) *Fordham International Law Journal* (2007), 1174–1211.

30   Alec Stone Sweet and Thomas L. Brunell, "The European Court of Justice, State Noncompliance, and the Politics of Override", 106(1) *American Political Science Review* (2012), 204–213.

31   Sadurski (2012), *op. cit.* note 13, 104–126.

32   In a series of cases from 1970s, the German and Italian constitutional courts expressed some reservations concerning the applicability of the EC law due to deficient protection of human rights as compared to the constitutions of Germany and Italy respectively.

33   The Court emphasized the need for action to be taken by the Parliament, which inevitably led to the amendment of the Polish Constitution.

narrow the Court's competences by amending the Fundamental Law. In its recent judgment concerning the constitutionality of the fourth amendment to the Hungarian Fundamental Law, the Constitutional Court referred openly to EU law and the necessity of applying the rules conferred by the supranational institutions as an argument in favor of its control over the amendments to the Constitution, stipulating that:

> The power of the Constitutional Court is a restricted power in the structure of division of powers. Consequently, the Court shall not extend its powers to review the constitution and the new norms amending it without an express and explicit authorization to that effect. [...] The Constitutional Court shall moreover consider the obligations Hungary undertook in its international treaties or those that follow from membership in the EU, along with the generally acknowledged rules of international law, and the basic principles and values reflected therein. All of these rules – with special regard to their values that are also incorporated into the Fundamental Law – constitute such a unified system (of values), that shall not be disregarded neither in the course of constitution-making or legislation, nor in the course of constitutional review conducted by the Constitutional Court.[34]

The Court simply stated that it had to take the international obligations of Hungary into account and thus it has to maintain the control over the process of the constitutional amendments set out by the 2/3 parliamentary majority. It seems that within the context of the Hungarian constitutional law and the system of constitutional control having been adopted in the recently amended Fundamental Law, the primacy doctrine may potentially serve as the argument of last resort in favor of the wider scope of control by the Hungarian Constitutional Court. In a sense, Sadurski is correct in linking the domestic struggle of power with the issue of adapting the primacy of EU law.

5   Conclusion

It seems that the evolutionary path dependence of the EU legal system takes such a direction to greater autonomy and cooperation of different supranational

---

34   The Constitutional Court of Hungary (2013.05.23) Press release regarding the constitutional review of the Fourth Amendment of the Fundamental Law of Hungary, decision II/00648/2013 of 2013-04-23.

and coexisting institutions. Whether the EU creates one complex legal system or a set of independent legal systems, it depends on the practice of the EU courts, the courts in Member States, and on the justification of these practices. It also seems that the alleged skepticism to (or at least partial refusal of) the unconditional acceptance of the primacy of the EU law by some constitutional courts does not give any significant argument against the spillover effect, stemming from the multilevel judicial dialogues among various courts within the EU. The application of EU law may enhance the coherence of judicial practice on the level of constitutional courts even when the courts adapts the doctrine of (national) constitutional supremacy.

The three doctrines adopted by the constitutional courts in Poland, the Czech Republic, and Hungary, namely constitutional supremacy, constitutional review, and separation, began to converge under the shadow of the German Federal Constitutional Courts' decision regarding the TFEU. At the same time, some constitutional courts in CEE are in the midst of political struggle for power, and their link to the CJEU aids to strengthen the judicial governance in each Member State. Such a Neofunctional understanding of European Integration based on spillover effects can explain the judicialization (or even constitutionalization) of the EU, while it softens the concern towards the adverse spillover effects characterized by the unified position among the Member States' Constitutional Courts against the principle of the primacy of EU law.

Bibliography

Arnull, Anthony. (2007) "Me and My Shadow: The European Court of Justice and the Disintegration of European Union Law", 31(5) *Fordham International Law Journal*, 1174–1211.

Arrighi, Giovanni. (1994) *The Long Twentieth Century: Money, Power and the Origin of Our Times* (Verso, London).

Beck, Urlich. (1992) *Risk Society: Towards a New Modernity* (SAGE, New Delhi).

Blutman, László and Chronowski, Nora. (2011) "Hungarian Constitutional Court: Keeping Aloof from European Union Law", 5(3) *Vienna Journal on International Constitutional Law*, 329–348.

Komárek Jan. (2013) "Czech Constitutional Court Playing with Matches: The Czech Constitutional Court Declares a Judgment of the Court of Justice of the EU *Ultra Vires*; Judgment of 31 January 2012, Pl. ÚS 5/12, *Slovak Pensions XVII*", 8(2) *European Constitutional Law Review*, 323–337.

Komárek, Jan. (2007) "European Constitutionalism and the European Arrest Warrant: In Search of the Limits of 'Contrapunctual Principles'", 44(1) *Common Market Law Review*, 9–40.

Kumm, Mathias. (2005) "The Jurisprudence of Constitutional Conflict: Constitutional Supremacy in Europe before and after the Constitutional Treaty", 11(3) *European Law Journal*, 262–307.

Kumm, Mathias. (1999) "Who is the Final Arbiter of Constitutionality in Europe?: Three Conceptions of the Relationship Between the German Federal Constitutional Court and the European Court of Justice", 36(2) *Common Market Law Review*, 351–386.

Laband, Paul. (1901) *Das Staatsrecht des Deutschen Reiches (The Constitutional Right of the German State)*, vol. 2 (Mohr, Tübingen).

Łazowski, Adam. (ed.) (2010) *The Application of EU Law in the New Member States: Brave New World* (T.M.C. Asser Press, The Hague).

Lindberg, Leon N. (1963) *The Political Dynamics of European Economic Integration* (Stanford University Press, Stanford).

MacCormick, Neil. (1999) *Questioning Sovereignty* (Oxford University Press, Oxford).

Sadurski, Wojciech. (2012), *Constitutionalism and the Enlargement of Europe* (Oxford University Press, Oxford).

Sadurski, Wojciech. (2008) "'Solange, Chapter 3': Constitutional Courts in Central Europe – Democracy – European Union", 14(1) *European Law Journal*, 1–35.

Sajo, András. (2004) "Learning Co-Operative Constitutionalism the Hard Way: The Hungarian Constitutional Court Shying Away from EU Supremacy", 3 *Zeitschrift für Staats- und Europawissenschaften*, 351–371.

Stone Sweet, Alec. (2007) "The Juridical Coup d'État and the Problem of Authority", 8 *German Law Journal*, 915–926.

Stone Sweet, Alec and Brunell, Thomas L. (2012) "The European Court of Justice, State Noncompliance, and the Politics of Override", 106(1) *American Political Science Review*, 204–213.

Weiler, Joseph H.H. (1994) "A Quiet Revolution: The European Court of Justice and its Interlocutors", 26(4) *Comparative Political Studies*, 510–534.

Weiler, Joseph H.H. (1991) "The Transformation of Europe", 100(8) *Yale Law Journal*, 2403–2483.

CHAPTER 2

Europeanization of the Hungarian Legal Order: From Convergence to Cancellation?

Tamas Dezso Ziegler and Balázs Horváthy

Abstract

Since the political transition of Hungary in the late 1980s, the law of the European Union has been the primary external influence on the modernization of domestic legislation. This chapter aims to illustrate that Hungary, as a passive and receptive actor, implemented all components of EU law which were prerequisites for EU membership. This has resulted in an intense convergence in rules and values of the domestic and EU legal order until its accession to the EU in 2004. After accession, however, Hungary started to move from a constructive to confrontational Member State, which has led to a substantial divergence between the laws of Hungary and EU law. This chapter analyzes these processes and attempts to identify the possible consequences of this alteration in the Hungarian stance to the adoption of rules, values, and regulatory models originating from EU law. It will be demonstrated with case studies ranging from recent Hungarian economic legislation to the constitutional reform, illustrating how this new role of Hungary negatively affects the adaptability of Hungarian legal order and leads to canceling the convergence to the European law.

Keywords

Hungary – harmonization – implementation – democratization – rule of law

1 Introduction

Hungarian law reforms in the last two centuries have been accomplished through the adoption and reception of foreign legal models,[1] and therefore

---

1 Disregarding some exceptional periods, e.g. the 1860s, when Hungarian legislation intensively resisted the reception of law forced on it by the Austrian Empire. For external influences and impacts on the Hungarian legal order, see Attila Harmathy (ed.), *Introduction to Hungarian Law* (Kluwer, The Hague, 1998).

the general attitude of Hungarian law is characterized as both open and adaptive towards foreign legal models. Over the past two decades since the political transition of Hungary in the late 1980s, the law of the European Union (and its predecessors) has been the primary external influence on the modernization of domestic legislation. As a passive and receptive actor, Hungary had implemented all components of EU law which were prerequisites for EU membership, resulting in an intense convergence in rules and values of the domestic and EU legal order prior to its accession to the EU in 2004. In the post-accession period, however, Hungary as a Member State has been able to directly influence legislative procedures at the EU level and become more of an active rather than receptive actor. In the first years of Membership, this position could be characterized as a constructive stance to EU legislation, but later Hungary shifted slightly towards a role of a confrontational actor and began to divert its legal order and policies from the value, principles, and norms of the European Union.

In the terminology of this chapter the *convergence* is conceptually an orientation of the legal order towards the models, rules, norms, and values of the European Union, while *divergence* is understood as detaching from such path, leading to more conflicts between the substance of EU and Members States' – here specifically the Hungarian – law.[2] Divergence can manifest itself in several forms, not only in incompatible legislation, but also in the practices of the government, authorities, and domestic courts. In this manner, the process of convergence and divergence is palpable not only in the formal operation of the legal orders, i.e. the "hard text" of the law, but also in informal ways, when the domestic legislators are accepting or refusing e.g. values, principles or even certain legal attitudes.[3]

The converging tendency of the domestic legal order to EU law is labeled here also as "Europeanization." Europeanization plays, however, also the role of an evocative term, since it can recall the permanent expansion of the legislative and rule-making procedures of the EU and refers to consequent fact that more and more areas of law have been becoming progressively subject to EU legislative procedures in the last decades. In other terms, the evolving process

---

2   See Pierre Legrand, "Public Law, Europeanisation, and Convergence: Can Comparatists Contribute?" in Paul Beaumont, Carole Lyons, and Neil Walker (eds.), *Convergence and Divergence in European Public Law* (Oxford University Press, Oxford, 2002), 225–226.

3   Lyons elaborates the role of aspirations ("*mentalité*") and states that "reading between the lines of the ordered "hard text" of the process of (legal) integration, there is an evolving sense of a European common good which can be said to represent an emergent European (legal) culture." Carole Lyons, "Perspectives on Convergence Within European Integration", in Beaumont, Lyons, and Walker, *ibid.*, 81.

of Europeanization requires more convergence at domestic level and attempts to minimize the diverging elements of the legal orders.[4] Therefore, the Member States face increasing level of legal sources, which originate from EU law and should be adapted and implemented at domestic level. Even though the trends of Europeanization are commonly used and well established in political science[5] (and partly within economics[6]), this chapter primarily contextualize Hungary within the legal scholarship through the lens of (legislative) convergence/divergence. Accordingly, the method of the analysis is restricted only to these concepts and can be understood as a simple legal-comparative narrative arranged in a chronological manner.

The following chapter analyzes these processes and attempts to identify the possible consequences of this alteration in the Hungarian stance to the adoption of rules, values, and regulatory models arising from EU law. It will be demonstrated with case studies ranging from recent Hungarian economic legislation to the constitutional reform of 2011, illustrating how this new role of Hungary negatively affects the adaptability of Hungarian legal order (divergent trends) and leads to canceling the convergence to the European legal order.

2   Convergence

Unilateral Adaptation of EU Law

The adaptation of the Hungarian legal order to EC/EU law until 1994 could be described as a *unilateral* process, which was mostly guided by economic and commercial interests within Hungary. The starting point of this period was not bordered by the political transition itself. As far back as two years before the

---

4   The concept of divergence is not applicable to the legal exceptions provided by EU law (e.g. public policy exceptions regarding the free movement of goods in Article 36 TFEU, or security exceptions in Articles 344 and 345 TFEU) as these exceptions merely illustrate the boundaries of the EU legal integration – unless the Member States exercise such exceptions without fulfilling all the criteria laid by EU law (i.e. divergence in procedural laws).

5   See e.g. Attila Ágh, *The Politics of Central Europe* (SAGE, London, 1998); Wade Jacoby, *Ordering from the Menu in Central Europe: The Enlargement of the EU and NATO* (Cambridge University Press, Cambridge, 2004); and Frank Schimmelfennig and Ulrich Sedelmeier (eds.), *The Europeanization of Central and Eastern Europe* (Cornell University Press, Ithaca, 2005). For definitions, see e.g. Tanja Börzel, "Europeanization: How the European Union Interacts with its Member States", in Simon Bulmer *et al.* (eds), *The Member States of the European Union* (Oxford University Press, Oxford, 2005), 45–76.

6   See e.g. Reiner Martin, *The Regional Dimension in European Public Policy: Convergence or Divergence?* (Palgrave Macmillan, Basingstoke, 1999).

first democratic parliamentary election, after having signed the general agreement on trade and cooperation with the EC and its Member States in 1988,[7] it was obvious that a significant part of Hungarian commercial regulations should be harmonized with the *acquis communautaire*, in order to expand market opportunities for the major export products of Hungary. The adaptation was characterized not only by the liberalization of export and import rules, but also the consideration of the entire set of EC single market regulations that played a central role in this process. In this period, the legislators were, sometimes spontaneously, implementing models of EC law, and therefore the *acquis* became a significant tool of Hungarian law reform. The reception of legal models and institutions of EC law was not always adequate, resulting in partial convergence with EC law in several cases (e.g. the 1988 reform of company law[8]). Nevertheless, EC Law certainly inspired the Hungarian regulators as in the case of the "grouping" of companies, based on the European Economic Interest Grouping,[9] adapted into a wide range of activities. A striking example of *full* harmonization was the improvement of the Hungarian product liability provisions, carried out by simply translating the relevant *acquis* in 1993.[10]

The basis of such approximation of Hungarian law to EC law was the institutional improvement which the government introduced in 1990 with the specific

---

7   Agreement Between the European Economic Community and the Hungarian People's Republic on Trade and Commercial and Economic Cooperation of 26 September 1988, [1988] OJ L327/14. The prerequisite of this agreement was the normalization of the relations between the EC and the Central and Eastern European countries, which was accomplished by the Joint Declaration on the Establishment of Official Relations (so-called Luxembourg Accord) in June 1988. This declaration led to opening of bilateral trade deals, resulting in removal of long-standing import quotas on a number of products and also the General System of Preferences was extended to the countries of this region. See John O'Brennan, *The Eastern Enlargement of the European Union* (Routledge, London, 2006), 15. Only specific quantitative trade restrictions remained in force until early 1990. See Allan F. Tatham, *Enlargement of the European Union* (Wolters Kluwer, Austin, 2009), 76–77.

8   Act VI of 1988 on Business Companies. The reformed law only partly implemented the compulsory disclosure requirements set forth by Council Directive 68/151/EEC of 9 March 1968, and the capital requirements for public limited liability companies set forth by Council Directive 77/91/EEC of 13 December 1976. See Magdalena Pajor-Bytomski, *Gesellschaftsrecht in Ungarn (Company Law in Hungary)* (Hüthig, München, 1994). The significance of this "selective" harmonization in the early transition legislation should not be underestimated. Tatham, *ibid.*, 340.

9   Council Regulation (EEC) No 2137/85 of 25 July 1985 on the European Economic Interest Grouping (EEIG).

10   Act X of 1993 on Product Liability.

requirements for harmonization into the domestic legislative procedures.[11] This Government Decision emphasized the importance of convergence between the Hungarian and EC legal orders, and obliged the Minister for Justice to discover the possible EC law relevance for all proposed legislation, including not only EC legislative acts, but also all international treaties concluded by the Community.[12] If the Hungarian legal instrument was proposed and detailed in accordance with the regulatory model of EC law, the proposal had to also encompass the cost estimation and an overall analysis of the possible horizontal consequences of implementation. Otherwise the proposal would include an explanatory memorandum why it intends to deviate from the provisions of EC law. The importance of the Government Decision lay in the fact that the adaptation of the Hungarian legal order was formally and institutionally incorporated into the domestic legislative procedures, therefore the spontaneous (ad hoc) legal harmonization was replaced by a general and permanent method. Although the economic interests remained central to this institutionalized harmonization process,[13] the attitude of Hungary towards Europe at that time was also a conscious choice of (mainly procedural) legal culture. Consequently, the unilateral character of legal adaptation meant that Hungary chose – or, to be precise, could now choose – the path of Europeanization of its own volition based on the values and norms of the Union.

Adaptation Governed by the Objective of EU Membership
In the period between 1994 and 2004, legal harmonization was no longer determined only by economic and commercial reasons, but also by the political objective of Hungary joining the EU, supported by a broad domestic consensus.[14] Hungary negotiated for a substantive reference to Membership

---

11   Decision 2006/1990 (HT 4) of the Government.

12   See paragraph 2 of the Decision.

13   This technocratic sentiment was well-matched to the objectives of the 1988 Agreement that predominantly aimed at the economic reforms and the complete conversion to a market economy. See David Phinnemore, *Association: Stepping-Stone or Alternative to EU Membership?* (Sheffield Academic Press, 1999), 44; and Tamás Sárközy, *A szocializmus, a rendszerváltás és az újkapitalizmus gazdasági civiljoga 1945–2005* (*The Economic-Private Law of the Socialism, the Transition and the New Capitalism 1945–2005*) (HVG-Orac, Budapest, 2007).

14   For detailed analysis, see Attila Fölsz and Gábor Tóka, "Determinants of Support for EU-Membership in Hungary", in Robert Rohrschneider and Stephen Whitefield (eds.), *Public Opinion, Party Competition, and the European Union in Post-Communist Europe* (Palgrave Macmillan, Basingstoke, 2006), 145–164.

in its Association Agreement (Europe Agreement)[15] with the European Communities (similar to that with Turkey), but only a unilateral and non-binding declaration by Hungary was included in the Agreement's preamble.[16] After the promulgation of the Agreement, on 1 April 1994, the application for EU Membership of Hungary was formally submitted to the European Communities.

The Agreement also encompassed a legislative approximation clause, which made clear that the major prerequisite for integration into the Community was the approximation of Hungarian legislation to EC law "as far as possible."[17] This formulation did not express an absolute obligation, but the provision had significant impact on the future process of adaptation and Europeanization of Hungarian law. Act I of 1994 that promulgated the Europe Agreement laid down the concrete legislative tasks arising from the approximation clause. First, the conformity with EU law had to be assured, and therefore subsequently, Hungary would only be able to conclude international agreements compatible with EU law.[18] Second, Act I of 1994 technically obliged the legislative bodies to assess the compatibility of all legislative proposals with EU law, and the conformity had to be indicated in all legal texts within a specific clause referring to equivalence with EU law. The Europe Agreement did not contain any provisions either on the method or on the extent of the approximation but referred

---

15 Europe Agreement establishing an association between the European Communities and their Member States, of the one part, and the Republic of Hungary, of the other part. [1993] OJ L347/2–266.

16 Paragraph 13 of the Preamble: "Considering Hungary's firm intention to seek full integration in the political, economic and security order of a new Europe", Europe Agreement [1993] OJ L347/3. Despite the Hungarian objective, the Communities were not willing to make any commitment concerning the future accession, see Attila Harmathy, "Constitutional Questions of the Preparation of Hungary to Accession to the European Union", in Alfred Kellermann *et al.* (eds.), *EU Enlargement: The Constitutional Impact at EU and National Level* (T.M.C. Asser Press, The Hague, 2001), 315.

17 Article 67 of the Europe Agreement. For detailed analyses, see Barna Berke, "Implementation of the Association Agreement, Approximation of Laws, Eventual Accession: Some Constitutional Implications", in Ferenc Mádl (ed.), *On the State of the EU Integration Process: Enlargement and Institutional Reforms* (EU Centre for Research and Documentation, Eötvös Loránd University, Budapest, 1997), 323–341; and Imre Vörös, "The Legal Doctrine and Legal Policy Aspects of the EU-Accession", 44(3–4) *Acta Juridica Hungarica* (2003), 141–163.

18 Act I of 1994 on Promulgation of Europe Agreement establishing an association between the European Communities and their Member States, of the one part, and the Republic of Hungary, of the other part, Article 3.

to branches of law that were "particularly" targeted areas for harmonization.[19] Moreover, the EU offered technical assistance regarding the implementation of EU law, which included provision of information, opportunities for expert exchange, and aid with the translation of Community legislation in relevant areas.[20] In 1995, following a White Paper of the European Commission,[21] the Hungarian Government reformed the coordination and institutional structure of legal adaptation and announced the first comprehensive program for harmonization in 1995.[22] The Government Decision laid down the framework for the planning and programming of legal harmonization. The entire legislative procedure from the identification of an obligation arising from EC law, through the drafting of legal texts up to its adoption fell under the scope of the Decision, and responsibilities were clearly allocated within the institutional structure of government. This framework for harmonization played a major role in the success of accession negotiations (1990–2002).

As a consequence of the stable policy objective of EU membership and the precise methods of legal harmonization, this period resulted in the largest law reform of the history of modern Hungary and led to intense convergence between the Hungarian and EU legal orders. The constitutional prerequisites of accession were also established during this period.[23] The 2002 amendment inserted the so-called Europe clause into the text of the Constitution of that time,[24] and additionally, another new provision on integration was included,

---

19   Art. 68 of the Europe Agreement. This list includes customs law, company law, banking law, company accounts and taxes, intellectual property, protection of workers at the workplace, financial services, rules on competition, protection of health and life of humans, animals and plants, food legislation, consumer protection including product liability, indirect taxation, technical rules and standards, transport, and the environment.

20   Art. 69 of the Europe Agreement.

21   White Paper – Preparing the associated countries of Central and Eastern Europe for integration into the internal market of the Union. COM (95) 163 final [1996] OJ C141/135.

22   Government Decision 2004/1995 (I. 20.) on the Hungarian Harmonization Plan Preparing the Accession to the European Union.

23   The preparatory process for the constitutional amendment concerning Hungary's prospective accession was launched by Government Decision 2319/2000. (XII. 21.). For comprehensive analyses (especially on Art. 2/A), see Balázs Horváthy and László Knapp, "The Relationship between the Hungarian and the EU Legal Orders", in Péter Smuk (ed.), *The Transformation of the Hungarian Legal System 2010–2013* (CompLex Wolters Kluwer, Budapest, 2013), 51–68; Márton Varju and Flóra Fazekas, "The Reception of European Union Law in Hungary: The Constitutional Court and the Hungarian Judiciary", 48(6) *Common Market Law Review* (2011), 1945–1984.

24   "By virtue of treaty, the Republic of Hungary, in its capacity as a Member State of the European Union, may exercise certain constitutional powers jointly with other Member States to the extent necessary in connection with the rights and obligations conferred by

which stresses that the Republic of Hungary shall participate in "establishing a European unity in order to achieve freedom, well-being and security for the peoples of Europe."[25] This rule formulated integration as a national constitutional objective, which while only symbolic and programmatic in nature, theoretically gave the government no choice but to follow the straight path of integration and cooperation with other European countries.

The process of legal harmonization and adaptation in this period was a success with few exceptions: e.g. the consumer protection provisions of the Hungarian Civil Code and the car registration tax, which had to enter into force on the day of accession, both inconsistencies with EU law were pointed out by legal scholars prior to accession. Not surprisingly, both disputes led to proceedings before the European Court of Justice after the accession. Following *Ynos*,[26] the Hungarian legislator modified the Civil Code and made clear how the unfair terms in consumer contracts could be contested before the Hungarian courts, while *Nádasdy* resulted promptly in the necessary corrections regarding the tax law inconsistencies.[27] Even though these discrepancies can be regarded as factors indicating less convergence, the outstanding activity of the Hungarian courts in the preliminary ruling procedures has obviously showed that the Hungarian courts were open to interactions and judicial dialogue with the European Court of Justice.[28] Institutionally coordinated harmonization, including adaptation and reception, resulted in high-level convergence between the Hungarian and EU regulatory models during this period.

---

the treaties on the foundation of the European Union and the European Communities [...]; these powers may be exercised independently and by way of the institutions of the European Union." See Act XX of 1949 on the Constitution of Republic of Hungary, paragraph 1 of Article 2/A. The English translation is available at <http://www.parlament.hu/angol/act_xx_of_1949.pdf>). The Constitution was repealed by the Fundamental Law of Hungary in 2011.

25   Act XX of 1949 on the Constitution of Republic of Hungary, paragraph 4 of Article 6.

26   C-302/04 *Ynos Kft.* v. *János Varga*. The Ynos case was the first Hungarian preliminary ruling procedure before the European Court of Justice. The decisive factor before the Court was that the facts of the case had been established before the accession of Hungary to the EU. For detailed analysis, see Balázs Horváthy, "After the First Lessons and Experiences: Cases Concerning Hungary before ECJ (2004–2007)", 49(1) *Acta Juridica Hungarica* (2008), 89–110.

27   C-290/05. Ákos Nádasdy v. Vám és Pénzügyőrség Észak-Alföldi Regionális Parancsnoksága. In the Nádasdy case, the ECJ regarded the Hungarian system of registration taxes discriminating and not proportionate to value, thus it was contrary to EU Law. *Ibid.*, 95.

28   Among countries of the region, Hungary's courts referred most actively to the ECJ for interpretation of EU Law within a preliminary ruling procedure. Hungary had 11 references, while the other nine Member States that joined in 2004 together had 14, between 2004 and 2007, i.e. in the first three years of membership. *Ibid.*, 110.

3   Divergence – or Cancellation of Convergence?

A Cooperative Member State

After joining the Union, the adaptation of the Hungarian legal order to EU law became a permanent obligation arising from Membership, but it is not merely a unilateral process. Hungary, as a Member State, is an actor in legislative procedures at the EU level, and this position needs other capabilities than those expected from a candidate country. The major question in this period was whether Hungary, as a formerly passive and receptive candidate country, could be an active yet co-operative Member State, without jeopardizing the convergence between the domestic and EU legal orders.

In the first four to five years after its accession, Hungary was one of the most cooperative Member States. Several examples prove this. The implementation of directives was very efficient and prudent, unlike in some of the older Member States, such as Italy.[29] The Hungarian Parliament ratified the Lisbon Treaty in an extremely short time on 17 December 2009, only three days after its signing, despite the then right wing opposition calling the action "unusual" and "inelegant" with the lack of public discourse. Hungary did not ask for an opt-out of the EU Charter of Fundamental Rights and it did not seek to extend the ban on foreign land buyers, which later became a crucial point of conflict within the country. Nor did Hungary formally ask for more rights for Hungarians who live in Transylvania when Romania joined the EU in 2007. Once again, it later became a source of conflict when more than 600,000 Hungarians living abroad in minority received citizenship without any negotiations with the countries concerned.

Even during this introductory period, there were signs that showed a lack of cooperation, or to be more precise, indicated that the country had yet to acquire the "thinking" of the Single Market.[30] The first Hungarian legislative effort clearly conflicting with the European rules was made by the left-wing Government, in power until 2010. In 2009, the Government sought to adopt a law which would have forced shops and supermarkets in Hungary to sell at least 80% Hungarian goods, a protective measure towards traditionally strong agriculture and the food industry. As passing such an act would have been

---

29   The EU Internal Market Scoreboard, available at <http://ec.europa.eu/internal_market/score/index_en.htm>.

30   The following paragraph is further elaborated in Tamas Dezso Czigler (Ziegler), "Protectionism – The Side Effect of Hungarian Nationalism", *Social Europe* (12 April 2012), available at <https://www.socialeurope.eu/2012/04/protectionism-the-side-effect-of-hungarian-nationalism/>.

contrary to EU law (free movement of goods), the Government pushed some of the representative organizations of domestic food producing and retailing companies into signing the "Code of Ethics on the Food Production Chain." This "recommandatory" and "non-binding" Code contained similarly discriminatory provisions, contrary to EU competition policy. In fact, it was also in conflict with Hungarian competition law. Consequently, the Hungarian Competition Authority (GVH) started an investigation into the case, although the case was closed based on the facts that the signed Code had never entered into force and that the representative organizations did not have authority from their member companies to bind them to such an arrangement.[31] However, with or without a strict rule, supermarkets still sell around 80% Hungarian food.[32] Another example is the case of the country's most important oil company, MOL. MOL is a public corporation limited by shares, one of Hungary's largest companies with a central role in the Eastern European oil industry. In 2007 Austria's OMV planned a takeover of MOL. The Government took several steps to counter this action, including the adoption of an act, which resembled the so-called "golden share" laws that have been ruled illegal in Western Europe. Later, the situation was moderated partly by the EU.[33]

On the Road to a Possible Cancellation of Convergence

In 2010, a right-wing Government was elected, led by Prime Minister Viktor Orbán and his party, Fidesz. Very quickly, hundreds of laws were passed that effected fundamental changes in society and governance, including a new

---

31 GVH, "No Food Production Chain Code, No GVH Proceedings", Press Release (6 August 2009), available at <http://www.gvh.hu/gvh/alpha?do=2&st=2&pg=133&m5_doc=5963>.

32 According to a survey conducted by Corvinus University (Budapest) in 2010, the portion of the food products produced or processed in Hungary in domestic retail was 76.45%. The research has shown a relatively lower portion at the international supermarket chains (72.8%) in comparison to the domestic owned stores (82%). See "Többségben a magyar élelmiszer a kereskedelmi láncok polcain (The Major Part of the Products on the Shelves of the Supermarkets are Hungarian Food Products)", *Trade Magazin* (9 November 2010), available at <http://www.trademagazin.hu/hirek-es-cikkek/piaci-hirek/tobbsegben-a-magyar-elelmiszer-a-kereskedelmi-lancok-polcain.html>. Recent estimates suggests the same portion of the Hungarian food products – 70–85% – in domestic retail, see "Egyre jobban fogy a magyar élelmiszer (Selling Hungarian Food is Getting Better and Better)", *Heti Világgazdaság* (21 March 2014), available at <http://hvg.hu/gazdasag/20140321_Egyre_jobban_fogy_a_magyar_elelmiszer/>.

33 Andrew Johnston, "Cross-Border Re-structuring, Company Law between Treaty Freedom and State Protectionism", in Ulf Bernitz and Wolf-Georg Ringe (eds.), *Company Law and Economic Protectionism: New Challenges to European Integration* (Oxford University Press, Oxford, 2010), at 171–172.

constitution, electoral laws, civil code, and penal code.[34] Several of them were criticized by the Commission and other EU institutions as they were against the concrete provisions of the *acquis*, or were in violation of international human rights standards (including Strasbourg law).[35] Hungary completed the presidency of the Council of the EU with relative success in 2011: the priorities were carefully selected and most of its goals were either achieved or prepared for approval. Even though the motto of the presidency was "Strong Europe", however, the government remained on the same path as it had been started earlier when it comes to domestic legislation, e.g. the aforementioned law offering the citizenship to all ethnic Hungarians abroad[36] and the new media law restricting its freedom.[37] The EU did not adopt effective sanctions against these actions, as the European People's Party in the European Parliament supported Orbán in many cases.[38] As a result, the government has a broad room to maneuver for divergence.

The core of rule of law problems in post-2010 Hungary is the newly introduced constitution (translated as "Fundamental law" or "Basic Law"),[39] which

---

34   For background materials see the website of Princeton University on Hungarian constitutional issues, available at <https://lapa.princeton.edu/newsdetail.php?ID=63#english>.

35   See e.g. Bojan Bugarič, "Protecting Democracy and the Rule of Law in the European Union: The Hungarian Challenge", *LSE "Europe in Question" Discussion Paper Series* (2014) No.79, available at <http://www.lse.ac.uk/europeanInstitute/LEQS/LEQSPaper79.pdf>; Kriszta Kovács and Gábor Attila Tóth, "Hungary's Constitutional Transformation", 7(2) *European Constitutional Law Review* (2011), 183–203, at 197; and "Editorial Comments: Hungary's New Constitutional Order and 'European Unity'", 49(3) *Common Market Law Review* (2012), 871–883, at 878.

36   Mónika Ganczer, "Hungarians outside Hungary: The Twisted Story of Dual Citizenship in Central and Eastern Europe", *Verfassungsblog* (8 October 2014), available at <http://verfassungsblog.de/hungarians-outside-hungary-twisted-story-dual-citizenship-central-eastern-europe/>.

37   Also see European Parliament Resolution of 10 March 2011 on Media Law in Hungary. P7_TA(2011)0094.

38   See e.g. "MEPs Voice Concerns over Constitutional Changes in Hungary", (17 April 2013), available at <http://www.europarl.europa.eu/news/en/news-room/content/20130416STO07356/html/MEPs-voice-concerns-over-constitutional-changes-in-Hungary>; and EPP, "EP Report on Hungary: EPP Group Rejects the Use of Double Standards", Press Release (3 July 2013), available at <http://www.eppgroup.eu/press-release/EPP-Group-rejects-the-use-of-double-standards>.

39   András Jakab and Pál Sonnevend, "Continuity with Deficiencies: The New Basic Law of Hungary", 9(1) *European Constitutional Law Review* (2013), 102–138; and Gábor Attila Tóth (ed.), *Constitution for a Disunited Nation: On Hungary's 2011 Fundamental Law* (Central European University Press, Budapest, 2012).

the public (e.g. NGOs and scholars) was not aware of its planning. The Fundamental Law was then amended six times: whenever the Constitutional Court found an act unconstitutional, the Parliament codified the act into the constitution.[40] The Commission raised concerns against some of these modifications,[41] as they began to curtail the powers and independence of the Constitutional Court itself through Government's exclusive power to nominate its judges. Additionally, the maximum retirement age of judges was reduced from 70 to 62 years (the general retirement age is 65 years), and the Head of the Supreme Court, among other nearly 300 judges, was replaced, without waiting the end of his mandate. The Constitutional Court found it unconstitutional and discriminatory, which again led to its inclusion in the Fundamental Law. The CJEU then found that the rule violated human rights, and that the judges had to be reinstated and compensated, which did not take place.[42] It also became common to put provisions into the so-called "cardinal laws", which require 2/3 majority to be amended in Parliament. By selecting a wide range of topics which are codified in cardinal laws, the Government is able to bind future governments' hands if the successors wish to modify them.

Even beyond these actions, the Government regularly criticized judges as "traitors" who serve the interests of banks and foreign actors, especially in the highly controversial case of foreign currency loans. In the preliminary procedure of *Kásler*, the Hungarian Supreme Court asked the CJEU whether foreign currency loan contracts was deemed invalid under EU law, especially under the Directive on unfair terms in consumer contracts.[43] The CJEU ruled that contractual terms relating to foreign currencies were not necessary exempt from an assessment as to whether they were unfair, and the evaluation of such

---

40 Tamas Boros, "Constitutional Amendments in Hungary: The Government's Struggle against the Constitutional Court", *Analyse* (Friedrich Ebert Stiftung Büro Budapest, 2013), available at <http://www.fesbp.hu/common/pdf/Nachrichten_aus_Ungarn_februar_2013.pdf>.

41 "The European Commission Reiterates its Serious Concerns over the Fourth Amendment to the Constitution of Hungary", available at <http://europa.eu/rapid/press-release_IP-15-4673_en.htm>.

42 Case C-286/12, European Commission v Hungary, ECLI:EU:C:2012:602; and Tamás Gyulavári and Nikolett Hős, "Retirement of Hungarian Judges, Age Discrimination and Judicial Independence: A Tale of Two Courts", 42(3) *Industrial Law Journal* (2013), 289–297. The ECtHR also proceeded in a related case. Baka v. Hungary (application no. 20261/12).

43 Case C-26/13: Request for a Preliminary Ruling from the Kúria (Hungary) Lodged on 21 January 2013 – Kásler Árpád, Káslerné Rábai Hajnalka v OTP Jelzálogbank Zrt. (2013) OJ C 156/18; Council Directive 93/13/EEC of 5 April 1993 on Unfair Terms in Consumer Contracts (1993) OJ L 95/29.

contracts may be done by local courts.[44] As a counteractive measure, the Government introduced a new law that the banks had to sue the Government and had to prove (in a 30-day long court procedure) that foreign currency loans were conformant with consumer law rules,[45] but courts were not allowed to accept the former arguments of banks that these contracts were conformant with the letter of the law at the time of signature. As a result, in most of cases banks lost the trials, which raised a constitutional problem of retroactive rules – roughly 3 billion Euros was lost.[46] Hostility towards foreign companies became visible in other sectors such as supermarket (e.g. the *Hervis* case[47]) resulted in several infringement procedures commenced by the European Commission.[48]

These actions follow a clear path: to turn away from the rules of the Single Market and to undermine the rule of law both on the domestic and EU level. This divergent trend from the values and norms of the Union leads to canceling the more than two decades of convergence to the European legal order. The response of the EU is divided into three different groups. First, there has been economic pressure applied which culminated in an excessive deficit procedure and halting of funds from the Union (although both of them were lifted eventually). Second, there was a political pressure from the European Parliament, symbolized in the so-called Tavares report and the discussion to commence the Article 7 procedure (i.e. suspension of EU voting rights based on human rights violations).[49] Thirdly, some infringement procedures were started by the Commission, mostly in connection with commercial issues. However, compared to the seriousness of the human rights violations, there

---

44   Judgment of the Court (Fourth Chamber) of 30 April 2014. Case C-26/13. ECLI:EU:C:2014:282.

45   Neil Buckley, "Hungary Struggles with Foreign Currency Loan Burden", *Financial Times* (25 July 2013), available at <http://www.ft.com/intl/cms/s/0/6c27cfbc-f50b-11e2-94e9 -00144feabdc0.html#axzz45X3O3LZl>.

46   "Banks Facing EUR 3 Billion Forex Bill, *Budapest Times* (14 September 2014), available at <http://budapesttimes.hu/2014/09/14/banks-facing-eur-3-billion-forex-bill/>.

47   Case C-385/12: Judgment of the Court (Grand Chamber) of 5 February 2014 (request for a preliminary ruling from the Székesfehérvári Törvényszék – Hungary) – Hervis Sport – és Divatkereskedelmi Kft v Nemzeti Adó – és Vámhivatal Közép-dunántúli Regionális Adó Főigazgatósága. OJ C 93, 29.3.2014, 10.

48   For further examples, see Tamás Dezső Ziegler, "The Links between Human Rights and the Single European Market: Discrimination and Systemic Infringement", 7(1) *Comparative Law Review* (2016), 1–23.

49   Report on the situation of fundamental rights: standards and practices in Hungary (pursuant to the European Parliament resolution of 16 February 2012) (2012/2130(INI)). A7-0229/2013, PE508.211v04-00.

were only a few lukewarm actions. The creation of a clearly written system that can effectively react to human right cases was proposed,[50] and the discussion seems to continue as Poland began to be mentioned.[51]

4   Conclusion: A Way Back or Total Cancellation

The process towards convergence between the Hungarian domestic legal order and the law of the European Union has its roots in the political transition period of the late 1980s, resulted in the implementation of the regulatory models, norms, rules, and values of the EU. Even though the method of adaptation – namely, the technique of harmonization – has not formally changed, Hungary's attitude to integration has in recent years transformed from a cooperative into confrontational one. Examples of this shift have been demonstrated by reference to Hungary's consistent pattern of refusing to fulfill certain obligations under EU law, or deliberately adopting domestic laws that are patently incompatible with EU law. The turning point was 2010 and this change in attitude has also been manifested in the increasing number of infringement procedures against Hungary.

Consequently, we must ask whether a path back exists. According to recent opinion polls, the governing parties sustain a strong support among voters.[52] Based on the amended electoral rules, the governing parties may retain their majority in the Parliament for the near future. For the EU, this will raise the question whether it seeks to be an economic community or a community based on democratic values, and whether it is ready to promptly intervene domestic legal procedures. Even if the current opposition gains a majority in Budapest, the provisions would be hard to be modified or "undone." For example, they cannot remove the pro-Orbán Constitutional judges, or remove the head of the National Bank, since that would be against the rule of law, while the Fundamental Law (or the items under the "cardinal laws") requires a 2/3 parliamentary majority to amend/revise. Thus, there is a fear that the

---

50   Kim Lane Scheppele, "What Can the European Commission Do When Member States Violate Basic Principles of the European Union? The Case for Systemic Infringement Actions", available at <http://ec.europa.eu/justice/events/assises-justice-2013/files/contributions/45 .princetonuniversityscheppelesystemicinfringementactionbrusselsversion_en.pdf>.

51   R. Daniel Kelemen and Mitchell A. Orenstein, "Europe's Autocracy Problem: Polish Democracy's Final Days?" *Foreign Affairs* (7 January 2016), available at <https://www .foreignaffairs.com/articles/poland/2016-01-07/europes-autocracy-problem>.

52   Median, available at <http://www.electograph.com/2016/02/hungary-february-2016-me-dian-poll.html>.

oppositions must use anti-democratic tactics in order to prohibit further human rights violations.

At present time, there seems to be a chance that the country moves into a repressive autocracy. Yet, it is in the Government's interest to try to remain in the EU as long as possible. One reason for this is that it receives support in the forms of funds from the EU. The EU's irrelevant and weak response further encourages "slow" divergence rather than rapid and dramatic takeover of the regime and the total cancellation of convergence to the European legal order. The refugee crisis has been used as a stimulus to induce fear and "nationalism" – absence of such "enemies" once again may lead people to revisit the Hungarian tradition of convergence and its democratic values.

Bibliography

Ágh, Attila. (1998) *The Politics of Central Europe* (SAGE, London).

Barna, Berke. (1997) "Implementation of the Association Agreement, Approximation of Laws, Eventual Accession: Some Constitutional Implications", in Mádl, Ferenc. (ed.), *On the State of the EU Integration Process: Enlargement and Institutional Reforms* (EU Centre for Research and Documentation, Eötvös Loránd University, Budapest), 323–341.

Boros, Tamas. (2013) "Constitutional Amendments in Hungary: The Government's Struggle against the Constitutional Court", *Analyse* (Friedrich Ebert Stiftung Büro Budapest), available at <http://www.fesbp.hu/common/pdf/Nachrichten_aus_Ungarn_februar_2013.pdf>.

Börzel, Tanja. (2005) "Europeanization: How the European Union Interacts with its Member States", in Bulmer, Simon *et al.* (eds.), *The Member States of the European Union* (Oxford University Press, Oxford), 45–76.

Bugarič, Bojan. (2014) "Protecting Democracy and the Rule of Law in the European Union: The Hungarian Challenge", *LSE "Europe in Question" Discussion Paper Series* No.79, available at <http://www.lse.ac.uk/europeanInstitute/LEQS/LEQSPaper79.pdf>.

"Editorial Comments: Hungary's New Constitutional Order and 'European Unity'", (2012) 49(3) *Common Market Law Review*, 871–883.

Fölsz, Attila and Tóka, Gábor. (2006) "Determinants of Support for EU-Membership in Hungary", in Rohrschneider, Robert and Whitefield, Stephen. (eds.), *Public Opinion, Party Competition, and the European Union in Post-Communist Europe* (Palgrave Macmillan, Basingstoke), 145–164.

Gyulavári, Tamás and Hős, Nikolett. (2013) "Retirement of Hungarian Judges, Age Discrimination and Judicial Independence: A Tale of Two Courts", 42(3) *Industrial Law Journal*, 289–297.

Harmathy, Attila. (2001) "Constitutional Questions of the Preparation of Hungary to Accession to the European Union", in Kellermann, Alfred *et al.* (eds.), *EU Enlargement: The Constitutional Impact at EU and National Level* (T.M.C. Asser Press, The Hague).

Harmathy, Attila. (ed.) (1998) *Introduction to Hungarian Law* (Kluwer, The Hague).

Horváthy, Balázs. (2008), "After the First Lessons and Experiences: Cases Concerning Hungary before ECJ (2004–2007)", 49 (1) *Acta Juridica Hungarica*, 89–110.

Horváthy, Balázs and Knapp, László. (2013) "The Relationship between the Hungarian and the EU Legal Orders", in Smuk, Péter. (ed.), *The Transformation of the Hungarian Legal System 2010–2013* (CompLex Wolters Kluwer, Budapest), 51–68.

Jacoby, Wade. (2004) *Ordering from the Menu in Central Europe: The Enlargement of the EU and NATO* (Cambridge University Press, Cambridge).

Jakab, András and Sonnevend, Pál. (2013) "Continuity with Deficiencies: The New Basic Law of Hungary", 9(1) *European Constitutional Law Review*, 102–138.

Johnston, Andrew. (2010) "Cross-Border Re-structuring, Company Law between Treaty Freedom and State Protectionism", in Bernitz, Ulf and Ringe, Wolf-Georg. (eds.), *Company Law and Economic Protectionism: New Challenges to European Integration* (Oxford University Press, Oxford).

Kovács, Kriszta and Tóth, Gábor Attila. (2011) "Hungary's Constitutional Transformation" 7(2) *European Constitutional Law Review*, 183–203.

Legrand, Pierre. (2002) "Public Law, Europeanisation, and Convergence: Can Comparatists Contribute?", in Beaumont, Paul, Lyons, Carole, and Walker, Neil. (eds.), *Convergence and Divergence in European Public Law* (Oxford University Press, Oxford).

Lyons, Carole. (2002) "Perspectives on Convergence within European Integration", Beaumont, Paul, Lyons, Carole, and Walker, Neil. (eds.), *Convergence and Divergence in European Public Law* (Oxford University Press, Oxford).

Martin, Reiner. (1999) *The Regional Dimension in European Public Policy: Convergence or Divergence?* (Palgrave Macmillan, Basingstoke).

O'Brennan, John. (2006) *The Eastern Enlargement of the European Union* (Routledge, London).

Pajor-Bytomski, Magdalena. (1994) *Gesellschaftsrecht in Ungarn (Company Law in Hungary)*, (Hüthig, München).

Phinnemore David. (1999) *Association: Stepping-Stone Or Alternative to EU Membership?* (Sheffield Academic Press, Sheffield).

Sárközy, Tamás. (2007) *A szocializmus, a rendszerváltás és az újkapitalizmus gazdasági civiljoga 1945–2005 (The Economic-Private Law of the Socialism, the Transition and the New Capitalism 1945–2005)* (HVG-Orac, Budapest).

Schimmelfennig, Frank and Sedelmeier, Ulrich. (eds.) (2005) *The Europeanization of Central and Eastern Europe* (Cornell University Press, Ithaca).

Tatham, Allan, F. (2009) *Enlargement of the European Union* (Wolters Kluwer, Austin).

Tóth, Gábor Attila. (ed.) (2012) *Constitution for a Disunited Nation: On Hungary's 2011 Fundamental Law* (Central European University Press, Budapest).

Varju, Márton and Fazekas, Flóra. (2011) "The Reception of European Union Law in Hungary: The Constitutional Court and the Hungarian Judiciary", 48(6) *Common Market Law Review*, 1945–1984.

Vörös, Imre. (2003) "The Legal Doctrine and Legal Policy Aspects of the EU-Accession", 44(3–4) *Acta Juridica Hungarica*, 141–163.

Ziegler, Tamás Dezső. (2016) "The Links between Human Rights and the Single European Market: Discrimination and Systemic Infringement", 7(1) *Comparative Law Review*, 1–23.

CHAPTER 3

The Use of Referendum in Central and Eastern Europe after EU Accession

Sergiu Gherghina

Abstract

The amount of referendums organized at national level in Central and Eastern Europe has gradually increased. This chapter analyzes the extent to which this development is related to the EU accession. It also provides several attempts to explain the possible mechanisms behind the observed changes. To this end, it provides a comparative analysis of the 11 newest Member States covering both the pre- and post-accession periods (up to 2013, i.e. ten years of accession). The chapter draws on a unique set of data and uses a statistical approach. It focuses on three dimensions: the type of referendum, popular participation, and the success (i.e. if the issue subjected to referendum has been approved) of the referendum.

Keywords

referendum – participation – citizens – institutional change

1 Introduction

The basic principle of direct democracy is that ordinary citizens express their preference on a public issue without an intermediary institution. As a recognition of referendums' importance in promoting democracy, all 11 post-2004 joiners to the EU have formalized mechanisms that trigger and govern referendums in their Constitutions (see Appendix 1). Unlike the principle of representation in which the electorate at large chooses delegates (and their political parties) to make choices, in direct democracy people vote for an outcome (policy). For scholars concerned about the democratic deficit and the growing gap between institutions and citizens, this alternative way to participate in politics may provide a fresh approach. At the same time, politicians and lawmakers may find the direct involvement of citizens beneficial for political legitimacy, conflict solving, and quality of government.

The direct democracy complements representative democracy and can have positive consequences for society. For example, in Switzerland direct democracy enhanced the creation of a consensus democracy in which decisions are taken through a process of discussion, rationalization and agreement rather than simply voting on "issues." This is possible partly because the individuals who participate in referendums are often better educated and more informed than the rest of the citizenry and thus more competent voters express opinions in direct democracy practices than in elections.[1] The existence of direct democracy initiatives (especially those coming from citizens) presupposes extensive interactions with the political elites that the state institutions are given time to consider policy-proposals and have the possibility to suggest alternative proposals.[2]

Accordingly, states have increasingly resorted to referendums – the most common form of direct democracy – as a tool for the decision-making process. In this sense, many European countries have approved direct democracy regulations over the last three decades.[3] Moreover, while binding referendums were almost unknown in Europe until the 1990s, 16 European states have institutionalized them with substantial variations in their national or regional constitutions.[4] The variety of referendums, in terms of type and policy addressed, increased considerably over time. Lithuania, for example, did not even specify in its 1992 constitution any types of referendum other than binding ones.[5] Only ten years later, in 2002, the consultative (i.e. non-binding) referendum was formally introduced and once organized in 2012 (as opposed to 10 binding referendums organized in the country since 1991 prior to 2012).

---

1 Hanspeter Kriesi, "Direct Democracy: Swiss Experience", in Brigitte Geissel and Kenneth Newton (eds.), *Evaluating Democratic Innovations: Curing the Democratic Malaise?* (Routledge, London, 2012), 39–55.

2 Graham Smith, *Democratic Innovations: Designing Institutions for Citizen Participation* (Cambridge University Press, Cambridge, 2009), 120.

3 David Butler and Austin Ranney (eds.), *Referendums around the World: The Growing Use of Direct Democracy* (Macmillan, Basingstoke, 1994); Matthew Mendelsohn and Andrew Parkin (eds.), *Referendum Democracy: Citizens, Elites and Deliberation in Referendum Campaigns* (Palgrave Macmillan, Basingstoke, 2001); Susan Scarrow, "Direct Democracy and Institutional Change: A Comparative Investigation", 34(6) *Comparative Political Studies* (2001), 651–665; and Lawrence LeDuc, *The Politics of Direct Democracy: Referendums in Global Perspective* (Broadview Press, Toronto, 2003).

4 Laurence Morel, "The Rise of 'Politically Obligatory' Referendums: The 2005 French Referendum in Comparative Perspective", 30(5) *West European Politics* (2007), 1041–1067.

5 Kestutis Lapinskas, "Referendum in Lithuanian Constitutional Practice", in European Commission for Democracy through Law (ed.), *Constitutional Justice and Democracy by Referendum* (Council of Europe Publishing, Strasbourg, 1996), 121–126.

In general, direct democratic rules found their way into almost all Central and Eastern European (CEE) constitutions adopted after the regime change.[6] Many of these countries have explicitly introduced mandatory referendums, i.e. constitutionally required upon particular issues. The most common issues are constitution approval or modification. Some countries mention the mandatory referendum when the country had to join the European Union (EU) (Croatia, the Czech Republic, Latvia) or when there are important modifications to the structure of state institutions such as the dissolution of legislature (Latvia) or dismissal of a President (Romania). In addition, many countries allow their citizens to initiate referendums based on a certain number of signatures that can be either a percentage of the total electorate or a specific number of signatures from citizens with the right to vote.[7]

Partly as a result of these formal provisions, the use of referendums is quite extensive in the CEE nations. An overview of the national-level referendums organized in Europe since 1990 indicates that approximately two-thirds of these have been conducted in CEE countries. This calculation does not take into account Ireland, Italy, and Switzerland, countries with considerable experience in organizing referendums on various topics.[8] The popularity of referendums in post-communist Europe becomes identifiable in the beginning of the 1990s when many countries from the former Soviet Union and Yugoslavia asked their citizens to express an opinion on the matter of state independence. The 2004 EU enlargement was another important event leading to a great number of referendums. Apart from these major changes, referendums have been used on many occasions with variation in terms of type, topic, and popular participation.

So far, in spite of such diversity, there is no systematic account about the use of referendums in CEE. This situation contrasts with Western Europe where extensive research has been conducted on the developments and causes of

---

6   Melanie Walter-Rogg, "Direkte Demokratie", in Oscar W. Gabriel (ed.), *Die EU-Staaten im Vergleich: Strukturen, Prozesse, Politikinhalte* (*The EU Countries in Comparison: Structures, Processes, Policy Content*) (vs Verlag für Sozialwissenschaft, Wiesbaden, 2008), 236–267.

7   Among the countries investigated in this chapter only Slovenia maintains the number of signatures required by citizens' initiatives to organize a referendum relative to a percentage of the electorate (10%). Croatia has been for a long period of time the other country, but is has recently shifted from percentage (10%, approximately 450,000 voters) to a specific number (415,000 voters).

8   Jane O'Mahony, "The Irish Referendum Experience", 35(4) *Representation* (1998), 225–236; Maija Setala, "Referendums in Western Europe – A Wave of Direct Democracy?" 22(4) *Scandinavian Political Studies* (1999), 327–338; and Hanspeter Kriesi, *Direct Democratic Choice: The Swiss Experience* (Lexington Books, Plymouth, 2005).

referendums.[9] In CEE countries, particular attention has been dedicated to the EU membership referendums.[10] To contribute to the existing literature, this chapter analyzes the use of referendums from a cross-national perspective before (starting with the regime change or the first year of independence) and after the EU accession (up to 2013, i.e. ten years of accession).[11] In doing so, it seeks to observe the evolution in the use of and content of referendums following the EU accession. Accordingly, this study focuses on the new EU Member States from CEE, including the most recent joiner Croatia.

The analysis is structured along three analytical dimensions: the type of referendum, the level of participation (turnout) and success (whether the referendums have made it). Each of these dimensions corresponds to one of the following sections as follows. The following section discusses the types of referendums relative to initiators and what happens after the direct voting takes place. The third section analyzes how many citizens participate over time. The next section reviews the referendum success (rate of adoption), while the conclusions summarize the main findings and discuss their implications.

2   Types of Referendum in CEE

The classification of referendums has been an ongoing concern in the literature. This section focuses on the introduction and outcome of a referendum. With respect to the introduction, Suksi has provided a compelling differentiation between mandatory and non-mandatory referendums.[12] The mandatory referendums are stipulated by law in certain circumstances which are normally issues of great political importance (e.g. constitutional revision, issues related to state sovereignty, transfer of competences to international organizations etc.).[13] This type has already been discussed in the introduction and occurs

9   Vernon Bogdanor, "Western Europe", in Butler and Ranney, *op. cit.* note 3; Michael Gallagher and Pier Vincenzo Uleri (eds.), *The Referendum Experience in Europe* (Macmillan, London, 1996); Setala *Ibid.*; and Sara Binzer Hobolt, "How Parties Affect Vote Choice in European Integration Referendums", 12(5) *Party Politics* (2006), 623–647.

10   Y.V. Tverdova and C.J. Anderson, "Choosing the West? Referendum Choices on EU Membership in East-Central Europe", 23(2) *Electoral Studies* (2004), 185–208.

11   The accession differs across countries: 2004 for eight of them, 2007 for Bulgaria and Romania, and 2013 for Croatia.

12   Markku Suksi, *Bringing in the People: A Comparison of Constitutional Forms and Practices of the Referendum* (Martinus Nijhoff Publishers, Dordrecht, 1993).

13   For a detailed account of the provisions of mandatory referendums in CEE, see Anneli Albi, "Referendums in Eastern Europe: The Effects of Reforming the EU Treaties and on the Candidate Countries' Positions in the Convention", *EUI Working Papers* (2002) No. 65.

in the case of specific issues of great importance to a political system that can be modified only through referendum. Mandatory referendums are also called law controlling.[14]

Within the non-mandatory category, Suksi identifies two types: active (introduced by citizens) and passive (introduced by state authorities). Following this typology, I distinguish between three types of referendums: mandatory, passive (introduced by the President, the Government, or Parliament) and active. The latter type includes all those referendum initiatives that rely on signatures gathered from citizens irrespective of the main supporter. Gathering signatures is an expensive endeavor that requires coordination. Since citizens can hardly do this without institutional help, political parties have often taken the lead in citizens' initiatives. In Western Europe, Italy is a well-known case where the Radical Party has organized many referendums in the last two decades. Similarly, many of the citizen-initiated referendums in CEE have been guided by political parties – usually in the opposition or extra-parliamentary.

What counts as a referendum? Since a referendum is defined as the process through which citizens vote on a public issue,[15] the emphasis should be on the issue itself. This is the functional equivalent of the choice made by voters (usually) between two alternatives. This choice is the answer to one question on the ballot. Following this reasoning, a referendum is the answer to such a question.[16] Accordingly, if more than one question is asked within an electoral in a single day, I consider them to be more than one referendum. Apart from this conceptual reason, three additional arguments can be brought to substantiate my operationalization. First, citizens can choose which of the questions they want to answer. In practice, even if more questions are asked at the same time, the turnout is fairly similar. However, there are cases, as in Slovenia in 2011, when the turnout differed for each question.[17] Second, the initiator of the questions asked the same day could be different. One example is Slovenia with the referendums organized in December 1996 to reform the electoral system when two questions came from Parliament, whereas the third was citizen-initiated.[18] Third, the questions asked during the same day are often very different. For example, in May 1997 the Slovak

---

14   Gallagher and Uleri, *op. cit.* note 9.

15   Butler and Ranney, *op. cit.* note 3.

16   This chapter does not differentiate between referendum and plebiscite.

17   In the analyzed countries there are not many instances in which more referendums are organized simultaneously. These cases are Croatia (1991), Hungary (2004 and 2008), Poland (1996), Romania (2009), Slovakia (1997 and 2010), and Slovenia (2003 and 2011).

18   The 1996 referendums in Slovenia is different than the other CEE referendums from the perspective of choices offered to citizens. A referendum usually offers the electorate two choices: either to accept or reject a proposal. In 1996 Slovenians were presented with

electorate was supposed to express their opinions on questions related to NATO – membership, nuclear weapons, and military bases – and the direct election of their president in the same day.[19] Similarly, in April 2004 they had questions about early elections, structure of the legislature, and legislation on fees for public broadcasters.

According to this measurement, the total number of referendums in CEE is 88 for the time period between 1990 and 2013 (i.e. prior to the ten year anniversary of their accession). The first included referendum took place in Hungary (29 July 1990) on the issue of direct election of the country's president and the last referendum (in this period) was organized in Croatia (1 December 2013) to amend the constitution to prohibit same-sex marriages. All 11 CEE Member States had organized at least one referendum, the country with most referendums being Slovenia, while Bulgaria and the Czech Republic have the least (only one). From the total number of referendums approximately 45% were organized before the EU accession and 55% after. The latter percentage includes referendums on EU membership.

Regarding the initiator, Figure 3.1 depicts the three types before and after the EU accession. The percentages illustrate that the number of mandatory referendums has increased after the EU accession. One possible explanation for this ascending trend is the constitutional provision of some countries like the Czech Republic or Latvia to hold referendums when sovereignty issues are involved. With respect to the referendums initiated by state institutions, there are fewer in the period following the EU accession. This decrease of state institutions' pro-activity in calling for referendums can be due both to an external EU influence and to democratic consolidation. In this respect, the executive and legislatures have gradually learned that political and policy conflicts can be solved in another way than through the involvement of mass public.

The bottom-up referendums (initiated by citizens) have gained considerable popularity when countries joined the EU (almost 70% compared to slightly more than 30% before the EU accession). The increased importance of citizens initiated is better observed when calculating their share within the post-accession period, compared to other types of referendums. Over the last decade, 19% of the initiated referendums were mandatory; state institutions

---

three alternative proposals of an electoral system and they could accept only one. They could, however, reject all three and almost 10% of those who voted proceeded as such.

19   In the end, the question about the direct election of the president was removed by the government from the ballots. As a result, the opposition and its supporters boycotted the entire process. The turnout in the other three referendums organized the same day was very low (9.5%) and thus did not meet the required threshold.

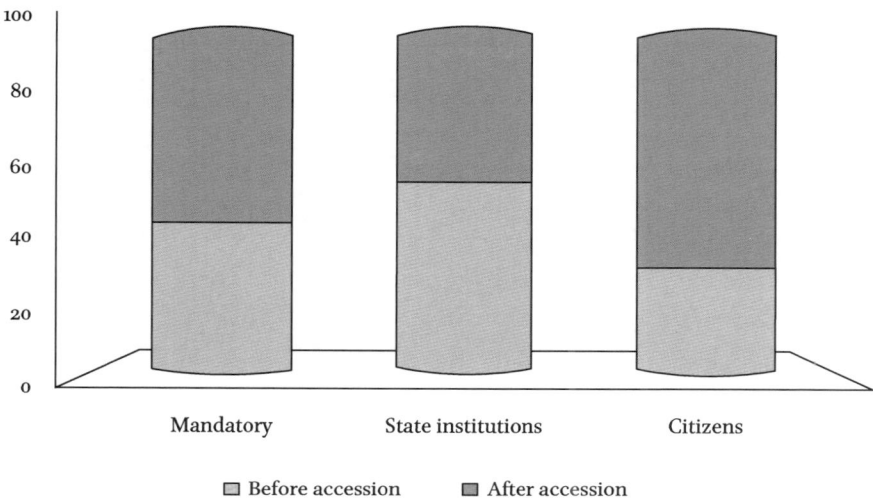

FIGURE 3.1 *The referendum initiators before and after the EU accession*

initiated 39%, whereas citizens initiated 42%. Such a percentage is more impressive if we consider that some of the CEE countries (Estonia, Romania) do not even allow their citizens to initiate referendums.

A second criterion to classify referendums is the way in which their outcome influences a country's structure of governance. In this sense, the key question is whether the referendum is binding or it is only consultative. In CEE the binding referendums are predominant (approximately 70%). Their number would have been even higher if Slovakia, a country that organized several referendums, would allow for binding referendums outside issues related to alliances with other countries (none of these has been subject to referendum since 1992). The amount of mandatory referendums is relatively small and always binding. Of the total number of referendums initiated by state authorities, 60% are binding. With respect to the citizen-initiated referendums, the percentage of binding referendums is higher (69%).

The EU accession makes no difference with respect to the outcome. The share of consultative vs. binding referendums is similar in the periods before and after the EU accession. Approximately 30% of the total number of referendums organized in either period is consultative. Looking within the two categories across the selected periods of time, they have a relatively equal increase: the consultative from 44% before the EU accession to 56% in the period after accession and the binding referendums from 46% to 54%.

To sum up, in the CEE countries the EU accession corresponds to an increase in the bottom-up and a decrease of state institutions' initiatives to organize referendums. The mechanisms behind this observation are likely to be related to the process of democratic learning and external pressure; both are subject to further empirical investigation. At the same time, most CEE referendums are organized with a binding character irrespective of the period of time.

3   Participation in Referendums

One core argument of the scholars who support the use of direct democracy is the improvement of decision-making quality and acceptance. The ordinary citizens are given the opportunity to directly influence government policies and the outcome is supposed to reflect the general will. Nevertheless, people do not always engage in this process. This section focuses on the popular participation in the CEE referendums and starts with a general comparison between the turnout rates.

The average turnout in the referendums after the EU accession is slightly smaller (42%) compared with the referendums organized before (46%). At the same time, the turnout in the post-accession period minimum presence of 11% and maximum of 71.5%) appears to be more homogeneous than before (minimum presence of 9,5% and maximum of 93.5%). Figure 3.2 depicts the turnout distribution for the two separate periods. It shows that the turnout in the post-accession referendums has been clustered in the 20–60% range with peaks at 20% and 40%. The referendums organized in this period do not have very high turnouts (above 80%) as it happened previously on several occasions.

While the frequency of participation reveals some differences, it is relevant to understand how they emerge. In this respect, the remainder of this section investigates the relationship between turnout, on the one hand, and the binding character of the referendum, existence of participation thresholds, and initiator, on the other hand. To better understand the signs of the coefficients presented in the following paragraphs, several details about coding are necessary. For the binding character of the referendums and for the existence of a participation threshold I have used a dichotomous coding 0 for consultative and 1 for binding; 0 if a threshold is not required and 1 if it is in place. For the referendum initiator a three-point scale has been used ordering the choices from the most top-down to bottom-up: the mandatory referendum was coded 1, the referendum initiated by institutions was coded 2, and the citizen-initiated referendum was coded 3.

Following the arguments presented above, there is likely to be a higher turnout when people perceive their decision as being important (i.e. referendums are binding). The correlation for the entire investigated period indicates that

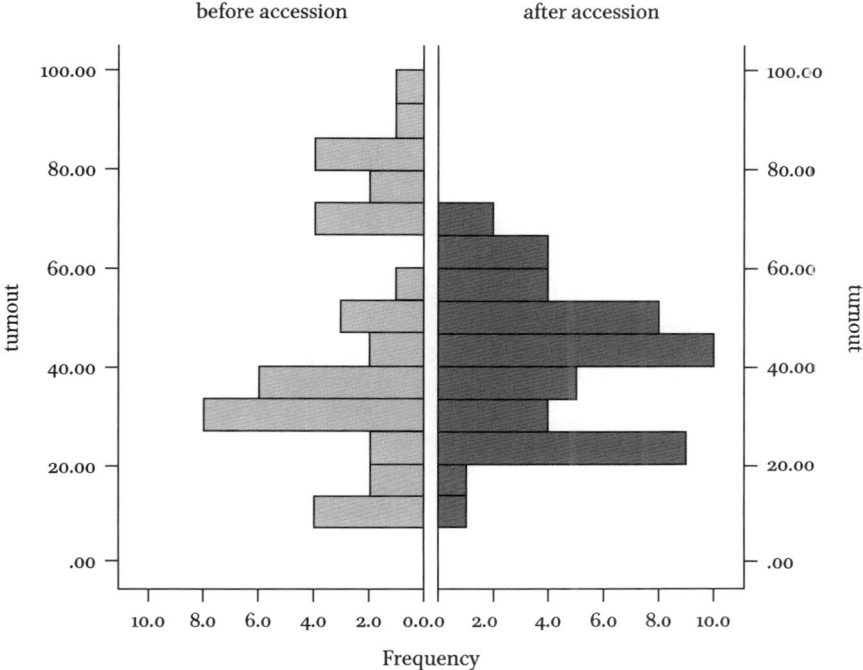

FIGURE 3.2 *The distribution of turnout in the CEE referendums*

this expectation is supported by evidence in CEE. The value of the coefficient is positive (0.43, statistically significant at 0.01) showing a medium to strong tendency of voters to show up at polls when the referendum is binding. When dividing the time period, we observe relevant differences. Before accession, the turnout was influenced much more by the existence of a threshold (correlation coefficient of 0.59, statistically significant at the 0.01 level) than in the post-accession phase (correlation coefficient of 0.26, not statistically significant).

In line with the general preference for binding referendums, many CEE countries have established turnout thresholds to validate referendums. In almost two-thirds of the organized referendums (65%) a threshold was required, the Czech Republic and Estonia being the only countries that have never used such thresholds. The most common threshold is half of the total number of voters, but sometimes the threshold was relative to the previous legislative elections (e.g. Bulgaria in 2013, Latvia in 2003). To test for the existence of a relationship between turnout and the existence of a threshold, I have run a bivariate correlation. For the period 1990–2012, the close to zero value of the coefficient (0.01) indicates the absence of a relationship between turnout and required threshold. In other words, the pressure of an existing threshold did not have any impact on people's participation. When running the same correlation for the before and after accession periods (Table 3.1) there is a slight difference between the pre and post-accession. Before accession, the value of the coefficient is similar to that of the entire period (0.01, not statistically significant) showing that the presence of threshold does not discourage voters to vote in referendums. Following the accession, the coefficient is negative but still very low (−0.03, not statistically significant). This reveals a weak negative relationship that can be interpreted as follows: in the isolated occasions when the presence of a threshold is related to popular participation in referendums, the threshold inhibits voter turnout. Differently put, following the EU accession there is a weak tendency among the voters to participate more in the referendums that do not require threshold.

The correlation between referendum initiator and turnout indicates that in CEE people attend the most the mandatory referendums (−0.40, statistically significant at the 0.01 level). One explanation is that the issues subjected to voters' choice are very important. In these situations, ordinary citizens realize that their voice counts and they participate more than in other referendums. Another possible explanation is the media coverage received by the event and the joint forces of political actors to persuade citizens to vote in the referendum. For example, the 2003 referendum in Romania was called to alter the constitution. The modifications were required by the EU accession. All political parties, with the exception of the radical right Greater Romania Party, joined efforts to make sure that the threshold (at least 50% of the total number of voters) was

TABLE 3.1   *Statistical analysis for the CEE referendum participation*

	Correlation		OLS regression	
	Before	After	Before	After
Binding character	0.59**	0.26	0.67** (7.04)	0.19 (4.37)
Participation threshold	0.01	−0.03	0.32* (7.14)	0.13 (4.10)
Initiator	−0.35**	−0.49**	−0.25* (4.73)	−0.48** (2.66)
R^2			0.45	0.23
N	40	48	40	48

Notes:
* significant at 0.05.
** significant at 0.01
Regression coefficients are standardized (standard errors in brackets).

reached. This was done at all costs, with independent observers reporting a number of frauds that augmented participation.

The coefficients reported in Table 3.1 indicate that the relationship is stronger in the aftermath of EU accession. In spite of a growing number of bottom-up initiated (i.e. active) referendums in this period, ordinary citizens are less attracted by such initiatives. The participation in state-organized referendums – either mandatory or called by president, government, or parliament – is high after EU accession. Thus, the turnout difference between top-down and bottom-up initiated referendums is higher in the most recent period. An additional explanation for such a result could be related to the high impact of participation threshold.

In addition to these bivariate tests, I have checked whether the determinants of turnout are different before and after the EU accession. To this end, I included all the above-mentioned variables in an OLS regression.[20] The results are also presented in Table 3.1 and they add relevant information to the observations made when interpreting the correlations. The explanatory power of the two models is different: the pre-accession model explains 45% of the variation in turnout and the post-accession model does a poorer job and explains 23% of this variation.

In essence, the multivariate models reveal that the strongest predictor of participation in referendums after the EU accession is the mandatory type. The second determinant is the binding character of the referendum. These results indicate that salient issues added to the agenda by state actors drive post-accession participation in referendums. In contrast, the binding character of a referendum is the most powerful predictor for turnout before accession. This is followed by the existence of a threshold and state-initiated referendums. It can be observed that the weakest predictor before accession (who initiates the referendum) has become the strongest after the CEE countries joined the EU. It should also be noted that the participation threshold has more explanatory power in the multivariate model than in the bivariate analysis. Accordingly, this variable can explain variations in turnout only in the presence of other variables. The main conclusions to be drawn on the basis of this regression analysis are that (1) the mandatory referendums gained importance in explaining participation in the post-accession period and (2) the binding aspect of referendums lost its relevance compared to the pre-accession period.

---

20   It is tested for multi-colinearity between the independent variables and the correlation coefficients indicate that this is not the case. The highest value is −0.40, statistically significant at 0.01 (between initiator and required threshold in the pre-accession period), the other values are between 0.14 and 0.30, the latter being statistically significant at 0.05.

One explanation for these trends is that the EU membership referendums have represented a turning point in the history of direct democracy in CEE: Although called in the vast majority of examined countries, most of them were consultative. Due to membership salience for the future of their country, people expressed their opinion on the matter because it was important, not because it was binding. Such an attitude could have a spillover effect over the referendums that followed. In this sense, ordinary citizens focus more on the importance of the issue at stake rather than on the procedural aspect that follows. This approach could also justify the high participation in state-initiated referendums since referendums that are mandatory or called by state institutions are likely to address the concerns of a large amount of the population. In contrast, the bottom-up referendums reflect concerns of particular groups – smaller or larger – in society and people belonging to other groups are less persuaded to participate. Of course, there are cases that do not follow this general line of argumentation. One of them is the 2012 referendum in Latvia regarding the use of Russian as a second official language. The referendum has been organized following the gathering of signatures coordinated by two Russian organizations and the participation rate was the highest since 1991.

4   Successful Referendums

The success rate of referendums is the last analytical dimension of this chapter. Success is conceptualized in a straightforward manner as the answer to the question: has the issue subjected to referendum been approved? Two criteria are used to assess if a referendum has been successful or not. In order to call it a success, both criteria should be met. First, it is important to know if the referendum has passed the participation or approval thresholds. The approval threshold is a supplementary (formal) provision that requires a certain percentage of the total electorate to vote in favor of the issue subjected to referendum in order to validate it. For example, in Lithuania a referendum is not valid only if 50% of the electorate participates; it is a necessary but not sufficient condition. For the referendum to pass, 50% of the electorate should vote "yes" to the referendum question. This is one reason for which the 1992 referendum on the restoration of the presidential institution in Lithuania has not been successful. Although the turnout was 59.18% and out of these 69.27% voted in favor, the percentage of favorable votes from the entire electorate was only 41%.

Second, the results of all the referendums passing the threshold(s) have been checked. If the majority of votes were cast in favor of the proposed issue, then the referendum is considered successful. If there are more votes against the proposal, then the referendum was coded as unsuccessful. Throughout the examined period, 39% of the called referendums were successful. Since all the EU accession referendums were validated the rate of success after that moment is slightly higher than before. Accordingly, after the EU accession 44% of the organized referendums were successful compared to 33% before that moment.

The success of referendums appears closely linked to the initiator. The role of the latter has been already dealt with in previous sections. Throughout the entire examined period, the mandatory referendums have the highest percentage of success – almost 70%. They are followed by the referendums proposed by state institutions with 40% and those initiated by citizens with 21%. Practically, one in five referendums initiated by citizens was successful. One of these has been the 2013 Croatian referendum about a constitutional amendment that defines marriage as being between two persons of different sex.

Figure 3.3 depicts the success of referendums for the two periods of time. The bars represent the percentage of successful referendums within each type. The major observation is that referendums became increasingly successful – for all three categories – since the EU accession. In absolute values, the highest increase is among the mandatory referendums but in relative terms, the biggest increase can be observed among the citizen-initiated referendums. This increase in success coincides with a general increase of this type of referendums from 9 in the period before accession to 20 after EU accession.

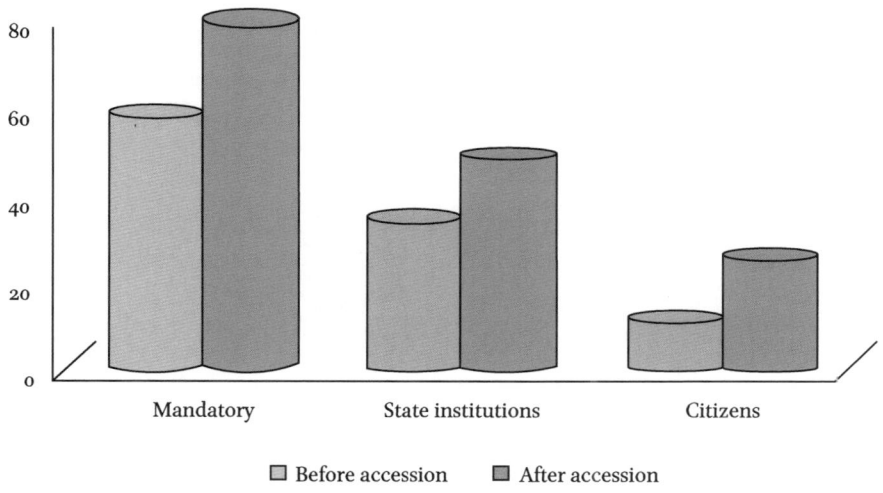

FIGURE 3.3 *The rate of success in CEE referendums*

5   **Conclusion**

All contemporary democracies rely extensively on representatives to formulate and implement policies. With many advantages in terms of efficiency, expertise and experience, the downside is that elected representatives may fail to pursue the public interest (i.e. the general will). The likelihood of such an ending is high especially in young democracies where institutions do not function properly and the plague of corruption spreads quickly. One solution to the "malaise" is to empower the electorate to have a direct say on policies. Building on these premises, this chapter has provided an overview on the use of referendums in 11 CEE countries during post-communism. The analysis has been divided in two major periods having as point of reference the EU accession. As earlier research shows, this moment has been a cornerstone in the political development of CEE countries.

While it is very difficult to assess the impact of Europeanization on the use of referendums, this study has shown the existence of important differences before and after the EU accession. In this respect, one key conclusion has been that in the most recent decade the number of citizen-initiated referendums has increased considerably. The role of the EU in this development remains to be empirically tested, but one general explanation can be sketched. The EU accession was both the official recognition of democratic developments and the openness to alternative ways of making decisions. On the one hand, countries did not have exclusive say with respect to some policies due to compliance with the EU. On the other hand, broader initiatives such as the European Citizens' Initiative could inspire national-level proposals.

A second important observation is that participation in referendums has slowly decreased after the EU accession and is mainly driven by the importance of the topic (i.e. in mandatory referendums). Along these lines, the EU accession referendums are illustrative since they attracted a large amount of the population at polls. Related to this issue, the third important conclusion is that referendums have become more successful after accession. This can be due to a general learning process in which a referendum is called if it has a good chance of making it through. In this sense, the EU-related referendums – organized not only in CEE but in Western Europe as well – may have served as useful examples.

The main purpose of this chapter has been exploratory. All these differences can be better understood if an in-depth causal analysis is conducted. This will help identifying how the Europeanization process is reflected in the use of referendums. To follow this avenue of investigation, a refinement of the concepts and measurement is necessary and new variables should be added. Further research can also focus on the ways in which referendums have become legal ways to promote democracy within post-communist politics. For example, some of the presented referendums have been abrogative, while others follow European norms – in particular in the post-accession period. Accordingly, future exploration can explain why these differences occur and how they are related to the legislation.

Appendix 1

The Constitutional Provisions and Number of Analyzed Referendums

Country	Constitution articles about national referendums	Number of referendums
Bulgaria	Art. 10, 42, 84, 98, 102	1
Croatia	Art. 80, 81, 87, 98, 125	4
Czech Republic	Art. 10a, 62, 87	1
Estonia	Art. 56, 65, 105, 106, 162, 163, 164	4
Hungary	Art. 8, 9	8
Latvia	Art. 14, 48, 50, 68	8
Lithuania	Art. 9, 69, 148, 151, 152	11
Poland	Art. 62, 90, 125, 144, 235	7
Romania	Art. 2, 73, 90, 95, 146, 151	7
Slovakia	Art. 7, 86, 93, 94, 95, 96, 97, 98, 99, 102	15
Slovenia	Art. 3a, 90, 97, 99, 170	22

Bibliography

Albi, Anneli. (2002) "Referendums in Eastern Europe: The Effects of Reforming the EU Treaties and on the Candidate Countries' Positions in the Convention", *EUI Working Papers* No. 65.

Bogdanor, Vernon. (1994) "Western Europe", in Butler, David and Ranney, Austin. (eds.), *Referendums around the World: The Growing Use of Direct Democracy* (Macmillan, Basingstoke).

Butler, David and Ranney, Austin. (eds.) (1994) *Referendums around the World: The Growing Use of Direct Democracy* (Macmillan, Basingstoke).

Gallagher, Michael and Uleri, Pier Vincenzo (eds.) (1996) *The Referendum Experience in Europe* (Macmillan, London).

Hobolt, Sara Binzer. (2006) "How Parties Affect Vote Choice in European Integration Referendums", 12(5) *Party Politics*, 623–647.

Kriesi, Hanspeter. (2012) "Direct Democracy: Swiss Experience", in Geissel, Brigitte and Newton, Kenneth. (eds.) *Evaluating Democratic Innovations: Curing the Democratic Malaise?* (Routledge, London), 39–55.

Kriesi, Hanspeter. (2005) *Direct Democratic Choice: The Swiss Experience* (Lexington Books, Plymouth).

Lapinskas, Kestutis. (1996) "Referendum in Lithuanian Constitutional Practice", in European Commission for Democracy through Law. (ed.), *Constitutional Justice and Democracy by Referendum* (Council of Europe Publishing, Strasbourg), 121–126.

LeDuc, Lawrence. (2003) *The Politics of Direct Democracy: Referendums in Global Perspective* (Broadview Press, Toronto).

Mendelsohn, Matthew and Parkin, Andrew. (eds.) (2001) *Referendum Democracy: Citizens, Elites and Deliberation in Referendum Campaigns* (Palgrave Macmillan, Basingstoke).

Morel, Laurence. (2007) "The Rise of 'Politically Obligatory' Referendums: The 2005 French Referendum in Comparative Perspective", 30(5) *West European Politics*, 1041–1067.

O'Mahony, Jane. (1998) "The Irish Referendum Experience", 35(4) *Representation*, 225–236.

Scarrow, Susan. (2001) "Direct Democracy and Institutional Change: A Comparative Investigation", 34(6) *Comparative Political Studies*, 651–665.

Setala, Maija. (1999) "Referendums in Western Europe – A Wave of Direct Democracy?" 22(4) *Scandinavian Political Studies*, 327–338.

Smith, Graham. (2009) *Democratic Innovations: Designing Institutions for Citizen Participation* (Cambridge University Press, Cambridge).

Suksi, Markku. (1993) *Bringing in the People: A Comparison of Constitutional Forms and Practices of the Referendum* (Martinus Nijhoff Publishers, Dordrecht).

Tverdova, Y.V. and Anderson, C.J. (2004) "Choosing the West? Referendum Choices on EU Membership in East-Central Europe", 23(2) *Electoral Studies*, 185-208.

Walter-Rogg, Melanie. (2008) "Direkte Demokratie", in Gabriel, Oscar W. (ed.), *Die EU-Staaten im Vergleich: Strukturen, Prozesse, Politikinhalte (The EU Countries in Comparison: Structures, Processes, Policy Content)* (vs Verlag für Sozialwissenschaft, Wiesbaden), 236–267.

CHAPTER 4

Special Economic Zones in Poland: A Black Hole Swallowing State Budget or a Messiah for Regional Development?

Hiroshi Kaneko

Abstract

Special Economic Zones (SEZs) in Poland have accumulated 35% of Foreign Direct Investment (FDI) flowing in for the manufacturing sector, as Poland celebrates its 10 years of European accession in 2014. With foreign capital playing a crucial role, SEZs were regarded as a major driving force for the Polish economy. As a Member State of the EU, Poland was required to reduce or even eliminate the tax incentives available in SEZs. The Government's response was an interesting blend of ensuring the compatibility with the EU's regional state aid policy and maintaining various financial and legal benefits in SEZs. Geographically speaking, however, the SEZs in south-western Poland remain popular among foreign investors, raising a question of SEZ's effectiveness as a regional development policy tool. This chapter assesses the Polish SEZs affirmatively, stating that the scheme contributed to draw a lesson from numerous legal amendments to create an investor-friendly environment in Poland. In other words, the Polish lawmakers and local municipalities learned to improve the quality of FDI promotion policy in this process of trial and error.

Keywords

Special Economic Zones – FDI promotion policy – investment incentives – EU regional state aid – EU Funds

1   Introduction

The Polish Government, under the strong initiative of the Ministry of Economy, introduced the Law on the Special Economic Zones (SEZ) in 1994.[1] The

---

1   Journal of Laws (1994), No 123, item 600.

Law aimed to reduce the structural unemployment in certain regions of the country by promoting new investments with attractive financial benefits.[2] Currently, 14 SEZs are in operation and the cumulative investment outlays in SEZS at the end of 2015 reached to 111.7 billion Polish Zlotys (PLN) (approx. EUR 26.2 billion) with almost 312,000 work places created.[3] The incentive scheme in SEZs takes a form of tax exemption from Corporate Income Tax (CIT) or Personal Income Tax (PIT) for both domestic and foreign investors.[4] By the end of 2015, 80.2% of the cumulative investment value had been realized by foreign investors (Germany 18.9%, USA 12.1%, Netherlands 10.3%, Japan 6.9%, Italy 6.5%, and South Korea 4.2%).[5] Approximately 37% of the total FDI flowing into the Polish manufacturing sectors was located within the terrain of SEZs.[6] The Polish SEZs can be classified as a successful policy to attract FDI.

However, the development path of SEZs in Poland was not on an easy track. During the accession talks between Poland and the European Commission initiated in 1998, the Commission repeatedly criticized in its "Regular Report on Poland's Progress Towards Accession" that the tax incentive scheme in SEZs does not comply with the EU rules for regional aid. As the Commission gradually loosened its restrictive attitude towards the Polish SEZs, the Polish Government also succeeded in harmonizing the Law on SEZs with the EU rules: multinational enterprises investing in SEZs became major aid recipients of the EU's Regional Development Fund for Poland. Somewhat ironically, a serious crisis for the further existence of SEZs was not brought by Commission's external pressure on the compliance of Polish national laws vis-à-vis the EU rules, but by an internal conflict between the Ministry of Economy and Ministry of Finance.

The purpose of this chapter is firstly to reveal the origin of the Law on SEZs as an investment promotion policy, and secondly, to examine the legislator's

---

2 Ministry of Economy, "Informacja o realizacji ustawy o specjalnych strefach ekonomicznych. Stan na 31 grudnia 2004 r. (Information on the realization of Law on SEZs. Current status on 31 December 2004)", (2005), 2.

3 Ministry of Development, "Informacja o realizacji ustawy o specjalnych strefach ekonom- icznych. Stan na 31 grudnia 2015 r. (Information on the realization of Law on SEZs. Current status on 31 December 2015)", (2016), 11 and 14.

4 Each SEZ was established based on the ordinance of Council of Ministers with 20 years of operational period. The period was prolonged for all SEZs twice, currently until 31 December 2026.

5 Ministry of Development, *op. cit.* note 3, 19.

6 The cumulative FDI in SEZs for the manufacturing sector is estimated at PLN 85.8 billion, while the nationwide cumulative FDI inflows to the manufacturing sector is estimated at PLN 229.6 billion at the end of 2015, according to the National Bank of Poland.

intentions of and the related parties' reactions for each amendment of the Law. The chapter concludes with prospects and suggestions for the regional development policy in Poland, weighing its responsibility to harmonize the policy with the rest of the EU.

2   Institutional Evolution of SEZs in Poland

The World Bank assesses SEZs quite favorably, understanding that for developing countries, SEZs traditionally have had both a policy and an infrastructure rationale. In terms of policy, SEZ can be a useful tool as part of an overall economic growth strategy to enhance industry competitiveness and attract FDI.[7] Indeed SEZs play an important role in the world economy today. The number of SEZs in the world has been constantly increased from 79 in just 25 countries in 1975 to approximately 3,500 in 135 countries in 2006, accounting for 40 million direct jobs and over USD 200 billion in gross export annually.[8] The World Bank categorizes the SEZs into the following 6 types:

(a) Free trade zones – "fenced-in, duty-free areas, offering warehousing, storage and distribution facilities for trade, transshipment, and re-export operations";
(b) Export processing zones (EPZ) – "industrial estates aimed primarily at foreign markets";
(c) Enterprise zones – "intended to revitalize distressed urban or rural areas through the provision of tax incentives and financial grants";
(d) Free-ports – "accommodat[ing] all types of activities, including tourism and retail sales";
(e) Single factory EPZs – "provid[ing] incentives to individual enterprises regardless of location; factories do not have to locate within a designated zone to receive incentives and privileges";
(f) Specialized zones – "includ[ing] science/technology parks, petrochemical zones, logistic parks, airport-based zones, and so on".[9]

According to the Law on SEZs in Poland, SEZs ("specjalne strefy ekonomiczne") are separated, non-residential areas of the country (Article 2). Investors are

---

7   World Bank, *Special Economic Zones – Performance, Lessons Learned, and Implications for Zone Development* (2008), 1.
8   *Ibid.*, 23; ILO, *ILO Database on Export Processing Zones Revised* (2007), 1.
9   World Bank, *Ibid.*, 3.

required to obtain a permit by which they are obliged to commit to the realization of a minimum investment outlays as well as creation of a certain number of new jobs to enjoy tax incentives in SEZs (Article 16). SEZs can be established for the purpose of accelerating economic development, in particular via:

- Developing certain areas of economic activities,
- Developing new technical and technological solutions as well as their application in the national economy,
- Developing export,
- Increasing competitiveness of manufactured goods and provided services,
- Utilizing the existing industrial assets and economic infrastructures,
- Creating new work places and;
- Utilizing non-used natural resources maintaining the principles of ecological balance (Article 3).

Thus, the Polish SEZs are mixtures of the World Bank's classifications of (b) export processing zones, (c) enterprise zones and (e) single factory EPZs, since development of export as well as utilization of the existing industrial assets from the communist era was described in the law. The Polish Government later amended the law to create a series of single factory-type sub-zones ("podstrefy") within the territory of SEZs.[10] The Government enlarged the allowed list of economic activities in SEZs to include ICT, R&D (Research and Development), and logistics businesses in the later stage.

There are criticisms toward SEZs in general. In particular, McCallum points out that "labour and civil society organizations claim that preferential standards often go too far, making corporate accountability impossible and promoting widespread labour abuse and discrimination. [...] While some countries explicitly suspend the freedom to unionize and other social legislation inside

---

10   There functioned an additional investment incentive package in Poland under the program of free customs areas ("wolne obszary celne"), however the scheme did not work well due to a lack of clarity in the relevant laws and malfunctions of the competent organs. In the end only a handful of entrepreneurs started business activities in the free customs areas, i.e. a computer assembler in Gliwice and duty free shops in the Warsaw International Airport. Finally all of 15 established free customs zones were liquidated. Leszek J. Jasiński, *Bliżej centrum czy na peryferiach? Polskie kontakty gospodarcze z zagranicą w XX wieku* (*Close to the Center or on the Peripheries? Poland's Foreign Economic Relations in the 20th Century*) (TRIO, Warsaw, 2011), 381–382.

EPZ territory."[11] However, as far as the Polish SEZs are concerned, there is no legal discrimination toward employees inside/outside of SEZs.[12]

The Beginning of FDI Promotion Policy in Poland and Establishment of SEZs

Although the first ever attempt in the post-war Poland to introduce foreign capital can be dated back to 1976, the first legal act which entitles foreign investors with so-called "tax holidays" (3-year CIT exemption from the beginning of economic activities) came into force in 1982.[13] The 1982 Law was replaced by a short-lived Law on Enterprises with Foreign Capital Participants in 1986.[14] The scheme allowed foreign investors to establish joint ventures with Polish state-owned enterprises, but it was further repealed by the 1988 Law which allowed foreign investors to establish *completely* foreign-owned entities in Poland. As the tax exemption schemes introduced by these acts were widely exploited,[15]

---

11   Jamie K. McCallum, "Export Processing Zones: Comparative Data from China, Honduras, Nicaragua, and South Africa", *ILO Working Paper* (2011) No. 21 3–4.

12   Though, there are academic papers in which hard labor conditions in the Polish SEZs is criticized. For example, see: Małgorzata Maciejewska, "Exhausted Bodies and Precious Products: Women's Work in a Special Economic Zone for the Electronics Industry in Poland", 6(2) *Work Organisation, Labour & Globalisation* (2012), 94–112.

13   The Basic Law on the Provision of Economic Activities by Foreign Enterprises and Natural Persons in Small Sized Manufacturing in the People's Republic of Poland (Journal of Laws (1982), No 19, item 146) succeeded to attract certain interests among the Polish society abroad ("Polonia"). By the end of 1989, 727 small sized enterprises with foreign capital were established with a total of 100,000 employment. Wojciech Burzyński, Ewa Sadowska-Cieślak, and Stefan Walter, "Results of FDI", in Ewa Sadowska-Cieślak (ed.), *Foreign Investments in Poland: Regulations, Experience and Prospects* (IKC: Foreign Trade Research Institute, Warsaw, 1990), 63 and 67. It is reminisced that "the [1982] Law was subject to many later modifications to be 'experimental field' for direct foreign investment in a centrally planned economy." Ewa Sadowska-Cieślak, Roland Pac, and Wojciech Kozyra, "The Goals of Direct Investments and Analysis of Relevant Legislation", in Ewa Sadowska-Cieślak (ed.) *Foreign Investments in Poland: Regulations, Experience and Prospects* (IKC, Foreign Trade Research Institute, Warsaw, 1990), 15.

14   Journal of Laws (1986), No 17, item 88.

15   The 1988 Law (Journal of Laws (1988), No 41, item 325) introduced the 3-year CIT exemption similar to the 1982 Law. However, the former only stipulated that all commercial companies with foreign participation whose share capital exceeds the equivalent for 25 million Old Polish Zlotys (approximately USD 50,000) were entitled to be exempted from CIT for the period of 3 years starting from the date of *issuing the first invoice* by the Company (Art.28, par.1, emphasis added). As a consequence, many domestic wealthy citizens established legal entities with foreign participation just to avoid taxes. Ewa Sadowska-Cieślak,

the post-communist government introduced the 1991 Law which stipulates that companies with foreign capital whose share capital exceeding the equivalent of ECU (European Currency Unit) 2 million may enjoy CIT exemptions with certain share capital caps (Article 23, paragraph 6). The companies with foreign capital were obliged to conduct businesses in a region suffered from structural unemployment, to introduce new technologies, or to gain at least 20% of the company's sales from exports in order to qualify for the tax benefits.[16] The 1991 Law conditions for tax exemption and those of which introduced by the Law on SEZs in 1994 were similar to each other.[17]

However, the tax incentives introduced by the Law on Companies with Foreign Capital are found contradicting to the WTO, EFTA, and CEFTA treaties, which forbid signatory countries to provide subsidies being tied with exports.[18] Finally the lawmakers abolished the Law on Companies with Foreign Capital and introduced the Law on Economic Activities based on the reciprocity principle. While the Law on SEZs introduced the national treatment for foreign investors, the tax exemption has been equally applied for all undertakings indifference to its capital origin. Currently the minimum investment outlays required to be qualified as an SEZ investor with tax exemption is lowered to EUR 100,000. Thus, the author classified all SEZs into the following 4 types:

1.   SEZs being set up in areas with old communistic industrial legacies, such as Katowice and Wałbrzych (for restructuring steel mills or coal mines), Legnica (for diversifying mono-culture economy heavily depending on

"Znaczenie zagranicznych inwestycji bezpośrednich dla polskiej gospodarki (The Meaning of FDI for the Polish Economy)", *Zeszyty BRE Bank-CASE* (2000) No. 48, 7–26.

16   The law (Journal of Laws (1991), No 60, item 253) was further replaced by Law on economic activities in 1999 which introduced a national treatment for foreign investors based on the reciprocity principle (Journal of Laws (1999), No 101, item 1178). Currently binding law on economic activities in Poland is Law on Freedom of Economic Activities enforced since 2004 (Journal of Laws (2004), No 173, item 1807).

17   Especially in the first years of the socioeconomic transformation in Poland, CIT rate was very high (40% in 1996). The rate had been regularly reduced from 38% in 1997 till current 19% in 2004. UNIDO, *How to do business in Poland* (2003), 129.

18   The Uruguay Round Agreement on Subsidies and Countervailing Measures (SCM Agreement) prohibits export subsidies for the WTO member countries. Such subsidies are classified as an actionable subsidy which can be offset by imposition of countervailing duties in the importing country. For the transition economies, the prohibited subsidies are to be lifted by the end of 2001. Jai S. Mah and Donatas Tamulaitis, "A Note on Investment Incentives in the WTO and the Transition Economies", 12(1) *Post-Communist Economies* (2000), 119–130, at 119–121. Law on SEZs originally contains the similar clause, though it was later repealed in 1997 (Journal of Laws (1997), No 120, item 757).

copper refinery as well as reuse of a former USSR army base), Mielec (for restructuring a state-owned licensed producer of the MiG air fighters or light planes), or Pomorska (for modernizing mono-culture industry overwhelmed by ship yards or solving unemployment problem after bankruptcy of a state-owned TV assembler etc.);

2. SEZs being set up in rural areas where former collective farms ("PGR") were dissolved, and high unemployment rate was observed, including Suwałki, Warmia-Mazury, and Słupsk;

3. SEZs being set up on border zones where investments from the neighboring countries were expected, including Kostrzyn-Słubice and Warmia-Mazury;

4. Kraków Technology Park where it was anticipated to become an incubator for R&D activities in connection to its well-developed science universities. The Park also was expected to attribute for restructuring of the former Lenin Steel Works.[19]

Perhaps contrary to the formal justifications to revive some regional economies, the Ministry of Economy clearly has aimed the a scheme at attracting as much FDI as possible into Poland. The concept of Polish SEZ itself was designed by Shannon Free Airport Development Company Ltd. (SFADCO) in 1993, a running company of the world's oldest EPZ, Shannon Free Zone in Ireland.[20] The Ministry of Economy mentioned in "Provisional project of establishing SEZs for 1996–1997" that SEZs should be located in such regions where foreign investors show their interests (for example, central trans-Odra River region for the reason of nearness to Berlin) or places with a potential to be frontiers for economic expansion to the eastern markets.[21] The later governmental

---

19   Hiroshi Kaneko, "Pōrando no keizai tokku – Gaikoku chokusetsu tōshi yūchi seisaku toshiteno hyōka (SEZs in Poland: An Evaluation as an FDI Promotion Policy)", 42(2) *Hikaku keizai taisei gakkai nenpō (Japanese Journal of Comparative Economics)* (2005), 13–25.

20   Agnieszka Bazydło, "Specjalna Strefa Ekonomiczna Euro-Park Mielec (Euro-Park Mielec SEZ)", in Elżbieta Kryńska (ed.), *Polskie specjalne strefy ekonomiczne (SEZs in Poland)* (Scholar, Warsaw, 2000), 56–85, at 56. The World Bank also mentioned that the Shannon Free Zone, established in 1958, inspires the development of EPZ in emerging markets worldwide. World Bank, *op. cit.* note 7.

21   Krzysztof Gwosdz, Wojciech Jarczewski, Maciej Huculak, and Krzysztof Wiedermann, "Specjalne strefy ekonomiczne w Polsce. Założenie a praktyka" (SEZs in Poland Assumption and Practice), in Bolesław Domański and Krzysztof Gwosdz (eds.), *Dziesięć lat doświadczeń pierwszej polskiej specjalnej strefy ekonomicznej Mielec 1995–2005 (Ten Years Experience of the First Polish SEZ Mielec 1995–2005)* (Instytut Geografii i Gospodarki Przestrzennej Uniwersytetu Jagiellońskiego, Krakow, 2005), 17–38, at 21.

documents also support the aim that SEZs should be a driving force to attract FDI in Poland.[22] In the period immediately after the collapse of communism in 1989 macroeconomic stabilization was the priority and it is not surprising that the "Balcerowicz Plan" hardly mentions regional policy and concentrates mainly on structural changes. The only significant regional policy innovation in the mid 1990s was the controversial experiment in setting up SEZs.[23]

There are some cases in which foreign investors succeeded to include the very place where they planned to invest as a territory of SEZs. The first case of such an annexation was done in Gliwice where local unemployment rate was not necessarily high, replying to a request from General Motors to build an assembly factory of Opel cars.[24] More obvious cases are inclusion of already existing factory site of Philips in Kwidzyń and FIAT in Bielsko-Biała into SEZs in exchange for commitments of further investments.[25] This kind of active lobbying activities organized by foreign investors is evident for the whole period of existing the SEZs till now.

Harmonization of the Law on SEZs with the EU Rules

The Commission repeatedly required the modification of Polish SEZs to comply with the EU rules. For example, "Regular Report on Poland's Progress Towards Accession for 2000" condemned the Polish Government that "[t]he Polish legislation in force on the Special Economic Zones (SEZ) includes elements contrary to the *acquis* and Poland's immediate obligations under the Europe agreement."[26] According to Article 63 paragraph 4 (a) of the Europe agreement, any public aid granted by Poland shall be assessed taking into account if any aid is provided in accordance with the provision of Article 92 par. 3 (a) of the Treaty of Rome. The relevant article stipulates that public aids intended to promote the economic development of regions where the standard

---

22   For example, in 1998, Ministry of Economy appealed that for the sake of achieving further FDI inflow, it is inevitable to facilitate privatization processes with participation of strategic foreign investors and promote investments in SEZs. Ministry of Economy, *Kierunki polityki przemysłowej do lat 1999–2002* (*Direction of the Industrial Policy for 1999–2002*) (1998), 24.

23   George Blazyca, Krystian Heffner, and Ewa Helińska-Hughes, "Can Regional Policy Meets the Challenge of Regional Problem in Poland?" in George Blazyca (ed.) *Restructuring Regional and Local Economies* (Ashgate, Hants, 2003), 25–42, at 33.

24   Małgorzata Mokrzyc, "Funkcjonowanie specjalnych stref ekonomicznych w Polsce (Functions of the SEZs in Poland)", *Gospodarka Narodowa* (*National Economy*) (1998) No. 8–9, 19–30.

25   Gwosdz, Jarczewski, Huculak, and Wiedermann, *op. cit.* note 21.

26   European Commission, *Regular Report on Poland's Progress Towards Accession* (2000), 42.

of living is abnormally low or where there exists serious under-employment may be deemed to be compatible with the Common Market.[27] The Commission pointed out particularly the following as serious discrepancies between the Law on SEZs and the EU rules:[28]

1. Aids are provided in the form of operational aids, i.e. aids directly related with current economic activities of undertakings. In accordance with the EU law, Member States are only allowed to provide aids related with investments in fixed assets including lands, buildings, machinery and appliances in principle;

2. Lack of strictly defined support limits for undertakings operating in SEZs. In the Member States the regional aids shall be provided based on so-called regional aid maps. Depending on each region's economic development level, maximum aid level shall be strictly capped.

In the end, two separate amendments of the Law on SEZs were introduced in November 2000 and in October 2003 to harmonize the Law on SEZs with the EU rules. The first amendment[29] applied standard EU rules for the regional aid for all investors who obtained SEZ permits after 1 January 2001, referring to the Law on the allowed conditions and supervision on the state aid provide for undertakings.[30] This amendment implements a principle that aids are provided solely for the purpose of supporting new investments or creating new work

---

27   See Art.107 para.3 (a) of the TFEU; The Commission interpreted Art.63 TFEU as such that the rights that investors obtained as result of 1994 SEZs legislation was prohibited because the law was originally enacted in violation with the EU rules. The Polish government viewed the Art.63 as inapplicable to the law because at that time "EA" lacked implementing rules. Monika G. Kislowska, "The Future of Special Economic Zones in the Aftermath of Poland's Accession to the European Union", 5(1) *Journal of International Business and Law* (2006), 174–202.

28   Agnieszka Bazydło and Maciej Smętkowski, "Specjalne strefy ekonomiczne – Światowe zróżnicowanie instrumentu (Special Economic Zones – Differentiated Instruments in the World)", in Elżbieta Kryńska (ed.), *Polskie specjalne strefy ekonomiczne (SEZs in Poland)* (Scholar, Warsaw), 17–55, at 41–42; Macjej Smętkowski, "Polish Special Economic Zones as an Instrument of Regional and Industry Policy", *Munich Personal RePEc Archive* (2002) Paper No.39184, 10. The EU law allows provision of operational aids only under exceptional conditions which include: the area is suffering from a huge economic problem with very high unemployment; such an aid shall be provided for a limited period; the main purpose of such an aid shall be to overcome serious structural problems occurred in the given region. Any operational aid is allowed for the automotive sectors.

29   Journal of Laws (2000), No. 117, item 1228.

30   Journal of Laws (2000), No. 60, item 704.

posts.[31] In contrast, the Law on SEZs originally allowed undertakings to enjoy 100% of income tax exemption for the first 10 years of operations and 50% for the following 10 years.

The other important change introduced by the 2000 amendment is that the Council of Ministers may change the borders of SEZs, as long as the total area of SEZs remains within the statutory maximum size (6,325 ha).[32] This modification was groundbreaking, since the authority is able to exclude non-usable lands such as forests from the territory of SEZs in exchange for the inclusion of totally different lands in remote municipalities ("gmina") as sub-zones ("podstrefy"). In this way, the government finally resigned from the original concept of establishing SEZs as a regional development policy, but as an FDI promotion tool.[33] The government has put a great stress on solving the unemployment problem by promoting SEZs as ideal investment sites for huge greenfield projects, but it is far from reducing the regional developmental gap.

The second amendment from 2003[34] deals with problems related to the old permit holders obtaining the permit before 1 January 2001. For them, different regional aid caps are applied in accordance with the size of undertakings and the year of obtaining permits.

The Ministry of Economy decided to enlarge the territory of SEZs from 6,325 to 8,000 ha in April 2004[35] to satisfy the foreign multinational enterprises' demands for large-sized investment in Poland. The enlarged territory of the SEZs are solely designated for such investment projects whose investment outlays exceed EUR 40 million or which create more than 500 new work places. In 2005 alone, 24 border changes of SEZs were implemented to realize 34 big investment projects.[36] The FDI boom was followed by Poland's accession to the EU in May 2004. While total FDI inflow in Poland in 2002 and in 2003 were EUR 4.37 and 4.31 billion respectively, the figure hiked to EUR 10.3 billion in 2004. The same level of high FDI inflow had been maintained until 2011 mainly thanks to Poland's ideal geographical location between the EU and Eastern markets as

---

31   Art.8 para.1.

32   Bazydło and Smętkowski, *op. cit.* note 28, 42–43.

33   Gwosdz, Jarczewski, Huculak, and Wiedermann, *op. cit.* note 21, 19.

34   Journal of Laws (2003), No. 188, item 1840.

35   Journal of Laws (2004), No. 123, item 129.

36   Ministry of Economy, "Informacja o realizacji ustawy o specjalnych strefach ekonomicznych. Stan na 31 grudnia 2005 r. (Information on the realization of Law on SEZs. Current status on 31 December 2005)", (2006), 1–2. In terms of the creation of new work places, LG Electrics, Johnson Controls, MAN Tracks, and Michelin were the biggest job creators in 2005 with 4,200 new job posted together. The largest FDI in SEZs in 2005 was Michelin's PLN 982 million worth investment project (approx. EUR 245 million).

well as relatively low investment costs, but the government's investment promotion policy seems to have played a significant role.[37]

Further Institutional Evolution of SEZs after Poland's Accession to the EU

As mentioned above, Poland's accession to the EU triggered an expansion of the average size of FDI projects in manufacturing. At the same time, the government also enlarged the "catalog" of allowed economic activities in SEZs in 2005, including BPO (Business Process Offshoring), such as accounting and bookkeeping services, call centers, and R&D (Research and Development) activities.[38] However, only a handful of investment projects in BPO or R&D sectors have been realized in SEZs. The main purpose of establishing SEZs was to attract as much FDI as possible in the manufacturing sectors, and the terrains often include industrial or rural areas. On the other hand, BPO or R&D specified investors by nature prefer to locate in urbanized areas where a good access to the highly skilled labor force is guaranteed.

The enlargement procedures of the total maximum area of SEZs continued. It was enlarged three times in 2006, 2008, and 2015 (to 25,000 ha). At the end of 2015, SEZs were operating in 421 municipalities all over the country with its present territory of 19,837 ha.[39] The investment procedures in the SEZs were simplified as well. In principle, investors willing to invest in SEZs should acquire a land by bidding for a public tender. However, the 2006 amendment[40] introduced a possibility to annex lands owned by the State Agricultural Land Agency (ANR) or National Army Property Agency (AMW) by non-pecuniary transfers into SEZs for big greenfield investment projects. By doing so, the lawmakers abolished the time-consuming public tender procedures for big investors. Qualified investors now only have to concentrate on land prices and its localization to invest in SEZs.[41] Even the Supreme Audit Office (NIK) claimed that the establishment of a new Łódź SEZ sub-zone in Warsaw for P&G's EUR

37   National Bank of Poland, "FDI in Poland" (various years).

38   Ministry of Economy, "Informacja o realizacji ustawy o specjalnych strefach ekonomicznych. Stan na 31 grudnia 2006 r. (Information on the realization of Law on SEZs. Current status on 31 December 2006)", (2007), 19.

39   Ministry of Development, "Informacja o realizacji ustawy o specjalnych strefach ekonomicznych. Stan na 31 grudnia 2015 r. (Information on the realization of Law on SEZs. Current status on 31 December 2015)", (2016), 5.

40   Journal of Laws (2006), No. 141, item 997.

41   Ministry of Economy, *op. cit.* note 38, 5. The standard procedures of public tender of lands in SEZs are regulated by the Ordinance of Council of Ministers in 2004 (Journal of Laws (2004), No. 254, item 2541).

100 million investment project, and the establishment of a Tarnobrzeg SEZ sub-zone in Wrocław via LG and Toshiba's symbolic 1 Euro land annexation from the ANR were "against the original idea of establishing SEZs [...] and resulted in encouraging unfair competition."[42] However, the government never lost sight of further liberalization of the SEZs' investment environment, and the 2008 amendment introduced *inter alia* the following changes:[43]

1. The conditions to alter SEZ permits were introduced. The Minister of Economy may change permits to reduce the number of committed new job creation but not more than 20%. This clause shall be applied only for the new permits issued after 3 August 2008. (Due to the financial crisis, the existing SEZ investors strongly demanded this reduction.);

2. The SEZ management companies are empowered with the right of issuing permits from the Ministry of Economy.

In 2012, FDI inflow to Poland declined from EUR 14.8 billion to 4.7 billion due to the global recession.[44] The number of withdrawn SEZ permits for the reason of failure to achieve or maintain the committed investment conditions has increased from 33 to 41, and the number of expired (i.e. not renewed) permits has increase from 41 to 47.[45] To counter this, the Ministry of Economy tried to extend the expiration of the SEZs operation from the end of 2020 to the end of 2026.[46] Many economic organizations (e.g. chamber of commerce) enthusiastically supported the idea, but the extension was not realized until

---

42   NIK (Supreme Audit Office), "Informacja o wynikach kontroli funkcjonowania i rozszer-zenia obszaru działania specjalnych stref ekonomicznych w latach 2006–2008 (Informa-tion on the results of control on functions and enlargement of the area of activities of SEZS in 2006–2008)", (2009), 27–30.

43   Journal of Laws (2008), No. 118, item 746. When NIK published the Report, both Parlia-ment and the government were under the control of the same political party, which partly explains the limited impact of the Report.

44   National Bank of Poland, *FDI in Poland*, (2013), 1–2.

45   Ministry of Economy, "Informacja o realizacji ustawy o specjalnych strefach ekonomic-znych. Stan na 31 grudnia 2012 r. (Information on the realization of Law on SEZs. Current status on 31 December 2012)", (2013), 9–10.

46   In 2011, Ernst & Young simulated that a typical investor from the automotive industry could only consume 18% of investment outlays as tax incentives in SEZs if the invest-ment is to be realized in 2015 under the condition that the tax incentives in SEZs were to be extinguished at the end of 2020. Ernst & Young, *Specjalne Strefy Ekonomiczne po 2020 roku –Analiza dotychczasowej działalności oraz perspektywy funkcjonowania (SEZs after 2020: An Analysis of their Activities up to Today and Future Perspectives of their Activities)* (Warsaw, 2011), 55.

10 September 2013. The then Minister of Finance, Jacek Rostowski, was against the extension, arguing that the SEZs did not contribute for the regional economic development nor reduction of unemployment.[47] The Minister's argument was mirrored in the Ministry's Report on preferential taxation in Poland:

> From 2008 it has been observed a succeeding reduction in the investment outlays in the SEZs. For example, in 2011 the income exempted from taxation was 9.5 billion PLN, while the investment outlays in SEZs were 6.4 billion PLN. The investment outlays in SEZs are suffering from a decline in comparison to other businesses functioning outside of SEZs.[48]

The Ministry of Economy objected to the Ministry of Finance arguing that on one hand, the state aids provided for the investors in SEZs generated costs for the state budget due to the CIT-exemptions, while on the other hand, the SEZs investors have contributed to the state coffers by paying PIT, CIT from the investors' income which did not qualify for exemption, or VAT.[49] A consulting firm KPMG predicted that six-year extension of the effective period of SEZs to 2026 could boost capital expenditures in SEZs by PLN 40 billion (approximately EUR 9.5 billion).[50] It seems that this internal conflict was brought forward by the fundamental differences in political views held by the two ministries. While the Ministry of Economy pursued FDI-led fast economic growths by providing investors tax exemptions in SEZs, the Ministry of Finance placed more stress on the state's fiscal stability as well as the maintenance of the institutional prudence of the state administrations.

On 6 January 2015, an amendment on the Law on SEZs introduced a detailed regulation on the financial sanctions in case of the withdrawal of a permit. On the other hand, it allowed all investors to ask the Minister of Economy to alter the SEZ permits to reduce the number of committed new job creation up to 20% regardless of its date of issue (recall, the 2008 amendment only allowed such a right for the permits issued after 3 August 2008). The amendment stipulates that representatives from the Ministry of Finance, Ministry of

---

47   "Rostowski kontra strefy (Rostowski vs. SEZs)", available at <http://www.uwazamrze.pl/artykul/1022455-Rostowski-kontra-strefy.html>.

48   Ministry of Finance, "Preferencje podatkowe w Polsce, Nr 3 (Report on the preferential taxation in Poland, No. 3)", (2012), 47. Author's own translation.

49   Ernst & Young, *op. cit.* note 46; Ministry of Economy, "Informacja o realizacji ustawy o specjalnych strefach ekonomicznych. Stan na 31 grudnia 2011 r. (Information on the realization of Law on SEZs. Current status on 31 December 2011)" (2012), 39.

50   KPMG, *Special Economic Zones 2011 Edition* (Warsaw, 2012), 40.

Economy, Office of Competition and Consumer Protection (UOKiK) as well
as regional autonomous bodies must be appointed to the supervisory board of
each SEZ management company, depending on their shareholder structures.
Furthermore, the Commission's new Guideline on Regional Aid for 2014–2020
(enforced on 1 July 2014)[51] has been implemented in Poland as well, symbol-
izing its harmonization with the EU Law.

The institutional evolution of SEZs in Poland became increasingly complicated, reflecting the growing interests from various parties as well as increasing number of judicial rulings on provisions of the Law.[52] The author wonders
if the on-going introduction of more transparent rules into the Law on SEZs
would lead to an improper, disproportional application of the Law without understanding the Law's purposes. One thinks of the wise Latin adage, "summum
ius, summa iniuria (extreme law, extreme injury)".

3   The Polish SEZs Today

At present, almost all SEZs possess sub-zones, even spreading into several
voivodeships (provinces). The Polish SEZs have been dynamically changed
from the World Bank's definition of the Export Processing Zones (EPZs) of
which territory is designated upfront by the authorities to the Single Factory
EPZs where it is available for the qualified investors to request the inclusion
of their private lands into the SEZs as the sub-zones. SEZs did not contribute
much in reshaping the existing spatial structure of the Polish industry due to
two conflicting policy goals: supporting the restructuring of the old industrial
regions and developing the peripheral regions without any industrial base.[53]
By the same token, despite a high level of FDI, the SEZ policy has not overcome
the legacy of the lagging regions since the investors in SEZs do not significantly

---

51   Official Journal of the European Union 2013/C209/01.
52   For example, Supreme Administrative Court issued a ruling on 11 March 2014 (Act No. II
      GSK 136/13) that all SEZ permits issued after 1 January 2001 should be valid until the end of
      functioning SEZs (31 December 2026) even when an earlier date of expiration is recorded
      on the permit. As well, the current Polish Government which aims to "reindustrialize"
      Polish economy recently amended Law on SEZs to include the possibility to enlarge the
      territory of SEZs for shipbuilding industry (Journal of Laws (2016), item 1206).
53   Maciej Smętkowski, "Rola specjalnych stref ekonomicznych w kształtowaniu struktury
      przestrzennej przemysłu w Polsce" (The Role of SEZs in Shaping the Spatial Structure
      of Industry in Poland), 10 *Prace Komisji Geografii Przemysłu Polskiego Towarzystwa Geo-
      graficznego* (*Studies of the Industrial Geography Commission of the Polish Geographical
      Society*) (2008), 204–216.

contribute to raise the remuneration levels.[54] The SEZs in Poland may have contributed to create new jobs both in SEZs and its neighboring areas, though the institution has not played a great role in regional development since almost no spillover investment effect to the regional economy is observed.[55]

Table 4.1 below shows the current status of the cumulative investment outlays and the maintained number of job post for each SEZ as of 31 December 2015.

TABLE 4.1   *The Polish SEZs*

The name of SEZ	Cumulative investment outlays (mln.PLN/mln.EUR)	Actual number of employment
Katowice	23 317/5 474	58 976
Wałbrzych	21 738/5 103	44 340
Łódź	13 623/3 198	33 719
Pomorska	10 626/2 494	19 654
Tarnobrzeg	8 082/1 897	25 270
Legnica	7 597/1 783	12 607
Kostrzyn-Słubice	5 327/1 250	22 182
Mielec	6 325/1 485	30 907
Warmia Mazury	4 221/991	17 355
Kraków Tech. Park	2 942/691	21 896
Kamienna Góra	2 179/512	6 736
Starachowice	2 134/501	6 973
Suwałki	2 079/488	8 004
Słupsk	1 492/350	3 403
Total Sum:	111 682.9/26 216.6	312 022

SOURCE: CALCULATED BY THE AUTHOR BASED ON THE MINISTRY OF DEVELOPMENT'S DATA FOR 2015.

---

54   Camilla Jensen and Marcin Winiarczyk, "Special Economic Zones – 20 Years Later", *CASE Network Studies and Analysis* (2014) No. 467.

55   Piotr Ciżkowicz, Magda Ciżkowicz-Pękała, Piotr Pękała, and Andrzej Rzońca, "The Effects of Special Economic Zones on Employment and Investment: Spatial Panel Modelling Perspective", *National Bank of Poland Working Paper* (2015) No.208; and Katarzyna Kopczewska, "NPV-based Econometric Modelling in the Assessment of Public Intervention Efficiency: The Case of Special Economic Zones in Poland in 1995–2012", paper presented at the Political Economy of Place-Based Policies with a Focus on Special Economic Zones, Warsaw School of Economics (23–24 April 2015).

Most of the successful SEZs listed above is located in the automotive industry hub in south-western Poland or in such an area with a good logistic connection with Western Europe by motorway or by sea. Therefore, it is most likely the case that FDI would have come to such regions even without establishing SEZs. That said, SEZs in Poland is nowadays highly evaluated by the world investors. For example, the Financial Times' *fDi Intelligence website* ranked several Polish SEZs as some of the world best SEZs from the perspectives of Supporting education and training, Start-up support, Infrastructure & Facilities upgrades, New investments, or China strategy categories in 2016.[56]

4   Conclusion

SEZs in Poland have been developed as an elastic FDI promotion vehicle by giving a wide range of freedom of the location choice for the investors, introducing "one-stop-shop" procedure to issue business permits or drawing a clear dividing line when amendments on the individual permits should be allowed etc. Since 1980s, the policy makers in Poland have tried to stimulate FDI inflow by providing foreign investors with investment incentive packages. The Law on SEZs ideally fits in this purpose, and as a result, both policy/law-makers and local authorities have accumulated soft knowledge in sophisticating FDI promotion policy before and after Poland's accession to the EU. However, as it is argued previously, there is a certain risk that the SEZs management should and would be too rigorous in near future.

The Ministry of Infrastructure and Development launched the Strategic Governmental Invention (SGI) program in 2013 in relation to receiving the 2014–2020 EU Cohesion Policy Funds. In its Assumptions to the Partnership Agreement, the Ministry lists the following five key regions for the Strategic Intervention:[57]

1.   Eastern Poland (Lubelskie, Podkarpackie, Świętokrzyskie and Warmińsko-Mazurskie Voivodeships);
2.   Voivodeship Cities (province capitals) and their Functional Areas;
3.   Cities and districts requiring revitalization;

---

56   Available at <http://www.fdiintelligence.com/index.php//Rankings/Global-Free-Zones-of-the-Year-2016>.
57   Available at <http://www.mir.gov.pl/english/european_funds/european_funds_2014_2020 /Programming_2014_2020/Partnership_Agreement/Documents/Broszura_UP_%20 ang%20Druk.pdf>.

4. Areas, in particular the rural areas, with the lowest access to goods and
    services; and
5. Border Zones.

Poland is expected to receive EUR 82.5 billion form the EU Cohesion Funds for
2014–2020. A new effective regional and industrial policy which can facilitate
an innovation-driven economic growth should be implemented with the existing investment incentive policy designed by the Law on SEZs.

Bibliography

Bazydło, Agnieszka. (2000) "Specjalna Strefa Ekonomiczna Euro-Park Mielec (The
    Euro-Park Mielec Special Economic Zone)", in Kryńska, Elżbieta. (ed.), *Polskie spec-
    jalne strefy ekonomiczne (SEZs in Poland)* (Scholar, Warsaw), 56–85.
Bazydło, Agnieszka and Smętkowski, Maciej. (2000) "Specjalne strefy ekonomiczne –
    Światowe zróżnicowanie instrumentu (Special Economic Zones: Differentiated In-
    struments in the World)", in Kryńska, Elżbieta. (ed.), *Polskie specjalne strefy ekonom-
    iczne (SEZs in Poland)* (Scholar, Warsaw), 17–55.
Blazyca, George, Heffner, Krystian, and Helińska-Hughes, Ewa. (2003) "Can regional
    policy meets the challenge of regional problem in Poland?" in Blazyca, George.
    (ed.), *Restructuring Regional and Local Economies* (Ashgate, Hants), 25–42.
Burzyński, Wojciech, Sadowska-Cieślak, Ewa, and Walter, Stefan. (1990) "Results of
    FDI", in Sadowska-Cieślak, Ewa. (ed.), *Foreign Investments in Poland: Regulations,
    Experience and Prospects* (IKC: Foreign Trade Research Institute, Warsaw).
Ciżkowicz, Piotr, Ciżkowicz-Pękała, Magda, Pękała, Piotr, and Rzońca, Andrzej. (2015)
    "The Effects of Special Economic Zones on Employment and Investment: Spatial
    Panel Modelling Perspective", *National Bank of Poland Working Paper* No. 208, 1–46.
Gwosdz, Krzysztof, Jarczewski, Wojciech, Huculak, Maciej, and Wiedermann, Krzysz-
    tof. (2005) "Specjalne strefy ekonomiczne w Polsce. Założenie a praktyka (SEZs in
    Poland. Assumption and Practice)", in Domański, Bolesław and Gwosdz, Krzysz-
    tof. (eds.), *Dziesięć lat doświadczeń pierwszej polskiej specjalnej strefy ekonomicznej
    Mielec 1995–2005 (Ten Year Experience of the First Polish SEZ Mielec 1995–2005)* (In-
    stytut Geografii i Gospodarki Przestrzennej Uniwersytetu Jagiellońskiego, Krakow),
    17–38.
Jasiński, Leszek J. (2011) *Bliżej centrum czy na peryferiach? Polskie kontakty gospodarcze
    z zagranicą w XX wieku (Close to the Center or on the Peripheries? Poland's Foreign
    Economic Relations in the 20th Century)* (TRIO, Warsaw).
Jensen, Camilla and Winiarczyk, Marcin. (2014) "Special Economic Zones – 20 Years
    Later", *CASE Network Studies and Analyses* No. 467.

Kaneko, Hiroshi. (2005) "Pōrando no keizai tokku – Gaikoku chokusetsu tōshi yūchi seisaku toshiteno hyōka (SEZs in Poland: An Evaluation as an FDI Promotion Policy)", 42(2) *Hikaku Keizai Kenkyū* (*Japanese Journal of Comparative Economics*), 13–25.

Kislowska, Monika G. (2006) "The Future of Special Economic Zones in the Aftermath of Poland's Accession to the European Union", 5(1) *Journal of International Business and Law*, 174–202.

Kopczewska, Katarzyna. (2015) "NPV-based Econometric Modelling in the Assessment of Public Intervention Efficiency: The Case of Special Economic Zones in Poland in 1995–2012", paper presented at the Political Economy of Place-Based Policies with a Focus on Special Economic Zones, Warsaw School of Economics (23–24 April).

Maciejewska, Małgorzata. (2012) "Exhausted Bodies and Precious Products: Women's Work in a Special Economic Zone for the Electronics Industry in Poland", 6(2) *Work Organisation, Labour & Globalisation*, 94–112.

Mah, Jai S. and Tamulaitis, Donatas. (2000) "A Note on Investment Incentives in the WTO and the Transition Economies", 12(1) *Post-Communist Economies*, 119–130.

McCallum, Jamie K. (2011) "Export Processing Zones: Comparative Data from China, Honduras, Nicaragua, and South Africa", *ILO Working Paper* No. 21.

Mokrzyc, Małgorzata. (1998) "Funkcjonowanie specjalnych stref ekonomicznych w Polsce (Functions of the SEZs in Poland)", *Gospodarka Narodowa* (*National Economy*) No. 8–9, 19–30.

Sadowska-Cieślak, Ewa, Pac, Roland, and Kozyra, Wojciech. (1990) "The Goals of Direct Investments and Analysis of Relevant Legislation", in Sadowska-Cieślak, Ewa. (ed.) *Foreign Investments in Poland – Regulations, Experience and Prospects* (IKC, Foreign Trade Research Institute, Warsaw).

Sadowska-Cieślak, Ewa. (2000) "Znaczenie zagranicznych inwestycji bezpośrednich dla polskiej gospodarki (The Meaning of FDI for the Polish Economy)", *Zeszyty BRE Bank-CASE*, No. 48, 7–26.

Smętkowski, Maciej. (2008) "Rola specjalnych stref ekonomicznych w kształtowaniu struktury przestrzennej przemysłu w Polsce (The Role of SEZs in Shaping the Spatial Structure of Industry in Poland)", 10 *Prace Komisji Geografii Przemysłu Polskiego Towarzystwa Geograficznego* (*Studies of the Industrial Geography Commission of the Polish Geographical Society*), 204–216.

Smętkowski, Maciej. (2002) "Polish Special Economic Zones as an Instrument of Regional and Industrial Policy", *Munich Personal RePEc Archive* Paper No. 39184.

PART 2

Politics – Skepticism

∴

(Dis)Trusting the European Union? On the Evolving Variety of Euroskepticism in Central and Eastern Europe

Boyka Stefanova

Abstract

This chapter revisits varying trends of Euroskepticism in Central and Eastern Europe (CEE), as the scope of public reluctance to uncritically accept the benefits of EU membership in these countries remains poorly understood.[1] The chapter examines key aspects of CEE Euroskepticism as a component of the institutional history of the 2004 EU enlargement. The organizing perspective is that of the unexpected emergence and intensity of Euroskepticism in the countries of the EU's eastward enlargement. By combining a variety of utilitarian, ideational, and attitudinal predispositions, significantly shaped by the national context, this evolving variety of Euroskepticism represents a valid measure of the public reaction to the purpose and policies of European integration.

CEE Euroskepticism is reflected in ambiguous and unsettled levels of public trust in the EU against the background of general dissatisfaction with the workings of national democracy. The CEE publics have become increasingly skeptical of their representation as citizens whose voice "counts" in the EU. They perceive the EU as less relevant to their personal situation although it represents well the interests of the Member States. Such contradictory dynamics suggests that the conventional measures of Euroskepticism as a pan-European phenomenon need to be re-examined by exploring trends of continuity and change in public support for the EU in CEE with a special focus on political variables.

Keywords

Euroskepticism – democratic legitimacy – political trust – political efficacy

---

1 Several segments of this chapter have appeared in Boyka Stefanova, "Returning to Europe as Reluctant Europeans: Revisiting Trends in Public Support for the European Union in Central and Eastern Europe Twelve Years after the 2004 EU Accession", *Croatian Yearbook on European Law and Policy* (2016) No.12, 275–297. This chapter contains more in-depth arguments

1   Introduction

> Enlargement is both an historic opportunity and an obligation for the
> European Union and so is one of our highest priorities. Our success in
> concluding this crucial undertaking, on which we have embarked togeth-
> er with the candidate countries, will depend on the vitality and rigour
> of our collective efforts and on engaging the support of the population,
> both in the candidate countries and in the current EU Member States.
> Enlargement must be duly prepared, and can be successful only if it has
> democratic support.
>
> GÜNTER VERHEUGEN[2]

The foundations of the EU's enlargement policy towards the countries of
Central and Eastern Europe (CEE) were laid down by the decisions of the Copenhagen European Council of December 1993 that established the political
and economic criteria for EU membership: democracy, the rule of law, respect
for human rights and the rights of minorities, market economy and ability to
withstand competitive pressure, and institutional capacity to implement EU
legislation (the community *acquis*) prior to membership.[3] Over a ten-year
period, starting with the first Pre-accession Strategy designed to prepare the
process to the eastward enlargement of 1 May 2004, the EU's institutions and
political actors had been preparing Eastern Europe's 'return to Europe.' The
Eastern enlargement was therefore not simply a big-bang event that changed
the map of Europe through the reunification of the east and the west. It was an
historic process of societal, political, and economic transformation of East-European societies into a component of Europe's organized political community
embedded in the European Union. The Eastern enlargement was the testing
ground for a laboratory of ideas, policy templates and governance mechanisms
designed to extend the EU's existing legal and institutional order into Eastern

---

and functions as an introduction providing an overview of Euroskepticism for the following
chapter on Czech Euroskepticism.

2 Member of the European Commission responsible for Enlargement. "Enlargement of the European Union: An Historic Opportunity", Statement in European Commission (2001), available
at <https://ec.europa.eu/neighbourhood-enlargement/sites/near/files/archives/pdf/press_
corner/publications/corpus_en.pdf>.

3 See European Council, *Presidency Conclusions Copenhagen European Council* (21–22 June)
Bulletin EC 6 (Brussels: European Council, 1993). The 1993 policy statement of the Copenhagen European Council was preceded by the Europe Agreements, signed with individual
CEE countries in the period 1991–1996 as a form of institutional cooperation, which included
areas as diverse as political dialogue, market competition, and the movement of persons, and
were designed to prepare a future enlargement of the Union.

Europe. The accession process, whose main mechanism was the *ex ante* adoption of EU law, was the principal site for the EU's enlargement policy to shape and consolidate itself. The policy focused on the obligations of the candidate countries, stressing that membership was conditional on compliance with EU rules and values. The Eastern enlargement established a process of interaction among the existing Member States, the EU institutional actors, and the candidate countries whereby the latter committed to adoption of the community *acquis* and political and economic adjustment to the criteria for EU membership. The approach was fundamentally top-down, based on compliance and rule adoption.[4] The anticipated broader consequences of the policy were positive security externalities creating stability and democratic consolidation (similarly to the South-European enlargements of the 1980s), and economic growth across the region.

The Eastern enlargement effectively extended the EU's legal order to the new Member States from CEE. As a process of institutional expansion, it was designed to strengthen the legitimacy and effectiveness of European integration through treaty development, growing application of the principle of qualified-majority voting in decision-making, and bringing the EU closer to the European citizens. The policy by far exceeded the objectives of implementing a process of merit-based territorial enlargement. In the context of the 2004 accession, the EU emerged as an external anchor for the democratic transformation of CEE. Yet, the CEE publics were reluctant to uncritically accept the benefits of the EU membership, and moreover, this variety of CEE Euroskepticism seems to differ from the other types of Euroskepticism.

2   The Puzzle of Euroskepticism in CEE

A necessary condition for a policy to perform and meet its objectives is public acceptance of its purpose and mechanism of implementation. In order to prepare the publics in the Member States in the West to endorse the Eastern enlargement, the EU institutional actors implemented a discursive strategy.[5] Enlargement was framed as a process designed to permanently abolish

---

4 The mechanism of conditionality in the Eastern enlargement is discussed in detail in Heather Grabbe, *The EU's Transformative Power: Europeanization through Conditionality in Central and Eastern Europe* (Palgrave, Basingstoke, 2006); and Frank Schimmelfennig and Ulrich Sedelmeier, *The Europeanization of Central and Eastern Europe* (Cornell University Press, Ithaca, 2005), among others.

5 Thomas Risse, *A Community of Europeans? Transnational Identities and Public Spheres* (Cornell University Press, Ithaca, 2010), 207.

divisions across Europe, improve living standards in the EU, enhance its geopolitical position, and promote a liberal political and economic order in CEE
based on the rule of law, democratic government, respect for human rights,
and a market economy. Such concepts were embedded in all keystone documents that had shaped the EU's enlargement policy from the formulation
of membership criteria by the Copenhagen European Council to the EU accession treaties.[6] "The European Union is set to achieve its most ambitious
enlargement ever. [...] We are putting behind us the old divisions in Europe,
consolidating peace, democracy and prosperity throughout the continent", a
2003 EU poster reads.[7] Obviously, ideational considerations were at the forefront of political discourse. Then President of the European Parliament Nicole
Fontaine remarked:

> Enlargement is, for all of us, a major opportunity in political and econom-
> ic terms. But enlargement is, above all, a historic moral obligation – the
> obligation to bring about the reunification of the great European family.[8]

The framing approach was instrumental, as it communicated individual dimensions of the Eastern enlargement to different segments of the European
publics.[9] While nominally, the principal frames of the 2004 Eastern enlargement were embedded in a common discursive framework, the predominantly
institutional and technical nature of the accession as a type of policy transfer did not develop an adequate communication strategy capable of generating public support for EU membership in the candidate countries. Political
actors expected that besides market liberalization and the consolidation of
democratic institutions across Eastern Europe, the accession process would
result in the gradual emergence of public space based on European values and
discourses about European citizenship, freedom of movement, and European
identity. Implicitly, in line with the already (out)dated but widely cited neofunctionalist mechanism of spillover as a related albeit indirect outcome, the
theoretical and policy expectation was that a EU membership would lead to
broad public acceptance of the tenets of European institutionalism and governance, and shifting loyalties to Europe.

---

6   See Document JOL_2003_236_R_0017_01. Official Journal L 236, 23.09.2003, 17–32.
7   European Commission (3 December 2003), available at <http://bookshop.europa.eu/en/
    bundles/posters-cbcWuep2Ixvv8AAAEuyyUDoUfc/>.
8   Nicole Fontaine, *Speech to the European Parliament*, 26 June 2001. On file with author.
9   Juan Diez Medrano, *Framing Europe: Attitudes to European Integration in Germany, Spain,
    and the United Kingdom* (Princeton University Press, Princeton, 2003).

Positive public attitudes in CEE were thus taken for granted in view of the benefits of EU membership and democratic reform. Conceptualizing the Eastern enlargement as an expansion of the EU-based democratic political order and the Western community of liberal values was effective in Western Europe but produced unexpected consequences for the acceding countries.[10]

The emergence and, with time, persistence of skeptical and opposing views of the EU in CEE is counter-intuitive. It represents a puzzle for most theoretical accounts of the European integration of CEE. The Eastern enlargement was dominated by the mega-discourse of the reunification of Europe and Eastern Europe's 'return to Europe', widely shared in scholarly, policy, and political circles.[11] The benefits of enlargement were positively viewed across Europe. Graph 5.1 shows that, at the time of the 2004 enlargement, broad majorities in both the Western and CEE Member States perceived enlargement as a positive process along the principal dimensions of transformative change that it brought to the organization of public life in Europe: free movement and travel, CEE's modernization, increased prosperity and competitiveness, enhanced security stability in Europe, and decreased levels of organized crime and illegal immigration.

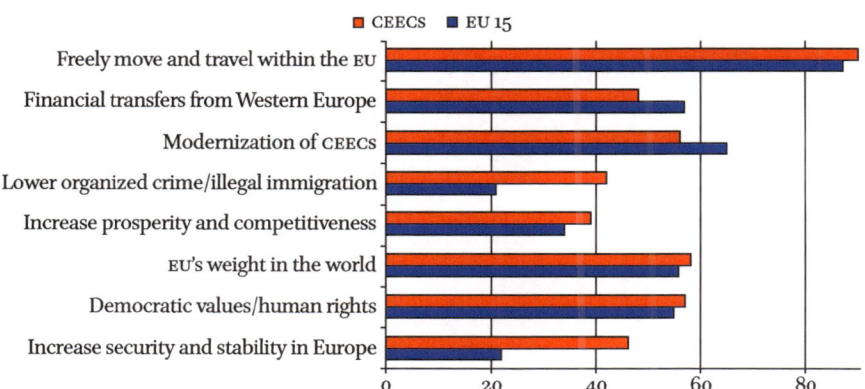

GRAPH 5.1   *The EU 2004 Enlargement in Retrospect (2009): The Consequences of the Integration of CEE into the EU, net positive responses (agreement with statement)*
SOURCE: EUROPEAN COMMISSION.[12]

---

10   Risse, *op. cit.* note 5, 208.

11   Simona Guerra, *Central and Eastern European Attitudes in the Face of Union* (Palgrave Macmillan, Basingstoke, 2013), 2.

12   European Commission, "Views on European Union Enlargement", *Flash Eurobarometer* (2004) No.257, available at <http://ec.europa.eu/public_opinion/flash/fl_257_en.pdf>, 21.

In the wake of the 2004 accession, CEE economies grew in real terms by 3.0% a year versus an average of 1.0% annual real GDP growth for the Member States in the West (EU 15).[13] Economic growth, however, was not linked to positive economic expectations. The CEE citizens joined the EU as more pessimistic with regard to their personal situation. At the time of the 2004 accession, 22% of respondents in CEE expected life to improve versus 32% in Western Europe. Only 15% (versus 33% in Western Europe) expected a better financial situation, although sociotropic assessments about the improvement of the national economy in both categories of countries were relatively similar (15%).

The difference between positive and negative evaluations of subjective well-being in CEE was narrowing. The net positive difference varied between 9 and 17 percentage points in Slovenia, Estonia, Latvia, and Lithuania with net negative differences in Hungary (−2%), the Czech Republic and Poland (−6%) and Slovakia (−12%).[14] Public perceptions of the rising adjustment costs on the road to EU membership were reflected in growing negative opinions on the personal situation for the preceding five years, ranging between 41 and 44%. On the eve of the 2004 Eastern enlargement, public attitudes in CEE were divided, although the citizens supported the systemic context and benefits of EU membership.[15]

Variation in utilitarian attitudes, however, is insufficient to explain Euroskepticism within the East-European publics. Similarly, the emergent CEE Euroskepticism may not be adequately explained by models applicable to public support for European integration in Western Europe.[16] CEE Euroskepticism lacks the trend of continuity typical of West-European Euroskepticism,

---

13   United Nations, *World Economic Situation and Prospects and Update* (United Nations publication, Sales No. E.14.II.C.2, 2014). Annex Tables, 153, available at <http://www .un.org/en/development/desa/policy/wesp/wesp_archive/2014wesp_annex_tables.pdf>. The new EU Member States from CEE registered a highest annual GDP growth rate of 6.0% in 2006 versus 3.4% for EU 15. CEE registered positive real GDP growth rates through the 10-year period since the 2004 accession with the exception of 2009, when the EU economy declined by 4.5% in real terms (−3.8% for CEE).

14   European Commission, "Public Opinion in the European Union", *Eurobarometer* (2004) No.61, Full Report, C 10, available at <http://ec.europa.eu/public_opinion/archives/eb/ eb61/eb61_en.pdf>.

15   Guerra, *op. cit.* note 11; and Jorg Jacobs and Detlef Pollack, "Support Based on Values? Attitudes toward the EU in Eleven Postcommunist Societies", in Robert Rohrschneider and Stephen Whitefield (eds.), *Public Opinion, Party Competition, and the European union in Post-Communist Europe* (Palgrave Macmillan, New York, 2006), 86.

16   Alex Szczerbiak, "Polish Public Opinion: Explaining Declining Support for EU Membership", 39(1) *Journal of Common Market Studies* (2001), 105–122; and Paul Taggart and Alex

centered on concerns about the loss of sovereignty as a result of EU membership and the poor standards of democratic legitimacy of the EU institutions
when compared to the democratic exercise of power at the national level.[17]

The Varieties of Euroskepticism

The question about loyalty, albeit limited to the level of transnational elites
as politically relevant actors, is at the core of neofunctionalism, the classical
theory of European integration.[18] According to Ernst Haas, European integration is measured by the extent to which it matches the economic expectations
of political actors, as well as their fears, interests, satisfaction with the national
political context, ideologies, and political efficacy.[19] Neofunctionalism did not
address the political relevance of public preferences and loyalties at the unit
level. As an elite-led process, European integration originally operated in the
context of a "permissive consensus", defined as a passive public approval of the
integration process and an assumption that the transfer of public loyalties to
the EU would be unproblematic, as a result of the efficiency and welfare gains
associated with European integration.[20] However, more recent theorizing has
determined that it is both normatively and empirically insufficient to examine
the potential convergence of the interests and loyalties of European citizens.[21]
Viewed from a legal-institutionalist perspective, the measures of public support for European integration should not only reflect the simple dichotomy
or additive effects of interests and identities but also perceptions of belonging to a democratically organized political community whose institutions are

---

Szczerbiak, "Parties, Positions and Europe: Euroscepticism in the Candidate States of
Central and Eastern Europe", paper presented at the Annual Meeting of the Political Studies Association (10–12 April 2001, Manchester).

17   See Marianne Sundlisæter Skinner, "Different Varieties of Euroscepticism? Conceptualizing and Explaining Euroscepticism in Western European Non-Member States", 51(1) *Journal of Common Market Studies* (2013), 122–139; Simona Guerra, "Does Familiarity Bring
Contempt? Determinants of Public Support for European Integration and Opposition
to it before and after Accession", 51(1) *Journal of Common Market Studies* (2013), 38–50;
and Sofia Vasilopoulou, "Continuity and Change in the Study of Euroscepticism: Plus ça
Change?" 51(1) *Journal of Common Market Studies* (2013), 153–168.

18   Ernst Haas, *The Uniting of Europe: Political, Social, and Economic Forces 1950–1957* (Stanford University Press, Stanford, 1968).

19   *Ibid.*, 15.

20   Leon Lindberg and Stuart Scheingold, *Europe's Would-be Polity: Patterns of Change in the
European Community* (Prentice-Hall, Englewood Cliffs, NJ, 1970).

21   Liesbet Hooghe and Gary Marks, "A Post-Functionalist Theory of Integration: From
Permissive Consensus to Constraining Dissensus", 39 *British Journal of Political Science*,
1–23; Lauren McLaren, *Identity, Interests, and Attitudes to European Integration* (Palgrave

representative of the aspirations and well-being of the EU citizens. Such measures, however, may not be as straightforward in CEE as they have been in the West.

Euroskepticism, or the departure from unconditional public support for European integration, has many faces: it pertains to party politics and public opinion while it may be issue-based or general. There is an agreement in the literature that attitudes towards the EU cannot be unidimensional and binary. Paul Taggart suggests that Euroskepticism is best studied as an encompassing term that "expresses the idea of contingent, or qualified opposition, as well as incorporating outright and unqualified opposition to the process of European integration."[22] In an elaboration to the original definition, Taggart and Szczerbiak include categories of "soft" and "hard" Euroskepticism. "Hard" Euroskepticism is an "outright rejection of the entire project of European political and economic integration, and opposition to joining or remaining within the EU", while "soft" Euroskepticism is an evolving "contingent or qualified opposition to European integration", the current or planned trajectory or transfer of competences.[23]

The distinction between "soft" and "hard" Euroskepticism is intertwined with differences between diffuse and specific support for European integration.[24] Diffuse support is support for the general ideas of European integration that underlie the EU. Specific support is support for the practice of integration; that is, the EU as is and as it is developing. From this more contextualized perspective, Taggart and Szczerbiak identify two dimensions of diffuse and specific support. The first dimension, "support for the ideas of European integration", separates the Europhiles from the Europhobes. Europhiles believe in the key ideas of European integration underlying the EU: institutionalized cooperation on the basis of pooled sovereignty (the political element) and an integrated liberal market economy (the economic element). The second dimension, "support for EU policies", separates the Euroenthusiasts from the Euroskeptics.[25] Strictly defined, Euroskepticism in CEE largely conforms to the

---

       Macmillan, Basingstoke, 2006); and Ignacio Sanchez-Cuenca "The Political Basis of Support for European Integration", 1(2) *European Union Politics* (2000), 147–171, among others.

22   Paul Taggart, "A Touchstone of Dissent: Euroskepticism in Contemporary Western European Party Systems", 33 *European Journal of Political Research* (1998), 363–388, at 366. Also, Petr Kopecky and Cas Mudde, "The Two Sides of Euroscepticism: Party Positions on European Integration in East Central Europe", 3(3) *European Union Politics*, 297–326.

23   Taggart and Szczerbiak, *op. cit.* note 16, 6.

24   Kopecky and Mudde, *op. cit.* note 22, 300.

25   Iván Llamazares and Wladimir Gramacho, "Euroskeptics among Euroenthusiasts: An Analysis of Southern European Public Opinions", 42(2–3) *Acta Politica* (2007), 211–232.

lack of specific support for EU policies and direction. It also includes the category of the Euroneutrals: citizens who consent to the idea of EU membership but are not enthusiastic about it.[26]

3   CEE Euroskepticism: A Special Variety?

According to Kopecky and Mudde, the measures of specific and diffuse support for the EU should be derived from the perspective of what Europe means to the citizens of CEE: a reflection of their interests, identities, aspirations, and community sentiment.[27] The appropriate measure of Euroskepticism needs to contextualize the conventional indicators of output legitimacy, conventionally applied with regard to the EU's democratic credentials,[28] by including the overlapping aspects of dissatisfaction with government performance, as well as with the workings of democracy at the national and EU level. Such broad-based indicators of legitimacy serve as a benchmark against which CEE Euroskepticism is measured. The emphasis on trust, legitimacy, and relevance to the political aspirations of European citizens is what distinguishes the CEE variety of Euroskepticism from forms prevalent in Western Europe.

Political Trust
The EU has failed to maintain its position of a trusted political actor in CEE. At the time of the Eastern enlargement, the average level of trust in the top three political and social institutions in the new Member States was on average 13% (ranging from 32% in Estonia to 6% in Poland).[29] The EU was the most trusted institution only in Slovenia (47% of respondents), the second most trusted institution in Hungary and Lithuania (54% and 50%, respectively), and the third most trusted institution in Slovakia (47%).[30] It is obvious that levels of trust have varied significantly across the region, but they tend to converge to those typical in the West.[31] In contrast to CEE, however, the EU institutions are generally less trusted by the publics in the West than their institutions of national

---

26   Szczerbiak, *op. cit.* note 16, 108.

27   Kopecky and Mudde, *op. cit.* note 22.

28   Fritz Scharpf, *Governing in Europe: Effective and Democratic?* (Oxford University Press, New York, 1999).

29   European Commission, *op. cit.* note 14, C 19.

30   *Ibid.*, C 25.

31   *Ibid.*, C 20.

democracy. The core of CEE Euroskepticism thus may be defined as the decline of trust and loyalty towards the EU, coterminous with low levels of satisfaction with government performance and national democracy.

The publics in four new Member States – Slovenia, Slovakia, Lithuania, and Estonia – tend to trust the EU more than the United Nations: however in three CEE countries – the Czech Republic, Hungary, and Poland – the publics have more confidence in the United Nations. In May 2012, for the first time since Poland joined the EU, the percentage of Poles who responded "not to trust" the EU (46%) was higher than the percentage of Poles who "trust" it (41%) – a remarkable development for a country that has traditionally been pro-European. That trend was only subsequently reversed.

The Declining Relevance of the EU to the Publics in CEE

One of the important aspects of CEE Euroskepticism reflects the EU's declining relevance to the citizens of CEE. While in the early stages of EU membership public trust towards the EU in general was higher than trust in the national government and institutions, pointing to expectations that the EU would act as a corrective to the national political system, such attitudes have gradually regressed. The current trend is one of declining levels of confidence in both the EU and the national political institutions. The national government is trusted by 25.5% of the CEE citizens, with net negative views of 38.6%.[32] The European Commission has been the most trusted EU institution in CEE (versus the European Parliament in Western Europe), on average by 41.3% of the CEE public.[33] Public attitudes nevertheless reflected a decline in satisfaction with EU democracy and trust towards the EU institutions, the European Parliament in particular. CEE Euroskepticism gradually evolved along measures of legitimacy, sense of political effectiveness ("my voice counts"), diverging perceptions of the benefits of EU membership for the Member States and for the citizens, and uncertainty with regard to the EU's actual impact on the lives of the EU citizens. In 2014, trust in the European Parliament had declined by nine percentage points in a single year to reach a record low level of 39.3%.[34]

Even prior to the 2004 enlargement, CEE public opinion was somewhat skeptical of European "integration", reflected in uncertainty with regard to the importance of diffuse support for the EU's systemic objectives relative

---

32   European Commission, "Public Opinion in the European Union", *Standard Eurobarometer* (2014) No.81, available at <http://ec.europa.eu/public_opinion/archives/eb/eb81/eb81_publ_en.pdf>, 63.

33   *Ibid.*, 89.

34   *Ibid.*

to specific support for its policies. This type of Euroskepticism may not be distinctly defined either as an outright rejection of the EU typical of "hard" Euroskepticism, or as a variety of "soft" Euroskepticism, characterized by disagreement with select EU policies or performance. The mismatch between the historical value of enlargement and its meaning for the citizens of CEE is the core of CEE Euroskepticism. It is reflected in less appreciation of the benefits of EU membership, less allegiance to the EU institutions, and less convergence in public views on the direction of European integration. Furthermore, in contrast with the tendency for the EU institutions to maintain higher approval ratings than the national political institutions in CEE, and in particular the national government, the EU appears to have lost its reputation as the anchor of stability for the CEE countries and as a continued source of inspiration for social and economic reform.

Euroskeptic Images of the EU in CEE: Democratic Effectiveness

In the wake of the 2004 accession, the EU emerged as a distant political object for the CEE citizens. Gradually, they have come to view the EU as less relevant to their living standards. On average, 10% of respondents in the eight CEE Member States consider the EU to have significant effects on their living standards, versus 51% for the national government and 34% for the regional and local level in 2009.[35] This is yet another measure of the EU's remoteness to the citizens and its limited output legitimacy.

A related measure of the CEE variety of Euroskepticism is the perception of a lack of relevance of the EU to the concerns and priorities of the European publics. While 49% of respondents in CEE agree that unemployment is a national priority, only 21% consider it a personal concern. Many of the EU's important outcomes address national, and not personal, priorities, such as the economic situation, crime, immigration, and terrorism. In contrast, issues such as pensions, healthcare, and rising prices, predominantly perceived as personal concerns, are either not directly addressed or are adversely affected by EU-level policy making.[36]

Furthermore, the CEE publics share negative views with regard to their political efficacy, reflected in the perception that their voice does not "count." As Graph 5.2 demonstrates, CEE public opinion remains skeptical of the effective representation of citizens' concerns in EU affairs. Measures of political efficacy

---

35   European Commission, "Public Opinion in the European Union", *Standard Eurobarometer* (2009) No.71, available at <http://ec.europa.eu/public_opinion/archives/eb/eb71/eb71_std_part1.pdf>, 81.

36   *Ibid.*, 62.

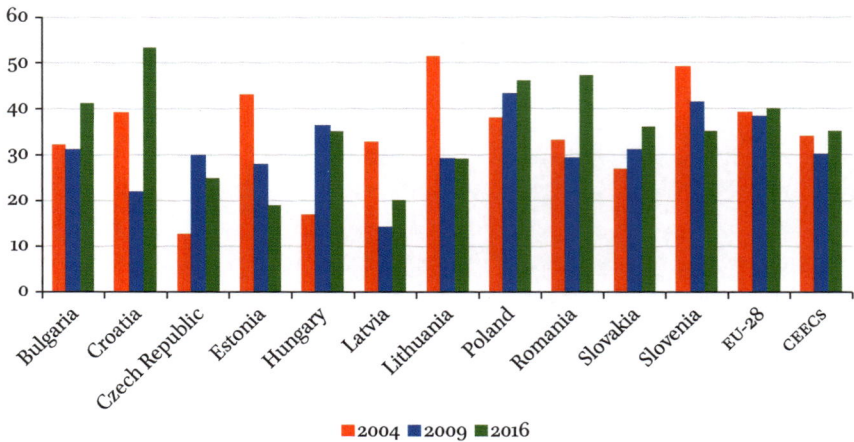

GRAPH 5.2   *Political Trust and Legitimacy: Comparative Data, 2004–2016*
Q (2004, 2009, 2016). D72: Please tell me to what extent you agree or disagree with
the following statement: My voice counts in the EU (agreement with statement).
SOURCE: EUROPEAN COMMISSION.[37]

are consistently low. More than 12 years after accession, the East-European
publics have yet to develop confidence that their voice "matters" in the EU.
In five Member States, citizens were overall less confident of their political efficacy in 2016 than they were in 2009, against the background of high variation
both longitudinally and cross-nationally.

Political Behavior

In 2009, at the height of the European economic and financial crisis, a majority of the citizens in CEE considered things in the EU to be "going in the right
direction."[38] The highest level of trust in the European Parliament among the
27 EU Member States, 67%, was recorded in Slovakia, against an average of
53.5% in CEE and an EU average of 48%.[39] At the same time, despite an overall positive EU image, the CEE citizens did not vote in large numbers in the
European elections.

The first elections for Members of the European Parliament in the eight
CEE countries in 2004 ushered in a long-term trend of CEE Euroskepticism
from the point of view of political behavior. Disappointment with the national

---

37   European Commission, "Public Opinion in the European Union", *Standard Eurobarometer*
(2004) No.62, 80; *Standard Eurobarometer* (2009) No.71, 101; and *Standard Eurobarometer*
(2016) No.86, 18.

38   European Commission, *op. cit.* note 35, 63.

39   *Ibid.*

government was the principal factor for voter participation in the elections. The European elections in CEE thus validated the concept of second-order elections, defined by a lower turnout rate than in national-level elections, losses for the principal parties in government, and electoral success for newer and smaller parties.[40]

While public attitudes towards the EU in CEE were positive at all three consecutive elections held in 2004, 2009, and 2014, voter turnout rates in CEE have been significantly lower than the EU average, as well as relative to all new Member States in previous enlargement rounds. Such behavioral outcomes reveal yet another aspect of the dynamics of democratic legitimacy in the countries of the 2004 EU enlargement. As the data in Table 5.1 demonstrate, voter turnout rates in the European elections in CEE have remained below the EU

TABLE 5.1   *Elections for Members of the European Parliament: Voter Turnout Rates in the New Member States (since 1981)*

Country	1981/1987	1989	1994	1999	2004	2009	2014	Mean 1981–2014, by country
Greece*	77.2	80.1	80.4	75.3	62.8	52.6	59.8	69.7
Spain*	68.9	54.7	59.1	64.4	45.9	44.9	43.8	54.5
Portugal*	72.4	51.2	35.5	40.4	38.7	36.8	33.7	44.1
Austria			67.7	49.0	41.8	46.0	45.4	50.0
Finland			57.6	30.1	39.4	40.3	41.0	41.7
Sweden			41.6	38.8	37.8	45.5	51.1	43.0
Czech Republic					28.3	28.2	18.2	24.9
Estonia					26.9	43.9	36.5	35.4
Hungary					38.5	36.3	29.0	37.4
Latvia					41.3	53.7	30.2	47.5
Lithuania					48.3	21.0	47.4	34.6
Poland					20.8	24.5	23.8	22.6
Slovakia					16.9	19.6	13.0	16.5 (EU lowest)
Slovenia					28.3	28.3	24.6	28.3

---

40   Karlheinz Reif and Hermann Schmitt, "Nine Second-Order National Elections: A Conceptual Framework for the Analysis of European Election Results", 8 *European Journal of Political Research* (1980), 3–44.

TABLE 5.1   *Elections for Members of the European Parliament: Voter Turnout Rates in the New Member States (since 1981) (cont.)*

Country	1981/1987	1989	1994	1999	2004	2009	2014	Mean 1981–2014, by country
Mean for election	59.0	58.4	56.7	49.5	45.5	43.0	42.5	
Mean for new members	70.5	62.0	55.6	37.3	36.8	**33.4****	**33.2****	

Notes: The results of new Member States in all respective elections are in bold.

* The electoral result of 77.2% refers to Greece's accession election in 1981. The mean for the 1979 elections was 61.2%. The first European elections in Spain and Portugal were held in 1987. The 1989 elections report an average turnout rate for Greece, Spain, and Portugal as new members (62.0%).

The first European elections in Austria, Finland and Sweden as new members were held in 1995 (Sweden) and 1996 (Austria and Finland). The 1999 elections report a separate average turnout rate for Austria, Finland, and Sweden as new members (37.3%).

** Reported mean for the eight CEE countries in 2009, 2014. No results for further new members are reported. Bulgaria and Romania (since 2007) and Croatia (since 2013) are excluded.

SOURCE: EUROPEAN PARLIAMENT.[41]

average in all consecutive elections. Electoral results display wide variation both regionally and across time. For example, voter turnout in Lithuania has varied between 48.3% in 2004 and 21.0% in the 2009 election; in Latvia – from 53.7% in 2009 to 30.2% in 2014; and in Estonia – from 26.9% in 2004 to 43.9% in 2009. In each election since 2004, voter turnout rates in Slovakia have been the lowest in the EU, with an average of 16.5%.

4   Understanding CEE Euroskepticism

The origins of CEE Euroskepticism are anchored in the very nature of the post-communist transition. Even prior to the opening of EU membership negotiations, the transition had developed into a process of contradictory dynamics and high social costs. As Václav Havel has noted:

---

41   European Parliament, "Results of the 2014 Elections", Turnout by Country (Table), available at <http://www.results-elections2014.eu/en/turnout.html>, with author's calculations.

We are witnesses to a bizarre state of affairs: society has freed itself, true, but in some ways it behaves worse than when it was in chains. [...] there are others, more serious and dangerous symptoms: hatred among nationalities, suspicion, racism, even signs of fascism; politicking, an unrestrained, unheeding struggle for purely particular interests, unadulterated ambition, fanaticism of every conceivable kind, new and unprecedented varieties of robbery, the rise of different mafias; and a prevailing lack of tolerance, understanding, taste, moderation, and reason. There is a new attraction to ideologies, too.[42]

On the one hand, the principal dimensions of an organized European society in CEE differ from those in the West, although studies of public opinion in the EU, and especially research on Euroskepticism, examine the phenomenon through a common lens. CEE is characterized by a less structured public space: lower levels of knowledge about Europe, limited domestification of European issues, less congruence between voters and parties, and low levels of cognitive mobilization.[43] As a result, public preferences for European integration have experienced high volatility typical of broader trends in domestic public opinion and electoral preferences.

On the other hand, it is important to place the evolution and scope of Euroskepticism in CEE within the EU context, characterized by a continued decline in public support for European integration, rejection of the idea of a EU constitutional treaty, lower levels of support for further EU territorial expansion, and deepening of the "constraining dissensus" coterminous with increasing public scrutiny of EU policy action at the national level.[44]

One of the arguments with regard to the sources of Euroskepticism in CEE suggests that the CEE accession was not informed by the constraining dissensus typical of EU policy making in the post-Maastricht environment. Although levels of support for the EU were volatile during the accession negotiations, they did not prohibitively constrain elite action in pursuing EU membership. The emerging CEE Euroskepticism at the time did not fully create a public atmosphere of "constraining dissensus" that could have restricted the scope and freedom of policy choice, or prevented the CEE Member States from adopting the policy prescriptions of the community *acquis* in its entirety.

---

42   Václav Havel, *Summer Meditations* (Faber and Faber, London, 1992), 2.

43   Richard Rose and Neil Munro, *Elections and Parties in New European Democracies* (cq Press, Washington DC, 2003).

44   Hooghe and Marks, *op. cit.* note 21.

CEE Euroskepticism thus emerged as a phenomenon in select spheres of public trust and democratic legitimacy, spanning the utilitarian-affective and instrumental-ideational dichotomy of public attitudes. Against the background of political euphoria and widely shared perceptions of systemic benefits, it persisted due to the bifurcation of public attitudes, diverging trends of egotropic and sociotropic, utilitarian and legitimacy assessments, and the growing importance of trust, communal solidarity, and social pessimism as a source of public skepticism vis-à-vis European integration. While at the early stages of the Eastern enlargement, the EU was a shorthand for freedom of movement, peace, and economic growth, recent views of the EU in CEE have become divided and more ambiguous. In parallel with peace and opportunities for travel and work, the public image of the EU is associated with bureaucracy and waste of money. Almost counter-intuitively, the image of the EU as a peace project is no longer a dominant perception for the citizens of CEE although it remains a widely shared view among the citizens of the West-European Member States.[45]

5   Conclusion

The EU's eastward enlargement policy was designed to bring the reunification of Europe, create economic prosperity, and consolidate democracy in Eastern Europe. It did not disappoint. Expectedly, enlargement added a modest increase in the EU's overall income but created significant opportunities for economic growth, employment, and cross-border cooperation. Public support for EU membership, however, was not directly and unequivocally linked to such positive performance evaluations. Euroskepticism emerged as an important shared feature of political support for the European integration of Eastern Europe, validating a common trend in public attitudes since the 2004 accession.

The East-European publics have shared a preference to break free from a totalitarian past and build open societies, modern democracies, and market economies. Based on the common legacies of the post-communist transition of CEE, there has been a tendency to treat CEE as a more or less coherent EU region. In reality, while embedded in the same historical context, the CEE

---

45   Eurobarometer, 2004–2014. According to Eurobarometer (Spring 2014) No.81, the EU was widely associated with the opportunity to travel, study and work everywhere in the EU (44%, highest), the Euro (35%), and peace (25%) but also waste of money (25%) and bureaucracy (24%).

citizens demonstrate diverse interests, aspirations, identities, and expectations of the EU.

This chapter has presented an argument that East-European Euroskepticism is multidimensional, spanning across issues along the utilitarian/affective dichotomy and dominated by aspirations for democratic legitimacy. By assuming that Euroskepticism in Eastern Europe is politically insignificant, and that ambiguous and low levels of public support could be accepted as "business as usual" due to the relatively low institutionalization of party systems and high volatility of public preferences in the process of the post-communist transition, the EU political actors failed to establish a salient connection between the European agenda and the representation of public demands. The resulting "expectations gap" is reflected reluctance, distrust, and a lack of direct identification with the EU as a political project. Taking stock of public support for the EU in Eastern Europe post-accession from the perspective of political trust and efficacy is therefore better positioned to explain CEE Euroskepticism than conventional utilitarian and identity-based measures.

The findings suggest that the East-European citizens share low levels of confidence in the European Parliament, the European Commission, and the national governments (in descending order). Regardless of the presence of direct elections for the European Parliament, the CEE publics still trust the United Nations more than the European Union and are less likely to vote in the European elections than citizens in the West-European Member States.

The lack of trust in the EU institutions reached an historic high in 2014 while support for a continued EU enlargement remained a standing preference of CEE public opinion. Such contradictory trends suggest that the conventional measures of Euroskepticism as a pan-European phenomenon need to be re-examined.

Bibliography

Diez Medrano, Juan. (2003) *Framing Europe: Attitudes to European Integration in Germany, Spain, and the United Kingdom* (Princeton University Press, Princeton).

Grabbe, Heather. (2006) *The EU's Transformative Power: Europeanization through Conditionality in Central and Eastern Europe* (Palgrave Macmillan, Basingstoke).

Guerra, Simona. (2013a) *Central and Eastern European Attitudes in the Face of Union* (Palgrave Macmillan, Basingstoke).

Guerra, Simona. (2013b) "Does Familiarity Bring Contempt? Determinants of Public Support for European Integration and Opposition to it before and after Accession", 51(1) *Journal of Common Market Studies*, 38–50.

Haas, Ernst. (1968) *The Uniting of Europe: Political, Social, and Economic Forces 1950–1957* (Stanford University Press, Stanford).

Havel, Václav. (1992) *Summer Meditations* (Faber and Faber, London).

Hooghe, Liesbet and Marks, Gary. (2009) "A Post-Functionalist Theory of Integration: From Permissive Consensus to Constraining Dissensus", 39 *British Journal of Political Science*, 1–23.

Jacobs, Jorg and Pollack, Detlef. (2006) "Support Based on Values? Attitudes toward the EU in Eleven Postcommunist Societies", in Rohrschneider, Robert and Whitefield, Stephen. (eds.), *Public Opinion, Party Competition, and the European Union in Post-Communist Europe* (Palgrave Macmillan, New York).

Kopecky, Petr and Mudde, Cas. (2002) "The Two Sides of Euroscepticism: Party Positions on European Integration in East Central Europe", 3(3) *European Union Politics*, 297–326.

Lindberg, Leon and Scheingold, Stuart. (1970) *Europe's Would-be Polity: Patterns of Change in the European Community* (Prentice-Hall, Englewood Cliffs, NJ).

Llamazares, Iván and Gramacho, Wladimir. (2007) "Euroskeptics among Euroenthusiasts: An Analysis of Southern European Public Opinions", 42(2–3) *Acta Politica*, 211–232.

McLaren, Lauren. (2006) *Identity, Interests, and Attitudes to European Integration* (Palgrave Macmillan, Basingstoke).

Reif, Karlheinz and Schmitt, Hermann. (1980) "Nine Second-Order National Elections: A Conceptual Framework for the Analysis of European Election Results", 8 *European Journal of Political Research*, 3–44.

Risse, Thomas. (2010) *A Community of Europeans? Transnational Identities and Public Spheres* (Cornell University Press, Ithaca).

Rose, Richard and Munro, Neil. (2003) *Elections and Parties in New European Democracies* (CQ Press, Washington DC).

Sanchez-Cuenca, Ignacio. (2000) "The Political Basis of Support for European Integration", 1(2) *European Union Politics*, 147–171.

Scharpf, Fritz. (1999) *Governing in Europe: Effective and Democratic?* (Oxford University Press, New York).

Schimmelfennig, Frank and Sedelmeier, Ulrich. (2005) *The Europeanization of Central and Eastern Europe* (Cornell University Press, Ithaca).

Sundlisæter Skinner, Marianne. (2013) "Different Varieties of Euroscepticism? Conceptualizing and Explaining Euroscepticism in Western European Non-Member States", 51(1) *Journal of Common Market Studies*, 122–139.

Szczerbiak, Alex. (2001) "Polish Public Opinion: Explaining Declining Support for EU Membership", 39(1) *Journal of Common Market Studies*, 105–122.

Taggart, Paul. (1998) "A Touchstone of Dissent: Euroskepticism in Contemporary Western European Party Systems", 33 *European Journal of Political Research*, 363–388.

Taggart, Paul and Szczerbiak, Alex. (2001) "Parties, Positions and Europe: Euroscepticism in the Candidate States of Central and Eastern Europe", paper presented at the Annual Meeting of the Political Studies Association (10–12 April 2001, Manchester).

Vasilopoulou, Sofia. (2013) "Continuity and Change in the Study of Euroscepticism: Plus ça Change?", 51(1) *Journal of Common Market Studies*, 153–168.

CHAPTER 6

Václav Klaus as a Driver of Czech Euroskepticism

Vratislav Havlík and Ondřej Mocek

Abstract

The development of party and non-party Euroskepticism in the Czech Republic is one of the most prominent phenomena in Czech political history in the last decade.[1] This phenomenon can be seen in the rise of a variety of parties and social movements whose goals fall along from a spectrum of opposition against the specific direction of European integration to outright opposition against the EU in general. Moreover, it is clear that in the past ten years (at the very least) where this increase in the visibility of Euroskepticism in the Czech media has occurred, it has often centered around the EU positions and opinions of the President at the time, Václav Klaus. This article examines the effect of Klaus on these movements, and demonstrates how he was the driving force both for their formation and their success.

Keywords

Václav Klaus – Euroskepticism – Czech Political Parties – Czech Republic – Lisbon Treaty

•••

[The Lisbon Treaty] will deepen today's problems of the EU, increase its democratic deficit, worsen the position of our country, and expose it to new risks.

VÁCLAV KLAUS, 9 October 2009

⁙

---

1 This chapter has been written as a part of the research project "Europe 2020: A Horizon of Change of Relevant Actors of the Czech Republic's Political System" (Czech Science Foundation Project GA13-24657S).

1   Introduction

The statement above is an excerpt from a speech by the then President of the Czech Republic, Václav Klaus, which he delivered around the time of the ratification of the Lisbon Treaty in 2009, just a few weeks before he ultimately signed the document. It was a peak time for Klaus' Euroskepticism from the perspective of the attention from the international media, possibly also of Czech Euroskepticism in general. The development of party and non-party Euroskepticism in the Czech Republic is one of the most prominent phenomena in Czech political history in the last decade. This phenomenon can be seen in the rise of a variety of parties and social movements whose goals fall along a spectrum of opposition to the EU, ranging from opposition to the specific direction of European integration to outright opposition against the EU in general. Moreover, it is clear that in the past ten years (at the very least) where this increase in the visibility of Euroskepticism in Czech media has occurred, it has often centered around the EU positions and opinions of the President at the time, Václav Klaus.[2] Therefore former President Klaus and his actions are the focus of this article.[3]

The main goals in this text are to draw attention to the dynamic development of Euroskepticism in between 2003 and 2015 and clarify the role of Václav Klaus in this process. While obviously it is not possible to quantify the influence of Klaus Euroskepticism on Czech citizens' attitudes about the EU, we can identify the role Klaus played in the formation of a public "Euroskepticism of the elite", which includes political parties and civil society movements. We therefore do not try to show Václav Klaus as a driver of the Euroskeptic attitudes of the Czech *public* (though by using Eurobarometer, we can see some parallels), but instead as a driver of Euroskepticism in *political parties* and *civic movements*. As a result, the Euroskepticism discussed in this text is not public-based, but rather rooted in parties and civic organizations. We begin by noting that the common denominator of Czech Euroskepticism is Václav Klaus himself, whose declarations of sympathy and support acted to legitimize the greater or lesser successes of various movements and activities, and without

---

2   Vít Hloušek and Petr Kaniok, "Czech Republic", in Nicolo Conti (ed.), *Party Attitudes Towards the EU in the Member States: Parties for Europe, Parties against Europe* (Routledge, Abingdon, 2014), 158–173.

3   Lubomír Kopeček, in his biography of Klaus, argues that the direction of European integration was a constant source of interest to Klaus; however, until 2003, it was a rather peripheral topic for Klaus. See Lubomír Kopeček, *Fenomén Václav Klaus (The Phenomenon Václav Klaus)* (Barrister & Principal, Brno, 2012), 134.

this support would have often rendered them barely viable. Secondly, we further hope to determine how Klaus used the office of President to pursue his Euroskeptic agenda. In other words, we try to determine whether Klaus truly influenced actual policy and delaying the adoption of EU primary law, or was only a source of rhetorical invective without any actual effect on the legislative process.

The rise of Euroskepticism is described as an unexpected externality of the Klaus Presidency. Before his election to the Presidency, Klaus focused his political energies on other topics, chiefly the (domestic) political situation in the Czech Republic,[4] and there existed no foreshadowing that the otherwise consistent and predictable Klaus would change course. It is necessary to outline the selection of Euroskeptic movements that arose during the time of the Klaus Presidency which our argument engages with. The text concentrates solely on those movements or parties that explicitly followed the ideas of Václav Klaus, or received direct support from him at the time of their founding.

The outline of this text on Czech Euroskepticism is logically divided along chronological developments, and sections are separated by key milestones. The first section characterizes developments from the election of Václav Klaus as President in 2003, and continues until the creation and resulting discussion around the EU's Constitutional Treaty. The next stage concerns this discussion, which was undoubtedly a key moment in Czech Euroskeptic thinking, and the chapter covers this discussion until Klaus' departure from the Civic Democratic Party (ODS).[5] The concluding phase we touch on covers the "Klaus' Post-Lisbon Era", lasting since 2009 and characterized by the establishment of a new think tank, the Václav Klaus Institute, and the discussion of the formation of a new Euroskeptic party under the auspices of the former President.

2   The Klaus Presidency, Part I

Václav Klaus has undoubtedly been a major figure in the development of Czech politics since 1989. First as Minister of Finance and later as Prime Minister, Klaus had a marked influence on the conceptualization of the Czech transition from the socialist era as well as leaving his mark on the Czech Republic's

---

4   Otto Eibl, Miloš Gregor, and Alena Macková, "O čem a jak hovořil Václav Klaus ve svých veřejných projevech (Issues and Tonality of Václav Klaus' Public Speeches)", *Czech Journal of Political Science* (2013) No. 4, 392–418, at 400.

5   ODS – Občanská demokratická strana. This was the main right-wing Czech party between 1992 and 2013.

integration into European and Western institutions. Although a critic of European integration, Klaus nevertheless presided over the Czech application to the EU in 1996 as Prime Minister.

Klaus was elected President of the Czech Republic about 14 months before the accession of the Czech Republic to the European Union. From the outset, it was clear that as the Republic's second President, as well as a political heavyweight in his own right, he would attract a great deal of media attention. The President enjoyed and took full advantage of this opportunity, and zealously brought to attention themes which until that time had been relatively unconsidered. Kopeček describes the situation:

> The skilled debater cleverly took advantage of the aura of the Presidency and successfully turned interviews toward topics that he wanted to discuss, or that he felt were a priority. He developed a full thematic repertoire, with specific modifications, additions, and emphases, which he maintained to the end of his presidency. Its most visible aspect was the criticism of the direction of the EU.[6]

This historical context, the combination of two circumstances – the entry of the Czech Republic to the EU and the beginning of the Klaus Presidency – is crucial for the following argument, which discusses this increase in party-based[7] and non-partisan[8] Euroskepticism during Klaus' ten-year Presidency. Quantitative research seems to confirm this thinking. A study of Klaus' speeches from 1995–2013 indicates that in the eight years when Klaus was politically active but before he became President (i.e. from 1995–2003), Klaus referred to the EU a mere 25 times, while during his first presidential term (2003–2008), the topic already occurred in 51 cases; during his second term (2008–2013), the topic continued to arise, coming up in 60 cases.[9] While it is true that Klaus gave speeches more often as President, the available data also indicates that the relative frequency of occasions on which Klaus spoke on European topics increased as well, from 13.6% to 21.7% (of all speeches). By any measures, the frequency of European themes (which with Klaus were typically approached skeptically) increased sharply.

Key Euroskeptic movements were already formed before the turn of the millennium. One was the Center for Economics and Politics (Centrum pro

---

6 Kopeček, *op. cit.* note 3, 157, translation by the authors.
7 Here, this means Euroskepticism in ideology and/or the platform of a political party.
8 This is understood as Euroskepticism in ideology of movements and think-tanks.
9 Eibl, Gregor, and Macková, *op. cit.* note 4, 400.

Ekonomiku a Politiku, CEP), founded by Klaus in 1999. During his Presidency, however, Klaus continued to have a considerable influence on the CEP, shown, for example, in his constant membership on the three-member CEP board of directors, a position he has held to date. Klaus was – and is – an "opinion-maker" for the organization, as evidenced, among other things, by his role at the *Newsletter*,[10] the monthly journal of the CEP. In this journal, before the beginning of his presidency, Klaus wrote columns nearly every month reflecting a particular key problem of the day. These "problems" were often those connected with the EU. In 2002–2003, this topic was especially important; however, it was not the only topic, but by 2005 at the latest, it became clear that together with Klaus' writings in regard to the EU, the number of Euroskeptic articles in CEP significantly increased. Typical titles of Klaus' texts at this time included "Mám strach o Evropu (I'm worried about Europe)" or "Evropské problémy a jejich neřešení (European Problems and their Non-Solutions)." At this time Klaus was not a hard-line Euroskeptic calling for an exit from the EU, but rather proposed an alternative form for it, as in the column "Mýtus tureckého nebezpečí (The Myth of the Turkish Danger)." Klaus maintained a constant influence on the outlook of the CEP and significantly helped to create its ideological focus even during his Presidency, as well as using these texts to launch the CEP to the forefront of intellectual interest and putting an agenda focused on opposition to the current form of the EU on the table. That said, circulation of the *Newsletter* (in 2008, 6,000 copies were printed monthly) never came close to that of other similarly-oriented journals, and was only distributed among an intellectual elite, particularly in universities, as well as to journalists and politicians.

One interesting aspect of this period, which laid the foundation for further argumentation, was the development of Klaus' relationship with the ODS, which he founded in the beginning of the 1990s and served as Chairman until 2002. Any result of the election of Klaus' successor to the chairmanship was bound to be of utmost concern for the future President. The vote was unexpectedly won by Mirek Topolánek, rather than Jan Zahradil or Petr Nečas,[11] two men whom Klaus strongly preferred. Topolánek was a rather different type of politician, and mutual antipathy did not take long to emerge. Nevertheless, in the following years, President Klaus remained loyal to the ODS and specific points of criticism only began to emerge at the beginning of the next ODS government headed by Topolánek. By the beginning of 2007, in an interview with

10   *CEP Newsletter*, available at <http://cepin.cz/cze/newsletter.php>.
11   Kopeček, *op. cit.* note 3, 142–143.

the Czech weekly news magazine *Týden*, Klaus indicated that the ODS was taking a direction that he did not like. One of the reasons had to do with the excessive concessions granted to ODS' coalition partners, the Christian Democratic Union–Czech People's Party (KDU-ČSL) and the Green Party (Strana Zelených), during the period of the formation of a government. Both KDU-ČSL and the Greens had a clearly pro-European program.[12] Klaus viewed these concessions to the smaller coalition with great apprehension and indicated his disappointment with ODS' alleged departure from the ideals on which the party was founded.[13] However, the President avoided any major disagreements with his party at the time he was up for re-election in 2008 and when ODS's support was critical. Only after Klaus' re-election did disagreement between Klaus and Topolánek (and thus the ODS) come to a head, in the context of the discussion of the Lisbon Treaty ratification. It is to this era we turn next.

3   Klaus' Battle of Lisbon

The second chronological period is Klaus' characteristic battle against the revision of the fundamental treaties of the European Union. As an opponent of further European integration, Klaus received the proposal for a Treaty Establishing a Constitution for Europe extremely negatively. Like the Treaty on European Union, he perceived it as a victory of a highly motivated group of Europeanists over hundreds of millions of people who simply were not thinking or paying attention.[14] The Constitutional Treaty nevertheless failed to be ratified in France and the Netherlands, and thus the process of ratification was scrapped. Because of this, in the Czech Republic a wider and deeper debate on the treaty did not occur, and thus the subject of alternative directions of European integration did not settle into Czech political discourse.

Nevertheless, renewed negotiations unleashed a corresponding new wave of Klaus' Euroskepticism. The first indicator that negotiations toward deeper

---

12   Dalibor Balšínek and Miroslav Korecký, "Smrtící zkušenost vládnutí (Lethal Governance Experience)", *Týden* (8 January 2007), available at <http://www.tyden.cz/rozhovory/smrtici-zkusenost-vladnuti_2034.html>.

13   Vlastimil Havlík, "A Breaking-up of a Pro-European Consensus: Attitudes of Czech Political Parties towards the European Integration (1998–2010)", *Communist and Post-Communist Studies* (2011) No. 2, 129–147.

14   Václav Klaus, "Nalijme si čistého vína ohledně evropské ústavy (Pour a Pure Wine about the European Constitution)", *CEP Newsletter* (March 2007), 8.

European integration might be problematic occurred at the beginning of 2007, when the EU issued the Berlin Declaration, celebrating 50 years since the foundation of the European Economic Community. Václav Klaus pointedly indicated that he would absolutely refuse to sign any text that made reference to a new constitution for Europe. Germany, which at the time chaired the Council of the EU, eventually gave in to the pressure from the Czech Republic and other Member States and removed any reference to a constitution from the text. Additionally, the text of the Declaration was eventually only signed by the heads of individual European-level institutions, rather than by Member States. Klaus thus defined and declared his position on the renewal of negotiations to revise the European treaties, even announcing that the prospect of a new treaty in 2009 was "just a dream."[15]

Klaus nevertheless failed to prevent the government led by Mirek Topolánek (ODS) from other negotiations regarding changes to primary legislation. The revised Constitutional Treaty, known as the Lisbon Treaty, was signed by the leaders of EU Member States in 2007; this fact and the resulting ratification process once again set off a new wave of the Czech Euroskepticism, once again with Václav Klaus at the head of it. For Klaus, the ruling ODS had lost all credibility. The party, which he had founded and for a long time headed, had become so ideologically divergent from the direction he felt it should take that at the party's convention at the end of 2008 he officially cut all his ties with the party, and resigned from the post of honorary chairman.[16] This opened a new space for Klaus' political action.

In 2008, like Václav Klaus, Petr Mach also left the ODS and resigned from its board. Mach was a long-time Klaus colleague and confidante, who ran the CEP from its beginning and in 2003 became its executive director. The same year he also became an adviser to President Klaus, and continued in this position until 2007. The wave of partisan and nonpartisan Euroskepticism, which in 2008 completely swept through the Czech Republic, also resulted in an additional political undertaking for Mach – he announced the formation of a new party. One of the main reasons was undoubtedly the Lisbon Treaty, which the party addressed in their introductory statement:

---

15   Paul Taylor and Noah Barkin, "Merkel Urges EU Renewal at 50th Birthday Ceremony", *Reuters* (25 March 2007), available at <http://uk.reuters.com/article/2007/03/25/uk-eu-anniversary-idUKL2363371620070325>.

16   Václav Klaus, "Vystoupení prezidenta republiky na 19. kongresu ODS (Speech of the President on the 19th Congress ODS)", (6 December 2008), available at <http://www.klaus.cz/clanky/1715>.

We are convinced that the implementation of the Lisbon Treaty would lead to the decline of Europe, would create a pretend democracy in which the will of voters in individual countries is circumvented by supranational institutions. We don't want the Lisbon Treaty, because we want to keep liberty, we want to keep functioning democracy, and we want to restore prosperity.[17]

The party, which took the name The Party of Free Citizens (Strana svobodných občanů – SSO) was officially established at the beginning of 2009, and filled a gap in the Czech political spectrum for a non-radical Euroskeptic party, which not incidentally had close links to Václav Klaus. Klaus himself appeared at the party's first convention, giving a speech in which he pointed out the party's focus "on the defense of individual liberty and national sovereignty."[18] However, he never officially endorsed the party, though not because of his obligations as President. In subsequent elections to the European Parliament, the SSO performed poorly, winning only 1% of the vote, and their program was considered too radical – the Free Citizens called for a total withdrawal from the EU, which Klaus refused to support.[19] It is obvious thus that on one hand, Klaus wished the party success and regarded it as a potentially capable advocate for his Euroskeptic ideas, but on the other hand (as in later cases), he hesitated to extend explicit support and lend his name to any movement that had only an uncertain likelihood of success. In other words, Klaus never wasted his political capital or his "brand image." Moreover, at this time, Klaus' Euroskepticism took a softer form than at the end of his presidential term. In a text from the beginning of 2009, he called for a decentralized Europe of states, rather than a Europe of regions, and at the same time rejected ever closer Union.[20] Calls for leaving the Union, however, were also absent from his speeches, and Klaus did not support such calls.

---

17   Petr Mach, "Ideový projev k založení strany svobodných občanů (Speech on the Occasion of the Establishment of the Free Citizens Party)", *Svobodní* (14 February 2009), available at <https://web.svobodni.cz/clanky/petr-mach-ideovy-projev-k-zalozeni-strany-svobod nych-obcanu>, translation by the authors.

18   Václav Klaus, "Zdravice prezidenta republiky na Ustavujícím sněmu Strany svobodných občanů (Welcome Message of the President at the Inaugural Assembly of The Party of Free Citizens)", *Svobodní* (14 February 2009), available at <http://www.svobodni.cz/media/clanky/27-zdravice-prezidenta-republiky/>.

19   Kopeček, *op. cit.* note 3, 228.

20   Václav Klaus, "Výzvy roku 2009: pohled z České republiky (Challenges of the Year 2009: View from the Czech Republic)", (8 Junuary 2009), available at <http://www.klaus.cz/clanky/2210>.

Another organization that protested against deeper integration and the Lisbon Treaty was Akce D.O.S.T.[21] This movement was founded at the end of 2007, with an ideological basis founded on conservative Christian values.[22] One of the main program points of the movement, however, concerned the defense of Czech statehood and sovereignty against the EU. The Lisbon Treaty thus became an especially important topic for Akce D.O.S.T., who attempted to mobilize to the public against it. During this time, the movement organized a number of protests and marches, as well as convening a number of discussion forums, during which they attempted to demonstrate to the broader public their decidedly negative opinion toward deeper integration. A few of the many examples include "Pochod na obranu svobody a státní suverenity (the March for the Defense of Freedom and National Sovereignty)", "Pochod za samostatný stat (the March for an Independent State)", and a demonstration called "Svoboda pro Irsko (Freedom for Ireland)", which reflected their opposition to a second Irish referendum on the Lisbon Treaty.[23] The movement closely parallels the arguments of Klaus, and is linked to him as well as his close advisers. Klaus himself also participated (and continues to participate) in their events, and has confirmed his agreement with the ideas that Akce D.O.S.T. has propagated, explaining, "I read your words, I understand them. I feel similarly to the way you do, but as President perhaps I use some weaker terminology."[24] In return, members and sympathizers of Akce D.O.S.T. showed their gratitude, and in times of crisis, when various people on the Czech political scene called for Klaus' resignation from the post of President due to his opposition to the Lisbon Treaty, members of Akce D.O.S.T. supported him, urging him to stay in the Prague Castle. The example of support for Akce D.O.S.T. shows that the President utilized a colorful palette of parties and movements in his "Euroskeptic battle", and did not limit himself to support from the CEP, his own think-tank. Klaus thus was not only a founder of Euroskeptic movements (e.g. CEP). He was also a driver of Euroskeptic movements that were founded independently, and which he lent support to only later. Support from the lips of the President of the Republic automatically meant media attention.

---

21   DOST is an acronym for the Czech words Důvěra (Trust), Objektivita (Objectivity), Svoboda (Freedom), and Tradice (Tradition). The word "dost" itself means "enough."

22   Available at <http://www.akce-dost.cz/>.

23   Available at <http://www.akce-dost.cz/20090927.htm>, <http://www.akce-dost.cz/2009 1026.htm>, and <http://www.akce-dost.cz/20091030.htm>.

24   D.O.S.T., "Na akci D.O.S.T. Pochod na Hrad promluvil prezident ČR (President of the Czech Republic has a Speech at the Event of D.O.S.T. March to the Castle)", (28 September 2010), available at <http://www.akce-dost.cz/20091005.htm>.

Klaus' ideas combined with his opposition to the Lisbon Treaty resonated not only with civic society, but also among political elites. In 2008, this meant a strengthening of the more Euroskeptic wing of the ODS. This was particularly evident in a group of Senators, who filed a complaint in the Czech Constitutional Court for a review of the Lisbon Treaty and its conformity with the constitutional order of the Czech Republic. After an unsuccessful attempt in the first half of 2008, the Senate group filed a new, more complex complaint at the end of the year. The President lent his support to both complaints, and during the second he, in fact, became the main critic of the Treaty.[25] However, even the second hearing turned out unsuccessful. Klaus was totally dissatisfied with the result, and had no intention of laying the matter to rest. He self-published a book on his statements made during sessions before the Constitutional Court,[26] so that they could be more widely circulated among the citizens. A final symbol of his opposition to the treaty was the attempt to negotiate an "opt-out" from the Lisbon Treaty's Charter of Fundamental Rights.[27] This was promised rather quickly and there were consequently no further obstacles Klaus could use to avoid signing the treaty.[28]

The run-up to the election for the European Parliament in May 2009 combined with the problematic ratification of the Lisbon Treaty accelerated the already negative perception of the EU among a considerable portion of the population. Two other political actors appeared on the scene to respond to this situation and give voice to a defense of national values and opposition to deeper integration.[29] The first of these was Libertas.cz, which was the Czech parallel to the Europe-wide movement Libertas, which sprang up in a variety of Member States before the election. The second organization was the Sovereignty Party (Suverenita), headed by Jana Bobošíková.[30] Both of these actors

---

25 Kopeček, *op. cit.* note 3, 226.

26 Václav Klaus, *Prezident republiky k Lisabonské smlouvě* (*The President of the Republic on the Lisbon Treaty*) (Euromedia Group, Banská Bystrica, 2009).

27 Václav Klaus, "Prohlášení prezidenta republiky ze dne 9. října 2009 k ratifikaci Lisabonské smlouvy (Statement of the President of the Czech Republic on the ratification of the Lisbon Treaty)", (10 October 2009), available at <http://www.klaus.cz/clanky/1307>.

28 Helena Bončková and Hubert Smekal, "Fragmentace společných hodnot? Výjimky z Listiny základních práv Evropské unie (Fragmentation of Common Values? Opt-outs from the Charter of Fundamental Rights of the European Union)", *Current Europe* (2010) No. 2, 61–81, at 72–73.

29 Sean Hanley, "Dynamics of New Party Formation in the Czech Republic 1996–2010: Looking for the Origins of a 'Political Earthquake'", 28(2) *East European Politics* (2012), 119–143, at 127.

30 Interestingly, Železný, founder of Libertas.cz, and Bobošíková campaigned for the EP together in 2004 as a single movement, the Independents (Nezávislí), which nevertheless fell apart after the election. Hloušek and Kaniok, *op. cit.* note 2, 164.

applauded the efforts of the Czech President to preserve Czech sovereignty and to refuse to sign the Lisbon Treaty.[31] Klaus himself, however, held back from supporting either of the two movements, even though both parties were based on the background and the popularity of his opinions. In the end, neither of these parties was able to clear the 5% minimum hurdle required to enter the EP. Libertas.cz eventually folded as a result.

As can be seen, the resulting movement was based on direct support from the President – or at least it took umbrage in his ideas. This proved to be a risky move. As a *homo politicus*,[32] Václav Klaus carefully weighed where to lend his support, as well as when to save his political capital. The occasional loss of interest by President Klaus in some Euroskeptic movements or parties understandably resulted in a decrease in media attention to them, which for the cases mentioned above proved to be fatal. This was the fate of the Party of Free Citizens, which Klaus initially supported but later withdrew his support from which then began the media's shift away from coverage of the party. Akce D.O.S.T. encountered a similar destiny, as well as the meteoric demise of the Chin Up party (see the next section). Libertas.cz completely disappeared. This does not mean that these groups deviated from Klaus' position on Europe, but instead their failure came from the collapse in support from voters. Thus when these movements lost Klaus, they also lost their ability to appeal to a broader audience and keep the public's attention. Nevertheless, Czech party- and nonpartisan Euroskepticism after the Klaus Presidency has been characterized by its continued abilities of reincarnation.

4   Klaus' Post-Lisbon Period

The period from the end of 2009 to the present has taken on an entirely different thematic attitude. After all the meanderings and delays, Václav Klaus eventually became the last head of state of an EU Member State to sign the Lisbon Treaty in November 2009, which symbolically brought the entire debate on the topic to a close. For most of the remainder of his Presidency, and with the economic and currency crisis raging, Klaus turned to the economy as a source of political debate. While he has continued in his criticism of the EU and its approaches to ending the crisis, the topic has not held enough society-wide salience to mobilize additional movements drawing on Klaus' ideas.

---

31   Jana Bobošíková, "Volební spot (Election spot)", (2009) available at <http://www.youtube
       .com/watch?v=drwCV57TjFY>; and Libertas.cz, "Volební spot (Election spot)", (2009)
       available at <http://www.youtube.com/watch?v=bTrmOxmvA-s>.

32   Kopeček, *op. cit.* note 3.

A renewal of this view coincides with the end of Klaus' presidential term. In 2012, the Václav Klaus Institute (IVK), a liberal-conservative think tank, was founded, with the goal of "developing the political and ideological legacy of Václav Klaus."[33] The institute therefore can perhaps be considered Klaus' vehicle to develop and propagate his ideas. These undoubtedly include a critical perspective on today's path of integration as well, and Klaus and his colleagues continue to disseminate their opinions through newsletters, political commentaries, polemics, columns, and other publications. For illustration, we have selected the titles of some of these – "Evropská vlajka na Hradě aneb oživování dávno mrtvé debaty (The European Flag over the Castle or Reviving a Long-dead Argument)" or "Evropa, její problémy a Rusko ve 21. Století (Europe, its Problems, and Russia in the 21st Century)", as well as Klaus' most recently published book, *Česká republika na rozcestí – Čas rozhodnutí* (*The Czech Republic at the Crossroads: A Time for Choosing*). At the same time, the IVK and the CEP have moved into the same address in Prague, and have planned for future closer cooperation with the eventual goal of merging the two organizations. IVK would thus come to be seen as the single flagship, to further disseminate the ideas of Václav Klaus and his ideological successors.

The influence of Klaus' ideas could still be seen at the beginning of 2012. Once again, a powerful Euroskeptic wing in the party continued to oppose a reduction in the powers of Member States vis-à-vis the EU. At the core of this dispute was the signing of the EU's "fiscal pact", which Petr Nečas, the Prime Minister of the Czech Republic, together with British Prime Minister David Cameron, refused to sign. For Nečas, this meant dividing his governmental coalition, as the other parties in the government were solidly supportive; however, for the backbenchers of the ODS, it was exactly what they wanted. Public support for Nečas' decision came from President Klaus, who thanked Nečas for refusing.[34] Even at the end of his term, Klaus did not hesitate to take the opportunity to influence actual policy. At the end of 2012, and into the beginning of 2013, he continued to refuse to sign the Treaty Establishing the European Stability Mechanism, even though both chambers of the Czech Parliament ratified the treaty and he was required to sign it. Nevertheless, Klaus did not

---

33   IVK, "O Institutu (About the Institute)", available at <http://www.institutvk.cz/o
-institutu>.

34   "Klaus pochválil Nečase: Jednal jako zodpovědný politik (Klaus Commends Nečas: He
Acted as a Responsible Politician)", *Lidovky* (31 Janary 2012), available at <http://www
.lidovky.cz/klaus-pochvalil-necase-jednal-jako-zodpovedny-politik-pps-/zpravy-domov
.aspx?c=A120131_164855_ln_domov_ogo>.

back away from his opinion, and the treaty was ratified by his successor in April 2013.[35]

A logical element of Klaus' post-Lisbon period also included his interactions with Jana Bobošíková, well-known in Czech media as a Euroskeptic. Despite previous failures, Bobošíková continued to head a campaign of Euroskepticism during the early elections of 2013, and ran for the Chamber of Deputies of the Czech Republic. This was Bobošíková's second attempt to enter the Chamber of Deputies. The first was in 2010, when she ran as the top candidate of the Sovereignty-Jana Bobošíková Block party (Suverenita–blok Jany Bobošíkové). At this time, she repeatedly referred to the thinking of Václav Klaus – the defense of national values, the preservation of sovereignty, etc. The vote count for the party came in just under the 5% hurdle, and therefore the party failed to receive any seats in the Chamber.[36]

After the end of his presidential term, media outlets naturally began to reduce their focus on Václav Klaus, and thus limit the scope of his arguments. At the same time, leaving the Presidency allowed Klaus to develop a far more partisan profile. At the first possible moment, Klaus decided to support the political actor that came closest to his political thinking. In the 2013 elections, this was Jana Bobošíková, this time campaigning as the top candidate for the party Chin Up (Hlavu vzhůru). Klaus did not merely offer expressions of support, but he put himself up as the symbol of the movement, and his image became the central visual element in the party's campaign, with his face appearing prominently on billboards across the country. Klaus' opinions, resting on their Euroskeptic foundations, for the first time completely engaged in electoral battle. When final vote was tallied, the Chin Up party nonetheless finished with a negligible 0.5%. While the result in 2010 marked a possible future entrance to the Chamber of Deputies, the party in 2013 suffered a fatal crash. Even though Klaus himself supported the party, the topic of Euroskepticism had by that point completely flickered out, and attracted very few voters found it to be a

---

35   Filip Horáček, "Vznik záchranného fondu eurozóny brzdí už jen Klaus, varoval Senát (Only Klaus is Blocking the Establishment of a Eurozone Rescue Fund, Senate Warns)", *iDNES* (6 December 2012), available at <http://ekonomika.idnes.cz/senat-vyzval-klause-aby-podepsal-vznik-fondu-esm-fbf-/ekonomika.aspx?c=A121206_103804_ekonomika_fih>, as well as "Zeman na Hradě podepsal euroval, s Barrosem vyvěsil vlajku EU (Zeman Signs ESM, Raises EU Flag with Barroso)", *iDNES* (3 April 2013), available at <http://zpravy.idnes.cz/na-hrade-uz-visi-vlajka-eu-zeman-podporil-i-euroval-fwr-/domaci.aspx?c=A130403_075730_domaci_kop>.

36   Sean Hanley, "Czech Republic: 'Sovereignty' a Party to Watch", (20 July 2011), available at <http://drseansdiary.wordpress.com/2011/07/20/czech-republic-sovereignty-a-party-to-watch/>.

total non-starter. Czech Euroskepticism as such remains, though it is no longer a main topic for political parties, and rather marginal (such as for ODS and the Communists); it has not been a wedge issue for voters in elections, as EU membership is uncontested by the established parties.[37]

Until the end of 2012, it was still evident that the development of Czech Euroskepticism was one of the main externalities of the Klaus Presidency, and thus of the first decade of Czech politics in a European context. The situation since Klaus left the office in March 2013 offers a completely different image. The media no longer writes about Akce D.O.S.T. or the IVK. The parliamentary elections of October 2013 illustrated that the party supported by Klaus, Chin Up, received less than half a percent of the votes nationwide. Commentators spoke of the end of Bobošíková; the more daring spoke of the end of Klaus as well.[38]

In 2014 and 2015, media interest in Klaus has waned. Euroskepticism thus has not been so pushed in the Czech Republic, and has been more and more marginalized in society. This decline of Euroskeptic attitudes in the Czech Republic can also be seen in opinion polls, which in 2014 showed a sharp increase in positive feelings about the EU. In 2014, 37% of respondents indicated they had a positive opinion about the EU, up from 24% in 2013. With this, the Czech Republic has started to fall into the European average, which in 2014 was 39%.[39] The only Euroskeptic organization which has experienced at least a little success was the SSO, which was not a conservative party (which Klaus supported at the beginning), but a libertarian party. In the 2014 elections to the EP, it received one seat. Nevertheless, this party, as mentioned above, was not associated with Klaus and did not have his support.[40]

---

37   Hloušek and Kaniok, *op. cit.* note 2. Also, Kateřina Hubertová, "Témata letošních voleb: zdravotnictví, nezaměstnanost i korupce (Topics of This Year's Election: Health Care, Unemployment and Corruption)", *ČT24* (27 October 2013), available at <http://www.ceskatelevize.cz/ct24/domaci/1068988-temata-letosnich-voleb-zdravotnictvi-nezamestnanost-i-korupce>.

38   Jakub Kalenský, "Ponurý konec Václava Klause (The Dismal End of Václav Klaus)", *Česká pozice* (30 October 2013), available at <http://ceskapozice.lidovky.cz/ponury-konec-vacla va-klause-dıc-/tema.aspx?c=A131029_102423_pozice_137092>.

39   European Commission, "Veřejné míněné v zemích Evropské unie – Národní zpráva Česká republika (Public Opinion in EU Countries – National Report of the Czech Republic)", *Eurobarometer* (2014), available at <http://ec.europa.eu/public_opinion/archives/eb/eb82/eb82_cz_cz_nat.pdf>.

40   "Voliči se k volbám nehrnuli. Vyhrálo ANO nebo TOP 09? (Voters didn't Flock to the Elections: Who Won ANO or TOP 09?)", *Týden* (24 May 2014), available at <http://www.tyden.cz/rubriky/domaci/eurovolby-2014/volici-se-k-volbam-nehrnuli-vyhralo-ano

Klaus, however, has had no intention of completely disappearing from the political scene and has presented his opinion on the two major issues of the day – the Russo-Ukrainian crisis and the refugee crisis. In the case of the Russo-Ukrainian conflict, he sided with Russia, criticizing the EU and the USA for being behind the whole situation.[41] Similarly, he has criticized EU officials for their handling of the refugee crisis.[42] The peak of his efforts in this area came in the form of a petition in September 2015 in which he called for rejecting quotas which the EU wanted to use to allocate refugees, as well as for securing the borders.[43] However, these facts have not been able to catalyze party and non-party Euroskepticism as much as when Klaus was still President. Other than the one seat held by the SSO, all other movements have been completely marginalized.

5   Conclusion

As noted in the introduction, the gradual spillover of Euroskepticism since the accession of the Czech Republic to the European Union has been indisputable and visible, but somewhat more interesting is the discussion of the reasons for this trend. The rise of Euroskepticism in the Czech society, as it has been observed, is not solely a phenomenon standing on its own feet, but has been dependent on the actions of Václav Klaus. When Klaus supported the individual movements discussed above in his capacity as President, we can speak of a vibrant Euroskeptic discourse; after the end of his term in 2013, however, there has been a decline in partisan as well as non-partisan Euroskepticism for which Klaus was the driving force.

-nebo-top-09_307990.html>; and Petr Mach, "Proč my Svobodní nejsme Klausovci (Why aren't We Members of the Party of Free Citizens the Klaus-folowers)", available at <https:// volby.svobodni.cz/aktualne/mach-proc-my-svobodni-nejsme-klausovci/>.

41   "Klaus. K tragédii na Ukrajině přispěly USA a EU. Putin jedná racionálně (Klaus: The USA and the EU Contribute to the Tragedy in Ukraine. Putin is Acting Rationally)", *iDNES* (6 March 2014), available at <http://zpravy.idnes.cz/klaus-o-situaci-v-rusku-a-na-ukra jine-dv4-/domaci.aspx?c=A140306_145211_domaci_maq>.

42   Václav Klaus, "Rozhovor Václava Klause pro týdeník Ekonom nejen o uprchlících, kvótách a české ekonomice (Ekonom Interview with Václav Klaus not only about Refugees, Quotas, and Czech Economics)", (10 September 2015), available at <http://www.klaus.cz/ clanky/3797>.

43   Václav Klaus, "Výzva občanů České republiky vládě a Parlamentu ČR (Call of Citizens of the Czech Republic on the Government and the Parliament)", (5 September 2015), available at <http://www.klaus.cz/clanky/3792>.

The development of Euroskepticism, ranging from criticism of the development of the EU to eventual calls for the Czech Republic leaving the EU, during the Klaus Presidency had always had one basic characteristic. It followed his ideas, both directly from his personal support as well as indirectly. Klaus employed both of these strategies, using formal as well as informal tools to support Czech Euroskepticism. The obstruction and delays regarding his signature of the Lisbon Treaty demonstrated Klaus' use of the formal powers the Czech President has to (refuse to) ratify international treaties. Klaus' appetite to engage in actual policy could also be observed later, when he supported Prime Minister Nečas during his opposition to the "fiscal pact", as well as in the waning months of his presidency, when he refused to sign the treaty on the European Stability Mechanism. At the same time, the majority of his Euroskeptic ideas sprang from an informal position, when he was able to take advantage of being at the center of the media's attention. Since the end of his term, however, we cannot observe the reincarnation of the Euroskepticism that was so visible during his Presidency.

This text can thus be concluded by noting that although it appeared that Czech Euroskepticism after 2000 was an ever-growing phenomenon, its solid foundation was Václav Klaus. This obviously implies a weakening of Euroskeptically-minded parties and movements after his passing from the presidential arena, since these parties and movements attract hardly any media attention. Klaus has not been capable of "driving" Euroskepticism as much as he did previously. Even the new issues around which the EU has been criticized have not helped him. In his post-presidency, he has only been able to take advantage of pre-prepared opportunities and has not been an agenda-setter. All this in the end has led to a decline in party and non-party Euroskepticism in the Czech Republic.

As Klaus himself has been marginalized in the media, so too have movements which he supported, or which have invoked his ideas. The SSO, which has distanced itself from Klaus, and which has chosen a completely different direction, has been able to achieve at least limited success. Klaus' abilities as a driver and ideological father of party as well as non-party Euroskepticism thus was folded into his role as a major political figure, and the media access associated with it.

Bibliography

Bončková, Helena and Smekal, Hubert. (2010) "Fragmentace společných hodnot? Výjimky z Listiny základních práv Evropské unie (Fragmentalization of Common

Values? Opt-outs from the Charter of Fundamental Rights of the European Union)", *Current Europe* No. 2, 61–81.

Eibl, Otto, Gregor, Miloš, and Macková, Alena. (2013) "O čem a jak hovořil Václav Klaus ve svých veřejných projevech (Issues and Tonality of Václav Klaus' Public Speeches)", *Czech Journal of Political Science* No. 4, 392–418.

Hanley, Sean. (2012) "Dynamics of New Party Formation in the Czech Republic 1996–2010: Looking for the Origins of a 'Political Earthquake'", 28(2) *East European Politics*, 119–143.

Havlík, Vlastimil. (2011) "A Breaking-up of a Pro-European Consensus: Attitudes of Czech Political Parties towards the European Integration (1998–2010)", *Communist and Post-Communist Studies* No. 2, 129–147.

Hloušek, Vít and Kaniok, Petr. (2014) "Czech Republic", in Conti, Nicolo. (ed.), *Party Attitudes towards the EU in the Member States: Parties for Europe, Parties against Europe* (Routledge, Abingdon), 158–173.

Klaus, Václav. (2009) *Prezident republiky k Lisabonské smlouvě* (*The President of the Republic on the Lisbon Treaty*) (Euromedia Group, Banská Bystrica).

Kopeček, Lubomír. (2012) *Fenomén Václav Klaus* (*The Phenomenon Václav Klaus*) (Barrister & Principal, Brno).

CHAPTER 7

Poland and the Re-categorization of the Eurozone Entry: From a Legal Obligation to a Political Issue

Anna Visvizi and Paweł Tokarski

Abstract

Although legally bound to adopt the Euro, since the outbreak of the Eurozone crisis, Poland, initially a great enthusiast of the Euro adoption, has been effectively postponing the Eurozone entry.[1] The objective of this chapter is to explore the rationale behind it. It is argued that while initially the Euro adoption constituted a predominantly legal challenge, over time it has been re-categorized into a political challenge. Three factors contributed to that. First, the indeterminate nature of the Maastricht convergence criteria opened-up a "temporal room for maneuver" for the EU Member States remaining outside the Eurozone to delay the introduction of the Euro. Second, the Eurozone crisis altered the cost-benefit analysis regarding the Eurozone entry and created additional incentives to exploit the Maastricht-induced "room for maneuver" as a means of shielding the Polish economy from external shocks. Third, the EU economic governance reform led to the emergence of new Eurozone membership criteria and new modes of decision-making in the Eurozone fora consolidated. In these circumstances, the prospect of the Eurozone entry turned into a political issue, whereby the attainment of nominal and legal convergence has become a function of a broader domestic and European political strategy of the Polish government.

Keywords

Eurozone expansion – Maastricht convergence criteria – Poland – Euro

---

1   This research project has been benefited from funding under the EU's Seventh Framework Programme for research, technological development and demonstration, grant agreement no. 320278 (RASTANEWS). An earlier and abbreviated version of this chapter was published as Paweł Tokarski and Anna Visvizi, "Poland's Winding Road to the Eurozone: From Cost-Benefit Stance to Risk Aversion", 24(3) *Polish Quarterly of International Affairs* (2015), 65–84, although the two works have overlapping, yet different conceptual foci.

1   Introduction

Fifteen years after the free election of 4 June 1989, Poland joined the European Union (EU) in May 2004. Prospective membership in the Economic and Monetary Union (EMU) was firmly inscribed in the Accession Treaty[2] signed in 2003. In line with the provisions of this Treaty as well as a result of Poland meeting the *acquis* membership criterion defined in Copenhagen in 1993, Poland is legally bound to join the Euro area as soon as it fulfills the nominal and legal convergence criteria. The prospect of joining the EU, and later on of adopting the Euro, has defined Poland's foreign and European policies since 1990. EU membership was seen as a "return" to Europe, a means of bypassing the historically-determined geopolitical problem of being locked in-between two powers, Russia and Germany, and a means of securing Poland's place in the EU decision-making process. Indeed, in early 2000s the Polish society and the political elite enthusiastically embraced the prospect of joining the EU and of adopting the Euro. As a result, the debate on the EU accession ran parallel with the debate on the Eurozone entry.[3] Eventually, the question of the Eurozone membership was included in the EU accession referendum that was held in June 2003. At that time 77.45% of voters expressed their support for the conditions of EU accession. Those included prospective participation in the currency union.[4] The consensus regarding Poland's Eurozone entry was reinforced right after Poland acquired the EU membership. Several governmental publications and reports of that time provided arguments that accession to the third stage

2   Treaty of Accession to the European Union, Official Journal of the European Union, L 236, 23 September 2003, available at: <http://eur-lex.Europa.eu/legal-content/en/ALL/?uri=OJ:L: 2003:236:TOC>.

3   The debate on the Eurozone entry can be traced back to 1997, when the Polish Ministry of Finance published a report "Euro-2006: Poland on the Path to the European Monetary Union", suggesting the introduction of the Euro in Poland in 2006. In 1999 when the Euro was launched, a special interdepartmental working group in charge of Poland's Eurozone accession was established, thus stirring the political and academic debate on Poland's Eurozone entry. Notably, the National Bank of Poland played a key role in producing well-founded arguments supporting the idea of a quick Eurozone entry. See, Zbigniew Polański, "Poland and the Euro Zone Enlargement: Monetary policy, ERMII, and Other Issues", 32(4) *Atlantic Economic Journal* (2004), 280–292.

4   Obwieszczenie Państwowej Komisji Wyborczej z dnia 21 lipca 2003 r. o skorygowanym wyniku ogólnokrajowego referendum w sprawie wyrażenia zgody na ratyfikację Traktatu dotyczącego przystąpienia Rzeczypospolitej Polskiej do Unii Europejskiej (The Official Announcement of the National Electoral Commission of 21 July 2003 on the Corrected Results of the Nationwide Referendum Concerning the Republic of Poland's Accession to the European Union), available at: <http://isap.sejm.gov.pl/DetailsServlet?id=WDU20031321223>.

of EMU would be beneficial to the Polish economy.[5] Not surprisingly, in 2007, the newly established coalition government was in favor of a quick Euro adoption; a relevant roadmap was approved in October 2008.[6]

Given the positive growth rates, good scores on the absorption of cohesion and structural funds, and undiminished popular enthusiasm for European integration, Poland's Eurozone membership was considered mainly as a matter of a legal obligation derived from the provisions of the Accession Treaty and the convergence criteria as enshrined in the Maastricht Treaty and related documents. Indeed, perceived as the "best pupil" of the EU, highlighting the success of enlargement policy,[7] Poland was expected to fulfill the Maastricht convergence criteria relatively quickly and thus join the Eurozone soon after acquiring the EU membership status. These expectations notwithstanding, more than a decade after Poland's EU entry, the prospect of the Euro adoption does not seem to be any nearer than it was in the early 2000s. In fact, the Eurozone crisis and its corollaries have had a catalytic impact on Poland's change of heart toward the Euro, turning it from an enthusiast of the Euro adoption to a skeptic. Three correlated factors have contributed to it. First, the indeterminate nature of the Maastricht convergence criteria opened-up a "temporal room for maneuver"[8] for the EU Member States remaining outside the Eurozone to delay the introduction of the Euro. Second, the Eurozone crisis altered the cost-benefit analysis regarding the Eurozone entry and created additional incentives to exploit the Maastricht-induced "room for maneuver" as a means of shielding the Polish economy from external shocks. Third, the EU economic governance reform led to the emergence of new EMU membership criteria and new modes of decision-making in the Eurozone fora consolidated.

---

5   National Bank of Poland, *Report* on the *Costs* and *Benefits* of *Poland's* Adoption of the *Euro* (March 2004), available at: <http://www.nbp.pl/en/publikacje/e_a/Euro_adoption.pdf>; and Government Plenipotentiary for Euro Adoption in Poland, Strategic Guidelines for the National Euro Changeover Plan in Poland (26 October 2010), available at: <http://www.mf.gov .pl/documents/764034/1010442/Strategic+Guidelines+for+the+National+Euro+Changeover +Plan_2010>.

6   Ministry of Finance, "Mapa drogowa przyjęcia Euro przez Polskę (The Roadmap toward the Euro Adoption Approved)", *Materiał Informacyjny* (*Information Bulletin*) (October 2008), available at: <http://archiwum-ukie.polskawue.gov.pl/HLP/moint.nsf/0/57EDCDBC29F5292 1C125754E003A73A6/$file/ME_54%28127%2902.pdf?Open>.

7   Ministry of Foreign Affairs , "Poland's 10 years in the European Union", *Report by the Ministry of Foreign Affairs of the Republic of Poland* (May 2014), available at: <http://www.msz.gov.pl/ resource/a23dff5d-8b90-4086-91b8-9a441cf861d9:JCR>.

8   Kenneth Dyson, "Euro Area Entry in East-Central Europe: Paradoxical Europeanisation and Clustered Convergence", 30(3) *West European Politics* (2007), 417–442, at 417.

In these circumstances, the prospect of the Eurozone entry turned into a political issue, whereby the attainment of nominal and legal convergence became a function of a broader domestic and European political strategy of the Polish government.

In this view, while initially the question of the Euro adoption was a predominantly legal challenge, since Poland's EU accession a significant recategorization of the challenge of the Euro adoption has taken place, rendering it an essentially political issue. As a means of substantiating these claims, the argument in this chapter is structured as follows. In the first part, the salience of the implicit and explicit EU/Eurozone membership requirements are elaborated. The specific nominal and legal convergence criteria that Poland needs to fulfill are elaborated and the contingencies inherent in them highlighted. Next, the cost-benefit analysis of Poland's Eurozone entry is discussed against the backdrop of the Eurozone crisis and its corollaries. Concluding discussion ensues at the end of this chapter.

2   Contemplating the Salience of Implicit and Explicit Membership Principles

The new Member States (NMSs) of the EU are bound to adopt the Euro by virtue of the *acquis* membership criterion and provisions of the 2003 Accession Treaty. Article 4 of that treaty states: "Each of the new Member States shall participate in Economic and Monetary Union from the date of accession as a Member State with a derogation[9] within the meaning of Article 122[10] of the EC Treaty."[11] What follows is that while the basic Eurozone eligibility criterion is the membership in the EU, other membership criteria exist and have been defined in several documents, with the reform of the EU economic governance adding another set. Overall, to adopt the Euro, *first*, in line with the Copenhagen criteria, the NMSs are required to adopt all EU legislation pertinent to the aims of economic and monetary union. *Second*, the exact nominal Eurozone membership criteria have been set in the Maastricht Treaty (Art. 140 TFEU). Referred to as *convergence criteria*, they define the nominal convergence benchmarks that a member-state needs to fulfill to be admitted to the third

---

9   "Member state with a derogation", i.e. "Member States in respect of which the Council has not decided that they fulfil the necessary conditions for the adoption of the Euro shall hereinafter be referred to as Member States with a derogation" (Art. 139 TFEU).

10   Currently, TFEU Articles 139 and 140.

11   Treaty of Accession to the European Union, *op. cit.* note 2.

stage of the EMU: price stability, fiscal soundness, two years of successful participation in the Exchange Rate Mechanism (ERMII), and the stability of long-term interest rate. As far as the real convergence is concerned – expressed in terms of the level of integration of markets, the situation and development of the balance of payments with regard to current account, and the development of unit labor cost and other price indices – although no specific numerical benchmarks have been set, it constitutes an equally important component of evaluation prior to the decision on the acceptance to the Eurozone. *Third*, the 2003 Accession Treaty reiterates the obligation of the NMSs to join the Eurozone. *Fourth*, apart from the applicant country's ability to fulfill the nominal convergence criteria, an equally important issue is that of making the applicant's legal system fully compliant with the provisions of TFEU as well as the European System of Central Banks and European Central Bank (ESCB/ECB). This criterion of legal convergence, interpreted in line with the provisions of Art. 140 TFEU, requires compatibility[12] of the national legal order with Articles 130 and 131 TFEU, which set formal independence of national central banks. Furthermore, compatibility of national law, including constitutional provisions concerning competences of monetary policy with the ESCB/ECB system,[13] is required.

The content and caveats of the Maastricht convergence criteria have been broadly debated in the literature. Contrary to initial expectations several NMSs did not opt for a fast Eurozone entry, and thus splitting into the "pacesetters" and "laggards."[14] Then, "[w]hy did the conditionality of Maastricht prove less potent than that of Copenhagen?"[15] Particularly for larger NMSs, the nominal convergence criteria of Eurozone entry "have not only allowed but encouraged the laggards to further delay their entry."[16] Certainly, several factors were at

---

12   "The requirement for national legislation to be 'compatible' does not mean that the Treaty requires 'harmonisation' of the NCBs' statutes, either with each other or with the Statute. National particularities may continue to exist to the extent that they do not infringe the EU's exclusive competence in monetary matters". ECB, *Convergence Report* (June 2013), 19, available at <https://www.ecb.Europa.eu/pub/pdf/conrep/cr201306en.pdf>.

13   Artur Nowak-Far, "Zasadnicze instytucjonalne i prawne wymiary przystąpienia Polski do strefy Euro (Essential Institutional and Legal Aspects of Poland's Eurozone Entry)", in Artur Nowak-Far (ed.), *Wprowadzenie Euro w Polsce – Za i Przeciw* (*The Introduction of Euro in Poland – Pros and Cons*) (Wydawnictwo Sejmowe, The Polish Sejm Press, Warsaw, 2013), available at <http://orka.sejm.gov.pl/WydBAS.nsf/0/3A95F9DFDA497743C1257B7F 004073A1/$file/Euro%20w%20Polsce.pdf>.

14   Dyson, *op. cit.* note 8.

15   Juliet Johnson, "The Remains of Conditionality: The Faltering Enlargement of the Euro Zone", 15(6) *Journal of European Public Policy* (2008), 826–842, at 827.

16   *Ibid.*, 826.

play in this process. The Euro area accession was shaped by combinations of "extreme 'formal' and 'informal' conditionality" and "of extreme [Europeanization] with limited Europeani[z]ation," and as a result, "the NMS [were given] a temporal room for manoeuver in managing 'misfit' with EMU conditionality requirements but not a room for manoeuver in redefining and renegotiating 'fit.'"[17]

It is quite interesting to look at the Eurozone membership criteria also from the following perspective. Joining the Eurozone, similarly as joining the EU itself, presupposes entering an existing entity, not the creation of a new one. This is what the logic of the *acquis communautaire* criterion dictates. Implicit in that criterion is the principle that transitional periods should be strictly limited and cannot contain serious derogation from the Treaty text and principles on which the Community is built.[18] That is, applicant countries are expected to adjust swiftly and efficiently to the rules defining the functioning of the EU. The successive rounds of enlargement, starting from 1973 through 2013, confirm that it was very difficult for the prospective members to successfully negotiate transitional periods in areas of their particular interest.

Also in context of the EMU, it would be reasonable to expect that the application of the *acquis communautaire* criterion would be accompanied by the principle of "limited transitional periods." In this view, transitional periods cannot contain serious derogation from the Treaty text as well as from principles on which the Community is built.[19] The Maastricht nominal convergence criteria deliberately ignored this principle, because the "transitional periods" were not clearly delineated. At the same time – as the case of the Stability and Growth Pact highlights – quite serious derogation from the Treaty text was allowed. Out of the four nominal convergence criteria only the ERMII sets a time-frame,[20] the remaining three criteria, apart from defining the numerical benchmarks, do not specify any time-period within which these should be attained. Certainly, the flexible nature of defining the transitional periods

---

17   Dyson, *op. cit.* note 8, at 417 and 441.

18   Dimitry Kochenov, "EU Enlargement Law: History and Recent Developments: Treaty –
        Custom Concubinage?" 9(6) *European Integration Online Papers* (2005), 1–34, available at
        <http://eiop.or.at/eiop/texte/2005-006a.htm>.

19   *Ibid.*, 12.

20   The ERMII criterion "shall mean that a Member State has respected the normal fluctuation margins provided for by the Exchange Rate Mechanism of the European Monetary
        System without severe tensions for at least the last two years before the examination."
        Protocol (No. 13) on the Convergence Criteria, art.3, Official Journal of the European
        Union C 115/281.

of attaining the nominal convergence benchmarks may have been justifiable from the economic policy perspective. From a legal perspective, though, it represents a remarkable omission that has left a significant leeway for the NMSs to postpone the implementation of the ERM II criterion as a means of delaying the Eurozone entry.

The problematic nature of the Maastricht convergence criteria resonated in the political debate. Many of the NMSs, especially the Visegrád Four (V4), lobbied for "a more flexible inflation rule, shorter waiting time in ERMII, and widening of the exchange rate band within the ERM"[21] in vein. The unwillingness of the Eurozone members to make the nominal convergence criteria more flexible[22] discouraged the NMSs from sustained reform drive and encouraged "minimalism in institutional and structural reforms."[23] By not rendering the Maastricht convergence criteria any more flexible for the NMSs, the Eurozone members resorted in fact to the so-called "selective inflexibility." This is because while some of the NMSs were barred from joining the Eurozone even if they would only marginally miss one of the criteria,[24] several Eurozone members were in clear breach of these criteria and no particular ado was made about it. This confirms the earlier claim that while the transitional periods have not been clearly delineated in the Maastricht criteria, quite serious derogation from the Treaty text has been allowed. Paradoxically, but not surprisingly, the "selective inflexibility"[25] and "temporal room for maneuver,"[26] both manifestations of a serious inconsistency inherent in the execution of the Maastricht convergence criteria, have had adverse impact on the process of Euro adoption by the NMSs. Poland represents in this context a very well placed example. The following sections highlight it.

---

21   Dorothee Bohle and Béla Greskovits, *Capitalist Diversity on Europe's Periphery* (Cornell University Press, Ithaca, 2012), 173.

22   Zsolt Darvas, "The Case for Reforming Euro Area Entry Criteria", 32(2) *Society and Economy* (2010), 195–219.

23   László Csaba, "Growth, Crisis management and EU: the Hungarian Trilemma", 58(3–4) *SüdEuropa Mitteilungen* (2013), 154–169, at 157.

24   For instance, in March 2006 the European Commission declined Lithuania's Eurozone entry bid arguing that its average inflation rate during 12 months, one of the Maastricht criteria, exceeded the reference value of 2,6% by 0,1 percentage point. European Commission, "Convergence Report on Lithuania, Convergence Report on Slovenia", 2 *European Economy* (2006), 12.

25   Anna Visvizi and Paweł Tokarski, "Poland and the Euro: Between Lock-in and Unfinished Transition", 36(4) *Society and Economy* (2014), 445–468.

26   Dyson, *op. cit.* note 8.

3   Poland and the Contingencies Inherent in the Nominal
     and Legal Convergence Criteria[27]

The fulfillment of the nominal convergence criteria remains one of the key barriers on Poland's entry into the euro area. As of August 2015,[28] Poland fulfilled three of these criteria, i.e. the price stability, long-term interest rate, and fiscal sustainability. Poland does not fulfill the exchange rate criterion because it does not participate in ERMII. Specifically, with regard to price stability, the average 12 month price increase based on the Harmonized Indices of Consumer Prices (HICP) was at a historically low level of −0.7% in August 2015 and thus was significantly lower than the reference value of 1.4 pp. In terms of the long-term interest rate criterion, the average long-term interest rate for the past 12 months was 2.7%, thus was 1.6 pp below the reference value of 4.3%. The situation is more complex as regards Poland's fiscal position, even if Poland complies with the benchmarks defining this criterion. That is, in line with the provisions of the Stability and Growth Pact (SGP), Poland had been under the Excessive Deficit Procedure (EDP) since 2009. Following the reversal of 1999 pension reform and a transfer of government bonds from private pension funds to the government sector in 2014, a significant improvement in Poland's fiscal position was recorded. In this way, technically speaking, Poland was able to meet the general government deficit and debt criteria; in fact, the Ecofin Council has lifted the EDP for Poland in June 2015.[29] General governance sector deficit and debt reached in 2015 respectively, 2.8% and 50.1%. Both were below the reference values of 3% and 60%.

The attainment of legal convergence means that Poland is bound to address two groups of legal incompatibilities embedded in the Polish legal system in order to make it fully compliant with the provisions of TFEU and the ESCB/ECB. That is, first, in line with Article 140 TFEU that requires compatibility of national legal order with Articles 130 and 131 TFEU, Poland needs to ensure formal independence of the National Bank of Poland (NBP). Second, changes need to be introduced in specific provisions of the Polish Constitution in order to

---

27   This section closely follows European Commission, "Convergence Report", 3 *European Economy* (2012).

28   Ministry of Finance, *Monitor konwergencji nominalnej* (*Nominal Convergence Bulletin*) (October 2015).

29   Council of the European Union, "Malta's and Poland's Deficits back below 3% of GDP, Council Closes Procedures", Press Release (19 June 2015), available at <http://www.con silium.europa.eu/en/press/press-releases/2015/06/19-malta-poland-deficits-back-below -three-percent-gdp/>.

ascertain independence of monetary policy decisions.[30] Specifically, the 2012 Convergence Report[31] points to the Act on the National Bank of Poland (NBP Act)[32] and the Constitution of the Republic of Poland as the key sources of legal incompatibility. The specific areas of incompatibility include: the NBPs independence, the NBPs integration with the ESCB, the prohibition of monetary financing by the NBP of other financing institutions, the definition of the objectives of the NBP, and the legal status of the NBP's external auditor.

As regards the required changes in the Constitution, three articles require amendment, including Article 198(1), i.e. "accountability to the State Tribunal"; Article 227, i.e. "responsibility for monetary policy"; and Article 203, i.e. "competences of Poland's Supreme Audit Office (NIK)." Subsequent amendments in related secondary law will have to follow. With regard to the NBP Act, it is Article 3(1) setting the objectives of the NBP that appears problematic. It says: "The basic objective of the activity of NBP shall be to maintain price stability, while supporting the economic policy of the Government, insofar as this does not constrain the pursuit of the basic objective of NBP."[33] In other words, Article 3(1) refers only to the economic policies of the Government, whereas it should also make reference to the general economic policies in the European Union, with the objectives of the latter taking precedence over the former. The next issue concerns undue influence through monetary guidelines. In line with the NBP Act, its President has *inter alia* to submit draft monetary policy guidelines to the Council of Ministers and the Minister of Finance. This procedure has been interpreted by the Commission as an opportunity for the government to exert influence on monetary and financial policies of the NBP. As such, in line with Article 130 of the TFEU and Article 7 of the ESCB/ECB Statute, it constitutes incompatibility in the area of independence of the NBP.[34]

Furthermore, in line with the provisions of the NBP Act, its President shall assume his/her duties after taking an oath before the Parliament. The text of the oath mentions the Polish Constitution and other laws, the economic development of Poland and the well being of its citizens.[35] As the oath does not

---

30   Nowak-Far, *op. cit.* note 13.

31   ECB, *op. cit.* note 12, 113–114.

32   The Act on the National Bank of Poland of 29 August 1997, Journal of Laws (2013), item 908 as amended, Art. 9(3).

33   *Ibid.*

34   *Ibid.*

35   The President of the NBP shall assume his/her duties after taking the following oath before the Sejm: "Assuming the duties of the President of the National Bank of Poland I do solemnly swear that I will strictly observe the provisions of the Constitution and other

contain any reference to the central bank's independence as defined in Art. 130 TFEU, it needs to be brought in line with the TFEU and the ESCB/ECB Statute. This is particularly important given the fact that after the Eurozone accession the President of the NBP acts in dual capacity as a President of NBP's Monetary Policy Council and the member of the ECB Governing Council. What follows is that also Article 9(3) of the NBP Act needs to be adapted to reflect the status and the obligations and duties of the President of the NBP as member of the relevant decision-making bodies of the ECB. Another problematic issue concerns the grounds for dismissal of the NBP's President, according to Articles 9(5) are going beyond those of Article 14.2 ESCB/ECB Statute, setting up additional grounds for dismissal.

Moreover, the Law on the State Tribunal Article 25(3) in conjunction with its Articles 3 and 1.1(3) define grounds for the NBP's President removal from the office should she/he violate the Constitution or a law. The power of the State Tribunal over the NBP is reiterated in Article 9(5) (3) of the NBP Act[36] that the grounds for the dismissal of the NBP President. Given the relationship of dependency of the NBP vis-à-vis the State Tribunal thus maintained, the above-mentioned provisions are considered as incompatible with Article 14.2 of the ESCB/ECB Statute. Finally, according to Article 203(1) of Poland's Constitution, NIK is entitled to examine NBP's activities as regards its legality, economic prudence, efficiency, and diligence. Given the fact that NIK's controls are not performed in the capacity of an independent external auditor as required by Article 27.1 of the ESCB/ECB Statute, Article 203(1) of the Constitution should be defined so as the provisions of Article 130 of the TFEU and Article 7 of the ECB/ESCB Statute are respected.[37]

4   The Cost-Benefit Analysis of the Eurozone Entry

Over the years eastward enlargement of the Eurozone has attracted considerable attention in academia and a variety of methodological and conceptual perspectives have been employed to discuss the likely threats and opportunities

---

laws and that in all my actions I will pursue the economic development of our Homeland and the well-being of its citizens." *Ibid.*

36   "The President of the NBP may be dismissed if: [...] the Tribunal of State has prohibited him/her from occupying managerial positions or holding posts of particular responsibility in state bodies." *Ibid.*

37   ECB, *op. cit.* note 12, 113–114.

of the Eurozone membership. While the debate was not devoid of suggestions of unilateral adoption of the Euro by the NMSs,[38] essentially, the argument oscillated around the question of the NMSs' degree of compliance with the Maastricht nominal convergence criteria, their overall structural fit with the Eurozone economies,[39] and the optimal policy strategies of Euro adoption and economic convergence in general.[40]

Overall, prior to the outbreak of the global and the Eurozone crises a quick path to the Eurozone accession was advocated in the literature.[41] However, voices were also heard, that aware of the uncertain cost-benefit analysis, advocated a more balanced approach towards the Eurozone accession.[42] In the particular case of Poland, some estimates[43] suggested that the adoption of the common currency in Poland would add to the annual GDP growth on average from 0.2 to 0.4 percentage points between 2004 and 2030; positive spillovers would emerge with regard to consumption level, FDI inflow, exports and imports. In 2007, these estimates were embraced by the political elites, and the

---

38   Andrzej Bratkowski and Jacek Rostowski, "Dlaczego jednostronna Euroizacja ma sens w przypadku Polski i (niektórych) innych krajów kandydujących (Why the Unilateral Euronisation Makes Sense in Poland's Case and (Some) Other Candidate Countries)", Paper presented at the Conference "Polska droga do Euro (Poland's Way to the Euro)" (National Bank of Poland, Falenty, 22–23 October 2001), available at <http://www.nbp.pl/konferencje/droga_do_Euro/bratkowski_rostowski_pl.pdf>.

39   Monika Błaszkiewicz and Przemysław Woźniak, "Do Candidate Countries Fit the Optimum-Currency-Area Criteria?" *Studies and Analyses* (2003) No.267, available at <http://www.case-research.eu/upload/publikacja_plik/1661295_267.pdf>; Paul de Grauwe and Gunther Schnabl, "Nominal Versus Real Convergence: EMU Entry Scenarios for the New Member States", 58(4) *Kyklos* (2005), 537–555; and Jarko Fidrmuc and Ikka Korhonen, "Meta-Analysis of the Business Cycle Correlation between the Euro Area and the CEECs", *CESifo Working Paper Series* (2006) No.1693.

40   Witold Maciej Orłowski, *Optymalna Ścieżka do Euro (The Optimal Pathway to the Euro)* (Scholar, Warsaw, 2004); Cezary Wójcik, *Integracja ze strefą Euro. Teoretyczne i praktyczne aspekty konwergencji (Integration with the Euro Area: Theoretical and Practical Aspects of Convergence)* (PWN, Warsaw, 2008); National Bank of Poland, *op. cit.* note 5; and Andrzej Sopoćko (ed.) *Polska w strefie Euro? Nowe Perspektywy wzrostu (Poland in the Eurozone? New Growth Perspectives)* (Wydział Zarządzania Uniwersytetu Warszawskiego, Warsaw, 2008).

41   Polański, *op. cit.* note 3, 285–287.

42   Dominik Sobczak and Katarzyna Żukrowska (eds.) *Rozszerzenie strefy euro na wschód. Raporty przygotowane na potrzeby projektu badawczego Ezoneplus (The Enlargement of the Eurozone to the East: Reports Prepared for the Research Project Ezoneplus)* (Instytut Wiedzy, Warsaw, 2004).

43   National Bank of Poland, *op. cit.* note 5.

PO-PSL coalition government established in November 2007 expressed its full support for a quick Euro adoption. Subsequently, in October 2008 a relevant roadmap was adopted, and in February 2009 special plenipotentiary for Euro adoption was appointed.

The Global Financial Crisis and especially the Eurozone crisis[44] changed the cost-benefit calculations and thus affected the estimates as to when Poland would introduce the Euro. Interestingly, although the 2009 NBP Report[45] on Poland's Eurozone accession pointed to the crisis as a risk factor, it would still offer a rather balanced assessment of possible benefits and threats of Poland's Eurozone entry. Similarly, the report "Strategic Guidelines" on Euro adoption published by the Ministry of Finance in October 2010[46] concluded that membership in the currency union would be beneficial for Poland both in short- and long-run. Overall net benefits for Poland's economy should reach 0.9–1.9% GDP in short term, and 2.5–7.5% GDP in the long term.[47] In detail, the benefits of Eurozone membership were identified as elimination of exchange risk, transaction cost reduction, interest rates' decrease, increase in foreign investment and consumption levels, and the resulting higher economic growth. As regards the projected downsides of Eurozone accession, the same report pointed to the risk of price level increase, the cost of meeting the Maastricht criteria, technical and administrative cost as well as risk of consumption boom related to access to cheap consumer loans. The risk of asymmetric shocks and loss of independent monetary policy were identified as the long-term cost of the Eurozone membership.[48] In contrast to earlier studies, the 2014 report by the National Bank of Poland is very cautious regarding the benefits of the Eurozone accession. The Report indicates that only a slight chance exists that membership in the third stage of EMU will trigger growth. At the same time the risk of a possible macroeconomic instability following the Euro adoption

---

44   Francesco Passarelli and Antonio Villafranca, "Eurozone Flaws: Uncovering the Holes in the Cheese", *RAstaNEWS Working Paper* (2014) No.04, available at <http://www.rastanews.eu/PWA_uploads/EuroEurozone-flaws-final.pdf>.

45   National Bank of Poland, Report on Full Membership of the Republic of Poland in the Third Stage of the Economic and Monetary Union (2009), available at <http://www.nbp.pl/en/publikacje/e_a/Euro_report.pdf>.

46   Government Plenipotentiary for Euro Adoption in Poland, Strategic Guidelines for the National Euro Changeover Plan (Ministry of Finance, 26 October 2010), available at <http://www.mf.gov.pl/documents/764034/1010442/Strategic+Guidelines+for+the+National+Euro+Changeover+Plan_2010>.

47   *Ibid.*, 3.

48   *Ibid.*

is highlighted. The Report stresses at the same time the salience of improving the competitiveness of Poland's economy.[49]

Similarly, one of the widely quoted research-papers, suggested that it was beneficial for Poland to keep flexible interest rate during the crisis as it contributed to the economy's resistance to external shocks during the economic and financial turmoil.[50] Remaining outside ERMII was in this way depicted as a way of dealing with the crisis. Overall, a cost benefit analysis is not possible because of the complexity of the issues involved. This is particularly true given the fact that irrespective of the attempts to contain the Eurozone crisis,[51] its main sources, such as gaps in competitiveness, weaknesses of the banking sectors and unsustainable sovereign debt levels, have not been effectively addressed yet. The following paragraphs expound on these issues.

5   Eurozone Entry: Exploring the Gray Sphere of the Cost-Benefit Analysis

Since the beginning of the Eurozone crisis substantial regulatory and institutional changes have been introduced in its design; several more are on their way. Given that, as part of the convergence criteria, a Member State must have been part of ERMII for at least two years, the decision to adopt the Euro is bound with at least a two-year waiting period. Given the pace of changes taking place in the Eurozone at the moment, any cost-benefit analysis of the Eurozone entry that is valid at the point of ERMII entry will be out-of-date upon the actual Eurozone entry. This puts Poland at a disadvantage and increases the political cost associated with the decision to introduce the Euro. The corollary of the above is that as a result of regulatory changes introduced in the EU right now, *de facto* new Eurozone entry requirements have been set. This is because upon joining the Eurozone, the entering MS will have to become a member of the European Stability Mechanism (ESM) Treaty,[52] fully comply with the

---

49   National Bank of Poland, The Economic Challenges of Poland's Integration with the Euro Area (November 2014), available at <http://www.nbp.pl/en/publikacje/inne/The-economic-challenges-of-Poland-s-integration-with-the-euro-area.pdf>.

50   Michał Brzoza-Brzezina, Krzysztof Makarski, and Grzegorz Wesołowski, "Would it Have Paid to be in the Euro-zone?" *National Bank of Poland Working Paper* (2012) No 128.

51   Passarelli and Villafranca, *op. cit.* note 44.

52   Treaty Establishing the European Stability Mechanism, available at <http://www.European-council.Europa.eu/media/582311/05-tesm2.en12.pdf>.

Fiscal Compact provisions,[53] and join the banking union. Poland is a signatory of the Fiscal Compact. The decision to join the third stage of the EMU will require that Poland signs the ESM treaty and contributes to the ESM's callable and paid-in capital. It is worth noting that financial obligations related to ESM membership, measured as a percentage of GDP, can be considerable. The case of Slovakia depicts that upon joining the third stage of EMU in 2009, and hence becoming member of the European Financial Stability Facility (EFSF) and its successor ESM, Slovakia's exposure to both assistance mechanisms amounted to 20% of its GDP.[54] Today, the value of Slovakia's subscription to the authorized capital stock of ESM is EUR 5.77 billion.[55] Should Poland become an ESM member, it is estimated that within the first 5 years upon joining, its share of paid-in capital (to be delivered in 5 years after the accession) would have to reach the value of EUR 3.15 billion, i.e. with total liabilities amounting to 8% of Poland's GDP.[56] Bluntly, this means that given the confines of Poland's fiscal soundness obligations under the Stability and Growth Pact (SGP) and the Fiscal Compact, in order to afford accommodating its contribution to the ESM, Poland will have to consider introducing serious spending cuts in its budgets following the Eurozone accession. This is politically very costly.

Participation in the ECB-led single supervisory mechanism (SSM) for the largest credit institutions across the Eurozone (and other countries willing to join the SSM) constitutes another factor that weighs heavily on the cost-benefit calculations of Poland's Eurozone entry. That is, on the one hand, theoretically-speaking, membership in the Euro area would give Poland an equal footing in the system of banking supervision. On the other hand, as a Eurozone member, Poland would be eligible to request financial assistance from the prospective banking union's single resolution fund and ultimately the ESM.[57] Essentially,

---

53   Treaty on Stability, Coordination and Governance in the Economic and Monetary Union, available at <http://European-council.Europa.eu/media/639235/stootscg26_en12.pdf>.

54   Martin Šuster "Slovak Experience with the Euro", in Gostyńska, Agata. et al. (eds.), Eurozone Enlargement in Times of Crisis: Challenges for the V4 Countries (Polish Institute of International Affairs, Warsaw, 2014).

55   ESM Factsheet, available at <http://www.esm.europa.eu/pdf/ESM%20Factsheet.pdf>.

56   "Droga do Euro wiedzie przez mniejszy dług (The Road to the Euro Leads through Less Debt)", Rzeczpospolita (19 April 2013), available at <http://www.ekonomia.rp.pl/artykul/1001733.html>.

57   In line with the Single Resolution Mechanism Regulation and Bank Recovery and Resolution Directive (BRRD), adopted by the European Parliament on 15 April 2014, it will take 8 years to merge national resolution funds and to reach the EUR 55 billion target level. The success of this strategy notwithstanding, EUR 55 billion is a negligible amount that falls short of any possible future needs.

the Polish banking system, unlike that of several Eurozone countries, already has deposit guarantee scheme *ex ante*. This implies, however, that the advantages of the new bail-in rules in case of the need to recapitalize banks are questionable for Poland. This is because these rules have been designed to hit bank owners and their creditors in the first place.

In spite of earlier declarations, the Eurozone banking union will not have any separate system of deposit guarantees at its disposal. Instead, it will rely on harmonization of the national systems. This notwithstanding, the truth is that regardless of whether Poland is a member of the Eurozone or not, it will be influenced by the new system of banking supervision in any case.[58] This is due to significant exposure of the Polish banking system to Eurozone credit institutions, i.e. through their subsidiaries, which make between 60 and 70% of the banking sector assets. In this view, it makes sense for Poland to secure a seat at the table of the SSM, at least for the sake of making its voice heard.

Another problem that looms on the banking supervision horizon concerns the way of constructing the mechanism's future Eurozone-wide deposit guarantee fund. One of the proposals that were aired at the EU fora suggested that capital contributions to the fund should mirror the subscription key to the ECB. Note that the latter reflects respective country's share in the total population and gross domestic product of the EU. Poland's share in the total EU population is 7.64% and its GDP is 2.9%, while its banking system is relatively small in relation to Poland's GDP. This means that in line with the above proposal, participation in the common system of deposit guarantees would be disproportionately costly for Poland, both in relation to the relative size of the Polish banks' assets and the scale of problems that they may generate. Even if the question of common system of deposit guarantees has been put on hold in the debate, it is likely to resurface in the near future and to further influence the cost-benefit calculations.

As the Eurozone crisis placed the notion of the EU economic governance reforms high on the agenda, considerable revival in the quality and density of debates in the European Council, Ecofin, but especially in the Eurogroup was observed. In other words, the Eurogroup has come to play a fundamental role in fostering process of deliberation and consensus building among the Eurozone Member States.[59] However, as the *modus operandi* of the Eurogroup

---

58   Patryk Toporowski, "A Post-Crisis Eurozone: Still an Attractive Offer for Central Europe", 22(124) *PISM Policy Paper* (2015), 5.

59   Uwe Puetter, "Europe's Deliberative Intergovernmentalism: The Role of the Council and European Council in EU Economic Governance", 19(2) *Journal of European Public Policy* (2012), 161–178.

is based on informal meetings (during which no minutes are taken!) and much shorter formal sessions during which decisions are made. This informal environment may in fact enable the practice of some countries silencing others. Ideally, by becoming a member of the Eurozone, Poland would acquire a seat at the Eurogroup's table, full access to the Euro area summits, and a seat in the ECB Governing Council. Therefore, it would be actively engaged with the process of shaping economic governance in Europe. The point is that becoming a member of the Eurozone does not guarantee influence on the decision-making process in the EU/Eurozone. Of course, as over the last decade Poland succeeded in establishing very good relations with Germany, Poland may not turn into a pariah in the Euro area after all. It does not mean, however, that it will be able to reclaim status comparable to that of the Netherlands. Similar considerations apply to other Eurozone decision-making bodies. The distribution of key posts in institutions such as the European Central Bank and relevant DGs in the European Commission seems to indicate that preference is given to some Eurozone members over others.[60]

The third factor that weighs heavily on the cost-benefit analysis is bound with the political cost of domestic-level reforms. Regardless the positive growth rates that the Polish economy displayed amidst widespread recession in Europe and beyond, Poland's economy faces several challenges that need to be addressed as soon as possible, including in particular long-term competitiveness and hidden public debt.[61] With regard to competitiveness, Poland occupies a relatively high position in the global competitiveness index.[62] However, this positive score is derived mainly from factors such as low labor cost and low prices of products/services. Following Poland's EU entry, gradual loss of these sources of Poland's competitive advantage was observed. As competitiveness is closely linked to innovation, it is worthwhile to stress that Poland is ranked relatively low among the EU countries as regards the innovation index, substantially below the Eurozone average.[63] This sheds negative light on

---

60   Peter Spiegel, "Do Triple-A Countries Have Monopoly on Top Euro Jobs?" *Brussels Blog, Financial Times* (22 January 2012), available at <http://blogs.ft.com/brusselsblog/2013/01/do-triple-a-countries-have-monopoly-on-top-Euro-jobs/>.

61   Marian Gorynia and Bożena Jankowska (eds.), *The Influence of Poland's Accession to the Euro Zone on the International Competitiveness and Internationalisation of Polish Companies* (Difin, Warsaw, 2013).

62   In Global Competitiveness Index 2013–2014, Poland was ranked as 42nd, superior to 13 other Member States, available at <http://www.weforum.org/reports/global-competitiveness-report-2013-2014>, 15.

63   Global Innovation Report (Cornell University, INSEAD and the World Intellectual Property Organization) ranks Poland as 49th place behind all MS, except for Greece, available at

long-term competitiveness of Poland. Innovation plays a crucial role in view of Poland's Eurozone entry, because its absence produces adverse effects for the medium- and long-term prospects for the Polish economy and hence makes it a vulnerable member of the Eurozone. Specifically, given the dwindling advantage of low cost of labor/products, in face of fading competitiveness Poland, once in the Eurozone, Poland may see a decrease in FDI flows. As maintaining Poland's pace of growth depends on foreign capital inflow, this would serious adverse impact on the Polish economy.[64] This observation coincides with the broader argument developed in the academic debate that emphasizes the necessity of long-term structural reforms prior to Poland's Eurozone entry.[65] The political calendar in Poland is not conducive to any major structural reforms. Note that the 2014 elections to the European Parliament were followed by the parliamentary and presidential votes in 2015. The government, established in autumn 2015, was initially not expected to make any bold, politically costly decisions. Overall, consensus consolidated in Poland that given the inconclusive risk-benefit calculations, prospective Eurozone accession demands a referendum on this matter. It is plausible though that a Euro adoption debate that such a referendum would require would trigger several adverse effects, both domestically and internationally.

Domestically, given the risk of high politicization of such a debate, it would distract voters and redirect their attention away from the necessity of structural reforms in the Polish economy. This in turn would make voters vulnerable to political manipulation. The risk of politicization of the Eurozone entry debate is particularly valid given the fact that, as elaborate earlier in this chapter, Poland is required to address several incompatibilities inherent in its legal system prior to joining the third stage of EMU. As some of them require amendment of the Polish Constitution, a clear 2/3 majority in the parliament is necessary to pass the necessary changes. This paves the way for political competition and politicking. *Externally*, a debate on Euro adoption, by casting

---

<http://www.globalinnovationindex.org/content.aspx?page=gii-full-report-2013#pdfo pener>.

64   Joanna Stryjek, "Economic Security Aspects of the Potential EMU Membership of Poland", in Anna Visvizi and Tomasz Stępniewski (eds.), 11(5) *Yearbook of the Institute of East-Central Europe* (2013), 47–64.

65   Gorynia and Jankowska, *op. cit.* note 61; Piotr Krajewski (ed.), *Gospodarka Polski w perspektywie wstąpienia do strefy Euro. Ujęcie ilościowe (Polish Economy in View of the Eurozone Entry: A Qualitative Approach)* (Polskie Wydawnictwo Ekonomiczne, Warsaw, 2012); and Paweł Tokarski, "Wejście Polski do strefy Euro wobec potrzeb modernizacyjnych polskiej gospodarki (Poland's Entry into the Eurozone vs. the Polish Economy's Modernisation Needs)", *Sprawy Międzynarodowe* (2013) No.2, 23–38.

shadow on the honesty and commitment of Poland to join the third stage of EMU, would affect Poland's image and leverage at the EU forum, not only vis-à-vis the Eurozone issues.

6   Conclusion

The objective of this chapter was to highlight that due to some very specific – economically justifiable – omissions in the EMU *acquis,* room of maneuver was established for Poland to essentially manage a misfit with the Maastricht nominal convergence criteria. As the Eurozone crisis altered the cost-benefit calculations of the Eurozone membership, powerful incentives were generated for Poland to flexibly manage the implementation of its legal obligation to join the Eurozone. Interestingly, although meeting the nominal convergence criteria remains a challenge for the Polish economy, currently Poland's Eurozone entry strategy is not driven predominantly by economic policy issues related to meeting the numerical criteria. Economic policy considerations as well as the question of regulatory changes related to attaining legal convergence have become a function of political concerns at domestic, EU and international[66] level.

As the discussion in this chapter highlighted, the challenge of adopting the Euro does not consist solely of the challenge of meeting the nominal and real convergence criteria. The biggest challenge consists in the choices that Poland needs to make and the battles that it needs to wage if it has the ambition to exert influence on developments in the EU and in the Eurozone specifically. It is impossible to quantify the concerns related to Poland's prospective Eurozone entry, yet their influence on the cost-benefit calculations is considerable. In this view, while initially the question of the Euro adoption was a predominantly legal challenge, today it is an essentially political issue bound with domestic politics considerations and the ability to engage with decision-making process

---

66   Given the developments in Ukraine, Latvia's portrayal of the Eurozone entry as under-
        pinned by security concerns gains on validity. The importance of making closer ties with-
        in the EU by means of introducing the Euro was repeatedly stressed by Latvian politicians
        prior to Latvia's Eurozone entry on 1 January 2014. The following statement of the then
        Latvian Finance Minister, Andris Vilks, is quite representative in this regard: "Russia isn't
        going to change. We know our neighbour. There were before, and there will be, a lot of
        unpredictable conditions. It is very important for the countries to stick together, and with
        the EU." qtd. Graeme Wearden, "Latvia Joins Eurozone at Midnight Despite Little Public
        Enthusiasm", *The Guardian* (31 December 2013), available at <http://www.theguardian
        .com/business/2013/dec/31/latvia-joins-Euro-single-currency>.

at the EU level. While at face value the relevance and validity of legal aspects of the Euro adoption have not changed, a case can be made that a remarkable re-categorization of the challenge of Poland's Eurozone entry has taken place consistent with turning it from a legal obligation to a matter of a broader two-level political strategy that the Polish authorities pursue to maximize their position at the domestic- and at the EU-level.

Remaining outside the Eurozone has some advantages, but it restricts the variety of formal channels of participation at Poland's disposal. Consider for instance, the barring of Poland from participating in the Eurogroup meetings during the Polish Presidency of the Council in 2011 or limited participation in the Euro area summits. Becoming a member of the Eurozone, however, although it would grant Poland a seat in the Eurogroup and in the ECB Governing Council, does not serve as a guarantee that Poland's voice would actually count.[67] What follows is that – and this is what current developments suggest – keeping its own currency with flexible exchange rate regime and not participating in financial assistance programs to some extent shields Poland from negative economic consequences of the uncertain developments in the Eurozone. Moreover, current developments concerning the UK (with a foot over the doorstep), Sweden (abandoned Eurozone membership aspirations), and Iceland (EU? – no, thank you, after all), suggests that following an alternative way of policy-making in the EU or in relation to it (as the case of Iceland suggests) is possible, even if within certain bounds.

Bibliography

Błaszkiewicz, Monika and Woźniak, Przemysław. (2003) "Do Candidate Countries Fit the Optimum-Currency-Area Criteria?" *Studies and Analyses* No. 267, available at <http://www.case-research.eu/upload/publikacja_plik/1661295_267.pdf>.

Bohle, Dorothee and Greskovits, Béla. (2012) *Capitalist Diversity on Europe's Periphery* (Cornell University Press, Ithaca).

Bratkowski, Andrzej and Rostowski, Jacek. (2001) "Dlaczego jednostronna Euroizacja ma sens w przypadku Polski i (niektórych) innych krajów kandydujących (Why the Unilateral Euronisation Makes Sense in Poland's Case and (Some) Other Candidate Countries)", Paper presented at the Conference "Polska droga do Euro (Poland's Way to the Euro)" (National Bank of Poland, Falenty, 22–23 October), available at <http://www.nbp.pl/konferencje/droga_do_Euro/bratkowski_rostowski_pl.pdf>.

---

67   Anna Visvizi, "Slovenia's Role in the V4: A View from Poland", 7(2) *European Perspectives* (2015), 87–113.

Brzoza-Brzezina, Michał, Makarski, Krzysztof, and Wesołowski, Grzegorz. (2012) "Would it Have Paid to be in the Euro-zone?" *National Bank of Poland Working Paper* No 128.

Csaba, László. (2013) "Growth, Crisis management and EU: the Hungarian Trilemma", 53(3–4) *SüdEuropa Mitteilungen*, 154–169.

Darvas, Zsolt. (2010) "The Case for Reforming Euro Area Entry Criteria", 32(2) *Society and Economy*, 195–219.

Dyson, Kenneth. (2007) "Euro Area Entry in East-Central Europe: Paradoxical Europeanisation and Clustered Convergence", 30(3) *West European Politics*, 417–442.

Fidrmuc, Jarko and Korhonen, Ikka. (2006) "Meta-Analysis of the Business Cycle Correlation between the Euro Area and the CEECS", *CESifo Working Paper Series* No. 1693.

Gorynia, Marian and Jankowska, Bożena. (eds.) (2013) *The Influence of Poland's Accession to the Euro Zone on the International Competitiveness and Internationalisation of Polish Companies* (Difin, Warsaw).

De Grauwe, Paul and Schnabl, Gunter. (2005) "Nominal Versus Real Convergence – EMU Entry Scenarios for the New Member States", 58(4) *Kyklos*, 537–555.

Johnson, Juliet. (2008) "The Remains of Conditionality: The Faltering Enlargement of the Euro Zone", 15(6) *Journal of European Public Policy*, 826–842.

Kochenov, Dimitry. (2005) "EU Enlargement Law: History and Recent Developments: Treaty – Custom Concubinage?" 9(6) *European Integration Online Papers*, 1–34, available at <http://eiop.or.at/eiop/texte/2005-006a.htm>.

Krajewski, Piotr. (ed.) (2012) *Gospodarka Polski w perspektywie wstąpienia do strefy Euro. Ujęcie ilościowe (Polish Economy in View of the Eurozone Entry: A Qualitative Approach)* (Polskie Wydawnictwo Ekonomiczne, Warsaw).

Nowak-Far, Artur. (2013) "Zasadnicze instytucjonalne i prawne wymiary przystąpienia Polski do strefy Euro (Essential Institutional and Legal Aspects of Poland's Eurozone Entry)", in Nowak-Far, Artur. (ed.), *Wprowadzenie Euro w Polsce – Za i Przeciw (The Introduction of Euro in Poland – Pros and Cons)* (Wydawnictwo Sejmowe, The Polish Sejm Press, Warsaw), available at <http://orka.sejm.gov.pl/WydBAS.nsf/0/3A95F9D FDA497743C1257B7F004073A1/$file/Euro%20w%20Polsce.pdf>.

Orłowski, Witold Maciej. (2004) *Optymalna Ścieżka do Euro (The Optimal Pathway to the Euro)* (Scholar, Warsaw).

Passarelli, Francesco and Villafranca, Antonio. (2014) "Eurozone Flaws: Uncovering the Holes in the Cheese", *RAstaNEWS Working Paper* No.04, available at <http://www.rastanews.eu/PWA_uploads/Eurozone-flaws-final.pdf>.

Polański, Zbigniew. (2004) "Poland and the Euro Zone Enlargement: Monetary Policy, ERM II, and Other Issues", 32(4) *Atlantic Economic Journal*, 280–292.

Puetter, Uwe. (2012) "Europe's Deliberative Intergovernmentalism: The Role of the Council and European Council in EU economic Governance", 19(2) *Journal of European Public Policy*, 161–178.

Sobczak, Dominik and Żukrowska, Katarzyna. (eds.) *Rozszerzenie strefy euro na wschód. Raporty przygotowane na potrzeby projektu badawczego Ezoneplus (The Enlargement of the Eurozone to the East: Reports Prepared for the Research Project Ezoneplus)* (Instytut Wiedzy, Warsaw).

Sopoćko, Andrzej. (ed.) (2008) *Polska w strefie Euro? Nowe Perspektywy wzrostu (Poland in the Eurozone? New Growth Perspectives)* (Wydział Zarządzania Uniwersytetu Warszawskiego, Warsaw).

Stryjek, Joanna. (2013) "Economic Security Aspects of the Potential EMU Membership of Poland", in Visvizi, Anna and Stępniewski, Tomasz (eds.), 11(5) *Yearbook of the Institute of East-Central Europe*, 47–64.

Šuster, Martin. (2014) "Slovak Experience with the Euro", in Gostyńska, Agata *et al.* (eds.), *Eurozone Enlargement in Times of Crisis: Challenges for the V4 Countries* (Polish Institute of International Affairs, Warsaw).

Tokarski, Paweł. (2013) "Wejście Polski do strefy Euro wobec potrzeb modernizacyjnych polskiej gospodarki (Poland's Entry into the Eurozone vs. the Polish Economy's Modernisation Needs)", *Sprawy Międzynarodowe* No.2, 23–38.

Tokarski, Paweł and Visvizi, Anna. (2015) "Poland's Winding Road to the Eurozone: From Cost-Benefit Stance to Risk Aversion", 24(3) *Polish Quarterly of International Affairs*, 65–84.

Toporowski, Patryk. (2015) "A Post-Crisis Eurozone: Still an Attractive Offer for Central Europe", 22(124) *PISM Policy Paper*.

Visvizi, Anna. (2015) "Slovenia's Role in the V4: A View from Poland", 7(2) *European Perspectives*, 87–113.

Visvizi, Anna and Tokarski, Paweł. (2014) "Poland and the Euro: Between Lock-in and Unfinished Transition", 36(4) *Society and Economy*, 445–468.

Wójcik, Cezary. (2008) *Integracja ze strefą Euro. Teoretyczne i praktyczne aspekty konwergencji (Integration with the Euro area: Theoretical and Practical Convergence Issues)* (PWN, Warsaw).

PART 3

Society – Education and Values

∵

Emerging European Geographies: The Erasmus Program and Its Effect on the East–west Divide in Time of Economic Crisis

Amelia Hadfield and Robert Summerby-Murray

Abstract

This chapter examines the conceptual assumptions that underlie Erasmus: the EU's most successful student mobility scheme. Originally designed to inspire a new "geography of European youth", Erasmus provides ambiguous outcomes in terms of generating a deepened sense of European identity. A European youth demographic clearly exists, but its ability to support European integration through specific dynamics of identity, association, and skill generation have been undermined internally by a lack of clarity regarding the current purpose of Erasmus, and externally by the upheavals of enlargement and the Eurozone crisis.

Keywords

Erasmus – education – youth – geography – identity

•••

A liberal education is at the heart of a civil society, and at the heart of a liberal education is the act of teaching.

A. BARTLETT GIAMATTI[1]

∴

---

1 August C. Bolino, *Men of Massachusetts. Bay State Contributors to American Society* (iUniverse, Bloomington, 2012), 300.

1   Introduction

Europe has a long and distinguished history of high quality education. It also
has a surprisingly substantive history of using education as an efficient vehicle
for political and social reform. The Socratic method and dialectical tools developed in ancient Greece set the stage for forms of inquiry that relied upon
both curiosity about the natural world, and critical thinking about social structures to provide a range of contestable answers. Greek modes of inquiry subsequently set the stage for Roman, neo-Platonic and Medieval knowledge which
itself laid the foundation for the High Middle Ages, Enlightenment, modern
and post-modern ages of education and research. The Middle Ages saw universities and monasteries operate not only as crucibles of sacred and secular
illumination, but as internationally linked centers of learning with a "broad
pan-European scope."[2]

The most recent change however is the greatest. Under the aegis of the European Union, this most ambitious of political projects has generated a series
of inter-locking institutions that governs, on the basis of integration, key aspects of its population of 508 million inhabitants across 28 Member States.
Equally, from the earliest days of the European Economic Community, there
has existed a clear need to construct and promote a European identity – chiefly
among the youth – by which to enhance political allegiance to the EU and
indirectly foster further economic integration. The natural crucible for constructing a European conscience, as well as the specific tools of "skilling" young
Europeans in the mechanics and modes of integration, is the area of education. More particularly as argued by Kuhn, "scholars and policy-makers alike
have put high hopes in the role of cross-border mobility and interactions as
harbingers of a common identity among the European public."[3] Attempting to
balance Member States jealous of losing their national competence in education, and an entrepreneurial European Commission keen to construct a multi-
faceted European identity, education policy has developed since the 1970s to

---

2   Inga Ulnicane, "Europe of Knowledge 2014: High Expectations and Complex Realities",
    Europe of Knowledge – UACES "Ideas on Europe" blog (7 January 2014), available at <http://era
    .ideasoneurope.eu/2014/01/07/europe-of-knowledge-2014-high-expectations-and-complex
    -realities/>.
3   Theresa Kuhn, "Why Educational Exchange Programmes Miss Their Mark: Cross-Border Mo-
    bility, Education and European Identity", 50(6) *Journal of the Common Market Studies* (2012),
    994–1010, at 994. See also Karl W. Deutsch *et al.*, *Political Community and the North Atlantic
    Area* (Greenwood Press, New York, 1957); Arend Lijphart, "Tourist Traffic and Integration Po-
    tential", 2(3) *Journal of Common Market Studies* (1964), 251–262; and Neil Fligstein, *Euroclash:
    The EU, European Identity and the Future of Europe* (Oxford University Press, Oxford, 2008).

produce a wide range of innovative projects. The most successful of these is the Erasmus program. Launched in 1987,[4] the Erasmus program was originally designed to promote staff and student exchange between (and beyond) all EU Member States, on the basis of mobility, with the specific purpose of enhancing both their vocational and educational content, and the broader goal of producing generations of well-informed, productive young European citizens.

Based on 2015 figures indicating results for 2012–2013, Erasmus has sent more than 3 million students abroad, with a record quarter of a million Erasmus students undertaking studies or work placements abroad in 2011–2012 alone, in addition to 46,500 academic and administrative staff undertaking training or teaching abroad. As described by the European Commission, this represents a sum total of experiences "designed to improve the quality of teaching and learning in the 33 countries which participate in the scheme (EU Member States, Iceland, Liechtenstein, Norway, Switzerland and Turkey)."[5] Such figures, and the prospect of envisaged expansion to four million students between 2014 and 2020 is not only "testament to the enduring success and popularity of the programme" but makes Erasmus one of the most heavily utilized EU policies.[6]

Given its hybrid goals of Europeanizing the EU's youth demographic, and simultaneously enhancing both education and training, the question this chapter poses is whether Erasmus is ultimately as effective as it is popular. In order to tackle this issue, this chapter first examines relevant EU policy documents, deconstructs the conceptual assumptions that underlie Erasmus, and then explores the impact of East–west enlargement and the Eurozone crisis. It concludes that the impact of Erasmus has moved from an experiment in heightening integrative allegiances to the EU itself, to an inter-cultural method of reinforcing both EU and national identities, and availing the European Commission of an area in which to slowly shift the overall policy objectives of EU education. The questions are salient indeed: has Erasmus created a new "geography of European youth", and if so, how does this new demographic support the concept of integration through specific dynamics of identity, association, skill generation, etc.? Does the act of traveling, studying, interacting abroad at a formative time in one's life have the power to develop bonds, values, norms associated not only with the educational program itself, but reflective of the overall "locale" of the European Union? Or do the majority of students return

---

4   Official Journal of the European Union, No L 166, 25.06.1987, 20.

5   European Commission, "Number of Erasmus Students Tops 3 Million", IP/13/657 Press Release (8 July 2013), available at <http://europa.eu/rapid/press-release_IP-13-657_en.htm>.

6   *Ibid.* The EU target for overall student mobility is at least 20% by the end of the decade.

socially *affected*, but not necessarily rendered *effective* in terms of their citizenship, either politically or economically?[7]

Mindful of the seminal themes of this volume, we look into the impact of enlargements have upon the project of trans-national educational exchange, and the socio-economic imbalances that it – and the Eurozone crisis – have brought about. With its "underlying rationale [...] [to] become aware of their commonalities and develop a supranational identity", Erasmus itself was a key instrument in the integrative ambitions of the European Commission, deployed to eradicate entrenched East–west macroeconomic imbalances and enhance employability, to embed a sense of political equality, and most importantly, to instill a socio-cultural similarity.[8] While our findings throw light on additional problématiques of the mobility-identity-integration triptych, we conclude that in enabling mobility, Erasmus, despite its various internal ambiguities and uneven application, ultimately contributes to the self-proclaimed goal of generating "stronger cohesion in Europe, as well as to European citizenship",[9] and is increasingly viewed as an "essential tool for helping to promote active European Citizenship."[10]

2   Hybrid Visions and Multiple Functions

Mobility programs like the Erasmus program are consciously designed to promulgate the philosophy of "identity construction." Following the multidisciplinary theory of constructivism, this two-fold concept argues first that collective identities can be strengthened by increased self-perception, on the basis of symbols, narratives, and modes of denoting inclusion and exclusion.[11] Second, constructivism suggests that collective identities are in large part socially constructed to enhance given societal – and in this case

7   DG Education and Culture (European Commission), The Impact of ERASMUS on European Higher Education: Quality, Openness and Internationalisation, Final Report (2008), available at <http://www.gri.ipt.pt/download/site/gri/impacto8.pdf>.

8   Kuhn, *op. cit.* note 3, 994.

9   Commission of the European Communities, Report on the Follow-up to the Recommendation of the European Parliament and the Council of 10 July 2001 on Mobility within the Community of Students, Persons Undergoing Training, Volunteers and Teachers and Trainers, COM (2004) 21 Final (January 2004), 3.

10   Official Journal of the European Union, No L 394, 30.12.2006, 6.

11   See for example Rogers Brubaker and Frederick Cooper, "Beyond 'Identity'", 29(1) *Theory and Society* (2000), 1–47.

institutional – goals.[12] Via identity-boosting socialization, a given population is "exposed to a certain set of institutions, [and] they gradually adopt their values and norms."[13] This dynamic puts identity-creating power in the hands of national and supranational institutions, and transforms policies into vehicles for ideational transformation and behavioral change. This allows collective identities to be effectively constructed from both policies themselves (e.g. education), *and* their content and internal logic structures (e.g. mobility). When applied to Erasmus, the pattern is similar, namely that a particular collective identity – in this case, a European youth demographic – is identified, enhanced, and ultimately strengthened through the Erasmus program, which in turn allows a new form of Europeanized youth identity to become socially constructed upon key structures like Erasmus, and mechanisms like mobility.

For this, and many similar policies, the EU relies upon top-down policy architecture for its form, and a persuasive, ideational core of common norms and values for its content. Key to this expanding project was an overarching identity by which Europeans were drawn together in, and as, a community:

> What is needed is not simply greater "consciousness of Europe", but the creation of a "European consciousness" that will transcend national divisions and mobilise Europe's [...] citizens towards a new image of themselves as "Europeans" rather than nationals.[14]

Reflecting its multi-national content, and its multidimensional composition, an EU identity is an emphatically post-national collective identity, that somehow knits together an individual's civic commitment and the cultural heritage of their national community. The salient question is *how* precisely a European identity should be constructed within the official discourse of the Union, in the area of education policy. In simple terms, official discourses use core mobility programs like Erasmus, and a variety of harmonizing policies to establish EU institutions as "authors of identity" for the citizenry of youth comprising the "target audience." Projects like Erasmus are constructed as conscious practices bolstering the integrationist philosophy underlying the entire EU, as evidenced

---

12   See in reference to European collective identity Thomas Risse, *A Community of Europeans? Transnational Identities and Public Spheres* (Cornell University Press, New York, 2010); and Jeffrey T. Checkel and Peter J. Katzenstein (eds.), *European Identity* (Cambridge University Press, Cambridge, 2009).

13   Kuhn, *op. cit.* note 3, 996.

14   Chris Shore, "Transcending the Nation-State?: The European Commission and the (Re)-Discovery of Europe", 9(4) *Journal of Historical Sociology* (1996), 473–496, at 476.

by the text of the Council's 1987 decision adopting the ERASMUS program, in which one of the primary six objectives was "[t]o strengthen the interaction between citizens in different Member States with a view to consolidating the concept of a People's Europe."[15]

Interaction, it was hoped, would boost a wide range of transactions: economic, political, symbolic, educational, etc. which would cultivate familiarity, socialization, and ultimately a common identity. As argued by Corbett,[16] this is the backdrop against which the Commission launched, from 1987 onward, a range of educational programs. Mobility early on was prioritized for its singular ability to promote an enhanced European identity, and thus deepen a commitment to the EU, its logic of integration, and the more instrumental rigors of its integrationist requirements.[17]

Detailed scrutiny of Erasmus however illustrates that "its declared objectives have changed repeatedly throughout its history"; while it is tempting to suggest that the initial goals of Europeanization of a terrain of youth are somehow purer, and therefore closer to the true heart of an integrationist project like the EU, the transactional benefits (particularly in economic terms) of a mobility scheme like Erasmus are just as likely to be upheld by policy-makers as its envisaged cultural effects.[18] Equally, the host of policy coalitions that carve out a policy as mammoth as Erasmus arrive at a compromise lodged within the policy itself, "leading to a certain vagueness about what the programme is actually *for*."[19] Papatsiba's 2005 review of official publications discovered no fewer than four key arguments propounded by the Commission in support of Erasmus, as is summarized by Wilson:

> a means to "create a European consciousness",[20] to help alumni transcend intra-European borders during their future careers (lubricating the common European labour market), to allow the transfer of skills, techniques and technology within Europe (dynamizing the economy), and to help students to acquire such personal characteristics as independence and intercultural sensitivity, as well as improving their language skills.[21]

---

15   Official Journal of the European Union, No L 166, 25.06.1987, 21.

16   Anne Corbett, *Universities and the Europe of Knowledge* (Palgrave, Basingstoke, 2005).

17   Vassilki Papatsiba, "Political and Individual Rationales of Student Mobility", 40(2) *European Journal of Education* (2005), 173–188.

18   Iain Wilson, "What Should We Expect of 'Erasmus Generations'?" 49(5) *Journal of Common Market Studies* (2011), 1113–1140, at 1115.

19   *Ibid.*, 1116.

20   Papatsiba, *op. cit.* note 17, 174.

21   Wilson, *op. cit.* note 18, 1116.

In taking a necessary step back, it becomes clear that the very goal of building Europe seems itself to have shifted from a civilization venture to a market-based project, from entrepreneurial institutionalism to full-blown, pan-continental governance. Education, as an effective fillip to all such goals, has simply transformed in parallel to the EU's own iterative developments. Small wonder that Erasmus, with a felicitous symmetry between its own mobility goals and borderless make-up of the EU, has been routinely employed as both an end and a means of various social, economic, and political objectives.[22] Erasmus' excessively multipurpose nature is increasingly visible in post-enlargement documents like the 2006 European Parliament and Council Recommendation on transnational mobility to launch the European Quality Charter for Mobility; witnessed by its unbearably long job description:

(1)   Mobility in education and training is an integral part of the freedom of movement of persons – a fundamental freedom protected by the Treaty – and one of the main objectives of the European Union's action in the field of education and training, based both on common values and on respect for diversity. It is an essential tool for creating a genuine European area of lifelong learning, for promoting employment and reducing poverty, and for helping to promote active European citizenship.
(2)   Mobility brings citizens closer to one another and improves mutual understanding. It promotes solidarity, the exchange of ideas and a better knowledge of the different cultures which make up Europe; thus, mobility furthers economic, social and regional cohesion.[23]

Based on the impossibly flexible underlying principle of mobility, Erasmus itself is subsequently infelicitously endowed with a variety of oppositions which effectively attempt to balance instrumental with non-instrumental objectives. In other words, Erasmus has from the outset contained both symbolic content implicit in constructing a European identity, and delineated goals that are functional and instrumental in nature, and which aim to (re)educating citizens along the political and economic templates favored by the Council and Commission: the former constructing an identity by schooling, the latter rendering practical the uses of identity by 'skilling.' Some may regard these various goals as simply too wide apart to permit Erasmus to operate with any degree of cohesion. Others however, including the authors of this chapter, believe that tensions can be relational as well as oppositional, and may more likely produce

---

22   Corbett, *op. cit.* note 16.
23   Official Journal of the European Union, No L 394, 30.12.2006, 5.

a greater availability of opportunity and choice, along which the ambitious goals of Erasmus can be calibrated, in both the short and long-term.

In addition to the tension of ideational vs. instrumental content and symbolic vs. commercial goals, two other tensions haunt higher education in general. First, the EU-Member State split in terms of actual competence over education. Member States continue to hold the upper hand in terms of determining the content and structure of their respective national educational systems, while the EU is restricted by the Article 165 of the Treaty on the Functioning of the European Union (TFEU) specifying:

> The Union shall contribute to the development of quality education by encouraging cooperation between Member States and, if necessary, by supporting and supplementing their action, while *fully respecting* [emphasis added] the responsibility of the Member States for the content of teaching and the organisation of education systems and their cultural and linguistic diversity.[24]

This would seem a recipe for two-level policy stasis. Yet despite acrimonious competence and policy tussles, European integration in higher education has taken off and remains one of the most successful integrative policies of the EU, having been launched in 1987 in the form of the Erasmus program, and having produced results credibly associated with integration as a result. Disconcerting top vs. bottom dynamics however increase with every attempt by the European Commission to promulgate a change to projects like Erasmus, or more tacitly, in its watchdog capacity overseeing post-Bologna structures, which "adds a supranational element to an otherwise primarily intergovernmental agreement."[25] The 2009 Council conclusions on European education training make pointed observations about the need "to ensure the development of national qualifications frameworks [...] and their link to the European Qualifications Framework", as well as continuing to use progress reports to evaluate specific national progress on education and training.[26]

Second, there remains an ambiguity about the *overall point* of an integrated higher education space. Should it primarily be focused upon teaching and harmonizing learning exchange, as laid out in the Bologna Process, and as central

24   Official Journal of the European Union, No C 326, 26.10.2012, 120.

25   Martina Vukasovic, "European Initiatives in Higher Education – Why Should One Care?"
      Europe of Knowledge – UACES "Ideas on Europe" blog (27 December 2013), available at
      <http://era.ideasoneurope.eu/2013/12/27/european-initiatives-in-higher-education>.

26   Official Journal of the European Union, No C 119, 28.05.2009, 2.

to Erasmus, or should the thrust instead be focused upon research, as supported by the Lisbon (now Europe 2020) program, interpreted to produce a holistic understanding of research bolstering humanities, politics, economics, and other scientific fields? The needs of the present EU militate efforts geared toward the latter. While higher education remains a key element of the profoundly socializing goals necessary to keep the EU a cohesive, unified, transformational entity, legitimate in the eyes of its citizens, education remains a usefully transformative method to mitigate both internal market shocks and external geopolitical shifts.

As well as a wellspring for a potent youth-based European identity, education clearly represented the single best method of ensuring that European youth obtained a commercially-focused, multi-lingual skill set by which to guarantee their internal market employability, which in turn could assist the EU in maintaining economic clout, and even permit it to gain a "knowledge-based" edge over increasingly rapacious competitors. Education has by necessity been re-conceptualized "as an economic commodity."[27] The 2009 Council conclusions confirmed tacitly that "education and training have made a substantial contribution towards achieving the long-term goals of the Lisbon strategy for growth and jobs";[28] a philosophy made explicit in the launch of the newest iteration of European mobility: Erasmus+. As defined in July 2013 by European Commissioner for Education, Culture, Multilingualism and Youth, Androulla Vassiliou:

> Erasmus is more important than ever in times of economic hardship and high youth unemployment: the skills and international experience gained by Erasmus students make them more employable and more likely to be mobile on the labour market. Erasmus has also played a tremendous role in improving the quality of higher education in Europe by opening up our universities and colleges to international cooperation.[29]

While lifelong learning and mobility remain strategic objectives of the Council, alongside improving the equality and efficiency of education and training, the only Europeanizing content is denoted in the promotion of "equity, social cohesion and active citizenship."[30] The demography of European youth – as perceived by the Commissioner – is driven exclusively by the skills necessary

---

27   Kuhn, *op. cit.* note 3, 997.
28   Official Journal of the European Union, op. cit. note 26, 1.
29   European Commission, *op. cit.* note 5.
30   Official Journal of the European Union, op. cit. note 26, 3.

to become employable, and conducive to use by the labor market; a view overlapping with the Council's own requirement that education and training be geared at engaging more fully with "creativity and innovation, including entrepreneurship."[31]

Are we, as recipients, observers, contributors to this process, entirely convinced? Is the end result indeed a persuasive synchronicity between the *means* of a youth geography educated in the positive ramifications of integration (or the risks of its fallout) and the *ends* of a renewed, post-Eurozone crisis political entity of 28 Member States capable of reasserting trade, diplomatic, security, and normative impact upon and beyond its borders? In what way can education policy itself assist in the EU's soft power ambitions to export its indigenous cultural values?

At present, we can but survey the geography of European integration in the higher education sector, and suggest, as does Vukasovic,[32] that it has three key dimensions. First, Commission-led initiatives such as Erasmus, as well as support to a widening group of stakeholders such as university associations in European education. Second, harmonizing initiatives like ECTS and Bologna, which impact higher education in both EU non-EU members. Bologna, Lisbon, and now Europe 2020, with their various emphases on teaching and research, have not only laid the foundations for the current *Europe of Knowledge* project, by covertly subjecting a variety of inter-governmental areas to supranational "management" if not outright authority, but have also quietly strengthened the overall philosophy of EU (rather than national) governance in higher education.[33] Third, educational initiatives designed to increase the EU's impact on non-EU regions in North America and Asia. As Vukasovic argues, this interaction has "served primarily to consolidate and legitimize [...] both EU and pan-European elements in the European governance layer."[34]

3   The Challenges of Enlargement

After the first enlargement in 2004, the integration of the new enlargement countries into the Erasmus program was certainly compelling. In a 2006 press

---

31   *Ibid.*

32   Vukasovic, *op. cit.* note 25.

33   Governance in this sense betokens an arrangement of overlapping and interacting supranational, intergovernmental and transitional power structures. See Tanja Börzel, "European Governance: Negotiation and Competition in the Shadow of Hierarchy", 48(2) *Journal of Common Market Studies* (2010), 191–219.

34   Vukasovic, *op. cit.* note 25.

release, Ján Figeľ, the former Director General for Education in the European Commission noted the 36% increase of participation in Erasmus exchanges among the new European Union Member States in the academic year 2004–2005. On the new figures the Commissioner stated:

> These figures reveal that the new Member States are fully taking part in the benefits of membership of the EU. Their rapid integration into the Erasmus scheme directly contributes to its continued success, ensuring that additional generations of Europe's bright young people can enjoy the benefits of academic, cultural and linguistic exchange. [...] The hundreds of thousands of students who have benefited from the scheme since 1987 form a growing body of highly educated Europeans with cross-cultural and multi-lingual experience, essential requirements for the dynamic, knowledge-based European Union of the future.[35]

In this sense, Erasmus and the wider European Higher Education Area has come of age. Its first stage was to fuse bottom-up participation of students and the voluntarism of universities and academics with top-down dynamic of well-funded projects to produce and to enhance the overall process of Europeanization.[36] Its second stage includes a high-stakes geopolitical component: not merely to constructing geopolitical familiarity to bridge East–west fault lines, but developing contemporary socio-economic skills to ensure employment, entrepreneurialism and competition in which a "Europe of Knowledge" operates on a genuine level-playing field. During its third stage, East–west discrepancies are ironed out to ensure an equal uptake of the Lisbon Strategy and the Europe 2020 Strategy.

Taking a step back, the 2004 and 2007 enlargements clearly contributed to a shift in the EU educational landscape. Although the enlargement countries of Central and Eastern Europe (CEE) had largely already begun to take part in the Erasmus program, there was an increased focus on the integration prospects of the region itself, and methods of aligning the new Member States within a pre-established European Community. DG Education had its role to play in utilizing higher education and mobility program as an instrument of promoting integration of a newly emerged demographic of European youth: Erasmus

---

35   European Commission, "Erasmus: University Exchanges Expand Rapidly among the New Member States", IP/06/319 Press Release (3 December 2006), available at <http://europa.eu/rapid/press-release_IP-06-319_en.htm>.

36   Jana Bacevic, *Higher Education and Citizenship in Central, Eastern and South-Eastern Europe: Exploring the Links,* available at <http://www.herdata.org/public/JBacevic_ECPR.pdf>.

was viewed as a direct vehicle for transforming the student population into European citizens.[37]

At the same time, the CEE countries were dealing with a dual transition; a transition away from a former communist economy and all the effects this incurred as their countries moved towards a market economy while simultaneously working towards integration into the European Union and all the reforms that membership entails. The universities of the CEE countries were also transforming, and it was DG Education's mindset that they would transition into a transnationalized, European higher education space.[38] A 2006 report by researchers at the International Centre for Higher Education Research at the University of Kassel in Germany on the impact of the Erasmus program on former students revealed interesting conclusions. Former participants from the CEE countries were far more likely than their Western European counterparts to attribute a high professional value to the program, and felt they had experienced a significant career enhancement due to their participation in the program. Their colleagues in the Western European countries did not report the same type of career enhancement after their own experiences, suggesting an uneven, but greater impact on students from the CEE countries. The report summarizes the results in this area:

> Most strikingly, former ERASMUS students from Central and Eastern European countries report advantageous employment and work in general and international assignments more frequently than their peers from Western Europe. They are a more select group, but they also benefit more strongly from the study period abroad.[39]

This finding in particular is striking, as the CEE countries had begun sending students to participate in Erasmus in 1999; as such, students from this region had participated in Erasmus for a solid six years prior to the completion of the 2004 enlargement process, with the result that their perception of the program's impact on their employment opportunities as largely positive. When taking a look at the figures of Erasmus participation, the increase of students coming from CEE is striking. In 2000–2001, the first academic year of Bulgaria's participation in the program, 134 Bulgarian students took part in an Erasmus exchange. By 2004, that number had almost tripled to 751 students and by the

---

37   Bacevic, *op. cit.* note 36, 6–7.
38   *Ibid.*, 11.
39   Oliver Bracht *et al.*, "The Professional Value of ERASMUS Mobility", *INCHER-Kassel* (2006), 19.

2009–2010 period, 1,549 students were able to enroll in an Erasmus exchange during their studies.

Other CEE countries such as the Czech Republic, Hungary, Poland, and Romania experienced similar increases in outgoing students. Romania sent 1,250 students in 1998–1999, reaching 4,604 outgoing students during the 2009–2010 academic year.[40] Still, the representation of CEE students in the Erasmus program is quite minimal compared with the students from Western Europe: Germany, France, and Spain claim the highest number of outgoing students in the overall program each year with between 14–15% of the total Erasmus participants while Bulgaria represents a mere 0.41% and Romania 1.47%.[41] Contrasting the figures with the 2006 study results presents an interesting observation; although there are more participants from Western Europe, Erasmus may have a stronger impact on the smaller demographic of participants from Central and Eastern Europe.

Another 2006 survey conducted by Eurobarometer on the socio-economic status of Erasmus students showed further results. While most respondents reported their parents' income as being slightly higher than average or higher than average, the majority of students who reported coming from a family income of lower than average was in CEE, in particular from Bulgaria, Romania, Slovakia, Latvia, and the Czech Republic.[42] The authors of the report also noted that participants from these countries receive a higher grant amount than their Western European counterparts and that perhaps the grant opportunity facilitates the ability to embark on an exchange program. The survey also looked into extent at which the personal financial situation of a student deters participation in an Erasmus exchange. In the CEE countries, over 90% of participants reported having university friends who could not participate in Erasmus for financial reasons, compared with only 25% of respondents in several Western European countries.[43]

Erasmus has also brought both cohorts to CEE, contributing to the development of its universities and increasing the cross-cultural understanding between the two different regions of Europe, a cornerstone goal of Erasmus. In the period of 2004–2005, the only university from CEE to make the top 100 list of Incoming Erasmus Students per Institution was Charles University in

---

40   *Ibid.*

41   *Ibid.*

42   Manuel Souto-Otero, "Survey of the Socio-Economic Background of ERASMUS Students", ECOTEC Research and Consulting (2006), 6.

43   *Ibid.*, 10.

the Czech Republic.[44] By 2010–2011, universities in the Czech Republic, Slovenia, Poland, and Hungary were all represented in the top 100 list of universities with the most incoming Erasmus students.[45] As mentioned earlier, the CEE countries have been engaged in a major transition period, as have the higher education institutions within the region. Increasingly attracting Erasmus students from other countries to study in CEE is also a positive indication towards integration between Western Europe and the newer Member States.

Still, with over a decade more of experience participating in Erasmus, students and universities in Western Europe are more equipped to participate in Erasmus and the participants are more likely to come from a stronger socio-economic background than students coming from the relatively new enlargement countries of the EU. There remains a problem of access to Erasmus for these students; the opportunity to participate in a mobility program is still very unequal across Europe's regions and it is still more likely for someone from a socially privileged background to participate in a study abroad program than a student of a different socio-economic status.[46] The Eurozone crisis, which has also hit Western Europe in full force, has the potential to halt and in some instances even reverse the development in CEE. The next section will explore the spillover effect of the Eurozone crisis on the Erasmus program, and how it may be increasing the divide between Western and Eastern Europe, threatening to reverse the integrationist projections of the European Commission.

4   **The Spillover Effect of the Eurozone Crisis on the International Component of Higher Education in Europe: An East–west Schism?**

A 2012 report from PwC Poland released during the 22nd Economic Forum highlighted the significant risks to the economies of CEE posed by the Eurozone crisis. The report summarized:

> The deep financial and economic crisis that has been developing over the last few years continues to have a strong and negative impact on the

---

44   DG Education and Culture (European Commission), Erasmus Student Mobility by Institution in 2005/2006: Top 100 Incoming (2006), available at <http://http://ec.europa.eu/education/tools/statistics_en.htm>.

45   DG Education and Culture (European Commission), Erasmus Student Mobility (studies + placements) by Institution in 2010/11: Top 100 Incoming (2011), available at <http://http://ec.europa.eu/education/tools/statistics_en.htm>.

46   Bacevic, *op. cit.* note 36, 7.

economies of Central and Eastern Europe. [...] A deep recession in the Eurozone represents, therefore, a great and imminent threat for the entire CEE region.[47]

There is clearly much at stake in the still-developing CEE region, including its prospects for European integration. While at one level, the construction of an active, educated, post-graduate *polis* from a loose and largely tacit student *demos* (through citizenship which is the form, education which provides the content, and civil society which cultivates the concept of European identity) is key to the success of an imagined European community, the geopolitics of youth – a collective identity sharpened as a result of the current crisis – is now threatening to splinter current conceptions of a European cultural community.

The EU is now afflicted by an emerging complexity between those who are mobile, multi-lingual, who move across a pan-Europe seamlessly and have grown up within its mandate of unity amid diversity, and youth facing severe socio-economic distress as a result of the quasi-failure of certain Member States' economies.[48] The question remains whether Erasmus can provide the buffer against the instinct to "remain at home" and the increasing economic divide between youth of various regions of Member States. Whether in the face of less mobile higher education students, rising economic nationalism and a range of economic, political and social (including educational) disenfranchisement, Erasmus may be a robust enough bulwark to keep alive the opportunity to go beyond such perceived or real limitations.

If Erasmus is successful, the above qualitative understanding of the benefits will likely continue to exhibit a pan-European appreciation of regional/ national cultures. However, if the EU remains mired in economic malaise, political destabilization and ensuing forms of disaffection, then Erasmus will be unsuccessful as a policy bulwark against the rising tide of identity politics. If there is now a strongly regionalized geography of disaffection emerging within youth populations in Europe, the EU certainly faces a new internal challenge.

As suggested above, the terrain of transnational European youth is a highly mobile one, characterized by frequent travel, multi-lingualism, a high degree

---

47 PwC Poland, Central and Eastern Europe and the Eurozone Crisis (2012), available at <http://www.pwc.pl/pl/publikacje/pwc_approaching_storm_report_on_transformation .pdf>.

48 Amelia Hadfield and Robert Summerby-Murray, "Vocation or Vocational? Reviewing European Union Education and Mobility Structures", 6(3) *European Journal of Higher Education* (2015), 237–255. The data and analyses presented in this section (and inevitably, a part of conclusion) overlap with those in the cited article.

of open-mindedness, competitive attitudes, and a largely positive outlook on the EU and the EU's ability to provide a decent social model in the long-term, based on a foundation of acceptable cultural and political values. But the Eurozone fallout has prompted untold fault lines across this terrain since 2011. The failure of a number of European economies to recover from the 2008 financial crisis – notably Greece, Italy, Spain, and Portugal – has opened significant rifts in the sense of European opportunity. Add to this, the reversal of development and growth opportunities in the recently integrated CEE countries signals that a serious social problem is emerging in Europe, affecting not only a sectorial issue like higher education, but also threatening to undo the positive integrationist attitudes of youth from these countries.

Under various austerity budgets, Member State governments under crisis have been forced to reduce social spending and the encouragement of job creation. The Multiannual Financial Framework, the 2014–2020 budget for the EU, however, promises that education will not see a cutback in funding, at least not in the next seven years. The final budgetary figures published in early 2014 for Erasmus + show it will operate with a budget of EUR 14.7 billion,[49] which represents a 40% increase in comparison to 2007–2013 budget for equivalent programs (Lifelong Learning Program and Youth in Action), which received EUR 7 billion and 885 million respectively. Erasmus + replaces seven individual programs[50] as of 1 January 2014 and unifies them into a single, streamlined, integrated system centrally run by the Education, Audiovisual and Culture Executive Agency (EACEA) divided into three key actions (Learning mobility, Co-operation, and Policy support) in addition to special activities: Jean Monnet and sport. Learning mobility of individuals, which is the first key action, amounts to 63% of the total budget alone, representing EUR 9.2 billion. In real numbers this means: mobility opportunities for approximately 2 million higher education students, 1 million teachers, trainers, youth workers and other staff, altogether enabling close to 5 million people to study, train, volunteer, and teach abroad between 2014–20, compared with 2.5 million mobility opportunities from 2007 to 2013.[51]

---

49   European Commission, Financial programming and Budget: Multiannual Financial Framework (2014), available at <http://ec.europa.eu/budget/mff/figures/index_en.cfm# documents>.

50   Erasmus + replaces seven programs bringing together the Lifelong Learning Program (Erasmus, Leonardo da Vinci, Comenius and Grundtvig), the Youth in Action program, five international cooperation programs (Erasmus Mundus, Tempus, Alfa, Edulink, the program for cooperation with industrialized countries) and the new sport action, available at <https://eacea.ec.europa.eu/erasmus-plus_en>.

51   DG Education and Culture (European Commission), The EU programme for Education, Training, Youth and Sport 2014–2020 (2014), available at <http://ec.europa.eu/program mes/erasmus-plus/documents/erasmus-plus-in-detail_en.pdf>.

At the level of the European Commission, there is clear evidence of the commitment towards the continued policy relevance of mobility in higher education. Within Member States themselves, however, the EU is a markedly less healthy environment for youth, both for students and for graduates than it once was. With the exception of Poland, in all of the large Member States (UK, France, Spain, and Germany) youth unemployment now reaches record highs (in excess of 52% in Spain, for youth aged 18–25). For Member States chronically hit by the Eurozone crisis fallout (Ireland, Portugal, Greece, and Cyprus), youth unemployment has tipped 65% in some areas. University admissions have seen a fall off of 10–20%; graduate completion rates declining between 20–25%. In CEE, youth unemployment has revealed itself as one of the most pressing social problems. In Bulgaria, youth unemployment is officially estimated at around 30%, but a 2012 survey by the Mediana Agency suggested at the time, that the actual figure is much higher.[52] The study also shows that the rates of jobless young people with secondary and higher education qualifications have continued to rise even faster than their less-educated counterparts.[53] Slovenia meanwhile has reached a youth unemployment rate of 27% and Slovakia is at over 35% for youth unemployment.[54] Poland and Romania are respectively showing rates of youth unemployment at 27% and 22%.[55]

There is anecdotal evidence (requiring further study) to suggest students in hardest hit states in Europe are now less inclined to take up the Erasmus exchange program, citing poor timing, unsuitability for their studies, or overall unsuitability for their envisaged educational and career structure. Taken together, there appears to be a broad downward trajectory in terms of educational incentives, post-educational opportunities, and broad-based confidence in the social model of the EU. If the EU as the envisaged social model cannot guarantee a productive outcome in the lived realities of these young people, why then invest in the content of a European identity, obtained via mobility projects like Erasmus? However, the crisis may avail policy-makers and educators alike of a positive opportunity to re-examine the original motives of

---

52   See also the 2016 survey conducted by Trading Economics which suggest the same trend, available at <http://www.tradingeconomics.com/bulgaria/youth-unemployment-rate>.

53   Mediana Agency, *Youth Unemployment in Bulgaria – Factors, Type of Unemployment, State Policy, Programmes, Effectiveness of Measures, and Problem Identification* (2012), available at <http://www.eurofound.europa.eu/ewco/2012/10/BG1210011I.htm>.

54   Richard Martin, "Youth Unemployment Increases in Slovenia", *Aljazeera* (02 June 2013), available at <http://www.aljazeera.com/video/europe/2013/06/201362162950776912.html>.

55   YCharts, *Poland Youth Unemployment Rate* (2012), available at <http://ycharts.com/indicators/poland_youth_unemployment_rate_lfs>.

education policy and overhaul them in the face of the greatly changed market reality found in many Member States.

Changes encouraging students from the worst hit Member States to, for example, continue to use Erasmus could be implemented. Failure to address the stresses that express themselves in current examples of youth-driven social protest, budget cuts for student mobility, growing disenchantment among educators to teach EU studies or support Erasmus initiatives – separately or together – threatens to uncouple the EU edifice that is the legitimating structure behind the entire education enterprise of Erasmus. Usefully, a few other scholars have contextualized the construction of European identity through mobility programs in an emerging Eurozone financial crisis. Fligstein for example observe the "unevenness of European integration",[56] and points to emerging divisions in national debates that threaten labor mobility, education-based mobility, and European-scale policy cohesion. Surprisingly perhaps, these authors conclude with positive views, suggesting that "a wide, if shallow, sense of European identity"[57] may prevail in determining future policy options.

5   Conclusion

What are the implications of these cultural and political attitudes for universities and governments, especially in terms of future directions for education policy in general and student mobility programs specifically? Is Austrian Chancellor Wermer Faymann indeed correct that the EU is doomed without a social model that supports social cohesion, itself based on epistemic communities, likeminded culture, EU *demos,* and functionality? As illustrated, the European Commission has been single-minded in pursuit of realigning the employability and market-potential content of Erasmus; its *Rethinking Education Strategy* of 2012 made clear that investment in higher education comes with the expectation of producing a reliable crop of "highly skilled and versatile people who can contribute to innovation and entrepreneurship", and that education must target both "the needs of students and the labour market."[58] Yet the ability to recreate a program that can serve multiple functions of both "skilling" would-be consumers and "schooling" future citizens in the full spectrum of economic,

---

56   Fligstein, *op. cit.* note 3, 120.

57   *Ibid.*

58   European Commission, "Commission Presents New Rethinking Education Strategy", IP/12/1233 Press Release (20 November 2012), available at <http://europa.eu/rapid/press-release_IP-12-1233_en.htm>.

socio-political dimensions seems to have waned. A failure to restore the balance may render prophetic Chancellor Faymann's warning that: "We can't have a Europe where young people are losing hope and expectations, where they don't have the opportunity to prove themselves."[59]

Two observations complete this chapter. First, the *youth voice*, and in particular, the potential for this to be transmitted as a *youth vote* (whether conveyed through formal electoral politics or non-electoral means such as social protest), now demonstrates signs of being significantly affected by the growing social, cultural and economic schism of the EU during this present time of crisis. Doug Saunders claims that Western European youth have "grown up with ethnic and sexual minorities around them and don't have the taste for identity politics."[60] This broad comment ignores the significant youth geopolitics of today's Europe and masks what is arguably an increasing dynamism and instability around political identities. Now, more than ever, close attention must be paid to these regional and identity dynamics if the EU as a cultural and political enterprise is to be preserved and not split along new north–south or East–west fault-lines.

Second, close attention to mobility programs and a few substantive changes to the ERASMUS program in particular may be enough to exploit the uneven but still dynamic and largely undirected European terrain of youth, directing them toward, rather than away from, the need to engage with a pan-European identity, alongside their national viewpoints. A favored policy option should therefore be to redirect student mobility programs selectively or collectively to address youth opportunity in countries currently suffering the brunt of Eurozone financial crisis. In this way, student mobility will continue to address the key role of education in affirming the European social model and social cohesion between the varying regions. Rather than simply a program under budget stress in the present situation, student mobility programming can be a remarkably effective way of addressing what appears to be an emerging "terrain of disaffection", a terrain which contains potential disenfranchisement politically and economically as youth seek non-electoral forms of protest and become progressively removed from the wage economy. It is ever more apparent that the way forward is to affirm the longstanding effectiveness of student mobility

---

59   Cillian Donnelly, "Feymann: EU Doomed without Social Model", *New Europe* (15 January 2013), available at <https://neurope.eu/article/feymann-eu-doomed-without-social-model/>.

60   Doug Saunders, "Conservatives Face New Reality: Embrace Immigrants and Gays, or Lose Power", *The Globe and Mail* (15 December 2012), available at <http://www.theglobeand mail.com/opinion/conservatives-face-new-reality-embrace-immigrants-and-gays-or -lose-power/article6373112/>.

programming as a significant means of maintaining and enhancing European civic identity.

The point is to make use of the current structure, but to acknowledge the current problems. As observed, there is something of a split personality in terms of the policy competence of education in general. Torn between top-down harmonizing attempts of the European Commission and bottom-up backlashes of Member States intent on teaching "their youth", "their culture", "their way", the only connective tissue that gives students with a given particularistic national outlook the chance to witness a greater Europe and build a two-fold identity is Erasmus. Indeed, with the greater "body politic" of the EU now significantly at risk of disenfranchising the political, economic, and social options of wide swathes of its youth population, Erasmus may be the only connective tissue left to reassure young Europeans that the EU of the future stands a chance.

Bibliography

Bacevic, Jana. (2011) *Higher Education and Citizenship in Central, Eastern and South-Eastern Europe: Exploring the Links,* available at <http://www.herdata.org/public/JBacevic_ECPR.pdf>.

Bolino, August C. (2012) *Men of Massachusetts. Bay State Contributors to American Society* (iUniverse, Bloomington).

Börzel, Tanja. (2010) "European Governance: Negotiation and Competition in the Shadow of Hierarchy", 48(2) *Journal of Common Market Studies*, 191–219.

Brubaker, Rogers and Cooper, Frederick. (2000) "Beyond 'Identity'", 29(1) *Theory and Society*, 1–47.

Checkel, Jeffrey T. and Katzenstein, Peter J. (eds.) (2009) *European Identity* (Cambridge University Press, Cambridge).

Corbett, Anne. (2005) *Universities and the Europe of Knowledge* (Palgrave, Basingstoke).

Deutsch, Karl W. *et al.* (1957) *Political Community and the North Atlantic Area* (Greenwood Press, New York).

Fligstein, Neil. (2008) *Euroclash: The EU, European Identity and the Future of Europe* (Oxford University Press, Oxford).

Hadfield, Amelia and Summerby-Murray, Robert. (2015) "Vocation or Vocational? Reviewing European Union Education and Mobility Structures", 6(3) *European Journal of Higher Education*, 237–255.

Kuhn, Theresa. (2012) "Why Educational Exchange Programmes Miss Their Mark: Cross-Border Mobility, Education and European Identity", 50(6) *Journal of the Common Market Studies*, 994–1010.

Lijphart, Arend. (1964) "Tourist Traffic and Integration Potential", 2(3) *Journal of Common Market Studies*, 251–262.

Papatsiba, Vassiliki. (2005) "Political and Individual Rationales of Student Mobility", 40(2) *European Journal of Education*, 173–188.

Risse, Thomas. (2010) *A Community of Europeans? Transnational Identities and Public Spheres* (Cornell University Press, New York).

Shore, Chris. (1996) "Transcending the Nation-State?: The European Commission and the (Re)-Discovery of Europe", 9(4) *Journal of Historical Sociology*, 473–496.

Wilson, Iain. (2011) "What Should We Expect of 'Erasmus Generations'?", 49(5) *Journal of Common Market Studies*, 1113–1140.

CHAPTER 9

Slovenian Soft Power Capabilities in the European Context: Missed Opportunities of Cultural Diplomacy and Erasmus Student Exchange Program

Ana Bojinović Fenko and Jure Požgan

Abstract

This chapter analyzes missed opportunities in one of the fields of soft power that Slovenia, as a small EU Member State, could have seized, namely in higher education exchange schemes. Due to limitations in their material foreign policy capabilities, small states have a strong national interest to turn to forms of soft power, especially culture and cultural diplomacy. An empirical analysis indicates a rise in Slovenia's soft presence; however, in comparison with other Central and Eastern European countries, Slovenia's performance in capitalization of presence in terms of influence in the EU is the poorest. The reason for this is not so much a lack of soft power capabilities but rather unprofessional policy-making and strategic governance, which have led to underdeveloped, substantially uncoordinated, and strategically misapplied capabilities. A case study based on an online survey among Slovenian and foreign exchange students who have come to the University of Ljubljana, Slovenia's largest university and its best educational soft power capability, for an educational exchange program between 2009 and 2013, as well as focus group interviews with foreign exchange students and e-mail interviews with home students abroad in 2013, confirm these findings.

Keywords

cultural diplomacy – soft power capabilities – soft power presence – foreign policy influence – student exchange

1   Introduction

In 2010, the European Commission (EC) proposed the so-called Europe 2020 Strategy, a strategy for smart, sustainable, and inclusive growth of the European Union (EU), through which the vision of Europe's social market economy for the 21st century would be fulfilled. As one of the seven main principles of action (flagship initiatives), this document presents the *Youth on the move* initiative aimed at catalyzing progress of the EU and its Member States. Accordingly, enhancing "the performance and international attractiveness of Europe's higher education institutions and rais[ing] the overall quality of all levels of education and training in the EU" is to be achieved by promoting mobility of students and trainees, and improving the employment situation for young people.[1] Since education policy is not a common EU policy, its implementation is merely coordinated at the EU level within the so-called open method of coordination.[2] Therefore, this article focuses on the socio-political rather than the pure legal dimension of this policy, evaluating the Erasmus exchange program for one of the Member States, i.e. Slovenia. The benefits for the people, especially in the fields of education, professional development, and job opportunities for the young population, were regarded as one of the main motivations for Slovenia to join the EU.[3] However, the EC's 2015 Country Report for Slovenia is pressingly critical with regard to the aforementioned flagship area of the Europe 2020 Strategy as youth unemployment has been steeply growing from 10.4% in 2008 to 21.6% in 2013.[4] The report states that Slovenia must address several inefficiencies in its higher education system such as an estimated 35% dropout rate and about 50% fictitious enrollment

---

1   European Commission, Communication from the Commission "Europe 2020": A Strategy for Smart, Sustainable and Inclusive Growth (2010), available at <http://ec.europa.eu/eu2020/pdf/COMPLET%20EN%20BARROSO%20%20%20007%20-%20Europe%202020%20-%20EN%20version.pdf>, 11.

2   Open method of coordination stands for a light but structured dialogue and exchange of good practice between EU countries with the aim of contributing to improvement of the design and implementation of cultural policies, including education, without regulatory instruments. Available at <http://ec.europa.eu/culture/policy/strategic-framework/european-coop_en.htm>.

3   Marko Lovec, "The European Union is no Free Lunch: Reconsidering the Eastern Enlargement of the EU from an Intergovernmental Perspective", 17(66) *Croatian International Relations Review* (2012), 31–58.

4   European Commission, Commission Staff Working Document. Country Report Slovenia 2015 (2015), available at <http://ec.europa.eu/europe2020/pdf/csr2015/cr2015_slovenia_en.pdf>, 7 and 57–58.

to post-secondary vocational education, which are "mostly due to the incentives and social benefits linked to the student status and weak administrative checks."[5] Additionally, an immense challenge for the state is keeping up with "the quality of implementation of tertiary [programs, which] risks being affected by the decrease in total expenditure on education."[6]

This indicates that Slovenia has not made good use of the opportunities offered by EU policies and instruments, most notably its higher education exchange schemes. Taking into consideration that student (and academic staff) exchange programs can be used as soft power instruments of a state's foreign policy, this result makes up another opportunity cost of Slovenia's membership in the EU. As shown by Atkinson in the case of the USA, student exchanges can be used as an instrument of cultural diplomacy to achieve promotion of the most important national values and goals as knowledge about American democratic governance is being built through networks with foreign citizens, former exchange students in the USA.[7] For Slovenia, a small and young state, the main foreign policy goals to be achieved are state promotion, positive image-building, and increasing visibility by influencing foreign audiences. This chapter thus demonstrates a missed opportunity of Slovenia in the field of European Higher Education Area (envisaged in the Bologna Declaration of 1999) in terms of potential spillover effects achieved through cultural diplomacy using student exchange programs. The methodology used is a triangulation of quantitative and qualitative research methods and a case study of one (the biggest) of the Slovenian universities, the University of Ljubljana (UL). For the latter we conducted on online survey in 2013 among 1,153 Slovenian and 873 foreign students who have come to the UL between 2009 and 2013 for an educational exchange program. An additional survey in 2013 carried out focus group interviews with foreign exchange students at the Faculty of Social Sciences, UL, and e-mail interviews with home students abroad.

2 Culture as a (Small) State's Soft Power Capability

From the perspective of international relations, culture as a phenomenon is defined as all-encompassing, and cultural relations are relations between national cultures and national societies that transcend national borders. Reeves

---

5 *Ibid.*

6 *Ibid.*

7 Carol Atkinson, "Does Soft Power Matter? A Comparative Analysis of Student Exchange Programs 1980–2006", 6(1) *Foreign Policy Analysis* (2010), 1–22.

places the beginning of so-called *international cultural relations* to the time of the First World War, when the idea that "[if] people became more cultured, then they would change their habits and behaviour; this would mean that they would become more civilised, which would, if all went as expected, affect the nature of international relations."[8] From a foreign policy analysis perspective, however, states have been using culture especially as a means of influencing other societies and states, e.g. during the Cold War by means of public diplomacy and propaganda, or lately in the field of intercultural dialogue. In this regard, small states were (and mostly still are) unable to invest greatly in cultural diplomacy because they needed to focus all their capabilities on surviving (providing security or staying neutral), finding a security guarantee or active engagement in international organizations.[9]

Fischer emphasizes that, out of foreign policy motives, culture and ideology are more contingent than material interests of states (i.e. security, prosperity, geographical influence).[10] Using culture in foreign policy is therefore perceived as an influence strategy[11] that accounts for the structure and substance of the ways by which states seek to promote their image with a foreign public.[12] However, this line of understanding culture is rather one-sided, as it only takes into consideration cultural diplomacy as an instrument of a state's foreign policy. The neglected view of the above reasoning is the fact that culture first needs to be identified as a foreign policy capability and developed as such for its later activation through diplomacy. This highlights the noteworthy difference between power as *capability* and power as *influence*.

Power as capability rests on states' material (tangible) or ideational (intangible, i.e. soft) resources. Thus, power is to be understood firstly as a static analytic element of what a state possesses materially and ideationally (capability), and

---

8   Julie Reeves, *Culture and International Relations: Narratives, Natives and Tourists* (Routledge, London, 2004), 41.

9   Jeanne A.K. Hey, "Introducing Small State Foreign Policy", in Jeanne A.K. Hey (ed.), *Small States in World Politics: Explaining Foreign Policy Behavior* (Lynne Rienner, London, 2003), 1–12; and Zlatko Šabič and Charles Bukowski (eds.), *Small States in the Post-Cold War Period: Slovenia and NATO Enlargement* (Praeger, Westport CT, 2002).

10   Markus Fischer, "Culture and Foreign Politics", in Brenda Schaffer (ed.), *The Limits of Culture: Islam and Foreign Policy* (MIT Press, London, 2006), 27.

11   Ben D. Mor, "The Rhetoric of Public Diplomacy and Propaganda Wars: A View from Self-Presentation Theory", 64(5) *European Journal of Political Research* (2007), 661–683.

12   Manheim speaks of the intended foreign policy effects of a government as "to bring about understanding for its nation's ideas and ideals, its institutions and culture, as well as its national goals and current policies." Jarol B. Manheim, *Strategic Public Diplomacy: The Evolution of Influence* (Oxford University Press, New York, 1990), 3.

only secondly as a relational analytic element of the state's actions towards the object addressed (influence).[13] As a consequence, *soft power* (culture) is a term encompassing both, a state's (non-material) capabilities and, on the other hand, the influence produced in the international community through the use of soft power instruments of foreign policy, including cultural diplomacy, traditional (*pure*) diplomacy, public diplomacy, economic and commercial diplomacy, and propaganda, i.e. any non-coercive means based on societal or governmental inducements. It is therefore important to realize, that (a) capability does not produce influence in world politics automatically by itself, and (b) it is not self-evident how to capitalize on resources or transform power as capability into power as influence. A detailed conceptualization of soft power along this line of differentiation has recently been applied by Ohnesorge, identifying three sub-units of soft power: resources/capabilities, instruments, and reception.[14]

Cultural societal incentives as attractions have been understood within the context of states' soft power since Nye's invention of this concept in 1990. Culture (if pleasing and attractive to others), values, and policies are the major elements of a country's soft power (in terms of capabilities). Accordingly, this brings people to act through cooperation rather than coercion.[15] Nye recently upgraded the influence element of soft power by defining *smartness* in power performance: "Power conversion strategies turn out to be a critical variable that does not receive enough attention. Strategies relate means to ends, and those that combine hard and soft power resources successfully in different contexts are the key to smart power."[16]

Culture as states' intangible capability has to be operationalized through instruments of foreign policy to be communicated to foreign recipients; Brighi and Hill underline in this respect a vigorous civil society, quality of civil service, and industrial and technology skills.[17] Warren has recently confirmed the

---

13   For a recent and more thorough insight into the definition of power in foreign policy see Joseph S. Nye, "Power and Foreign Policy", 4(1) *Journal of Political Power* (2011), 10–13.

14   Hendrik W. Ohnesorge, "Making the Intangibles Tangible: Soft Power and its Subunits", paper presented at the Emerging Scholars Forum at the ISA West Annual Conference 2014 (Pasadena CA, 26 September 2014). Several other authors have also pointed to Nye's conceptually underdeveloped definition of soft power, especially its element of attraction. Janice Bially Mattern, "Why 'Soft Power' isn't so Soft: Representational Force and Attraction in World Politics", in Felix Berenskoetter and M.J. Williams (eds.), *Power in World Politics* (Routledge, Oxon, 2007), 98–119.

15   Joseph S. Nye, "Get Smart", 84(4) *Foreign Affairs* (2009), 160–163.

16   Nye, *op. cit.* note 13, 15.

17   Elisabetta Brighi and Christopher Hill, "Implementation and Behaviour", in Steve Smith, Amelia Hadfield, and Tim Dunne (eds.), *Foreign Policy: Theories, Actors, Cases* (Oxford University Press, Oxford, 2008), 117–135.

success of states in achieving large-scale normative influence through political communication generated by densely constituted mass media systems as a strictly soft power capability.[18] Being a means of persuasion (soft power) rather than coercion (hard power), cultural diplomacy enables small states to better cope with being restricted to fewer financial and human resources, intellectual centers and professional services.[19] Nevertheless, such niche diplomacy needs to be supported by adequate resources of attraction to achieve legitimate persuasion, e.g. the use of information, communication technology, and multilateral institutions,[20] promotion of national audio-visual arts, educational and research scholarship schemes, etc., where small states again find themselves in a disadvantaged position.[21] Culture as a foreign policy instrument can therefore be used by a state to influence the international community whereas culture *per se* may also be an *agency* of (state) influence. However, in this case state government bodies are not the (leading) agency but are complemented by non-official representatives of the state – the citizens (non-governmental and market-related agency).

Recently, an index of soft power has been introduced by McClory, in which he underlines that practitioners of state foreign policy should first understand what exactly soft power assets (capabilities) of states are, whether they can be mobilized by the state, and, if so, where they may be deployed.[22] In the past few years, soft power's rising value as an explanatory concept resulted in attempts to measure various aspects of countries' economic, political, social, and cultural realities in order to determine their influence on the global stage. An important part of these empirical analyses is the novel concept of *presence*.

---

18   T. Camber Warren, "Not by the Sword Alone: Soft Power, Mass Media, and the Production of State Sovereignty", 68(1) *International Organization* (2014), 111–141.

19   Anders Wivel, "The Security Challenge of Small EU Member States: Interests, Identity and the Development of the EU as a Security Actor", 43(2) *Journal of Common Market Studies* (2005), 393–412.

20   Ronald M. Behringer, "Middle Power Leadership on the Human Security Agenda", 40(3) *Cooperation and Conflict* (2005), 305–342.

21   Jure Požgan and Ana Bojinović Fenko, "Kulturna diplomacija in kultura v mednarodnih odnosih: študija primera slovenske zunanje politike (Cultural Diplomacy and Culture in International Relations: A Case Study of Slovenian Foreign Policy)", 28(69) *Družboslovne razprave* (2012), 8–29.

22   Jonathan McClory, *The New Persuaders: An International Ranking of Soft Power* (Institute for Government, London, 2010), available at <http://www.instituteforgovernment.org .uk/pdfs/new_persuaders_soft_power.pdf>, 5; and *id., The New Persuaders II: A 2011 Global Ranking of Soft Power* (Institute for Government, London, 2013), available at <http://www .instituteforgovernment.org.uk/sites/default/files/publications/The%20New%20 PersuadersII_0.pdf>.

Olivie and Molina define global presence as "a country's effective positioning, or projection" in the world with which the country tries "to occupy an intermediate level between available internal assets and their conversion into the relative capacity of a country to effectively shape globalization."[23] Accordingly, "global presence is a prerequisite for the exercise of influence through diplomacy."[24] In short, a country-related all-encompassing presence is in the international realm, whereas soft power capabilities are an element of a state's domestic environment. However, they both determine the soft power influence of states.

Education is a sub-index in these scales, and is measured by the quality of primary and secondary education, the quality of universities, the number of foreign students studying in a given country, and by academic publishing.[25] Culture, however, is defined by McClory as a different sub-index (measured by metrics such as tourism, reach of state-sponsored media outlets, language, Olympic profile, music market, art gallery attendance, world heritage, status in international football, etc.). *Education* is therefore a separate component of soft power compared to the more generally understood sub-index of *culture* (as cultural and art production and societal influence). Nevertheless, the line is not clear-cut. Thus, exchange programs, like the EU scheme Erasmus, offer states a tool for enlarging their material capabilities with respect to internationalization of higher education (number of partner institutions and number of outgoing and incoming exchange students and teachers). Additionally, exchange programs provide potential to achieve foreign policy influence by positive image projection if relations with foreign students are kept after the exchange program ends.[26] As small states usually do not have the material capabilities at their disposal to individually assure the necessary cultural diplomacy infrastructure, multilateral schemes for raising soft power

---

23   Iliana Olivie and Ignacio Molina, *Elcano Global Presence Index* (Real Instituto Elcano, Madrid, 2011), 3.

24   Bretherton and Vogler also define presence, referring to the EU's ability as a foreign policy actor "to exert influence externally; to shape perceptions, expectations and behavior of others." However, their definition significantly differs from the one above since it denotes presence as a "mere consequence of being" and does not mean purposive external action. Charlotte Bretherton and John Vogler, "Conceptualizing Actors and Actorness", in Charlotte Bretherton and John Vogler (eds.), *The European Union as a Global Actor* (Routledge, London, 2006), 27.

25   McClory, *op. cit.* note 22.

26   Atkinson, *op. cit.* note 7.

capabilities – like international exchange programs – are of even higher relevance to them.

The above discussion has established that, due to material limitations in their foreign policy capabilities, small states, firstly, have a strong national interest to use cultural elements in their foreign policies as much as they can in terms of capability. And secondly, to produce influence, they commit themselves to using soft power instruments, especially culture and cultural diplomacy, including student exchange programs. Between domestic capabilities and achieving international influence, states rely on international presence of their entire society. In all three aspects of soft power, small states have proven weaker in absolute terms. Nevertheless, in the field of culture (including education), they may overcome this deficiency through smart specialization by using international exchange schemes for intangible capability-building and linking the latter with material capabilities.

3   Slovenian Soft Power Presence

The assumption that Slovenia as a small state also has little soft power (i.e. weak capabilities, presence and influence) in world politics is well supported by various soft power indices. According to Olivie and Molina, these are:

- mostly focused on power and influence rather than presence, therefore prioritizing large(r) states;
- limited in size (number of countries) and scope (issue areas/indicators) of the sample, which is biased in favor of large(r) states and hard(er) power (mostly economic);
- used as support or tools for policy-making rather than academic purposes;
- based on perceptions (public opinion surveys), or at best on perceptions combined with objective data (composite metrics across various indicators);
- relative rather than absolute, focusing on *de facto* capabilities rather than on potential for power/presence/influence.[27]

---

27   Olivie and Molina, *op. cit.* note 23, 23–24.

Accordingly, Slovenia is either not included in soft power surveys at all (Soft Power Index 2012[28] and 2014,[29] Anholt-GfK Roper City Brands Index,[30] Global Cultural Diplomacy Ranking,[31] Ernst&Young Emerging Markets Soft Power Index[32]) or is ranked at the bottom of soft power indices such as the European Union Cultural Diplomacy Ranking 2011[33] (rank 20 out of 27), the Elcano Global Presence Index (IEPG) 2014[34] (rank 71 out of 80) and the Elcano European Presence Index (IEPE) 2014[35] (rank 22 out of 28). From a global perspective, one possible conclusion would be that non-Western European small states in

---

28   The index assesses 30 countries based on five categories: business/innovation, culture, government diplomacy, and education. The culture sub-index includes measures like the annual number of tourists visiting a country, the global reach of a country's native language, and Olympic sporting success, but not student mobility (student exchange programs). See McClory, *op. cit.* note 22.

29   Cesare Serventi, "Soft Power Survey 2014/15", *Monocle* (November 2014), available at <http://monocle.com/film/affairs/soft-power-survey-2014-15/>.

30   The index measures the power and quality of 50 countries' *brand image* according to six dimensions: exports, governance, culture and heritage, people, tourism, investment and immigration. See Anholt-GfK Roper City Brands Index (2013), available at <http://www .gfkamerica.com/practice_areas/roper_pam/placebranding/cbi/index.en.html>.

31   The ranking focuses on the degree to which cultural diplomacy used as a tool of foreign policy by the governments of 40 states. The components of the index are government cultural diplomacy actions, cultural diplomacy initiatives (education, *exchanges*, performing arts, film industry, visual arts, music, sports) and international perception and media policy. See Institute for Cultural Diplomacy, *Cultural Diplomacy in the Public Sector: Executive Summary of the Public Sector Ranking 2012* (Berlin, 2012), available at <http://www .culturaldiplomacy.org/culturaldiplomacynews/content/pdf/Cultural_Diplomacy_Outlook_Report_2011_-_01-01.pdf>.

32   The index assesses 20 emerging market economies by measuring variables that define soft power according to three major categories: global image (*TIME* 100, media exports, most admired companies, Olympics, language enrollments), global integrity (freedom index, voter turnout, rule of law, CO_2 emissions) and global integration (immigration, tourism, English fluency, university ranking). See Ernst&Young, *Rapid Growth Markets Soft Power Index* (2012), available at <http://emergingmarkets.ey.com/wp-content/uploads/ downloads/2012/05/TBF-606-Emerging-markets-soft-power-index-2012_LR.pdf>.

33   The ranking follows the same methodology as the Global Cultural Diplomacy Ranking but only for 27 EU Member States.

34   The IEPG 2014 was measured for 80 countries, including the world's top economies, OECD and EU Member States. It assesses countries' global presence in three fields: economic, military and *soft* (cultural, social, sporting, internationalization of higher education system). See Real Instituto Elcano, *Elcano Global Presence Index* (2014), available at <http:// explora.globalpresence.realinstitutoelcano.org/en/country/iepg/global/SI/SI/2014>.

35   The IEPE assesses internationalization of EU Member States following the same methodology as the IEPG. See Real Instituto Elcano, *Elcano Global Presence Index* (2013), available

general are under-represented in favor of the emerging market economies, especially Brazil, Russia, India, China, and South Africa (BRICS). From a regional (EU) perspective, Slovenia definitely does worse compared to other small states in the EU – especially with the group of Central and Eastern European Countries (CEECs) where Czech Republic and Hungary rank 37–39th in the IEPG index and 14–15th in the IEPE index, Slovakia ranks 58th in the IEPG and 20th in the IEPE – or even compared to the EU's newest member Croatia, which ranks 17th among the 20 emerging market economies in the Ernst&Young Soft Power Index (where Slovenia is not even listed), 64th in the IEPG and 21st in the IEPE.

With regard to the relevance of these indices for the empirical analysis of Slovenian capabilities and instruments of cultural diplomacy, we decided to use two indices, namely the IEPG and the IEPE, since they escape some of the above-mentioned limitations. Firstly, they do not directly measure the influence of states but rather their international positioning (presence) by using entirely quantitative (non-perception-based) data. Secondly, as Slovenia is included in both indices, this allows for comparison between its two main foreign policy settings, i.e. the global and the EU, and an analysis of the differences in the application of its soft power capabilities. Thirdly, the structure of the two indices is such that it considers soft presence issue areas[36] (46%) relatively more than economic (38%) and military (16%) fields. Fourthly, both indices have been assessing presence annually since 2010 – the IEGP every five years since 1990 (1995, 2000, 2005, 2010) and annually since 2010, while IEPE data is available from 2005 – allowing an analysis of the evolution and trends in soft power projection.

Looking at the data for Slovenia we can conclude that after remaining level between 1995 and 2000 (3.5) its global presence index (IEPG) has seen rapid growth (in absolute terms) since 2000 (Graph 9.1). Steep increases in 2005 (6.2) and 2010 (9.3) can be attributed to Slovenia's accession to the EU but also to the non-governmental factors of presence in the index (Slovenian FIFA World Cup appearances in 2002 and 2010, good performance at the Beijing Olympic Games in 2008). The growth has slowed down since 2010, most probably as a result of a grave economic situation in Slovenia. The index value nevertheless reached its peak in 2012 at 10.4, but then slid to 10.05 in 2013, only to improve

---

at <http://explora.globalpresence.realinstitutoelcano.org/en/country/iepe/global/SI/SI/2013>.

36 These include immigrant population, tourist arrivals, results in major sporting competitions, exports of audiovisual activities, international dissemination of information through the internet, volume of foreign-oriented patents, internationalization of academic and university system (through academic publications and by number of foreign students) and development assistance. *Ibid.*

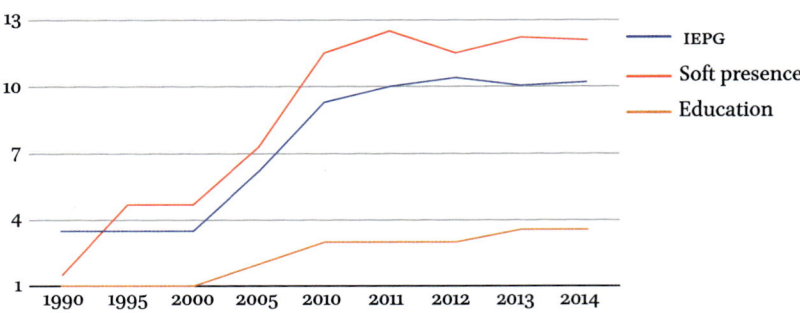

GRAPH 9.1   *Global presence index (IEPG)[37] – Slovenia*

again in 2014 to an index value of 10.20. In relative terms, however, Slovenia's
IEPG index record has not been impressive. On the contrary, Slovenia ranked
53rd among 60 sample countries in 1995, and has only ranked lower ever since –
54th in 2000, 2010 and 2011, and 55th in 2005 and 2012. In 2013, the number of
countries included in the index increased to 80; however, Slovenia still ranks
among the lowest 10 as 71st.

Similarly, Slovenia's soft presence sub-index, after the country gained independence in 1991, stagnated (at value 4.7) from 1995 to 2000. A steep rise
in its soft presence began in 2005 (7.3) and continued throughout 2010 (11.5)
and 2011 (12.5), before dropping back to the 2010 value in 2012 and then rising
again in 2013 (12.39) and decreasing slightly in 2014 (12.09). In relative terms, we
can see that the result reflects that of the overall IEPG index where Slovenia
ranked the highest among all indices in 1995 (49th out of 60 countries), before falling to 56th place in 2000, and has since settled at rank 50 (2011) and 51
(2005, 2010, 2012). In 2013 it ranked 60th (out of 80 countries) and 62nd in 2014.
This indicates a relative failure of its foreign policy to use soft power tools for
state promotion and branding in the immediate post-independence period.
With respect to education as one of the indicators measuring soft presence,
Slovenia's performance is even poorer, ranging from best performance rank 53
in 2010 (out of 60 countries) to rank 62 in 2013 and 2014 (out of 80 countries).

As for the European presence index (IEPE), which has been measuring the
internationalization of EU Member States since 2005 (Graph 9.2), Slovenia has
seen steady growth – starting with 10.3 in 2005 and rising to 15.4 in 2010, 18.6 in
2011, 20.4 in 2012, 23.3 in 2013, reaching its peak value of 23.46 in 2014. In relative
terms, however, this has not transformed into significant changes in Slovenia's
ranking, since other EU countries have also experienced similar growths.

---

37   *Ibid.*

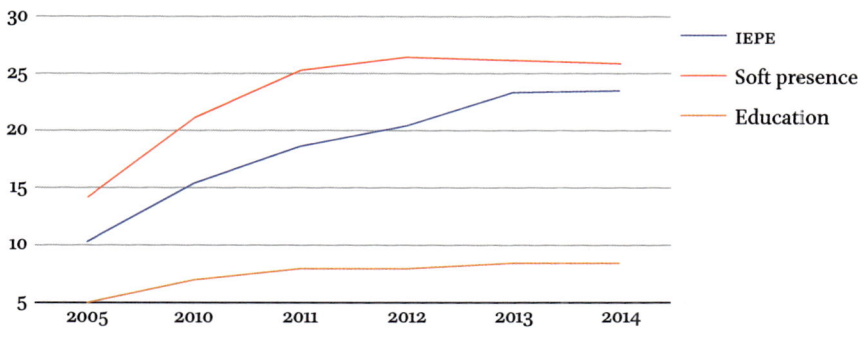

GRAPH 9.2   *European presence index (IEPE)*[38] *– Slovenia*

In 2005, Slovenia ranked 20th out of 25 member countries, and it has been in rank 22 since 2010.

A similar steady growth has been recorded in Slovenia's soft presence sub-index, with values increasing from 14.2 (2005) to 21 (2010), 25.2 (2011) and to 26.3 (2012), and then sliding to 26.06 (2013) and 25.79 (2014), which put Slovenia's European soft presence in relative terms at rank 23 in 2005, then at rank 22 (2010, 2011, 2012) and at rank 23 again in 2013 and 2014. This means that in the EU context only Malta, Cyprus, Lithuania, Latvia, and Estonia display less soft presence than Slovenia. In education performance, Slovenia ranks similarly low – 23rd in 2005, 22nd in 2010, dropping to rank 24 in 2011 and 2012 and rising to rank 21 in 2013 and 2014.

To sum up, the IEPG and IEPE indices show Slovenia's global as well as European soft presence increasing mostly as a result of its independence in 1991 and EU accession in 2004. This increase is nevertheless lower than those of other comparable states (CEECs), which have managed to increase not only their presence but also their influence potential despite the economic crisis. The following paragraphs therefore try to analyze reasons for this failure of Slovenia to turn its capabilities into presence and influence.

4   Slovenian Cultural Capabilities and Diplomacy

Three main aims in Slovenia's cultural diplomacy can be identified in the time since it declared independence in 1991. Firstly, Slovenia attempted to distance itself from historically negative images of the political and economic system of former Yugoslavia in order to redefine itself as a Central European country and

---

38   *Ibid.*

develop a more positive external image. Slovenia therefore chose to develop and communicate a new identity to the outside world (through political and economic elites, tourists, scientists, investors). This included its *away-from-the-Balkans* foreign policy strategy.[39] Secondly, one of the main objectives was to (re)position itself as a stable and reliable member of the international system, underlining its commitment to the principles of democracy, freedom, rule of law, human rights, and market economy by joining the international governmental institutions, mainly the Euro-Atlantic organizations. Preference was thus given to political and economic rather than cultural/educational capability-building. Finally, Slovenia has attempted since its EU accession in 2004 to position itself as a regional center and transition leader by engaging predominantly in intense political, economic and cultural relations with countries on the European periphery (Western Balkans).[40] Additionally, it tried to include culture in the framework of presiding over the decision-making bodies of regional international organizations (e.g. Council of Europe, Council of the EU, and the Organization for Security and Cooperation in Europe (OSCE)).[41]

If we look at culture as one of the areas of state promotion, besides the above-mentioned multilateral activities, Slovenia also concludes bilateral framework cooperation agreements in culture, education, science, and sport, particularly with states in its geographical and cultural proximity (neighboring states, the EU, and the Western Balkans). Also of special importance are its bilateral agreements with third states that are relevant in terms of scientific, technological and research cooperation.[42] However, the Slovenian Ministry of Culture (MC) does not consider bilateral agreements as a foreign policy tool in its 4-year national plan for culture. Under the title "International Cooperation," it only mentions

---

39   For a detailed analysis of Slovenia's *away-from-the-Balkans-towards-Central-Europe* foreign policy strategy see Ana Bojinović, "Geographical Proximity and Historical Context as a Basis of Active Foreign Policy Strategy of Small European Sates – the Case of Austria and Slovenia Regarding the Western Balkans", 1(1) *Politics in Central Europe* (2005), 8–29; and Ana Bojinović Fenko and Jure Požgan, "Regionalisation of Slovenian Foreign Policy: Back to the Balkans", 14(1) *Studia Historica Slovenica* (2014), 217–230.

40   This re-orientation is part of the *back-to-the-Western-Balkans* strategy, which includes Slovenia's role as a mediator between the EU and the countries of the region. *Ibid.*

41   Ana Bojinović Fenko and Zlatko Šabič, "Continuity and Change in Slovenia's Foreign Policy: A Comparison to Yugoslavia and an Analysis of the Post-Independence Period", in Soeren Keil and Bernhard Stahl (eds.), *The Foreign Policies of Post-Yugoslav States: From Yugoslavia to Europe* (Palgrave Macmillan, Basingstoke, 2014), 47–67.

42   Slovenia has signed 45 such bilateral agreements altogether. A detailed list of countries is available at <http://www.mzz.gov.si/si/zunanja_politika_in_mednarodno_pravo/kul turno_sodelovanje/>.

taking advantage of international and regional organizations and networks.[43] This, however, is not consistent with the declared "broad conception of culture and [promoting] its linking with the areas of foreign policy, public diplomacy, international development aid, education and neighborhood policy, cultural and creative sectors."[44] This still reproduces a rather narrow understanding of cultural cooperation in multilateral international cultural relations and instruments of foreign policy in this field, while no holistic capability-building or active state-image promotion through presence in world politics is planned.[45]

In other areas of a comprehensive understanding of culture, such as tourism, immigration and sports, capabilities are immense but are unfortunately weakly brought to operation. Volasko points out that Slovenia does not use its natural resources (biodiversity, water resources, forests) as soft power capability to its fullest potential. Consequently, there is no state-coordinated and state-driven comprehensive approach to linking tourism (as its biggest asset) with other associated sectors (such as agriculture, traffic and industry) into a unique offer that would enable Slovenia to act as a tourism brand and attract visitors from the EU and the rest of the world.[46] Similar missed opportunities with respect to country promotion include a poorly developed migration policy, where the transition period for adopting EU-*acquis* was not used for attracting sufficient highly skilled labor from abroad (e.g. former Soviet Union, Western Balkans), and an ambivalent attitude toward sport, with no strategic investment in infrastructure and rather sporadic promotion of outstanding sport results by some athletes (e.g. Tina Maze, Primož Kozmus, Urška Žolnir, the Slovenian ski jumping team).[47]

---

43   Ministry of Culture of the Republic of Slovenia, "Nacionalni program za kulturo 2014–2017 (National Program for Culture 2014–17)", available at <http://www.mk.gov.si/fileadmin/mk.gov.si/pageuploads/Ministrstvo/Drugo/novice/NET.NPK.pdf>, 134–136.

44   *Ibid.*, 134.

45   The document merely indicates this as part of the "cross-cutting implementation of international obligations of the Republic of Slovenia in the field of culture, human rights, specifically cultural rights and cultural diversity." *Ibid.*, 136.

46   Human resource capital, which could become a comparative advantage of Slovenia in tourism, has been poorly used. For example, promotion of traditional skills, arts and crafts has not been linked with the trend of sustainable and ecological production. Peter Volasko, Science Division at the Directorate of Science in the Ministry of Education, Science and Sport, interview by Ana Bojinović Fenko, Ljubljana (6 August 2013).

47   *Ibid.* An indication of the state's awareness of the importance of this kind of comprehensive strategic planning is Slovenia's participation at EXPO 2015, which for the first time exposed Slovenian cultural, economic, tourism, sports, and societal "production" under a common slogan of innovation and sustainable development.

Slovenian cultural diplomacy capabilities in the field of education are assessed to be the weakest. The state only started seriously addressing internationalization of higher education as late as its 2011 National program,[48] where
measure 28 envisages a national strategy on internationalization of higher
education to be formulated by 2013. According to the Center of the Republic of Slovenia for Mobility and European Educational and Training Programs
(CMEPIUS), academic capabilities of Slovenian universities are relatively high,
but the main problem has been achieving the wholesome perception of international exchanges as a student/teacher/researcher experience and as an
opportunity for state promotion.[49] We will illustrate this with two examples.

The different aspects of longer stays of foreign students that fall under the
competences of different ministries are very poorly coordinated among the
ministries and with universities.[50] CMEPIUS reports that no contact is kept
with Erasmus students after they leave Slovenia, but bilateral and Central
European Exchange Program for University Studies (CEEPUS for CEECs and
the Western Balkans) participants are included in a CMEPIUS-coordinated
alumni network. However, the latter is not used for any state-promotion activities. There is also no contact between Slovenian embassies and CMEPIUS
for promoting cultural, educational and scientific events in Slovenia or abroad
with former participants in exchange schemes, except for very rare occasions
of CMEPIUS asking an embassy to publish on its website information about
an academic work resulting from an exchange program of a foreign author in
Slovenia. The one positive development is a recent introduction of a Facebook
group called *Foreign students in Slovenia*, created by CMEPIUS in 2013, but the
day-to-day activities in this group are more of a side track for the CMEPIUS
personnel and would require additional staff to manage the group in the sense
of quality state promotion.[51]

A second critical point of assessment is the geographical focus of student
exchange programs, where the above mentioned CEEPUS for the Slovenian

---

48   Resolution on the National program for higher education 2011–2020, passed by the Nation-
      al Assembly on 24 May 2011, available at <http://www.uradni.ist/1/content?id=103885>.
49   CMEPIUS, interview with Ms. Sonja Mavsar and Ms. Marja Medved, employees at the
      Center of the Republic of Slovenia for Mobility and European Educational and Training
      Programs, by Ana Bojinović Fenko, Ljubljana (6 September 2013).
50   e.g. the Ministry of the Interior, the Ministry of Labor, Family and Social Affairs, and the
      Ministry of Foreign Affairs dealing with student preparation periods, long-term resi-
      dence, accompanying family members, payment of potential work, health insurance, etc.
      in case of long-term student/teacher exchanges. *Ibid.*
51   *Ibid.*

foreign policy priority area – the Western Balkans – is not taken into consideration by many faculties. They remain mainly focused on the Erasmus exchange program, from which this area is excluded. Moreover, the bilateral scholarships that Slovenia provides do not reflect a specific focus on the area, as during the academic year 2013/14 Serbia, Bosnia and Herzegovina, Kosovo, and Albania are not even included and this remained the same during the previous academic year however including Bosnia and Herzegovina.[52]

Underdeveloped internationalization of higher education programs is another missed opportunity where, despite the fact that Slovenia's largest university, the University of Ljubljana, is ranked among the top 500 universities of the world,[53] this institution was and is unable (or unwilling) to attract more foreign teachers, researchers and students – its international visibility is therefore declining. Some reasons for this lie in the very strict national regulation of obligatory use of the Slovenian language in class or in program accreditation procedures, as it is demanded by the Slovenian Quality Assurance Agency for Higher Education (NAKVIS) even for joint degrees.[54] According to Volasko, science was the only field where, as a result of increased investment,[55] Slovenia was able to project some soft power.[56] Namely, it succeeded in setting up a coalition of new Member States to gain support for the initiative for *widening participation* within Horizon 2020 (an EU-financed 7-year research program for 2013–2020), offering new Member States extra funds in research projects due to their objective limitations to equal participation in research networks and projects.

As for the application of existing soft power capabilities, Slovenia is mostly limited by the lack of a broader network of cultural centers organized to explicitly promote national cultural goals. Contrary to the practice of many other (CEE) states that have developed this institution, Slovenia only has two

---

52   There are 26 months of scholarships provided for Croatia, 20 for Macedonia and 18 for Montenegro. Other states (Poland, China, Mexico, Czech Republic, Slovakia, and Israel get more scholarship support). See the list of bilateral scholarships for various academic years (2015), available at: < http://www2.cmepius.si/en/higher-education/bilaterals/call .aspx>.

53   Center for World-Class Universities, "Shanghai Index – Academic Ranking of World Universities" (2013), available at <http://www.shanghairanking.com>.

54   CMEPIUS, *op. cit.* note 49.

55   From 1.66% of GDP in 2008 to 1.86% of GDP in 2009, 2.11% of GDP in 2010 (the figure is not comparable due to a change in methodology) and 2.47% of GDP in 2012. Available at <http://www.stat.si/novica_prikazi.aspx?id=5120>.

56   Volasko, *op. cit.* note 46.

operational cultural centers (SKICA and Korotan) in Vienna, Austria and one *in the making* in Berlin, Germany.[57] In spite of excellent cooperation among three institutional promoters of Slovenian culture in Vienna (SKICA, the Slovenian Scientific Institute, and the Representation of Slovenia to the OSCE), two institutions – SKICA and Korotan – should develop a better level of cooperation for more efficient implementation of cultural goals in Vienna and Austria in general.[58]

Save for Vienna, embassies remain the main actors of cultural diplomacy by implementing bilateral agreements on cultural cooperation and organizing cultural events. There have been several attempts to strengthen "the network of diplomatic and consular representations with cultural attachés or by establishing cultural information centers as part of the embassies [...] but such attempts have been abandoned in 2000 just before their realization."[59] Furthermore, the Ministry of Education, Science and Sport launched an initiative in 1999 to progressively establish seven special scientific attachés in Brussels, Berlin, New York, Tokyo, Vienna, New Delhi, and Paris. Currently, only one scientific attaché holds office in Brussels, and the Ministry of Foreign Affairs (MFA) only started to develop scientific diplomacy in 2012.[60]

We can sum up that Slovenia has tried to develop its cultural foreign policy tools in order to profit from its soft power capabilities. However, the country has been developing predominantly general multilateral cultural capabilities in international (regional) organizations. The state was, unfortunately, less successful in targeted multilateral education exchange schemes (like Erasmus), bilateral agreements and individual instruments (cultural centers). One could explain this low soft power capability and consequently poor presence of Slovenia by referring to some of the findings from Szondi's study of the reasons for unsuccessful branding in CEECs:

---

57   See Slovenski kulturni center Korotan (2013), available at <http://www.korotan.com/ korotan_dom/kultur/C59>; and Slovenski kulturnoinformacijski center (2013), available at <http://www.skica.at/Skica>. Korotan is registered as a non-profit association and is only partly co-financed by the Slovenian government. Nevertheless, its main goal is to promote Slovenian culture and art in Vienna. Slovenian Cultural Centre in Berlin opened in June 2016. See <http://www.culture.si/en/Slovenian_Cultural_Centre_in_Berlin>.

58   Volasko, *op. cit.* note 46.

59   Ministry of Culture of the Republic of Slovenia, "Analiza stanja na področju kulture s predlogi ciljev za nacionalni program za kulturo 2012–2015 (Analysis of the Situation Regarding Culture with Suggested Goals for the National Program for Culture 2012–2015)" (2011), available at <http://www.mk.gov.si/fileadmin/mk.gov.si/pageuploads/Ministrstvo/ Podatki/Letna_porocila/2011/Analiza_stanja_na_podrocju_kulture_s_predlogi_prednost-nih_ciljev-marec_2011_popravljeno28032011.pdf>.

60   Volasko, *op. cit.* note 46.

- lack of coordination among the elements of reputation management (destination of country branding, public and cultural diplomacy);
- absence of strategic coordination among institutions and actors involved in country promotion;
- relative infancy of the countries (since the early 1990s);
- politicized country promotion (domestic politics);
- lack of continuity and strategic approach; government instead of country promotion.[61]

For Slovenia, the lack of coordination and strategic planning in the MFA according to the state's needs has been a central problem. This was also stressed by CMEPIUS[62] and Volasko,[63] who note that it had a negative impact on the development of specific (soft power) capabilities.[64] Accordingly, key instruments for strengthening Slovenia's influence (not only its presence) in the field of science and education should be(come):

(1)   internationalization of education, science and industry by linking research networks to joint degree programs with renowned universities that are attractive for foreign audiences (students and researchers);
(2)   sufficient human resource investment in order to facilitate creativity, innovations, individual and collective responsibility both at the level of public administration as well as the private sector;
(3)   building strategic (bilateral) partnerships.[65]

To conclude, Slovenian cultural diplomacy has encountered some typical problems that especially small states should avoid. Two of them appear to be particularly challenging. Firstly, internally uncoordinated formulation and implementation of soft power foreign policy tools[66] along with politicization

---

61   György Szondi, "Central and Eastern European Public Diplomacy: A Transitional Perspective on National Reputation Management", in Nancy Snow and Philip M. Taylor (eds.), *Routledge Handbook of Public Diplomacy* (Routledge, London, 2009), 17–19.

62   CMEPIUS, *op. cit.* note 49.

63   Volasko, *op. cit.* note 46.

64   For instance, the Department for International Cultural Relations has been reorganized and transferred between different administration structures four times since 1991 and is seriously understaffed. As a consequence, its competences also constantly change. These changes are entirely dependent on the changes in the political system and the recruitment of public officials. Ministry of Culture, *op. cit.* note 59, 366–367.

65   Volasko, *op. cit.* note 46.

66   As we have shown, these agents are: the MFA, the MC, the Ministry of Higher Education, Science and Technology, the Ministry of the Interior, the Ministry of Labor, Family and

have caused under-development of capabilities and policy substance. Secondly, poorly developed strategies have focused on multilateral implementation of cultural international relations rather than on capacity-building in the field of targeted multilateral (education) and strategic bilateral (in the geographical proximity) cultural diplomacy where Slovenia's soft power presence and influence could be achieved with more success.

5   Slovenian Implementation of Cultural Diplomacy and Erasmus
         Educational Exchange Program

The data in this part of the chapter are based on an online survey conducted in the spring of 2013 among 1,153 Slovenian students at the University of Ljubljana (UL)[67] who have been included in an exchange program abroad and among 873 foreign students who have come to the UL for an educational exchange program, both in the last 4 academic years (2009/10–2012/13).[68] An additional survey was conducted subsequently in 2013 using two different methods of questioning, namely small focus groups (with foreign students) and e-mail interviews (with students at the UL).

       The quantitative survey shows that most students coming to the UL are from CEECs, followed by Southern and then Western European students. The least populous group of students is the one from the countries of former Yugoslavia,

---

Social Affairs, the Government Communication Office and the Slovenian Tourist Board. The government seems to have realized this problem and in 2012 it merged the agencies for promotion of investments, tourism and technology into a single agency SPIRIT Slovenia (Public Agency of the Republic of Slovenia for the Promotion of Entrepreneurship, Innovation, Development, Investment and Tourism). See <http://www.spiritslovenia.si/en>.

67   The University of Ljubljana (UL) is the largest and the oldest Slovenian university, public in nature, encompassing 22 faculties and 3 academies, covering fields from social sciences and humanities to natural sciences, (bio-)technical sciences and medicine. More information available at <http://www.uni-lj.si/en/>.

68   The aim of the survey was to establish where UL-based students and exchange students at the UL see the differences in knowledge, skills and study conditions between their home and host universities. The qualitative part of the survey also looked into micro dynamics of the study process, which is not the focus of this chapter. See Ana Bojinović Fenko and Ana Slavec, "Primerljivost študentov UL in tujih študentov na UL na mednarodni izmenjavi: znanje, veščine in pogoji za študij (Comparability of Students at the UL and Foreign Exchange Students at the UL: Knowledge, Skills and Study Conditions)", an online survey,

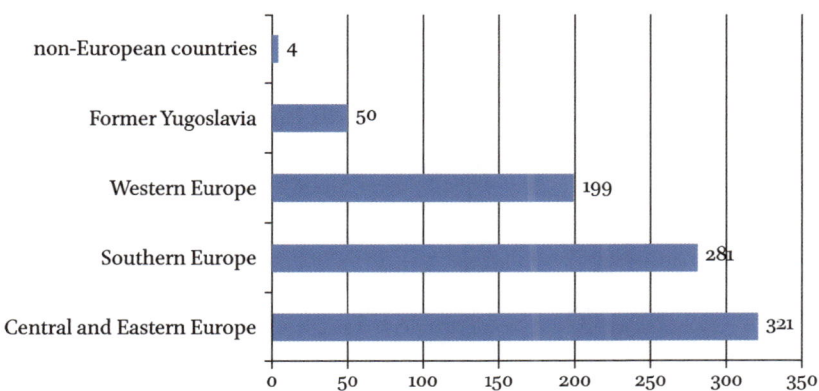

GRAPH 9.3   *Origin of foreign exchange students at the UL in the last 4 Years*[69]

which was not covered by Erasmus in the research period, but by programs such as Basileus and CEEPUS(Graph 9.3).

The focus group interviews additionally showed that the foreign students had decided to come to study to the UL, and to Slovenia, for various reasons – mainly to explore the Slovenian culture, because of its proximity to the Balkans and also to be able to travel to the Balkans.[70] Their references were also their home university professors, who recommended the UL for academic excellence, and former exchange students at the UL, who recommended the UL because they experienced Ljubljana as an excellent city with a highly student-friendly environment.[71] In general, the study shows that a higher share of Slovenian exchange students assesses their knowledge and skills as better compared to those of domestic students' at their host universities than foreign exchange students at the UL assess their knowledge as better compared to Slovenian domestic students.[72] Moreover, the average grade of a UL-based student abroad was higher in 42% of the cases, whereas only 32% of the exchange students at the UL polled had a higher average grade during their time

---

as part of the week of Slovenian university movement "Svobodna univerza" (Free university) (15–18 April 2013).

69   *Ibid.*

70   Focus group interviews – foreign, focus group and e-mail interviews with foreign exchange students at the University of Ljubljana, Faculty of Social Sciences by Ana Bojinović Fenko, Ljubljana (5 June–3 July 2013).

71   Bojinović Fenko and Slavec, *op. cit.* note 68.

72   UL-based exchange students assessed their knowledge as better in higher rates (foreign languages 69%, skills of academic writing 55% and information research 45%) compared

at the UL.[73] Study conditions[74] at the UL were assessed as the same (40%) or better than at the foreign students' home universities, although the conditions vary notably among different faculties of the UL, especially in terms of offering classes in English.[75] Finally, a greater share of foreign exchange students at the UL would recommend the university to their peers for purely academic reasons (94%) compared to only 85% of UL-based students who would do the same for their exchange host university. Other general positive aspects of Slovenia and those related to the university and academic society, as reported by foreign exchange students, refer to: good organization of the exchange (Erasmus exchange office at the UL), good organization of student social events, good infrastructure and system for students, and the positive effects of the UL being situated in a small but still a capital city.[76] This analysis confirms that, in the case of the UL, the potential for good image-building of the Slovenian academic environment and thus also a positive image of the state is quite high. In August 2013, two Erasmus Master's students from the Netherlands and Austria even published a music video shot in Ljubljana, and named it the *Erasmus anthem "Feelin Fine"*, portraying Ljubljana as "the best Erasmus city".[77]

However, in terms of benefiting from this positive image created with exchange students in the sense of long-term effects (turning presence into influence), the state is poorly organized. The most important piece of data that shows the low profile of the (non-existent) strategy on cultural diplomacy through exchange programs is the fact that the state does not give exchange students any organized information on the Republic of Slovenia (e.g. on the history, statehood, political system, geography, culture, educational system, etc.).[78] The foreign students, however, do get a possibility to learn (for a charge) Slovenian for a month before they start their exchange.[79] Furthermore, the

---

to that of domestic students at foreign universities. Focus group interviews – foreign, *op. cit.* note 70.

73   *Ibid.*

74   As study conditions, the survey measured: the amount of obligatory work per week, severity of conditions to be fulfilled before taking the final exam, access to literature, conditions for studying in the library, research equipment, accessibility of teachers, and opportunities to engage in additional research activities. *Ibid.*

75   *Ibid.*

76   *Ibid.*

77   Available at <http://www.youtube.com/watch?v=4WpjGSsZTfE>.

78   Focus group interviews – foreign, *op. cit.* note 70.

79   For comparison, some European universities promote their national language, history, and culture within the so-called orientation week for all exchange students; this would be organized together with language courses by a university-affiliated language or similar

management of exchange students' experience in Slovenia is extremely poor after they leave the country. The choice of the UL for our case study is very relevant as the share of foreign exchange students in the total number of students is only about 4%.[80]

The UL does not collect any data from foreign exchange students after they leave the UL, which means that no feedback on their experience is received nor is a body of alumni formed that would enable foreigners in their individual professional careers to keep contact with the Slovenian state (e.g. with invitations to events at the Slovenian embassy).[81] This is confirmed by the first-ever analysis and evaluation of effects of the Erasmus exchange program on Slovenian higher education; a survey conducted by CMEPIUS in 2013, in which almost 40% of exchange students reported that: "No one is interested in their Erasmus exchange experience at their home institution."[82] The lack of a systematic approach is thus the main reason for the missed opportunity of the Slovenian state to profit from the EU's Erasmus educational exchange program and to transform its soft power capability into influence in the EU. This is also reflected in CMEPIUS's recommendations to all Slovenian higher education institutions, which can be extrapolated to improving the state's systemic environment for internationalization of higher education: (1) "a systematic approach to organizing education for foreign students", (2) "the formulation of an international education profile" and "developing networks of preferred partner institutions", (3) developing "a greater share of programs and courses in foreign languages", (4) "a reform of the curricula with greater emphasis on internationalization", and (5) "increasing services and capabilities in order to successfully implement the internationalization strategy."[83]

---

center. In some countries, students are invited to presentations of national cuisine. E-mail interviews – home, e-mail interviews with exchange students from the University of Ljubljana, Faculty of Social Sciences by Ana Bojinović Fenko, Ljubljana (29–31 July 2013).

80   UL International Office, a telephone interview with Ms. Helena Deršek Štuhec, officer of the UL International Office by Ana Bojinović Fenko, Ljubljana (11 June 2013). Figures for academic year 2014/15: the total number of students at the UL was 42,921, while the total number of foreign exchange students was 1865. See University of Ljubljana, "Business Report by the Chancellor" (2014), available at <https://www.uni-lj.si/o_univerzi_v _ljubljani/organizacija__pravilniki_in_porocila/poslovno_financno_in_letno_porocilo _ter_program_dela/>.

81   *Ibid.*

82   Evalvacija učinkov programa Erasmus na visoko šolstvo v Sloveniji (Evaluation of Effects of the Erasmus Program on Higher Education in Slovenia), CMEPIUS (2013), available at <http://www.cmepius.si/wp-content/uploads/2014/02/Evalvacijska-studija-vpliva-na -visoko-solstvo_web.pdf>.

83   *Ibid.*

6   Conclusion

Despite its small size, Slovenia does possess some capabilities of soft power, such as natural attributes, tourism opportunities, rich and diverse culture, and especially academic excellence. We have demonstrated that Slovenia's EU accession and high profile within important regional governmental organizations during its presidencies, and some successes in non-political or economic issue areas have raised its presence on the European and even global scale (indices IEPG and IEPE), but the state is still incapable of demonstrating such influence in the fields of soft power – such as internationalization of education and science or through cultural centers – to be included in the top ranks of soft power indices. As seen in the case study of the implementation of student exchange programs at the biggest Slovenian university, the University of Ljubljana, the institution has a very high academic potential, which can be operationalized into foreign policy capability, but the state and occasionally the university itself lack crucial elements of a quality policy-making process and strategic governance, namely: coordination among areas of country promotion, and strategic coordination between supporting institutions for student exchanges and actors involved in country promotion. The biggest problem seems to be generally inept human resource management, which merits immediate political benefits over professionalism, independent expertise, and healthy mutually reinforcing cooperation with agents of the civil society. As the state has recognized and started addressing some of these underdeveloped cultural capabilities – particularly academic potential also by conducting a nation-wide analysis and developing national strategic documents – we can only hope to see them transformed into powerful tools of foreign policy influence, which so far remain one of the missed opportunities of Slovenian EU membership.

Bibliography

Atkinson, Carol. (2010) "Does Soft Power Matter? A Comparative Analysis of Student Exchange Programs 1980–2006", 6(1) *Foreign Policy Analysis*, 1–22.

Behringer, Ronald M. (2005) "Middle Power Leadership on the Human Security Agenda", 40(3) *Cooperation and Conflict*, 305–342.

Bojinović, Ana. (2005) "Geographical Proximity and Historical Context as a Basis of Active Foreign Policy Strategy of Small European Sates: The Case of Austria and Slovenia Regarding the Western Balkans", 1(1) *Politics in Central Europe*, 8–29.

Bojinović Fenko, Ana and Požgan, Jure. (2014) "Regionalisation of Slovenian Foreign Policy: Back to the Balkans", 14(1) *Studia Historica Slovenica*, 217–230.

Bojinović Fenko, Ana and Šabič, Zlatko. (2014) "Continuity and Change in Slovenia's Foreign Policy: A Comparison to Yugoslavia and an Analysis of the Post-Independence Period", in Keil, Soeren and Stahl, Bernhard. (eds.), *The Foreign Policies of Post-Yugoslav States: From Yugoslavia to Europe* (Palgrave Macmillan, Basingstoke), 47–67.

Bretherton, Charlotte and Vogler, John. (2006) "Conceptualizing Actors and Actorness", in Bretherton, Charlotte and Vogler, John. (eds.), *The European Union as a Global Actor* (Routledge, London), 11–34.

Brighi, Elisabetta and Hill, Christopher. (2008) "Implementation and Behaviour", in Smith, Steve, Hadfield, Amelia and Dunne, Tim. (eds.), *Foreign Policy: Theories, Actors, Cases* (Oxford University Press, Oxford), 117–135.

Fischer, Markus. (2006) "Culture and Foreign Politics", in Schaffer, Brenda. (ed.), *The Limits of Culture: Islam and Foreign Policy* (MIT Press, London), 27–64.

Hey, Jeanne A.K. (2003) "Introducing Small State Foreign Policy", in Hey, Jeanne A.K. (ed.), *Small States in World Politics: Explaining Foreign Policy Behavior* (Lynne Rienner, London), 1–12.

Lovec, Marko. (2012) "The European Union is no Free Lunch: Reconsidering the Eastern Enlargement of the EU from an Intergovernmental Perspective", 17(66) *Croatian International Relations Review*, 31–58.

Manheim, Jarol B. (1990) *Strategic Public Diplomacy: The Evolution of Influence* (Oxford University Press, New York).

Mattern, Janice Bially. (2007) "Why 'Soft Power' isn't so Soft: Representational Force and Attraction in World Politics", in Berenskoetter, Felix and Williams, M.J. (eds.), *Power in World Politics* (Routledge, Oxon), 98–119.

McClory, Jonathan. (2013) *The New Persuaders II: A 2011 Global Ranking of Soft Power* (Institute for Government, London), available at <http://www.instituteforgovernment.org.uk/sites/default/files/publications/The%20New%20PersuadersII_0.pdf>.

McClory, Jonathan. (2010) *The New Persuaders: An International Ranking of Soft Power* (Institute for Government, London), available at <http://www.instituteforgovernment.org.uk/pdfs/new_persuaders_soft_power.pdf>.

Mor, Ben D. (2007) "The Rhetoric of Public Diplomacy and Propaganda Wars: A View from Self-Presentation Theory", 64(5) *European Journal of Political Research*, 661–683.

Nye, Joseph S. (2011) "Power and Foreign Policy", 4(1) *Journal of Political Power*, 9–24.

Nye, Joseph S. (2009) "Get Smart", 84(4) *Foreign Affairs*, 160–163.

Ohnesorge, Hendrik W. (2014) "Making the Intangibles Tangible: Soft Power and its Subunits", paper presented at the Emerging Scholars Forum at the ISA West Annual Conference 2014 (Pasadena CA, 26 September).

Požgan, Jure and Bojinović Fenko, Ana. (2012) "Kulturna diplomacija in kultura v mednarodnih odnosih: študija primera slovenske zunanje politike (Cultural Diplomacy and Culture in International Relations: A Case Study of Slovenian Foreign Policy)", 28(69) *Družboslovne razprave*, 8–29.

Reeves, Julie. (2004) *Culture and International Relations: Narratives, Natives and Tourists* (Routledge, London).

Šabič, Zlatko and Bukowski, Charles. (eds.) (2002) *Small States in the Post-Cold War Period: Slovenia and NATO Enlargement* (Praeger, Westport CT).

Szondi, György. (2009) "Central and Eastern European Public Diplomacy: A Transitional Perspective on National Reputation Management", in Snow, Nancy and Taylor, Philip M. (eds.), *Routledge Handbook of Public Diplomacy* (Routledge, London), 292–313.

Warren, T. Camber. (2014) "Not by the Sword Alone: Soft Power, Mass Media, and the Production of State Sovereignty", 68(1) *International Organization*, 111–141.

Wivel, Anders. (2005) "The Security Challenge of Small EU Member States: Interests, Identity and the Development of the EU as a Security Actor", 43(2) *Journal of Common Market Studies*, 393–412.

CHAPTER 10

The Harmonization of Laws on Same-Sex Unions in Post-Communist Post-Accession Countries

Alar Kilp

Abstract

EU law on same-sex unions (SSU) expects Member States to legally recognize the family life of same-sex couples in the form of marriage, partnership, or cohabitation. The normative expectation, which in about 2010 became a principled position of the EU institutions and the European Court of Human Rights, has not been endorsed by one Western European Member State (Italy) as well as the majority of the post-Communist Member States (Bulgaria, Latvia, Lithuania, Poland, Romania, and Slovakia). There are a number of causes behind the failure to enact SSU laws: the legacies of the communist regimes, the prevalence of a certain interpretation of Christian doctrine, the medium level of economic affluence, and an unfavorable balance of power between the change and blocking coalitions of social, religious, and political actors.

Unlike Western European countries, where the family life of same-sex unions was legally recognized primarily due to pressures from below (due to changes in public opinion and shifts in cultural values), governments and legislatures in most Central and Eastern European Member States are encouraged more from above (by the European Union and the Council of Europe). Therefore, the prospects for legal recognition of same-sex unions are slim in countries where the European normative agenda meets no significant support from domestic social values or religious and political actors. This conflict of national and EU forces is most likely to persist in Member States which are post-Soviet, culturally Orthodox, not shifted from materialist to post-materialist values, and governed by right-wing governmental coalitions.

Keywords

veto-players – same-sex unions – European Court of Human Rights – value change

1   Introduction

Twelve years after the extension of the European Union to Central and Eastern Europe (CEE), the European Union is internally split as far as the legal recognition of the same-sex couples is concerned. Despite the unwavering commitment of European institutions to consider legal recognition of the family life of same-sex couples as a part of universal human rights, this principle is not followed by a significant group of EU Member States (Bulgaria, Italy, Latvia, Lithuania, Poland, Romania, and Slovakia) which do not legally recognize same-sex unions, partnerships, cohabitations, or marriages. Additionally, six of EU member nations (Bulgaria, Croatia, Hungary, Latvia, Lithuania, Poland, and Slovakia) have adopted constitutional bans on same-sex marriage.

This chapter will proceed in two parts. It will firstly start with an outline of the formation of EU law on same-sex unions (SSUs) since the Treaty of Amsterdam, which, for the first time, included "sexual orientation" within the EU framework on anti-discrimination policy. Thereafter, the first accession round of post-Communist countries (1998–2004) was characterized by relatively weak conditionality as far as the rights of homosexuals were concerned. The main points of focus were on the decriminalization of consenting same-sex relations, the protection of homosexuals in labor relations, and their rights of assembly. In about 2010, the institutions of the European Union and the European Court of Human Rights (ECtHR) started to adopt a position, which does not mandate the legalization of same-sex marriages, but expects Member States to recognize the family life of same-sex couples.

The second part of this chapter will assess the response of post-Communist Member States to the agenda and law of the EU and European institutions on SSUs against four alternative explanations. The failure to legally recognize the "family life of same-sex unions" is explained by: the political legacy of types of communism in the post-Communist and post-Soviet regions of Europe; the cultural legacy of the religious (Catholic, Orthodox, Lutheran) tradition; variations in the level of socioeconomic development; and the dependence of the policy outcome on the balance of power between the change and the blocking coalitions that consist of social, political and religious actors.

2   Formation of European Law on Same-Sex Unions

As of February 2016, the majority of EU countries have introduced same-sex union (SSU) laws either by legally recognized same-sex partnership, civil union, or marriage. At the national level, same-sex marriage was legalized first in the Netherlands in 2001, but the transition from legal hetero-normativity to homo-normalization surpassed the threshold of recognition of registered partnerships for same-sex couples first in Denmark in 1989.[1] Both changes in the legal recognition of SSUs were positively conditioned by a cultural trend toward widespread tolerance of homosexuality.[2] By 2016, same-sex marriages were legal in Belgium, Denmark, France, Iceland, Ireland, Luxembourg, the Netherlands, Norway, Portugal, Spain, Sweden, and the UK. Other forms of SSU registration schemes exist in the remaining Western European countries with the exception of Italy, which does not legally recognize SSUs. In the post-Communist region, Croatia recognized unregistered same-sex cohabitations in 2003, and registered partnerships were recognized in the Czech Republic and Slovenia in 2006, and in Hungary in 2009.[3] In October 2014, the Estonian parliament passed the gender-neutral Cohabitation Act, which allows cohabitating couples to register their relationship at a notary. SSUs are legally unrecognized in Bulgaria, Latvia, Lithuania, Poland, Romania, and Slovakia.[4]

Some of Member States from CEE have limited marriage constitutionally to heterosexual couples *after* EU accession, and the related clauses have been adopted in Latvia (2005), Hungary (2011), and Croatia (2013). Constitutional bans on same-sex marriage from the pre-accession era continue to exist in Bulgaria, Lithuania, Poland, and Romania.[5] On the surface, the latter policy

---

1   The conceptualization of a shift from hetero-normative to homo-normalized legislation is borrowed from Sasha Roseneil *et al.* who conceptualize the shift from hetero-normativity towards legal "homo-normalization" as a process which starts from the decriminalization of homosexuality and the protection of homosexuals from violence, and ends with the legal inclusion of homosexuals "as full and equal citizens" with their intimate relationships and parenting relationships recognized and protected on equal grounds with the heterosexual couples. Sasha Roseneil *et al.*, "Changing Landscapes of Heteronormativity: The Regulation and Normalization of Same-Sex Sexualities in Europe", 20(2) *Social Politics* (2013), 165–199, at 186.

2   For an outline and discussion of the process of transition from hetero-normative to homo-normalized legislation, see Judit Takács and Ivett Szalma, "Homophobia and Same-Sex Partnership Legislation in Europe", 30(5) *Equality Diversity and Inclusion* (2011), 356–378, at 358.

3   Ian Curry-Sumner, "Interstate Recognition of Same-Sex Relationships in Europe", 13(1) *Journal of Gender, Race & Justice* (2009), 59–80, at 61–63; and Aleksander Štulhofer and Ivan Rimac, "Determinants of Homonegativity in Europe", 46(1) *Journal of Sex Research* (2009), 24–32.

4   Website of the European Commission, available at: <http://europa.eu/youreurope/citizens/family/couple/registered-partners/index_en.htm>.

5   ustin Borg-Barthet, "The Principled Imperative to Recognize Same-Sex Unions in the EU", 8(2) *Journal of Private Law* (2012), 359–388, at 374.

choice on SSUS seems more continuous or even legally "coherent" as the national authorities do not recognize *any* form of "family life" between same-sex partners. On the contrary, Hungary and Croatia constitutionally exclude same-sex *marriages* while they both legally recognize same-sex *partnerships* or *cohabitations*. In Hungary, various types of same-sex partnerships were legally recognized long before accession to the EU (unregistered same-sex cohabitations have been recognized since 1996). Nevertheless, immediately *after* EU accession in December 2005, a constitutional ban on same-sex *marriages* was adopted[6] and the new Hungarian Constitution of 2011 defined marriage "to be the conjugal union of a man and a woman."[7] Similar contradiction remains also in Estonia, where the Cohabitation Act recognizes same-sex cohabitations, while Family Law Act limits the definition of marriage to heterosexual couples.[8]

On the European level, the Court of Justice of the European Union (CJEU) and the European Court of Human Rights (ECtHR) approach the issue by the doctrine of the "margin of appreciation."[9] Both expect all Member States not to discriminate between same-sex and different-sex cohabitations in situations where domestic law extends certain benefits to cohabiting different-sex partners, but do not mandate the legal recognition of same-sex *marriages*. In *Römer v. Freie und Hansestadt Hamburg* (2011), the CJEU argued that even when member-state restricts marriage to opposite-sex couples, it has to grant same-sex couples access to all the employment benefits granted to married couples.[10] Recently in *Oliari and Others v. Italy* (2015), the ECtHR insisted that the absence of legal recognition of homosexual relationships violates the right to respect for private and family life guaranteed by Article 8 of the European Convention of Human Rights.[11] While Member States of the EU and of the Council of Europe (CoE) are bound by similar set of principles and norms, countries which are neither EU members nor applicants (such as the Russian Federation) face significantly less "pressure from above", because "[t]he CoE

---

6   Kate Spencer, "Same Sex Couples and the Right to Marry: European Perspectives", 6(1) *Cambridge Student Law Review* (2010), 155–176, at 172.

7   Renáta Uitz, "Lessons from Sexual Orientation Discrimination in Central Europe", 60(1) *The American Journal of Comparative Law* (2012), 235–264, at 250.

8   Estonia's Family Law Act defines marriage as a contract "between a man and a woman" (§1.1.). Conformably, "a marriage is void if persons of the same sex are married" (§10.1). Family Law Act of the Estonia, available at: <archive.equal-jus-.eu/193/>.

9   Spencer, *op. cit.* note 6, 160.

10 *Römer v. Freie und Hansestadt Hamburg* (10 May 2011) C-147/08.

11 *Oliari and Others v. Italy* (21 October 2015) Nos. 18766/11 and 36030/11.

does not have the same enforcement mechanisms as the EU, which has clear rules on the superiority of European law over national law and special powers of enforcement."[12]

EU commitment to a principle whereby all human rights apply to homosexuals as they apply to heterosexuals is manifested in the "Guidelines to Promote and Protect the Enjoyment of All Human Rights by Lesbian, Gay, Bisexual, Transgender and Intersex (LGBTI) Persons" of 2013, which states:

> LGBTI persons have the same rights as all other individuals – no new human rights are created for them and none should be denied to them. The EU is committed to the principle of the universality of human rights and reaffirms that cultural, traditional or religious values cannot be invoked to justify any form of discrimination, including discrimination against LGBTI persons.[13]

Similar commitment is recognizable in three recent cases adjudicated by the ECtHR. In *Schalk and Kopf v Austria* case (2010), the ECtHR recognized that cohabiting same-sex couple living in a stable partnerships falls within the notion of "family life."[14] The Court did not expect the states to have a uniform SSU law, but proclaimed clearly that the states should recognize the family life of same-sex couples.[15] In 2013, the ECtHR upheld during *Vallianatos and Others v. Greece* case that Greek civil union law which does not extend to same-sex couples violates Articles 8 (right to respect for private and family life) and 14 (prohibition of discrimination) of the European Convention on Human

---

12   Ronald Holzhacker, "State-Sponsored Homophobia and the Denial of the Right of Assembly in Central and Eastern Europe: The 'Boomerang' and the 'Ricochet' between European Organizations and Civil Society to Uphold Human Rights", 35(1–2) *Law & Policy* (2013), 1–28, at 5.

13   The Council of the European Union, "Guidelines to Promote and Protect the Enjoyment of All Human Rights by Lesbian, Gay, Bisexual, Transgender and Intersex (LGBTI) Persons" (24 June 2013), available at <http://www.consilium.europa.eu/uedocs/cms_Data/docs/pressdata/EN/foraff/137584.pdf>. Earlier, the same principle was affirmed by Council of the European Union, "Toolkit to Promote and Protect the Enjoyment of All Human Rights by Lesbian, Gay, Bisexual and Transgender (LGBT) people" (17 June 2010), available at <http://www.consilium.europa.eu/uedocs/cmsUpload/st11179.en10.pdf>.

14   *Schalk and Kopf v. Austria* (24 June 2010) No. 30141/04. For an extended discussion of this case, see Jens M. Scherpe, "The Legal Recognition of Same-Sex Couples in Europe and the Role of the European Court of Human Rights", 10 *The Equal Rights Review* (2013), 83–96.

15   Scherpe, *ibid.*, 91–92.

Rights.[16] Another important step in framing European law on ssus was taken in the case *Alekseyev v. Russia* (2010), which focused primarily on the right of freedom of assembly for homosexuals. By considering the discourses of "public safety", protection of "public morality" and the special status of a dominant religion in society as invalid justifications for limiting the rights of homosexuals, the Court made a strong statement that the rights of homosexuals extend beyond the domestic sphere.[17] In the *Alekseyev* case, however, the Court confirmed the "margin of appreciation" that national authorities can use in granting or withholding the legal right to marry for same-sex couples.[18] This expectation is further expressed in recent resolutions of the European Parliament, which expects all Member States to recognize same-sex families and condemns the policies of Member States that exclude same-sex couples from the definition of "family."[19] The watershed for the progressive normalization of same-sex sexualities reached a point where EU law adopted a principled position regarding the legal protection of the "family life" of same-sex couples. Still, the regulation of transnational family law has largely been beyond EU competence.[20]

Although the EU had already advised Poland (as well as Malta and Italy) in May 2006 to legalize homosexual partnerships,[21] the emphasis on the "conditionality" of accession criteria during the period from 1998 to 2004 focused

---

16   "Reasons for Excluding Same-Sex Couples from 'Civil Unions' under Greek Law were not Convincing", press release issued by the Registrar of the Court, ECtHR 329 (7 November 2013), available at <http://www.tanea.gr/files/1/2013/europeancourt.pdf>.

17   *Alekseyev v Russia* (21 October 2010), No. 4916/07, No. 25924/08 and No. 14599/09. For a detailed analysis of the Judgment, see Paul Johnson, "Homosexuality, Freedom of Assembly and the Margin of Appreciation Doctrine of the European Court of Human Rights: Alekseyev v Russia", 11(3) *Human Rights Law Review* (2011), 578–593, at 582–589.

18   Holzhacker, *op. cit.* note 12, 15.

19   European Parliament, Resolution of 13 March 2012 on Equality between Women and Men in the European Union, available at <http://www.europarl.europa.eu/sides/getDoc.do?type=TA&language=EN&reference=P7-TA-2012-69>; *id.*, Resolution of 29 March 2012 on the EU Citizenship Report 2010: Dismantling the Obstacles to EU Citizens' Rights (2011/2182(INI)), available at <http://www.europarl.europa.eu/sides/getDoc.do?type=TA&language=EN&reference=P7-TA-2012-120>; and *id.*, Resolution of 24 May 2012 on the Fight against Homophobia in Europe (2012/2657(RSP)), available at <http://www.europarl.europa.eu/sides/getDoc.do?type=TA&language=EN&reference=P7-TA-2012-222>.

20   Borg-Barthet, *op. cit.* note 5, 359.

21   Anja Hennig, "Morality politics in a Catholic Democracy: A Hard Road Towards Liberalization of Gay Rights in Poland", in Jeffrey Haynes (ed.), *Religion and Politics in Europe, the Middle East and North Africa* (Routledge, London, 2010), 212.

on the protection of homosexuals from violence and discrimination, but did not lay much focus on the laws on ssus. During that period, EU law on homosexuality was focused primarily on the decriminalization of consenting same-sex relations (e.g. Romania),[22] rights of assembly, and labor laws. "Sexual orientation" was included in EU anti-discrimination policy within Article 13 of the Amsterdam Treaty (entered into force on 1 May 1999), forbidding "discrimination based on sex, racial or ethnic origin, religion or belief, disability, age or sexual orientation."[23] The framework for equal treatment was further expressed in the directive of the European Council,[24] included within the Charter of Fundamental Rights of the European Union[25] and the Treaty on the Functioning of the European Union.[26] In general, however, pre-2004 EU conditionality on gay rights was weak,[27] as it lacked a clear-cut position on the legal recognition of ssus. Since 2010, the harmonization of national legislation on ssus has become both a major concern and unresolved issue for the EU.

---

22   Jürgen Gerhards, "Non-Discrimination towards Homosexuality: The European Union's Policy and Citizens' Attitudes towards Homosexuality in 27 European Countries", 25(1) *International Sociology* (2010), 5–28, at 8.

23   Treaty of Amsterdam amending the Treaty on European Union, the Treaties Establishing the European Communities and Related Acts, available at: <http://eur-lex.europa.eu/ en/treaties/dat/11997D/htm/11997D.html>. Before the Amsterdam Treaty, which was the first to mention "sexual orientation" as part of anti-discrimination policy, the "EU could not legislatively prohibit discrimination based on sexual orientation" and "gay people in the EU did not have a specific prohibited ground of discrimination to rely on, should discrimination occur." Dimitry Kochenov, "Gay Rights in the EU: A Long Way Forward for the Union of 27", 3 *Croatian Yearbook of European Law and Policy* (2007), 469–490, at 476; and *id.*, "On Options of Citizens and Moral Choices of States: Gays and European Federalism", 33(1) *Fordham International Law Journal* (2009), 156–205, at 173.

24   Council Directive 2000/78/EC of European Council of 27 November 2000 required equal treatment of homosexuals and heterosexuals in employment and occupation, and forbid discrimination on the ground of sexual orientation, available at <http://eur-lex.europa. eu/LexUriServ/LexUriServ.do?uri=CELEX:32000L0078:en:HTML>.

25   Since 2000, Article 21 of the Charter of Fundamental Rights of the European Union includes prohibition of discrimination on the grounds of sexual orientation, available at <http://www.europarl.europa.eu/charter/pdf/text_en.pdf>.

26   Articles 10 and 19 of the Treaty on the Functioning of the European Union (TFEU) express the commitment to combat discrimination based on sexual orientation, TFEU is available at <http://eur-lex.europa.eu/LexUriServ/LexUriServ.do?uri=OJ:C:2008:115:0047:0199 :EN:PDF>.

27   Conor O'Dwyer and Katrina Z.S. Schwartz, "Minority Rights after EU Enlargement: A Comparison of Antigay Politics in Poland and Latvia", 8(2) *Comparative European Politics* (2010), 220–243, at 221.

This can be attributed to the fact that as long as the same-sex couples are not legally recognized in all Member States, the "families of same-sex couples do not enjoy the same free movements rights as opposite-sex couples."[28] The related discrepancies of national legislation have persisted mostly, but not only, within the post-Communist region.

The following discussion outlines the patterns of responses to EU law and influence among eleven post-Communist Member States in general, and in Poland and Latvia in particular. The accession processes and their aftermath stirred up interaction between the EU and national governments as well as social and political activism over the rights of homosexuals in all new Member States. From the perspective of the European Union, however, Poland and Latvia have been markedly problematic both in terms of EU-national government relations with respect to delays in bringing national labor laws into conformity with EU directives,[29] and also with regard to high levels of anti-gay prejudices at the societal level.[30]

3   Regional and National Patterns of SSU Law

Despite variations in national policies towards SSUs, a substantial consensus over morality policies existed among the pre-2004 EU-15. In particular, the EU had become "a community of liberal norms, including civil rights for sexual

---

28   Borg-Barthet, *op. cit.* note 5, 361. In 2009, Kochenov observed that due to divergent national legislation on same-sex unions, "a Dutch same-sex marriage is treated in Belgium, France, Spain, and Sweden, it is not recognized at all in Poland and treated as a registered partnership in the United Kingdom." Kochenov (2009), *op. cit.* note 23, 182.

29   Poland and Latvia were the last Member States to adjust their labor laws in accordance with the EU anti-discrimination norms. In Poland, the tensions with the EU lasted from the 2000s, when the European Parliament mandated changes to the labor code that would remove anti-gay provisions, until the beginning of 2011 when a new anti-discrimination law entered into force and the Polish labor code finally met the EU standards. Conor O'Dwyer, "Does the EU Help or Hinder Gay-Rights Movements in Post-Communist Europe? The case of Poland", 28(4) *East European Politics* (2012), 332–352, at 342; O'Dwyer and Schwartz, *op. cit.* note 27, 225–226; and Richard Mole, "Nationality and Sexuality: Homophobic Discourse and the 'National Threat' in Contemporary Latvia", 17(3) *Nations and Nationalism* (2011), 540–560, at 541.

30   Holzhacker, *op. cit.* note 12, 4; O'Dwyer and Schwartz, *op. cit.* note 27; and Mole, *ibid.* Kochenov has classified Poland and Latvia as both particularly homophobic new Member States and societies with widespread anti-gay prejudices. Kochenov (2007), *op. cit.* note 23, 486.

minorities."[31] Consequently, as the accession process opened up the opportunity for change in this dimension of morality policy, national publics of the post-Communist countries were soon split between those willing to use this situation for changing the legal, cultural, and social status quo, and others increasingly alarmed about potential transformations concerning the social regulation of sexuality and the rising level of perceived sexual permissiveness.

By the beginning of 2016, the national laws on ssus follow a pattern where: (1) no post-Communist Member State has legalized same-sex marriages and Estonia is the only post-Soviet state that has legally recognized same-sex unions; (2) Cyprus and Greece are the only culturally Orthodox countries that have legally recognized same-sex unions, culturally Catholic and Lutheran countries are *split in* the East and are overwhelmingly liberal in the West; (3) the enactment of ssu law is conditioned by the level of socioeconomic development and therefore expected in Eastern Europe "if and when" the antecedent socioeconomic conditions are fulfilled; (4) the successes and failures of the attempts to introduce ssu laws can also be explained by the balance of power among the change and blocking coalitions formed by alliances of social, political, national, transnational and supranational actors and institutions.

First, as the shared experience of communist regimes correlates with the absence of legally recognized same-sex marriages, to what extent can the communist legacy explain cross-national variations in ssu laws? Western European countries that have legally recognized ssus have done so primarily because of the pressures from below (due to changes in public opinion and shifts in cultural values) and not due to the pressures from above (from the EU, European institutions or courts).[32] Eastern European post-Communist governments and legislatures are mainly under the pressure from above. For example, when Latvia adopted a constitutional limitation restricting marriage to heterosexual couples in 2006, this decision was assessed negatively by the EU as an indicator of homo-negativity and the European Parliament called for a "tough action" against Latvia (and also against Poland) on the ground of Article 13 of the Treaty on European Union.[33] Article 13 empowers the Union "to promote its values."

---

31   O'Dwyer and Schwartz *op. cit.* note 27, 221; and Agnieszka Graff, "We Are (Not All) Homophobes: A Report from Poland", 32(2) *Feminist Studies* (2006), 434–449, at 445.

32   Legalization of same-sex marriages in the Netherlands, Belgium and Spain resulted from "a governmental reaction to a shift in public opinion and a recognition of same sex marriage as a human rights issue." Spencer, *op. cit.* note 6, 173.

33   Paul Belien, "Europe's Culture War: Secularism on the March", available at <http://www.brusselsjournal.com/node/2144>. Originally published on *The Washington Times* (23 May 2007).

Had there existed a significant social demand for legal recognition of SSUS (or against of it) among the electorate of the governing parties, the national parliaments and governments could have avoided the (democratic) impasse. At present, however, governments and legislatures in Poland, Romania, and Latvia face neither a clear-cut social demand nor a political incentive to recognize SSUS: the dominant parties may not risk losing the support of constituencies when they preserve the status quo. At the same time, the pressure from the European institutions – and also from transnational social movements – can result in cases of discrimination being brought before the national and European-level courts. The pro-change coalition of supranational institutions and transnational movements may hope that once SSU legislation is passed, the related laws will function as socializing agents and social tolerance of homosexuality will rise accordingly.[34] This logic makes sense as disapproval towards homosexuality tends to be lowest in countries where law permits homosexuals to marry.[35] Consequently, legal recognition of SSUS can be expected to influence positively the levels of social approval towards homosexuality. On the other hand, a strong correlation also exists between high levels of social approval toward homosexuality already at the moment of adoption of SSU laws. Among the post-Communist Member States, major exceptions to this rule are Hungary and Slovenia, which have legally recognized SSUS despite the relatively low level of social acceptance for homosexuality.[36] In situations like these, the leeway for the government is limited as relatively wide-spread homophobic sentiments can be exploited by those social and political actors in order to mobilize anti-gay sentiment and to block legislative change favorable to the gay rights cause.[37]

---

34   The legal recognition of SSUS and social approval of homosexuality are reciprocally influential – higher social tolerance of homosexuality contributes to the adoption of SSU laws and the adopted laws contribute also to the rise of social tolerance of homosexuality.

35   Hanneke van den Akker, Rozemarijn van der Ploeg, and Peer Scheepers, "Disapproval of Homosexuality: Comparative Research on Individual and National Determinants of Disapproval of Homosexuality in 20 European Countries", 25(1) *International Journal of Public Opinion Research* (2013), 64–86, at 69–70. The research findings allow Takács and Szalma to advise policy-makers in countries where "equal treatment of lesbian and gay citizens has not yet been achieved", not "to sit back and wait until society will slowly 'mature' by itself, and homophobia would not prevail any longer", but to speed up this process "by introducing and using legal institutions providing equal rights for all." Takács and Szalma, *op. cit.* note 2, 375.

36   Uitz has argued that the legal changes in Hungary and Slovenia are "clearly not driven mainly by changing social attitudes or by a new social consensus which overwhelmingly accepts gays and lesbians", because "animosity towards gays and lesbians remains tangible." Uitz, *op. cit.* note 7, 252.

37   *Ibid.*

According to a Eurobarometer survey in 2006 (when the Czech Republic and Slovenia initiated the some legalization of SSUs), overall social attitudes regarding homosexual marriage demonstrated a strong correlation between the types of SSU laws and public attitudes. The Netherlands, which legalized same-sex marriages first, had the highest (82%) approval of homosexual marriages, while the Southern European countries which do not recognize SSUs in any form, had the lowest levels of approval (14% in Cyprus, 15% in Greece, 18% in Malta, and 31% in Italy). The only post-Communist country above the European average (44%) was the Czech Republic (52%). Among the post-Communist countries, the support for same-sex marriages was lowest in Romania (11%), followed by Latvia (12%) – which held the lowest level regarding approval of same-sex marriage among Member States of EU-25 in 2006 – Bulgaria (15%), Poland (17%), Hungary (18%), Slovakia (19%), and Estonia (21%).[38]

The EU accession process opened up a "window of opportunity" for changes in morality policies, brought the rights of homosexuals into public debates, and stirred up the grassroots mobilization of the gay-rights movement both before and after accession. In both Poland and Latvia, during the immediate aftermath of EU accession (from 2004 until 2007), rising, but relatively weak pro-gay activism attempted to confront the hegemonic anti-gay mobilization.[39] At that time, the clash between pro- and anti-gay agendas and coalitions centered mostly on gay parade marches, which tended to bring the homosexual lifestyle out from the closet and into to the public sphere. Anti-gay mobilizations were headed by national governments and capital city mayors representing (in this dimension of morality) illiberal, conservative, and nationalist right-wing political parties, which either attempted to ban, or did ban, gay parades planned for 2005 and 2006.[40] For European institutions, the bans on gay marches indicated state-sponsored homophobia.[41] In January 2006, the European Parliament issued a resolution on homophobia in Europe, which had Poland and Latvia as the main targets of concern.[42] Likewise, the ECtHR, in *Baczkowski v.*

---

38 European Commission, "Eurobarometer 66: Public Opinion in the European Union- First Results" (2006), available at <http://ec.europa.eu/public_opinion/archives/eb/eb66/eb66_highlights_en.pdf>.

39 O'Dwyer and Schwartz, *op. cit.* note 27; and Graff, *op. cit.* note 31, 434–435.

40 O'Dwyer and Schwartz, *op. cit.* note 27, 221.

41 Holzhacker, *op. cit.* note 12.

42 O'Dwyer and Schwartz, *op. cit.* note 27, 233; and European Parliament, Resolution on Homophobia in Europe, available at <http://www.europarl.europa.eu/sides/getDoc.do?pubRef=-//EP//TEXT+TA+P6-TA-2006-0018+0+DOC+XML+V0//EN>.

Poland, declared the ban on the 2005 Warsaw parade a violation of freedom of assembly, as protected by Article 11 of the European Convention.[43] After 2007, the tensions between pro- and anti-gay rights coalitions in Poland dissipated. While limiting of the rights of association and labor rights of homosexuals is unlikely, the same can also be said for the extension of homosexual rights in the form of legal recognition of same-sex unions.[44] As the status of SSU law is similar in highly religious Poland, a state with a strong church-nation connection, as well as in the relatively secular and multi-confessional (Lutheran, Catholic, Orthodox) Latvia,[45] it is likely that the communist legacy helps to explain the unsuccessful attempts to introduce of bills recognizing SSUs in both Latvia and Poland.

Unlike Poland, Latvia is a post-Soviet country, where homosexuality was decriminalized (in 1992) only after the collapse of the Soviet Union. The situation of homosexuals in the Soviet Union was far more repressive than in the Communist Poland, or Hungary and Czechoslovakia where the legal status of homosexuals was, during the Cold War era, better than in some Western European countries.[46] Accordingly, among the reasons as to why not only Latvia, but also every other post-Soviet country has not legally recognized same-sex unions has to also take into account the legacy of both the law and social practices under Communism.

---

43   Uitz, *op. cit.* note 7, 242; and O'Dwyer, *op. cit.* note 29, 345.

44   O'Dwyer, *op. cit.* note 29, 347.

45   Holmes has classified Poland as a strong-church nation. Stephen Holmes, "Church-State Entanglements in the Post-Soviet Era", 6(4) *East–west Church & Ministry Report* (1998), available at <http://www.eastwestreport.org/articles/ew06409.htm>. Poland is among the most religious and most religiously affiliated nations in Europe, Latvia figures at about the European average in both categories. Estonia has the least religiously affiliated population in Europe. According to the European Values Study Surveys from 1999, 95.7% of Polish respondents claimed to belong to a religious denomination, 98.4% of religiously affiliated respondents belonged to the Catholic Church and 78.2% claimed to visit the Church more than once a month. Loek Halman, *The European Values Study: A Third Wave. Source book of the 1999/2000 European Values Study Surveys* (Tilburg University, WORC, 2001), 74, 75, and 78. For a cross-national comparative analysis, see Alar Kilp, "Secularization of Society After Communism: Ten Catholic-Protestant Societies", 12 *ENDC Proceedings* (2009), 194–231, available at <www.ksk.edu.ee/toimetised/kvuoa-toimetised -nr-12/>.

46   Mole, *op. cit.* note 29, 544. For a comprehensive historic overview of the decriminalization of same-sex acts in Western and Eastern European states, see Achim Hildebrandt, "Routes to Decriminalization: A Comparative Analysis of the Legalization of Same-Sex Sexual Acts", 17(1/2) *Sexualities* (2014), 230–253.

The second observed pattern is that no culturally Orthodox post-Communist country has legally recognized same-sex unions and traditionally Orthodox Romania was the last of EU Member States to decriminalize homosexual conduct.[47] To what extent can cultural legacies explain cross-national variations in SSU laws? The religious dimension of cultural traditions cannot be overlooked, as traditionally Orthodox societies are regularly the least approving homosexuality, while predominantly Protestant societies tend to be most approving.[48] Despite the principled homo-negative positions proclaimed by universal Catholicism,[49] Catholic countries are split in CEE (e.g. Poland does not recognize SSUs in any form, while Slovenia and predominantly Catholic Hungary recognize them to a certain extent). Traditionally Lutheran countries are split between the West and the East in terms of both social values and the value orientations of the national Lutheran churches. The 1999/2000 round of the World Values Surveys demonstrated a vast rift in the social values of traditionally Lutheran Latvia, Estonia, and the Scandinavian societies. When only 9% of Swedish respondents considered homosexuality to be "never justifiable", the Swedes were close to respondents from other Scandinavian societies (12% in Iceland, 13% in Finland and 21% in Denmark). However, in this respect, every Scandinavian country stood in stark contrast to the patterns of opinion expressed by the Estonian (57%) and Latvian (77%) respondents.[50]

---

47   Homosexual conduct was finally decriminalized in 2001. Kochenov (2007), *op. cit.* note 23, 483. In 1996, private homosexuality was decriminalized in spite of steadfast opposition on the part of the Romanian Orthodox Church. Sabrina Petra Ramet, "Redefining the Boundaries of Human Rights: The Case of Eastern Europe", 9 *Human Rights Review* (2008), 1–13, at 6.

48   A cross-cultural study by van der Akker *et al.* demonstrated that Orthodox societies are the least and Protestant societies are the most supportive of homosexuality. Van der Akker *et al.*, *op. cit.* note 35, 67 and 70. The findings of Štulhofer and Rimac demonstrated that four of the five least homo-negative countries were predominantly Protestant, while four of the five least accepting countries (Lithuania, Romania, Ukraine, Russia, and Belarus) were Eastern Orthodox. Štulhofer and Rimac, *op. cit.* note 3, 27.

49   Congregation for the Doctrine of the Faith, "Considerations Regarding Proposals to Give Legal Recognition to Unions between Homosexual Persons", available at <http://www.vatican.va/roman_curia/congregations/cfaith/documents/rc_con_cfaith_doc_20030731_homosexual-unions_en.html>. Pope Benedict XVI, Joseph Ratzinger, has also stated that the demand for legal recognition of same-sex unions "would fall outside the moral history of humanity." Joseph Ratzinger, "The Spiritual Roots of Europe: Yesterday, Today, and Tomorrow", in Joseph Ratzinger and Marcello Pera (eds.), *Without Roots: The West, Relativism, Christianity, Islam* (Basic Books, New York, 2006), 77.

50   World Values Surveys 1999/2000 referred in to Alar Kilp, "Patterns of Lutheran Politics in a Post-Communist State: The Case of Estonia", 6 *Kultura i Polityka* (2009), 65–76, at 68.

Additionally, the contrasting the morality positions of the Lutheran Church-es were evident in March 2007, when the decision of the Swedish (Lutheran) Church to bless same-sex partnerships during church services (since October 2009 the Church of Sweden has blessed same-sex marriages in church servic-es) resulted in a public letter to the Swedish Church and to the Lutheran World Federation by Archbishops from both the Estonian (Andres Põder) and the Latvian Lutheran Churches (Janis Vanags), as well as the Lithuanian Bishop of the Lutheran Church (Mindaugas Sabutis), where they protested against the decision of the Swedish Church to allow the blessing of registered partnerships of homosexuals during church services.[51] Scandinavian Lutheran societies are well known for having the highest levels of approval for homosexuality in Eu-rope. In the post-Communist realm, however, cultural value orientations are as disapproving of homosexuality to roughly the same degree in traditionally Lutheran Latvia and in predominantly Catholic Poland. As observed by Conor O'Dwyer and Katrina Schwartz, in both Latvia and Poland, "[o]utside the ranks of gay activists, there has been little desire to reconsider existing sexual norms or to emulate Western Europe's. Support from human rights advocates never rose to the level of active policy entrepreneurship."[52]

The third observed pattern is that a comprehensive explanation should not exclude the possibility that next to cultural and political legacies, the enactment of ssu legislation is also conditioned by the level of socioeco-nomic development. Several studies confirm the existence of correlation between economic modernization and cultural value shifts from materialist, traditional, authoritarian, and survival value orientations to post-materialist self-expression and tolerance values: the former limits sexual relationships to the nuclear family and heterosexual marriage while the latter tends to re-shape both religious orientations, gender roles, sexual norms, and patterns of cohabitation.[53] Conformably, more permissive and tolerant attitudes towards sex, abortion, and homosexuality replace traditional norms that formerly regu-lated the institutions of marriage, the relations of gender and the norms of sex-uality.[54] Against this background, the shift from materialist to post-materialist

---

51   "Baltic Bishops are Worried about the Unity of the Church", *Eesti Kirik* (15 March 2006).

52   O'Dwyer and Schwartz, *op. cit.* note 27, 236.

53   Ronald Inglehart *et al.*, *Human Beliefs and Values: a Cross-Cultural Sourcebook Based on the 1999–2002 Values Surveys* (Siglo XXI Editores, México, 2004), 9–10.

54   Russell J. Dalton, *Citizen Politics: Public Opinion and Political Parties in Advanced Indus-trial Democracies* (Chatham House, London, 1996), at 90 and 104; Juan J. Fernández and Mark Lutter, "Supranational Cultural Norms, Domestic Value Orientations, and the Diffu-sion of Same-Sex Union Rights in Europe, 1988–2009", 28(1) *International Sociology* (2013), 102–120, at 104; Štulhofer and Rimac, *op. cit.* note 3; and Amy Adamczyk and Cassady Pitt,

values started in Western Europe during the 1960s,[55] but began in the post-Communist Europe only during the 1990s. This may proceed successfully if related antecedent socioeconomic conditions start to be, and remain, fulfilled in Europe's East as they were in the Europe's West.

Fourth, the success and failure of the attempts to introduce SSU laws can be explained not only by legacies or by the emergence of a new kind of social consensus, but also by the balance of power between the change (mostly supranational courts and institutions and transnational activist networks) and blocking coalitions (alliance of mostly national religious, social and political actors), by the capacity to form a congruent coalition on both sides,[56] and, in particular, by the actions and relative powers of significant "veto-players" on the side of the blocking coalition.[57] On the side of the coalition for change, the SSU agenda and EU law has opened up a "window of opportunity" for gay-rights movements and activists, which were boosted both before and after EU accession not least by the support they received from European organizations, courts and INGOs.[58] The discourse of activists framed the equal treatment of hetero- and homosexuals as a democratic responsibility for all Member States of the EU,[59] and as a right associated with Europeanness and European

---

"Shaping Attitudes about Homosexuality: The Role of Religion and Cultural Context", 38(2) *Social Science Research* (2009), 338–351, at 339–340.

55   Until the 1960s, the traditional heterosexual form of marriage and sexual relations within the boundaries of marriage were social norms in the Western European countries. The major shits from traditional family arrangements took place in the 1960s and 1970s when homosexuality was decriminalized. The traditional connection between church and public norms of marriage started to break during the 1990s, when same-sex partnerships became publicly recognized. Same-sex marriages have been introduced since 2001.

56   Sophie Schmitt, Eva-Maria Euchner, and Caroline Preidel, "Regulating Prostitution and Same-Sex Marriage in Italy and Spain: The Interplay of Political and Societal Veto Players in Two Catholic Societies", 20(3) *Journal of European Public Policy* (2013), 425–441 at 428.

57   The "veto-player" approach has been used to explain the reasons why bills on SSUs introduced in national parliaments have failed. Hennig, *op. cit.* note 21; Uitz, *op. cit.* note 7; and Schmitt, Euchner and Preidel, *op. cit.* note 56. According to Tsebelis, veto player "is an individual or collective actor whose agreement is required for a policy decision." George Tsebelis, "Decision Making in Political Systems: Veto Players in Presidentialism, Parliamentarism, Multicameralism and Multipartyism", 25(3) *British Journal of Political Science* (1995), 289–325, at 293.

58   O'Dwyer, *op. cit.* note 29; and Holzhacker *op. cit.* note 12, 7.

59   Phillip M. Ayoub, "Cooperative Transnationalism in Contemporary Europe: Europeanization and Political Opportunities for LGBT Mobilization in the European Union", 5(2) *European Political Science Review* (2013), 279–310.

norms.[60] At critical junctures, both the national courts and the ECtHR supported their agenda.[61] Typically, the success of the change coalition has also been conditioned by the presence of predominantly left or center-left governments (or legislatures) and the relatively widespread support for gay rights at the grass-roots level of society.[62] Unfortunately, neither in Poland nor in Latvia, there has emerged no significant left-wing party advancing gay rights.[63] Additionally, in Latvia, a left or center-left presence has been constantly missing in governmental coalitions since 1991.[64] Finally, in both Poland and Latvia, *religious* actors are missing from change coalitions. Consequently, despite repeated efforts to pass the bills that would introduce ssu law, the change coalitions in Latvia and Poland have so far remained unsuccessful.

On the side of the "blocking coalition", eu accession stimulated the growing presence and popularity of conservative nationalism in the form of right-wing parties with ultra-nationalist and anti-gay positions,[65] which obtained offices of political power in both national governments and within the city councils of the capital cities. Consequently, from 2004 to 2007 pro-gay rights activists probably had to face the most nationalistic, populistic and anti-gay governments ever experienced in post-Communist Poland or Latvia.[66] Conservative nationalists framed their case by linking their non-negotiable moral positions with the protection of "traditional family values" as the moral foundations of Polishness and Latvianness respectively.[67] Hence, homosexuality was constructed

60   O'Dwyer, *op. cit.* note 29, 339.

61   During the rising clash of discourses, the Polish court condemned the banning of gay parades in Warsaw in 2004 and 2005. In Latvia, the first gay pride march took place in 2005 after court intervention. Kochenov (2007), *op. cit.* note 23, 475; and O'Dwyer and Schwartz, *op. cit.* note 27, 227. In *Baczowski and Others v. Poland* (2007), the ECtHR adjudged the ban of a gay pride march in Warsaw to be lacking legitimate justification. Holzhacker, *op. cit.* note 12, 10.

62   ssu legislation is usually adopted by left-wing governments while right-wing coalitions tend to block related legal reforms, e.g. same-sex marriage was legalized in Spain *after* the 2005 election victory of the Spanish Socialist Workers Party and in France shortly *after* the election victory of the Socialists in 2012. Schmitt, Euchner and Preidel, *op. cit.* note 56, 427; and Marc Olivier Baruch and Jean-Christian Vinel, "Gay Marriage and the Limits of French Liberalism", 60(4) *Dissent* (2013), 24–27.

63   Mole, *op. cit.* note 29, 554. For example, the constitutional amendment, which limited marriage to heterosexual couples was passed in the Latvian parliament with 65 votes out of 100 mps with only 5 mps opposing this move. O'Dwyer and Schwartz, *op. cit.* note 27, 230.

64   Mole, *op. cit.* note 29, 547.

65   O'Dwyer, *op. cit.* note 29, 342.

66   Graff, *op. cit.* note 31, 445.

67   O'Dwyer, *op. cit.* note 29, 339; Mole, *op. cit.* note 29, 547; and Uitz, *op. cit.* note 7, 252.

as a threat to core values of (Polish and Latvian) national identity.[68] Besides conservative nationalist parties, the blocking coalition also included traditional churches whose social authority the sexual morality change coalitions had to both face and challenge.[69] The moral messages of the dominant churches (Catholic Church in Poland; Lutheran, Catholic and Orthodox Churches in Latvia) played both an influential and instrumental role in the public clash of discourses.[70] The aforementioned churches articulated a strong and outspoken antipathy towards homosexuality and gay rights so that they were perceived to be the most powerful social forces opposing changes in morality and the "sex/gender" order.[71] However, somewhat unlike the conservative nationalists, the churches equated homosexuality with either sin, sickness, or sexual deviance.[72] Conformably, the dominant churches refrain from discourses that include the rights of homosexuals among universal human rights.[73]

The strong political and socio-cultural opposition towards extending the rights of same-sex couples, which besides Poland and Latvia, has also been identified in Lithuania and Romania,[74] does not automatically mean that the

---

68   Mole, *op. cit.* note 29, 549, 552, 557.

69   O'Dwyer, *op. cit.* note 29, 339.

70   Hennig, *op. cit.* note 21, 206, 212. When a gay pride parade was planned in Riga during the summer of 2005, leaders of the Latvian Lutheran, Catholic, Orthodox, and Baptist Churches published a joint public announcement where they assessed the event to have potential for moral degradation. "Rīga Cancels 'Pride' Parade, but Debate Continues", *Latvians Online* (20 July 2005), <http://latviansonline.com/index.php/news/article/269/>. At the same time, dean of the University of Latvia's Theology Faculty, Juris Calitis, was excommunicated from the Latvian Lutheran Church for hosting an ecumenical service at the end of the gay parade in Riga's Anglican Church in June 2005. "Ban on Gay Marriage Passes Second Reading", *The Baltic Times* (7 December 2005), available at <http://www.baltictimes.com/news/articles/14181/>.

71   O'Dwyer and Schwartz, *op. cit.* note 27, 237–238; and Gordon Waitt, "Sexual Citizenship in Latvia: Geographies of the Latvian Closet", 6(2) *Social & Cultural Geography* (2005), 161–181, at 167 and 170.

72   Jacqueline Heinen and Stéphane Portet, "Reproductive Rights in Poland: When Politicians Fear the Wrath of the Church", 31(6) *Third World Quarterly* (2010), 1007–1021, at 1011. The heads of Lutheran, Catholic and Orthodox Churches in Latvia signed an open letter that reacted to a bill drafted by the national Human Rights Office that would have extended to same-sex couples the rights enjoyed by married couples, which said: "We cannot have special rights for homosexual orientation as a special condition. No one provides laws for kleptomania, vampires, alcoholics and drug addicts. Regardless of whether these sicknesses are inborn or obtained in practice, we have to fight them and not provide new laws favourable to them." Quoted in Mole, *op. cit.* note 29, 543.

73   D.Ø. Endsjø, "Lesbian, Gay, Bisexual, and Transgender Rights and the Religious Relativism of Human Rights", 6(2) *Human Rights Review* (2005), 102–110, at 107.

74   Štulhofer and Rimac, *op. cit.* note 3.

blocking coalition is aiming to restore "family values" as they were "traditionally" thought of half a century ago. This coalition is integrated by a symbolic opposition to same-sex marriage and/or recognized unions and not (necessarily) by a commitment to reverse other processes that have disintegrated traditional marriage (such as linearly rising levels of births out of wedlock, to name one such process).[75] For them, opposition to same-sex marriage or unions serves as a symbol of a broader set of conservative, religious, moral, and cultural values.[76]

4   Conclusion

During the decade that has followed EU enlargement to CEE, European institutions have successfully implemented their normative agenda for the protection of homosexuals from prosecution on the grounds of their sexual orientation and its practice, from discrimination at workplace and from the illegitimate restriction of their right of assembly. In this regard, homosexuality as a lifestyle is not banned anywhere in Europe and homosexuals are protected from discrimination in all Member States of the EU. Starting from approximately 2010, legal recognition of same-sex unions became an unambiguous part of EU law. By January 2016, the number of Member States that legally recognized same-sex marriages rose from 2 (Netherlands and Belgium) in 2004 to eleven, while the number of Member States that limit marriage exclusively to heterosexual couples was also growing.

The conflict between European and domestic jurisdictions regarding the legal recognition of same-sex unions persists mostly in the post-Communist Member States that do not extend to same-sex couples legally recognized forms of cohabitation, civil partnership, civil union, or marriage otherwise available to heterosexual couples. The attempts of the European institutions to harmonize national laws in this regard have been mostly unsuccessful in Member States that are post-Soviet, culturally Orthodox, have not shifted from materialist to post-materialist values due to a medium level of economic development or are governed by right-wing governmental coalitions.

---

75   By 2009, the percentage of births outside of wedlock had risen in Poland to the level of
      20% and in Latvia over 40%. OECD, Social Policy Division, Directorate of Employment,
      Labour and Social Affairs, "SF2.4: Share of Births out of Wedlock and Teenage Births",
      available at <http://www.oecd.org/els/family/SF2.4_Births%20outside%20marriage%20
      and%20teenage%20births%20-%20updated%20240212.pdf>.
76   Spencer, *op. cit.* note 6, 168.

In the decade since 2004, the harmonization of SSU laws has been European-driven rather than local driven due to a lack of significant support from domestically held social values, and religious and political actors at the national level. In the coming decade, however, those post-Communist Member States, which have resisted the legal recognition of same-sex unions, will most likely not recognize same-sex marriage that is not supported by social value orientations and not mandated by the European institutions. On the other hand, however, it is also likely that the number of Member States not recognizing SSUs in any form will be linearly decreasing particularly after the *Vallianatos* and *Oliari* cases, which have provided both an example and an opportunity for domestic actors to challenge national legislation not in conformity with EU law on SSUs.

Bibliography

Adamczyk, Amy and Pitt, Cassady. (2009) "Shaping Attitudes about Homosexuality: The Role of Religion and Cultural Context", 38(2) *Social Science Research*, 338–351.

van den Akker, Hanneke, van der Ploeg, Rozemarijn, and Scheepers, Peer. (2013) "Disapproval of Homosexuality: Comparative Research on Individual and National Determinants of Disapproval of Homosexuality in 20 European Countries", 25(1) *International Journal of Public Opinion Research*, 64–86.

Ayoub, Phillip M. (2013) "Cooperative Transnationalism in Contemporary Europe: Europeanization and Political Opportunities for LGBT Mobilization in the European Union", 5 (2) *European Political Science Review*, 279–310.

Baruch, Marc Olivier and Vinel, Jean-Christian. (2013) "Gay Marriage and the Limits of French Liberalism", 60(4) *Dissent*, 24–27.

Borg-Barthet, Justin. (2012) "The Principled Imperative to Recognize Same-Sex Unions in the EU", 8(2) *Journal of Private Law*, 359–388.

Curry-Sumner, Ian. (2009) "Interstate Recognition of Same-Sex Relationships in Europe", 13(1) *Journal of Gender, Race & Justice*, 59–80.

Dalton, Russell J. (1996) *Citizen Politics: Public Opinion and Political Parties in Advanced Industrial Democracies* (Chatham House, London).

Endsjø, D.Ø. (2005) "Lesbian, Gay, Bisexual, and Transgender Rights and the Religious Relativism of Human Rights", 6(2) *Human Rights Review*, 102–110.

Fernández, Juan J. and Lutter, Mark. (2013) "Supranational Cultural Norms, Domestic Value Orientations, and the Diffusion of Same-Sex Union Rights in Europe, 1988–2009", 28(1) *International Sociology*, 102–120.

Gerhards, Jürgen. (2010) "Non-Discrimination towards Homosexuality: The European Union's Policy and Citizens' Attitudes towards Homosexuality in 27 European Countries", 25(1) *International Sociology*, 5–28.

Graff, Agnieszka. (2006) "We Are (Not All) Homophobes: A Report from Poland", 32(2) *Feminist Studies*, 434–449.

Heinen, Jacqueline and Portet, Stéphane. (2010) "Reproductive Rights in Poland: When Politicians Fear the Wrath of the Church", 31(6) *Third World Quarterly*, 1007–1021.

Hennig, Anja. (2010) "Morality politics in a Catholic Democracy: A Hard Road Towards Liberalization of Gay Rights in Poland", in Haynes, Jeffrey. (ed.), *Religion and Politics in Europe, the Middle East and North Africa* (Routledge, London), 208–225.

Hildebrandt, Achim. (2014) "Routes to Decriminalization: A Comparative Analysis of the Legalization of Same-Sex Sexual Acts", 17(1/2) *Sexualities*, 230–253.

Holzhacker, Ronald. (2013) "State-Sponsored Homophobia and the Denial of the Right of Assembly in Central and Eastern Europe: The 'Boomerang' and the 'Ricochet' between European Organizations and Civil Society to Uphold Human Rights", 35(1/2) *Law & Policy*, 1–28.

Johnson, Paul. (2011) "Homosexuality, Freedom of Assembly and the Margin of Appreciation Doctrine of the European Court of Human Rights: Alekseyev v Russia", 11(3) *Human Rights Law Review*, 578–593.

Kilp, Alar. (2009) "Patterns of Lutheran Politics in a Post-Communist State: The Case of Estonia", 6 *Kultura i Polityka*, 65–76.

Kilp, Alar. (2009) "Secularization of Society After Communism: Ten Catholic-Protestant Societies", 12 *ENDC Proceedings*, 194–231, available at <www.ksk.edu.ee/toimetised/kvuoa-toimetised-nr-12/>.

Kochenov, Dimitry. (2009) "On Options of Citizens and Moral Choices of States: Gays and European Federalism", 33(1) *Fordham International Law Journal*, 156–205.

Kochenov, Dimitry. (2007) "Gay Rights in the EU: A Long Way Forward for the Union of 27", 3 *Croatian Yearbook of European Law and Policy*, 469–490.

Mole, Richard. (2011) "Nationality and Sexuality: Homophobic Discourse and the 'National Threat' in Contemporary Latvia", 17(3) *Nations and Nationalism*, 540–560.

O'Dwyer, Conor. (2012) "Does the EU Help or Hinder Gay-Rights Movements in Post-Communist Europe? The case of Poland", 28(4) *East European Politics*, 332–352.

O'Dwyer, Conor and Schwartz, Katrina Z.S. (2010) "Minority Rights after EU Enlargement: A Comparison of Antigay Politics in Poland and Latvia", 8(2) *Comparative European Politics*, 220–243.

Ramet, Sabrina Petra. (2008) "Redefining the Boundaries of Human Rights: The Case of Eastern Europe", 9 *Human Rights Review*, 1–13.

Ratzinger, Joseph. (2006) "The Spiritual Roots of Europe: Yesterday, Today, and Tomorrow", in Ratzinger, Joseph and Pera, Marcello. (eds.), *Without Roots: The West, Relativism, Christianity, Islam* (Basic Books, New York), 51–80.

Roseneil, Sasha *et al.* (2013) "Changing Landscapes of Heteronormativity: The Regulation and Normalization of Same-Sex Sexualities in Europe", 20(2) *Social Politics*, 165–199.

Scherpe, Jens M. (2013) "The Legal Recognition of Same-Sex Couples in Europe and the Role of the European Court of Human Rights", 10 *The Equal Rights Review*, 83–96.

Schmitt, Sophie, Euchner, Eva-Maria, and Preidel, Caroline. (2013) "Regulating Prostitution and Same-Sex Marriage in Italy and Spain: The Interplay of Political and Societal Veto Players in Two Catholic Societies", 20(3) *Journal of European Public Policy*, 425–441.

Spencer, Kate. (2010) "Same Sex Couples and the Right to Marry: European Perspectives", 6(1) *Cambridge Student Law Review*, 155–176.

Štulhofer, Aleksander and Rimac, Ivan. (2009) "Determinants of Homonegativity in Europe", 46(1) *Journal of Sex Research*, 24–32.

Takács, Judit and Szalma, Ivett. (2011) "Homophobia and Same-Sex Partnership Legislation in Europe", 30(5) *Equality Diversity and Inclusion*, 356–378.

Tsebelis, George. (1995) "Decision Making in Political Systems: Veto Players in Presidentialism, Parliamentarism, Multicameralism and Multipartyism", 25(3) *British Journal of Political Science*, 289–325.

Uitz, Renáta. (2012) "Lessons from Sexual Orientation Discrimination in Central Europe", 60(1) *The American Journal of Comparative Law*, 235–264.

Waitt, Gordon. (2005) "Sexual Citizenship in Latvia: Geographies of the Latvian Closet", 6(2) *Social & Cultural Geography*, 161–181.

PART 4

EU Policy – From Within to Without

∵

CHAPTER 11

Poland and the Common Security and Defense Policy: Potential Leader?

Laura Chappell

Abstract

From a skeptical participant, Poland has gradually transformed into a potential leader of the Common Security and Defense Policy (CSDP). This chapter charts this evolution, underlining the country's stance towards a number of key initiatives including Permanent Structured Cooperation and the solidarity clause as set out in the Treaty of Lisbon. The country's role in influencing the development of CSDP is examined through the use of strategic culture which underlines a country's approach concerning when, where and how it uses force. It is argued that key elements of Poland's strategic culture have enabled the country to play a leadership role. These include Poland's emphasis on "nothing about us without us", its pro-activity concerning the use of force and the country's shift from an instinctive to pragmatic Atlanticist. Whilst the country's focus on transforming its own armed forces to the potential detriment of participating in military operations might be interpreted as a signal that Poland's leadership ambition may be showing signs of fatigue, this is not necessarily the case. Rather Poland wants to ensure that CSDP is relevant to its own security, which is combined with a pragmatic stance as to what can be achieved.

Keywords

CSDP – Poland – strategic culture – Atlanticism – use of force

1 Introduction

In 2009 the Treaty of Lisbon came into force. Within it were a number of measures on CSDP including Permanent Structured Cooperation in defense (PESCO), a name change (from ESDP to CSDP), expanding the number of tasks which could be carried out under CSDP as well as extending and listing the competencies of the European Defense Agency (EDA). CSDP originated from the Anglo-Franco declaration at St Malo in 1998 in which both countries had agreed to pursue an autonomous European defense policy as long as it did not duplicate NATO. It was then brought into the EU framework at the Cologne European Council and further developed at the Helsinki European Council including the Helsinki Headline Goal to deploy 50–60,000 armed forces. Throughout the 2000s the policy gathered pace with new initiatives (EU Battlegroups, Headline Goal 2010, the European Security Strategy (ESS), the EDA) and a myriad of civilian and military operations from Europe, to Africa and Asia. Yet the EU is still gripped by a capabilities-expectations gap,[1] hampered by a lack of Member State political willingness.

This Chapter sets out to underline continuity and change in Poland's approach to and role within the evolution of CSDP, as briefly outlined above, from 1999 to 2013. From a skeptical participant, Poland has transformed into a potential leader of CSDP – a noteworthy change within a short space of time. This may seem somewhat surprising considering Poland's Atlanticism which entails a pro-US rather than a pro-European stance regarding ensuring Poland's security. However as will be underscored below, a change in the strength of Polish Atlanticism combined with a civil-military approach to CSDP has ensured Poland's support.

In order to understand Poland's approach to CSDP, strategic culture is employed as the analytical framework. As will be highlighted in more detail in the next section, this approach focuses on when, where and with whom a country uses force. In the case of Poland we see at least three factors that ensure its prominent role in CSDP; first, a desire to be included in decisions affecting its interests, second a more pragmatic Atlanticism and, third a pro-active view on using force which has ensured that it has played an active role in CSDP. However Poland's transition has not been an easy one, underlined by the way in which its strategic culture has had to shift due to the new international security environment which began to materialize after the end of the Cold War and incorporates new defense threats. These include the proliferation of Weapons of Mass Destruction, international terrorism, state failure and regional conflict as highlighted in the EU's European Security Strategy.[2] This has involved a slow but steady change not only in Polish security thinking but also in the structure of its armed forces to account for its more active international defense role.

---

1   Christopher Hill, "The Capability-Expectations Gap, or Conceptualizing Europe's International Role", 31(3) *Journal of Common Market Studies* (1993), 305–328.

2   Javier Solana, *A Secure Europe in a Better World – European Security Strategy* (Council of the European Union, Brussels, 2003).

Poland's transformation has implications for CSDP. Since Lisbon, the policy has come to a standstill as initiatives such as Permanent Structured Cooperation in Defense (PESCO) have failed to materialize whilst the EU Battlegroups have never been deployed since they became fully operational in 2007. The launch of new EU operations also slowed down. Thus the EU needed an actor to get CSDP out of its post-Lisbon impasse, particularly in the context of the original rationale behind CSDP – to acquire a greater military capability in order to provide security in its neighborhood. As will be highlighted, Poland used its Presidency to try and do just that. The question remains as to Poland's success and whether its leadership role has been maintained following its moment in the spotlight.

2   Polish Strategic Culture

Strategic culture looks at the ideational components of a country's approach to using force and is based on social constructivism, a key theoretical approach in International Relations. Hence whilst "seen" factors such as the size and structure of a country's armed forces or its defense spending may give a guide to its power projection, these offer no understanding regarding why a country has a particular force structure or when or how it may use force. Strategic culture looks beneath these seen elements and focuses on the "unseen" or "ideational" which includes a range of different elements such as attitudes, norms and historical perceptions.

Strategic culture is defined as the "beliefs, attitudes and norms held by a security community towards the use of force which has had a 'unique historical experience.'"[3] Meyer understands norms to mean, "beliefs about what is appropriate, legitimate or just regarding the goals, ends and modalities."[4] In this respect norms relate to the legitimacy and appropriateness regarding deploying force whether this is regarding when it is deployed, where (geographically) or with whom (i.e. as part of a coalition of the willing or under the EU, NATO or the UN). Attitudes encompass behavior which is expected of a group whilst beliefs are deep seated approaches to using force based on experience, or an

---

3   Laura Chappell, *Germany, Poland and the Common Security and Defence Policy. Converging Perspectives in an Enlarged EU* (Palgrave Macmillan, Basingstoke, 2012), 419; and Colin. S. Gray, "Strategic Culture as Context: The First Generation of Theory Strikes Back", 7(1) *International Affairs* (1999), 49–69, at 51–52.

4   Christoph. O Meyer, *The Quest for a European Strategic Culture: Changing Norms on Security and Defence in the European Union* (Palgrave Macmillan, New York, 2006), 20.

understanding as to what is right. The final element of strategic culture relates to historical experience. However of key importance is how these historical experiences have been interpreted and how this in turn shapes (rather than determines) a country's approach to when, where and how it uses force. As Gray stresses, "culture shapes the process of strategy-making, and influences the execution of strategy."[5] This makes a security community's strategic culture unique.

Strategic culture lends itself to continuity because, once socialized and institutionalized over time, cultures stick. As Berger highlights "formal institutions play a key role in anchoring broader societal beliefs and values and provide context and permanency to them."[6] This is because institutions incorporate rules, traditions, practices as well as deeper seated norms. Whilst this emphases the constraints that institutions impose on actors (e.g. policy-makers) nonetheless, it is the elites who have to interpret and thus operationalize a strategic culture. Hence strategic culture offers a guide to policy-makers as to which options are feasible thus ruling out certain actions whilst affirming others. This underlines that it is the security and defense elites who are the agents of strategic culture as they formulate defense policy, rather than society in general.[7] Indeed policy-makers do not always act according to public opinion.

However change can occur. Whilst dramatic change, where a country's strategic culture is completely replaced by another due to war/conflict for example, is rare, incremental change is far more likely.[8] The latter occurs when two aspects of a strategic culture are conflicting or an altered security environment involves the replacement of certain policies (for example the abandonment of conscription). Nonetheless "incremental change" can give the false impression that all change under this label is minor. This is not necessarily the case and can involve substantial policy shifts and changes in underlying beliefs and attitudes which underpin its policies. Even so these fall short of a complete overhaul of a country's strategic culture.

So how can strategic culture be applied to the Polish case? Due to the importance of a security community's historical experience it is necessary to uncover the key events which have shaped Poland's perception of defense issues. These

---

5   Gray, *op. cit.* note 3.

6   Thomas Berger, *Cultures of Antimilitarism: National Security in Germany and Japan* (John Hopkins University Press, London, 1998), 11–12.

7   John Duffield, *World Power Forsaken* (Stanford University Press, Sandford, CA, 1998), 33–34; and Kerry Longhurst, *Germany and the Use of Force* (Manchester University Press, Manchester, 2004), 22.

8   Longhurst, *ibid.*

include the final partition of Poland in 1795 when the country ceased to exist as a geographical entity and regaining and then losing independence during the interwar years. Poland was invaded (1939) and divided between Nazi Germany and the USSR which was coupled with the UK and France failing to meet their alliance obligations. However of great significance was the "betrayal" of Poland by the Allied force at the Yalta Conference in 1945. Here the country was placed in the Soviet Union's sphere of influence and it lost territory in the East although it did gain land in the West from Germany.[9] Whilst the Communists subsequently tried to use Polish nationalism to legitimize their presence by underlining their role in rescuing the country from Nazi Germany, their failure to grant Polish independence meant that they failed in this endeavor.[10]

These historical events became integral factors in the formulation of Polish strategic culture. Therefore the core of this is founded on Poland's history of heroic defeat and its geographical position which made it a victim of Realpolitik.[11] This means that Poland's sovereignty is sacrosanct and its strategic culture was formulated to ensure the country's independence. Stemming from this are other interconnected key lessons learned for Poland. These included being a reliable ally, supporting self-determination as well as "nothing about us without us" whereby Poland should be included in decisions affecting its interests none of which occurred at Yalta.[12] In order to protect Polish independence, it turned to NATO's Article Five Security Guarantee underwritten by the Americans. This cemented the country's pro-Atlanticism as well as ensuring a pro-active view on the use of force to support Poland's allies if necessary.[13] This underlines Poland's skepticism regarding its European allies' ability to provide for its security following lessons from 1939 and 1945 as underscored above. Additionally it highlights that Poland's threat perception is based primarily on its region and therefore it prioritizes both regional and territorial defense. These central themes (Atlanticism, "nothing about us without us", regional and territorial defender and promoter, reliable ally, using force pro-actively) are of importance to understanding Poland's approach to CSDP as will be highlighted below. In order to explore them the next sections will underline Poland's role in the political development of CSDP as well as participation militarily in CSDP operations.

---

9   Chappell, *op. cit.* note 3, 38–39.

10 *Ibid.*, 39–40.

11 *Ibid.*, 42.

12 Olaf Osica, "Poland: A New European Atlanticist at a Crossroads?" 13(4) *European Security* (2004), 301–322.

13 Laura Chappell, "Poland in Transition: Implications for a European Security and Defence Policy", 31(2) *Contemporary Security Policy* (2010), 225–248, at 229.

3   Poland's Initial Reaction: A Skeptical but Pragmatic Participant

The country's approach to the initiation of CSDP reflected US concerns as articulated by Madeline Albright's 3 D's (no duplication, no decoupling, no discrimination). Poland did not want to be excluded from a policy which was evidently in its interests ("nothing about us without us") whilst concerns were raised regarding the potential for duplication with NATO – key to Polish security and reflecting its Atlanticism.[14] Poland however dealt with its concerns pragmatically by creating the 15 + 6 framework to discuss security issues, in which the 15 EU Member States were brought together with the 6 then non-EU European countries (Czech Republic, Hungary, Iceland, Norway, Poland, and Turkey).

Even so, the rationale behind the policy was not convincing for the then non-EU Poland and its concerns about being included in CSDP remained. This was not helped by CSDP initiatives which had been incorporated within the EU Constitution including PESCO and the solidarity clause. The former was problematic because as the previous Polish Defense Minister Bogdan Klich outlined, "we found ourselves faced with a concept of a 'select club', with just a few participating states."[15] Hence inclusion was Poland's concern here. In the case of the latter there was an evident concern about duplicating NATO's Article Five guarantee thus undermining the guarantee and by extension the US who under-wrote it. This underlines Poland's Atlanticist stance because only the US could protect Poland's security. Neither did the European Security Strategy (ESS), signed in 2003, represent Poland's view of the security and defense environment which is focused far more on the region and territorial defense. This resulted in an indifferent reaction although some influence of the document can be seen in Poland's National Security Strategy from the same year.[16] Despite this, Poland did participate in early CSDP operations taking part in three out of four of the operations deployed prior to Polish accession.

---

14   David Dunn, "Poland: America's New Model Ally", in Marcin Zaborowski and David Dunn (eds.), *Poland – A New Power in Transatlantic Security* (Frank Cass Publishers, London, 2003), 63–86; and Kerry Longhurst and Marcin Zaborowski, *The New Atlanticist Poland's Foreign and Security Policy Priorities* (Blackwell Publishing, Oxford, 2007).

15   Nicolas Gros-Verheyde "Interview with Bogdan Klich, Polish Defence Minister: Poland Backs Integrated Defence Mechanisms", *European Report* (27 May 2008).

16   Chappell, *op. cit.* note 3; and Antoni Podolski, "Polska Strategia Bezpieczeństwa Narodowego jako praktyczna implementacja Europejskiej Strategii Bezpieczeństwa – między teorią a praktyką (Polish National Security Strategy as a Practical Implementation of the European Security Strategy – between Theory and Practice)", *Raporty i Analizy* (2005) No.1, available at <http://www.csm.org.pl/pl/files/raporty/2005/rap_i_an_0105.pdf>.

Thus Poland's involvement in CSDP highlighted that whilst it was politically skeptical it was also pragmatic as Poland wanted its views to be heard and taken into consideration. They could only do this by engaging with the policy. Additionally in 2003 Poland participated in the controversial Iraq war bringing its European credentials into disrepute particularly from a French and German perspective. Thus it was important that the country demonstrated that it was a reliable ally.[17] Polish accession however was the beginning of the end of the country's skepticism as the country had the ability to be included in decisions on CSDP.

4   An Increasing Role: Poland's Approach beyond Accession

Poland's role gradually began to evolve as it was able to put forward its views from within the EU framework. However there appeared to be some disconnect between Poland's regional security concentration and its participation in a variety of operations whether within the context of CSDP (e.g. EUFOR Congo, EUFOR TChad/RCA), NATO (Afghanistan) or the US Coalition of the Willing (Iraq) as will be explored below. This section will highlight Poland's approach regarding the political development of CSDP, concentrating on the ESS and the Report on its update as well as initiatives within the Lisbon Treaty. Second it will examine the country's military contribution to CSDP operations. Finally it will assess Poland's approach towards capability development initiatives particularly the EU Battlegroup Concept. These three elements will form the basis for an analysis of continuity and change in Polish strategic culture and the subsequent impact on its armed forces.

The main focus of Poland's threat perception is Russia which is viewed as a "source of instability."[18] As previously highlighted the ESS failed to take Poland's security stance fully into account with an emphasis on an international role for the EU in contrast to Poland's concentration on regional security and more traditional security tasks and threats.

Poland's lack of influence on the 2003 ESS can be contrasted to its involvement in the Report on the Implementation of the ESS in 2008. As a fully-fledged member of the EU and supportive of looking again at the ESS, Poland made suggestions concerning the content of the document. These reflect Polish security concerns and priorities including Russia as a security challenge, energy security, the development of capabilities including rapid response,

---

17   Chappell, *op. cit.* note 3, 233.

18   *Ibid.*, 78.

civil-military coordination and the Eastern Partnership.[19] Poland's record of getting these areas incorporated into the Report on the Implementation of the ESS was rather mixed. Whilst many of its suggestions were included such as an emphasis on energy security and explicit reference to the Eastern Partnership, others were less successful including Poland's approach to Russia. Whilst the Report did not completely correspond to Polish threat perceptions, the Poles were generally satisfied with it, in particular its emphasis on energy security.[20] The suggestions Poland made also underlined its emphasis on the region and its support for the EU as a civil-military actor in contrast to NATO's overt military role. This underlined that Poland had gradually come to understand the role of CSDP vis-à-vis NATO thus representing a change in the country's approach to European security.

Poland's views towards other initially controversial areas were also in flux which included policies incorporated into the now defunct constitution such as PESCO and the solidarity clause.[21] This change in stance can be highlighted by former Polish Defense Minister Bogdan Klich who in relation to PESCO stated that "the concept that was endorsed in the end, and which is laid down in the Lisbon Treaty, was made more flexible and enlarged. And so we are now an ardent supporter of the idea."[22] Thus key to Poland's approach was the idea of 'nothing about us without us'. It also underlines Poland's desire to support and participate in initiatives thus emphasizing that Poland is an active participant within CSDP's political initiatives.

Poland's stance on the political development of CSDP is matched by its attitude towards the policy's operational component. Despite having few direct national security interests in Africa, Poland participated in EUFOR RD Congo (130 personnel) and EUFOR TChad/RCA (400 personnel) where Poland was the joint second largest contributor in addition to EUFOR Althea in Bosnia and Herzegovina. This decision was influenced not only by the idea of being a reliable ally in CSDP but also viewing CSDP in the context of needing potential contingencies.[23] Thus if Poland participates in an area which incorporates another EU Member State interests, then the expectation is that Poland's goodwill

---

19   Poland, *Examining the Impact of the European Security Strategy – Polish Input* (Brussels, 2008). The Eastern Partnership is part of the European Neighborhood Policy and was initiated in 2009.

20   Confidential interview with a Polish official (2010). This chapter cites six interviews conducted between 2006 and 2013.

21   Clara Marina O'Donnell, "Poland's U-turn on European Defense: A Missed Opportunity?" *U.S.-Europe Analysis Series* (2012) No.53, 1–5.

22   Gros-Verheyde, *op. cit.* note 15.

23   Confidential interviews with a Polish official 2006 and researcher 2007.

would be reciprocated if a mission was suggested in Poland's neighborhood. This reflects the country's continued emphasis on its neighborhood. Indeed Komorowski has underlined that CSDP should be made "more geographically balanced."[24]

Another area where Poland is a keen advocate is the EU Battlegroup concept which was included in the Headline Goal 2010. A Battlegroup is formed of 1,500 armed force personnel, should be sustainable for 30 days and extendable for up to 120 days. They are capable of rapid deployment and thus "the decision to launch an operation should be taken five days after the agreement by the Council and should be deployed 10 days after the decision by the EU."[25] The Battlegroups have been fully operational since 2007 where two Battlegroups are on standby at a time and rotated every six months. It is within this concept that Poland began to show its leadership potential by being a Framework Nation for all the Battlegroups in which it is participating. These include: 1. Poland, Germany, Latvia, Lithuania and Slovakia Battlegroup (2010), 2. The Weimar Triangle Battlegroup (Poland, Germany, France) (2013), and 3. The Visegrad Four Battlegroup (Poland, Czech Republic, Slovakia, Hungary) (2016).[26]

The reasoning behind Poland's participation underlines three elements. First is the idea that Poland needs to have influence over areas that affect its security which involves taking a positive approach to CSDP. The second is proving its predictability and reliability, particularly in the context of the Kaczynski government where Poland was seen to be unpredictable in other areas. Finally as the sixth largest country, Poland had responsibilities to fulfill.[27] However, the problem with the Battlegroups is that they have yet to be deployed. To this end, Poland is supportive of making them more usable and this aim was included in their Presidency program as will be highlighted below.[28]

Whilst the key elements of Polish strategic culture remained, the way they have been applied to CSDP has resulted in a rethink concerning the country's approach to the policy. As underlined above Poland's emphasis on 'nothing about us without us' has ensured that the country has engaged with the policy,

---

24 Stanisław J. Komorowski, "Poland's objectives in European Security & Defence", paper presented at the 7th congress on European Security and Defence (Berlin, 10 November 2008), available at <http://www.european-defence.com/Review/2008/binarywriterser vlet?imgUid=d4e30a99-62fb-2031-0648-01f307b988f2&uBasVariant=11111111-1111-1111-1111 -111111111111>, 4.

25 Chappell, *op. cit.* note 3, 140.

26 *Ibid.*, 141–142.

27 Confidential interview with a Polish official (2006).

28 Confidential interviews with Polish officials (2010 and 2013); and Marcin Terlikowski, "Polish-led EU Battle Group", 3(79) *PISM Bulletin* (2010), 157–158, at 158.

seeking to act as an active participant and where possible, a potential leader. This has combined with the desire to act as a reliable ally and its pro-active approach to the use of force to ensure that Poland has participated in a policy which does not always reflect its regional and territorial focus for its security. This points to its threat perception as being slightly less important than other elements within its strategic culture.

However an alteration has occurred within Polish Atlanticism. This has become more realistic due partly to Iraq where Poland got few returns for being a 'reliable ally' to the Americans with expectations ranging from loosened visa restrictions to business opportunities for Polish companies.[29] The cancellation of the missile defense shield did not help matters, in particular how it was communicated (on the 70th anniversary of the Soviet invasion of Poland after the first reports had already appeared in the press).[30] However in return for Poland agreeing to the missile defense shield, they had pressed for US investment in Polish defense, learning the lessons of Iraq.[31] Whilst Poland was included in the subsequent plan to host SM-3 missiles which included symbolically, the stationing of US troops on Polish soil, the whole episode underlined a weakening of Polish Atlanticism. This is not to say that it has dispersed altogether as Poland still relies on the US for its hard security but rather that it has become a pragmatic Atlanticist representing a more substantial incremental change. Thus whilst the US is certainly important, the EU is now seen as an independent security and defense actor, particularly within the civil-military realm.

Poland's increased activeness and alteration in the role it can play internationally has been assisted by the modernization of the Polish Armed Forces with the abandonment of conscription, the reduction in the size of the armed forces, and the announcement in 2013 concerning the much needed modernization of its equipment with 60% of it dating back to the Soviet era.[32] It will include 13 core programs including a short-range missile defense system as well as "new helicopters, transport planes, unmanned aerial 'drones', jet

29   Mark Melamed, "Polish-American Relations in the Aftermath of War in Iraq", 5(2) *The Polish Foreign Affairs Digest* (2005), 7–21, at 10.

30   Jan Puhl, "Warsaw Fears Washington Losing Interest in Eastern Allies", *Spiegel Online* (17 September 2009), available at <http://www.spiegel.de/international/europe/0,1518, 649688,00.html>.

31   Radosław Sikorski, *The Minister of Foreign Affairs on the Republic of Poland's Foreign Policy for 2008* (Ministry of Foreign Affairs, Warsaw, 2008), 10.

32   Jan Cienski, "Defence: Polish Military Prepares for Modernisation", *Financial Times* (22 May 2013), available at <http://www.ft.com/cms/s/0/d46e4d06-bbba-11e2-82df-00144fe-ab7de.html#axzz2ty1JkJvu>.

trainers, armored personnel carriers and modernized tanks"[33] helped by the fact that the Polish economy has avoided recession but also reflecting Poland's leadership.[34] Hence, "the share of the defense budget going on equipment will rise from 15% to 33%."[35] This is a reflection of the generally positive state of the Polish economy combined with the country's leadership aspirations[36] in addition to a desire to contribute "to the security of the North Atlantic Alliance."[37] These areas were underlined during their presidency.

5   The Polish EU Presidency and beyond: Fulfilling Its Destiny?

Poland's Presidency gave it the opportunity to become a fully-fledged leader. In relation to CSDP, Poland's Program had already been illuminated through the Weimar Initiative which it presented along with France and Germany in December 2010. This underlined that a "fresh impetus to European Security and Defense Policy, in full complementarity with NATO" was required.[38] Thus Poland's focus included putting forward plans to make the Battlegroups more flexible and thus more usable as well as pushing the 'Pooling and Sharing' initiative to create more capabilities. Additionally it advocated creating a standing civil-military HQ as well as improving EU-NATO relations and incorporating Eastern European countries into CSDP activities.[39] However Poland's emphasis on a standing civil-military HQ ran into problems in the form of the UK who strongly opposed it. Indeed France, Germany, Italy, Poland, and Spain wrote a letter to the High Representative Catherine Ashton encouraging her to "examine all institutional and legal options available to member states, including

---

33   *Ibid.*

34   Confidential interview with a Polish official (2013); and "East European Defence: Flexing its muscles", *The Economist* (17 August 2013), available at <http://www.economist.com/ news/europe/21583679-only-big-country-europe-increasing-defence-spending-poland-wants-more-say>.

35   *Ibid.*

36   Confidential interview with a Polish official (2013).

37   Ministry of Foreign Affairs, *Polish Foreign Policy Priorities 2012–2016* (March 2012), available at <http://www.msz.gov.pl/resource/d31571cf-d24f-4479-afo9-c9a46cc85cf6:JCR>, 16.

38   France, Germany, and Poland, *Weimar Letter* (6 December 2010), available at <http://www. europarl.europa.eu/meetdocs/2009_2014/documents/sede/dv/sede031011weimarletter_/ sede031011weimarletter_en.pdf>.

39   See Ministry of Foreign Affairs, *Programme of the Polish Presidency of the Council of the European Union 1 July 2011 – 31 December 2011* (Ministry of Foreign Affairs, Warsaw, 2011), 8–10.

Permanent Structured Cooperation, to develop critical CSDP capabilities, notably a permanent planning and conduct capability."[40] Eventually the standing civil-military HQ was downgraded to launching the previously unused Operations Centre for missions in the Horn of Africa.

The Council Conclusions on CSDP (1 December) underlined where progress has been made.[41] Eleven areas for cooperation were endorsed by the EU Member States' Defense Ministers under the Pooling and Sharing initiative. In relation to the Battlegroups, a number of areas were highlighted where further work was required and the Council invited the High Representative to present the results of the work strands identified in the first part of 2012. Additionally, the Council emphasized that strengthening EU-NATO cooperation was important and asked the High Representative to continue work on this, although progress was not seen due to continuing political difficulties. Meanwhile cooperation with Eastern and Mediterranean countries will be further developed on an individual basis. Finally declarations on a number of operations were made. This included the extension of EUNAVFOR Somalia's mandate, the announcement of a potential new operation for a civilian CSDP mission with military expertise in Somalia and the Horn of Africa as well as potential assistance in Libya.

Whilst Pomorska and Vanhoonacker underline that "no substantial progress was achieved" within CSDP,[42] Poland had nothing to build upon. Instead Poland's task was to insert some momentum into the policy. Thus it was a success to initiate something at a time when people were giving up on CSDP,[43] which was achieved through the initiation of Pooling and Sharing and getting discussions on the reform of the Battlegroups going again. Additionally it underlined to Polish decision-makers the limits of what could be achieved. As Sikorski highlights, "the experiences of the Polish Presidency show us that EU Common Security and Defence Policy is impossible to implement in a group of 27 countries, and that we must initiate tighter cooperation between willing countries, in line with the provisions of the Lisbon Treaty."[44] Hence Poland's

---

40   France, Germany, Italy, Poland, and Spain, *Letter to Baroness Catherine Ashton* (2 September 2011), available at <http://www.europarl.europa.eu/meetdocs/2009_2014/documents/sede/dv/sede051211weimarletter5_/SEDE051211Weimarletter5_EN.pdf>.

41   Council of the European Union, *Council Conclusions on Common Security and Defence Policy* (1 December 2011).

42   Karolina Pomorska and Sophie Vanhoonacker, "Poland in the Driving Seat: A Mature Presidency in Turbulent Times", *50 JCMS Annual Review* (2012), 76–84, at 81.

43   Confidential interview with a Polish official (2013).

44   Radosław Sikorski, *The Minister of Foreign Affairs on Polish Foreign Policy for 2012*, (2012), available at <http://www.msz.gov.pl/resource/2b624fd4-d5f9-4c36-8b43-91543bc1e36c:JCR>.

commitment to CSDP has not waned but rather it is seeking ways to create a stronger CSDP through coalitions. Indeed Poland has been doing this in the frameworks of the Weimar "Plus" (Poland, Germany France, Italy, and Spain) as well as within the Visegrad group.[45]

In the case of the former, the summary of their meeting in November 2012 underlined the importance of a comprehensive approach to crisis manage-ment underlining civil military instruments including "true civilian-military structures to plan and conduct missions and operations."[46] It also highlighted EU-NATO coherence, support for more capabilities including through Pooling and Sharing as well as a sustainable European Defense and Technological In-dustrial Base and the exploration of dual use technologies.[47] This underlines a continuation of the program put forward during Poland's Presidency and thus stresses key areas of importance for Poland including a focus on the civil-military dimension and EU-NATO relations. In the case of the Visegrad Group, action within CSDP has mainly focused around the creation of the Visegrad Four Battlegroup. However without agreement from 27 countries[48] concern-ing the direction of CSDP, it is difficult to see how progress on the policy can be made. Poland's continued drive to make progress is down to maintaining Poland's independence which relies on its security. This is being weakened by budget cuts across Europe, along with the US pivot towards Asia and thus away from Europe which impacts both CSDP and NATO. Therefore Poland's CSDP reform agenda "can be seen purely as a means of preventing Europeans from losing sight of the importance of defense",[49] a point which is further under-lined in the country's foreign policy priorities 2012–16.[50] This in turn means en-suring that Europeans are capable of maintaining their own regional defense. Therefore Poland is looking to play a leading role in ensuring the progression of CSDP.

The accumulation of the Polish Presidency's impact on CSDP was fully re-vealed at the end of 2013 which can be seen as a follow up process to what was

---

45   Marcin Terlikowski, "No One Left Behind? European Defence and 'Brexit'", 158(4) *The RUSI Journal* (2013), 26–30, at 27–28.

46   France, Germany, Italy, Poland, and Spain, *Meeting of the Foreign Affairs Ministers and Ministers of Defence of France, Germany, Italy, Poland and Spain* (15 November 2011), available at <http://www.diplomatie.gouv.fr/IMG/pdf/121114_Outcome_proposal_Final_cle821c1b.pdf>.

47   *Ibid.*

48   Denmark has an opt-out from CSDP and therefore is not included.

49   Terlikowski, *op. cit.* note 45, 28.

50   Ministry of Foreign Affairs, *op. cit.* note 37, 14.

started by Poland.[51] For the first time since 2008, CSDP was discussed at the European Council. Three areas were emphasized: increasing the effectiveness of CSDP (e.g. the Battlegroups and operations); the development of military capabilities (e.g. Pooling and Sharing, the code of conduct); the defense market and industry. Poland's approach towards transforming the Battlegroup concept was made clear during its presidency. In its position paper Poland stated that "we should make the BGs more flexible, fit-for-purpose, and therefore, potentially more attractive for Member States as an effective military tool."[52] The ideas put forward included differentiating the capabilities of the Battlegroups on standby, inserting the cost of strategic lift into the Athena mechanism for the Battlegroups as well as the exploration of the Battlegroups within humanitarian and evacuation operations including making them more flexible.[53] Poland's approach towards the Battlegroups reflects that of CSDP: it should be a tool for civil-military operations and it should be usable.

In terms of making CSDP more capable, another item on the Presidency agenda was Pooling and Sharing which Poland supports. The then Polish Defense Minister Tomasz Siemoniak stated that "in order to meet the challenges more effectively it is worth to cooperate closer (sic) within the EU and NATO. Joining and pooling some capabilities, 'lending' or buying them from each other we can do more, at lower cost and more effectively."[54] Pooling and Sharing is certainly seen as a project which has some longevity.[55] This instrument was extended to a further four projects in 2012. Additionally the European Council 2013 welcomed development of Remotely Piloted Aircraft Systems (RPAS), air-to-air refueling capacity, work on satellite communication and cyber.[56] However, Poland will still look for project cost efficiency and for partners which give the best price.[57] Although Poland is participating in certain projects such as Maritime Surveillance Networking, the European Satellite Communication Procurement Cell, and Air-to-Air Refuelling, it has not taken any project ideas to the EDA.[58]

51   Confidential interview with a Polish official (2013).
52   Polish Presidency, *Increasing Flexibility of the EU's Battlegroups Position Paper* (Brussels, 2011), 1.
53   *Ibid.*, 1–2.
54   Tomasz Siemoniak, "Savings or Security – Tomasz Siemoniak, Gazeta Wyborcza Daily" (Warsaw, 9 July 2012), available at <http://archiwalny.mon.gov.pl/en/artykul/13387>.
55   Confidential interview with a Polish official (2013).
56   European Council, Conclusions: Common Security and Defence Policy. Brussels 20 December EUCO 217/13 (2013).
57   Confidential interview with a Polish official (2013).
58   *Ibid.*

This brings about the final component of the European Council – the defense industry. As underlined above Poland has announced an overhaul of its military equipment. Nonetheless, the idea is to ensure work for Poland's own defense industry including state owned Bumar. Indeed Siemoniak has been quoted as stating that "whoever promises us a greater share of technology transfer and work in Poland will be favoured"[59] which appears to conflict with the EU's defense procurement directive which Poland has signed. However Poland does aim in the medium to long term to integrate "the Polish defense sector with the European defence sector, while protecting the former and consciously raising its level of competitiveness."[60] Currently, however Poland's approach to CSDP highlights that it views it as a civil-military instrument as well as highlighting the core of Poland's strategic culture: its independence which is based on its security.

Evidently to be a reliable partner Poland has to back this up with being a more capable one as underlined above with the country's military transformation program and support for capability development initiatives. However what it means to be a reliable partner has also come up in the context of the former President Komorowski's comments in 2013. In particular Poland's defense budget should be focused on the country's military transformation rather than on foreign operations although Poland would continue to be a reliable ally and participate in operations "within the scope of its needs and possibilities."[61] The catalyst for this is the ending of NATO's Afghanistan Operation which has in turn made Poland re-assess its previously "'overzealous' policy of 'eagerly sending Polish forces to the world's antipodes.'"[62] Again this emphasizes Poland's regional threat perception although the fact that Poland's reliable ally status still matters is palpable. In the context of the Polish military transformation Siemoniak stated that the main challenge is "making them an effective instrument of defending state's territory but at the same time contributing what is expected to the Euro-Atlantic security architecture."[63] Also Sikorksi underlines that "security largely depends on our own defence potential."[64] Beyond

---

59   Cienski, *op. cit.* note 32.

60   Ministry of Foreign Affairs, *op. cit.* note 37, 15.

61   President of the Republic of Poland, "President: No More Far-off Military Missions" (2013), available at <http://www.president.pl/en/news/news/art,485,president-no-more-far-off-military-missions.html>.

62   *Ibid.*

63   Siemoniak, *op. cit.* note 54.

64   Radosław Sikorski, "Address by the Minister of Foreign Affairs on the Goals of Polish Foreign Policy in 2013" (2013), available at <http://www.msz.gov.pl/resource/b67d71b2-2537-4637-91d4-531b0e71c023:JCR>, 22.

2013, this has become more prominent not least with Russian intervention in Ukraine and annexation of the Crimea.

Evidently there is a continuing conflict in Polish strategic culture between Poland's regional and territorial threat perception and its desire to be a reliable ally and leader. To lead, you not only have to be at the decision making table but also participate. Whilst Komorowski's comments were made in the context of the end of NATO's Afghanistan operation, more recent geopolitical (Russia) and domestic (the rise of the euro-sceptic, anti-Russian and nationalistic Law and Justice Party) changes may mean that territorial defense is prioritised over expeditionary operations. Whether this will impact on Poland's role in CSDP is questionable considering that CSDP operations are much smaller and are primarily civilian missions. However Politically at least, Poland has been determined to push forward with the reform of CSDP.

6   Conclusion: Poland as a Leader in CSDP?

This Chapter underlined key components of Poland's strategic culture: Atlanticism, "nothing about us without us", regional and territorial defender and promoter, reliable ally, using force pro-actively which have all had an impact on how Poland approaches CSDP. It has traced the transformation of Poland's attitude towards CSDP from a skeptical participant to a military and potentially political leader up until 2013. The question is whether Poland can be considered a "go to" player in European defense in light of Komorowski's comments and more recent events.[65] Clearly at the political level, Poland is determined to make CSDP more efficient and capable. However, Poland also wants to see that CSDP is relevant to its own security perceptions including an emphasis on regional security. Therefore Komorowski's comments underline a lessening of Poland's overt use of force particularly when it comes at the expense of the country's own defense transformation and thus its security. This is backed up by the country's announcement not to participate in any military action in Syria. However considering that Poland is continuing to contribute in CSDP operations including recently the EU's EUTM mission in Mali underlines that being a reliable ally is important and that CSDP operations will still include Polish support and participation.

---

65   Nick Witney, *Re-energising Europe's Security and Defence Policy* (European Council on Foreign Relations, London, 2008), available at <http://www.ecfr.eu/page/-/ECFR-06-RE -ENERGISING_EUROPES_SECURITY.pdf>, 24.

This highlights that Poland has become more realistic concerning what it can expect in return for its support and participation as well as what is feasible when 27 out of 28 Member States need to agree. At the same time, CSDP needs to be useable and it is this which is driving Poland's approach. Therefore Poland is looking to build coalitions within the EU to try and create a policy which is fit for purpose in line with its focus on being included in decisions which impact on its security. Thus what we are seeing is not a wholesale change in Polish strategic culture but rather a shift in stance reflecting changes in the international security environment which has brought about conflict within the country's strategic culture. Whilst Polish threat perceptions have altered, new security threats sit beside traditional defense tasks which results in Poland's Atlanticism. This has been conflicting with the country's desire to be included in defense decisions which impact on its security ("nothing about us without us"), its leadership role, its reliable ally status and its pro-activism to use force as this often requires Poland to participate in operations outside the region.

Hence modifications have been made which have resulted in slightly altered meanings concerning Poland's Atlanticism (which is more pragmatic), its use of force (which is less overt) and its reliable ally status where Poland will not automatically participate in any operation of its allies choosing but rather is more balanced. Being a "reliable ally" works both ways. However this does not make Poland any less of a leader particularly in the context of CSDP. Indeed, the country's stance concerning its ability to lead has completely shifted from an "active participant"[66] to a country actively seeking a leadership role.[67] In the post-Lisbon era, when countries who wish to provide a motor for CSDP are thin on the ground, Poland has tried to step up to the challenge. Whether Poland can maintain this position in consideration of more recent events remains to be seen.

Bibliography

Berger, Thomas. (1998) *Cultures of Antimilitarism: National Security in Germany and Japan* (John Hopkins University Press, London).

Chappell, Laura. (2012) *Germany, Poland and the Common Security and Defence Policy. Converging Perspectives in an Enlarged EU* (Palgrave Macmillan, Basingstoke).

---

66   Chappell, *op. cit.* note 3.

67   Radosław Sikorski, *The Minister of Foreign Affairs on Polish Foreign Policy for 2011* (2011), available at <http://www.mfa.gov.pl/resource/86efef22-d645-4dd8-9532-9e244ed41b1e: JCR>, 5–6.

Chappell, Laura. (2010) "Poland in Transition: Implications for a European Security and Defence Policy", 31(2) *Contemporary Security Policy*, 225–248.

Duffield, John. (1998) *World Power Forsaken* (Stanford University Press, Stanford).

Dunn, David. (2003) "Poland: America's New Model Ally", in Zaborowski, Marcin and Dunn, David. (eds.), *Poland – A New Power in Transatlantic Security* (Frank Cass Publishers, London), 63–86.

Gray, Colin S. (1999) "Strategic Culture as Context: The First Generation of Theory Strikes Back", 7(1) *International Affairs*, 49–69.

Hill, Christopher. (1993) "The Capability-Expectations Gap, or Conceptualizing Europe's International Role", 31(3) *Journal of Common Market Studies*, 305–328.

Komorowski, Stanisław J. (2008) "Poland's Objectives in European Security & Defence", paper presented at the 7th congress on European Security and Defence (Berlin, 10 November), available at <http://www.european-defence.com/Review/2008/binarywriterservlet?imgUid=d4e30a99-62fb-2031-0648-01f307b988f2&uBasVariant=1111111-1111-1111-1111-111111111111>.

Longhurst, Kerry. (2004) *Germany and the Use of Force* (Manchester University Press, Manchester).

Longhurst, Kerry and Zaborowski, Marcin. (2007) *The New Atlanticist Poland's Foreign and Security Policy Priorities* (Blackwell Publishing, Oxford).

Melamed, Mark. (2005) "Polish-American Relations in the Aftermath of War in Iraq", 5(2) *The Polish Foreign Affairs Digest*, 7–21.

Meyer, Christoph. O. (2006) *The Quest for a European Strategic Culture: Changing Norms on Security and Defence in the European Union* (Palgrave Macmillan, New York).

O'Donnell, Clara Marina. (2012) "Poland's U-turn on European Defense: A Missed Opportunity?" *U.S.-Europe Analysis Series* No. 53, 1–5.

Osica, Olaf. (2004) "Poland: A New European Atlanticist at a Crossroads?", 13(4) *European Security*, 301–322.

Podolski, Antoni. (2005) "Polska Strategia Bezpieczeństwa Narodowego jako praktyczna implementacja Europejskiej Strategii Bezpieczeństwa – między teorią a praktyką (Polish National Security Strategy as a Practical Implementation of the European Security Strategy – between Theory and Practice)", *Raporty i Analizy* No.1, available at <http://www.csm.org.pl/pl/files/raporty/2005/rap_i_an_0105.pdf>.

Pomorska, Karolina and Vanhoonacker, Sophie. (2012) "Poland in the Driving Seat: A Mature Presidency in Turbulent Times", 50 *JCMS Annual Review*, 76–84.

Terlikowski, Marcin. (2013) "No One Left Behind? European Defence and 'Brexit'", 158(4) *The RUSI Journal*, 26–30.

Witney, Nick. (2008) *Re-energising Europe's Security and Defence Policy* (European Council on Foreign Relations, London), available at <http://www.ecfr.eu/page/-/ECFR-06-RE-ENERGISING_EUROPES_SECURITY.pdf>.

CHAPTER 12

Prague on a Mission: Emphasizing Democracy Promotion within EU Foreign Policy

Marek Neuman

Abstract

This contribution studies the implications of widening on the EU foreign policy domain. By means of a detailed case study, the more specific focus is on how, and whether, the Czech Republic succeeded in reflecting its strong stance on human rights and democracy promotion in the EU's foreign policy. The contribution finds that the overall impact Prague has had on injecting the EU's external democratization policy with new impetus is limited at best, certainly if juxtaposed against its ambitious national preference. Yet, the study is also able to conclude that it should be hardly surprising that the Czech Republic would set out to remedy what it regarded to be the EU's ailing approach to democracy promotion. As such, it adds to EU integration scholarship by arguing that what are often termed "unexpected" consequences of the 2004 EU enlargement should have been "expected" all along.

Keywords

legislative history – Czech Republic – Czech Council Presidency – EU foreign policy – external democratization policy

1 Introduction

During the opening session of the "Building Consensus about EU Policies on Democracy Support" conference held during the Czech Republic's 2009 Council Presidency, former Czech President Václav Havel called upon the EU to take action against countries "where the violation of human rights is most flagrant, where there are political prisoners, where journalists are murdered, or where citizens are harassed in any way."[1] With this statement, Havel confirmed what

---

1 "Report from the Conference", paper presented at the Building Consensus about EU Policies on Democracy Support Conference (Prague, 2009), 30.

many scholars concerned with the implications of the 2004 EU enlargement had long suspected – new Member States would seek a shift in the European Union's foreign policy, including areas that were not foreseen prior to the widening itself. The general sentiment among scholars was that the soon-to-be new Member States would push for a more unified – and somewhat firmer – approach towards Russia, Eastern Europe, and the Commonwealth of Independent States (CIS). Based on their proximity to Russia and the rest of Eastern Europe, and due to their collective histories, new Member States were expected to upload their bilateral foreign policy preferences *vis-à-vis* their Eastern neighbors onto the EU level, thereby causing a geopolitical shift in the EU's foreign policy agenda.[2] However, Havel's call also indicated that within the EU foreign policy domain, new Member States would also pursue preferences beyond those strictly pertaining to Russia, often in areas not deemed strategic or salient by the other members.

Consequently, this contribution scrutinizes one of the "unexpected results" of the EU's 2004 enlargement to the East. The EU-15 was soon confronted with the desire of some of the new Member States to shift the EU's foreign policy in line with their domestic preferences, including in the domain of the EU's external democratization policy. As one of the most vocal proponents of such a shift, the focus of this contribution is on the Czech Republic. Prague planned to take full advantage of its 2009 EU Council Presidency to translate its own foreign policy preferences regarding democracy promotion into EU-wide policy. As such, this study sets out to answer three interrelated questions: (i) what was the Czech domestic preference on external democratization that Prague would upload to Brussels?; (ii) how did Prague go about uploading the preference onto the supranational level and which mechanisms did it rely upon during the multiple negotiation rounds?; and (iii) to what extent was the Czech Republic successful in its endeavor? By answering these questions, this study

---

2   See, for instance, Richard G. Whitman, "The Common Foreign and Security Policy after Enlargement", in Victoria Curzon Price, Alice Landau, and Richard G. Whitman (eds.), *The Enlargement of the European Union: Issues and Strategies* (Routledge, London, 1999); Jackie Gower, "EU-Russian Relations and the Eastern Enlargement: Integration or Isolation?" 1(1) *Perspectives on European Politics and Society* (2000), 75–93; Karen E. Smith, "The Outsiders: The European Neighbourhood Policy", 81(4) *International Affairs* (2005), 757–773; Jackie Gower, "The European Union's Policy on Russia: Rhetoric or Reality?" in Jackie Gower and Graham Timmins (eds.), *Russia and Europe in the Twenty-First Century: An Uneasy Partnership* (Anthem Press, London, 2007); and Kristi Raik, "A Europe Divided by Russia? The New Eastern Member States and the EU's Policy towards the East", in Jackie Gower and Graham Timmins (eds.), *Russia and Europe in the Twenty-First Century: An Uneasy Partnership* (Anthem Press, London, 2007).

hopes to add to the rather threadbare literature on the impact of the new Member States in shaping the EU's legislative process. This contribution will reveal the policy process preceding the (non)adoption of particular legal acts – more specifically, the European Consensus on Democracy and the statutes of the Civil Society Forum – and should be seen as a stepping stone for further legal research into the (non)binding nature of these very acts.

In trying to answer the above-stated questions, this contribution is anchored within Europeanization scholarship, more precisely its bottom-up dimension. This enables placing focus on both the concept of policy misfit (and the degree thereof) and the processes of national preference uploading to the EU level as one of the possible venues to reduce the previously identified misfit.[3] Such theoretical grounding is particularly relevant with regard to the EU policy domain scrutinized within this chapter. The EU's Common Foreign and Security Policy (CFSP) largely remains intergovernmental and analyses of individual Member States' policy input thus becomes merited.[4] The case study is completed by employing detailed process tracing, which is complemented by an analysis of primary and secondary sources, as well as over thirty interviews conducted with relevant policy makers on both the national and European levels.

The article begins by establishing the degree of misfit between the EU's and the Czech Republic's approaches to external democratization, thereby identifying the foreign policy preference Prague would pursue in Brussels. The next section discusses how the Czech Republic went about influencing two concrete proposals on EU structures – a Consensus on Democracy and the Civil Society Forum as part of the Eastern Partnership. It continues by assessing the

---

3   See, for instance, Simon Bulmer and Martin Burch, "Coming to Terms with Europe: Europeanisation, Whitehall and the Challenge of Devolution", *Queen's Papers on Europeanisation* (2000) No.9; Thomas Risse, Maria Green Cowles, and James A. Caporaso, "Europeanization and Domestic Change: Introduction", in Maria Green Cowles, James A. Caporaso, and Thomas Risse (eds.), *Transforming Europe: Europeanization and Domestic Change* (Cornell University Press, Ithaca, 2001); Tanja Boerzel, "Shaping and Taking EU Policies: Member State Responses to Europeanisation", *Queen's Papers on Europeanisation* (2003) No.2; and Michael Baun and Dan Marek (eds.), *The New Member States and the European Union: Foreign Policy and Europeanization* (Routledge, Abingdon, 2013).

4   See, for instance, Geoffrey Edwards, "The New Member States and the Making of EU Foreign Policy", 11(2) *European Foreign Affairs Review* (2006), 143–162; Peter Viggo Jakobsen, "Small States, Big Influence: The Overlooked Nordic Influence on the Civilian ESDP", 47(1) *Journal of Common Market Studies* (2009), 81–102; and Marek Neuman, *Too Small to Make an Impact?: The Czech Republic's Influence on the European Union's Foreign Policy* (Peter Lang, Frankfurt am Main, 2015).

mechanisms Prague utilized to garner support for its proposals among its European partners in the numerous negotiation rounds. The concluding section summarizes the main findings and establishes the extent to which the Czech Republic can be deemed a successful norm entrepreneur, before ending with a more general discussion on whether the "unexpected" consequences of the EU enlargement should have been "expected" from the beginning.

2   Identifying a Misfit between the EU's and the Czech Republic's External Democratization Policies

External democratization policy is usually closely intertwined with external human rights policy, which both the European Union as a whole and the Czech Republic as one of its Member States duly recognized in their statements.[5] Disregarding this conceptual consensus, the policy approach adopted by Brussels and Prague could not have been more divergent. The European Union has traditionally not been a conscious democracy and a human rights promoting actor abroad. Since the 1973 Copenhagen Declaration on European Identity, the Member States have reiterated to "defend the principles of representative democracy, of the rule of law, of social justice – which is the ultimate goal of economic progress – and of respect for human rights."[6] Yet, the statement was strictly inward-looking, which cannot come as a surprise when understood in light of the European Union's *raison d'être* at that point in time – to facilitate enhanced *economic* relations among the Member States. Such an isolationist approach became unviable in light of the global events that shaped the late 1980s/early 1990s. The collapse of the Soviet Union provided the EU with a new impetus to develop an efficient toolkit of mechanisms that could be employed to actively co-shape the newly developing countries' stance towards both democracy as a legitimate political system and human rights observance as an integral part of democracy.[7] The EU's operationalization of this sudden policy interest left much to be desired. Most importantly, Brussels seemed to

---

5   "EU Strategic Framework and Action Plan on Human Rights and Democracy" (Council of the European Union, Luxembourg, 12 June 2012); and "Conceptual Basis of the Foreign Policy of the Czech Republic" (Ministry of Foreign Affairs, Prague), as approved by the Government of the Czech Republic on 20 July 2011, 21–22.

6   "Declaration on European Identity", in *Bulletin of the European Communities* (Office for Official Publications of the European Communities, Luxembourg, 14 December 1973), 1.

7   Karen E. Smith, "The EU, Human Rights and Relations with Third Countries: 'Foreign Policy' with and Ethical Dimension?" in Karen E. Smith and Margot Light (eds.), *Ethics and Foreign Policy* (Cambridge University Press, Cambridge, 2001), 187.

systematically prioritize the promotion of human rights over the promotion of democracy. Consequently, during the ensuing EU "rights turn",[8] human rights promotion abroad – previously a non-issue – was integrated into the EU's communitarized trade, development, and aid policies, alongside its intergovernmental external dimension as manifested by the CFSP.[9] These policies resulted in the development of several human rights promotion instruments throughout the 1990s, with Smith identifying four: conditionality, aid, diplomacy, and the deployment of civilian and military missions.[10]

Whereas some headway was achieved in streamlining human rights promotion into the EU's external relations policies, the policies' external democratization aspect remained underdeveloped.[11] This was not only the result of a discussion among individual Member States as to how to implement the EU's democratization agenda, but also the result of a more fundamental disagreement about whether democracy as a governing system can be – and should be – promoted in the first place, and to what extent this would need to be driven by domestic demand for external assistance in the targeted countries. Accordingly, by the early 2000s, the EU's framework for external human rights and democratization policy suffered from many shortcomings. Brussels not only failed to systematically and consistently define both terms,[12] but was also accused of creating both an internal-external and rhetoric-practice gap in its external human rights and democratization approach.[13] Most importantly, rather than developing one comprehensive policy that would stress the promotion of both democratization and human rights observance as two inseparable sides of the same coin, the EU – in practice – decided to focus on these issues separately, sending an inconsistent message to the many potential recipients of its policy.

---

8   Agustín José Menéndez, "Human Rights: The European Charter of Fundamental Rights", in Walter Carlsnaes, Helene Sjursen, and Brian White (eds.), *Contemporary European Foreign Policy* (SAGE, London, 2004), 240.

9   Karen E. Smith, *European Union Foreign Policy in a Changing World*, 2nd edition (Polity Press, Cambridge, 2008), 121.

10   See, for instance, *ibid.*, 127–136.

11   The one obvious exception is the European Union's contribution to the democratic transitions in the countries of Central and Eastern Europe.

12   Landman and Larizza show in a comprehensive discourse analysis of some twenty-three EU documents that the terms remain undefined, and are often being presented as means to the achievement of other ends, particularly economic development. Todd Landman and Marco Larizza, "EU Policy Discourse: Democracy, Governance, and Human Rights" (International Institute for Democracy and Electoral Assistance, Stockholm, 2010), 14–52.

13   See, for instance, the discussion in Smith, *op. cit.* note 9, 114–116 and 167.

At the beginning, the Czech Republic's human rights and democratization policy was internally-geared to guide its own transition efforts and to distance itself from its communist past. Its own historical experience with a communist political regime was soon also reflected in Prague's newly emerging foreign policy, where both human rights and democracy became an inherent component. In essence, since the early 1990s, Prague began to position itself as a human rights and democratization actor who should be taken seriously, greatly aided by the support of the likes of Václav Havel, Karel Schwarzenberg, Jiří Dienstbier, and Šimon Pánek. While Prague's policy focus thus overlapped with the one articulated in Brussels, the Czech Republic vocally opposed the EU's above-described separation of the two policy strands. To give its protest form, the Czech Ministry of Foreign Affairs (MFA) created the Department for Human Rights and Transformation Politics (LPTP), which articulated the Czech Republic's *transition policy* would support projects abroad only if they would couple human rights support with democracy promotion. In terms of operationalization, Prague's efforts focused on strengthening civil society in ten initial priority countries, spanning the globe from Latin America (Cuba), to Europe (Belarus, Bosnia and Herzegovina, Kosovo, Moldova, Georgia, Serbia, Ukraine) and the Middle East (Iraq), and Asia (Burma).[14] Over time, Prague came to realize that it could "use its transition experience particularly in relation to countries that are culturally, geographically, historically or otherwise similar [and] therefore focuse[d] on collaboration with partners in Eastern Europe and the Western Balkans."[15] In addition to its geographic scope, the Czech transition policy was characterized by two additional features. First, in terms of democracy promotion, the Czech Republic was willing to brace for short periods of instability if the long-term prospects of establishing democratic rule in the target country so require.[16] Second, the bulk of the responsibility for the success of the mission was to be assumed by the many participating non-governmental organizations (NGOs). Each transition project supported

14   Veronika Bílková and Šárka Matějková, "Šíření demokracie jako národní zájem? Legitimizace české transformační politiky (Democracy Promotion as National Interest? The Legitimazation of Czech Transition Politics)", in Petr Drulák and Ondřej Horký (eds.), *Hledání českých zájmů: Obchod, lidská práva a mezinárodní rozvoj (In Search of Czech Interests: Trade, Human Rights and International Development)* (Ústav mezinárodních vztahů, Institute of International Relations, Prague, 2010), 128.

15   "Transition Policy" (Ministry of Foreign Affairs, Prague, 2010), 3.

16   Gabriela Dlouhá and Jan Šnaidauf, "Toward a Common Approach to the Global Pro-Democracy Agenda and a Revival of Democracy Promotion in the Arab-Muslim World", in *Policy Brief by the MFA of the Czech Republic* (Ministry of Foreign Affairs, Prague, 2011), 3.

by the Czech MFA was implemented by at least one specific Czech NGO as is illustrated elsewhere.

Recognizing a certain degree of misfit between the Czech and EU-wide approach towards external human rights and democratization promotion, it may come as no surprise that once a full EU member, Prague set out to have its own domestic preference translated onto the EU level. The period prior to its 2009 EU Council Presidency saw the most activity, supporting Tallberg's notion of the strategic importance individual Member States attach to the rotating Council Presidency, as it enables them to (partially) shape the EU policy agenda.[17] Before uploading its preference to the supranational level, the Czech MFA took stock on which aspects of its transition policy should form the locus of its domestically defined preference *qua* EU external human rights and democracy promotion. While previous research has shown that the Czech Ministry of Foreign Affairs was inconsistent in providing access points for civil society actors interested in co-shaping the Czech national preference,[18] with regard to its transition policy, the MFA's approach differed substantially. The level of cooperation between the institutional actors (the LPTP in particular) and the civil society sector was unprecedented, at times making a differentiation of the contribution each of these made to the national position difficult, if not outright impossible. Indicative was the MFA's initiation and funding of the establishment of the Association for Democracy Assistance and Human Rights (DEMAS), which was founded in 2008 initially to bring together eleven of the most prominent Czech NGOs. The purpose was to streamline the LPTP's communication with the NGO sector. Besides non-governmental organizations, prominent individuals – mostly united under the banner of the former dissent and considered the moral authority – made their voices heard either directly in the MFA or through various seminars, workshops, conferences, and media appearances.

---

17   Jonas Tallberg, "The Agenda-Shaping Powers of the EU Council Presidency", 10(1) *Journal of European Public Policy* (2003), 1–19. Note that since the Lisbon Treaty entered into force, the newly created Foreign Affairs Council – as the only one of the ten existing Council constellations – no longer is subject to the rotating Council Presidency. Yet, the entire remaining structure of the Council of the European Union – including all the working groups dealing with foreign policy matters and both COREPER and COPS – continue to be led by a representative of the presiding country. As such, further research into whether the Member States' ability to co-shape the EU's foreign policy agenda has remained intact is necessary. This is irrelevant to the present study as the Czech Republic held its Council Presidency before the Lisbon Treaty entered into force on 1 December 2009.

18   Marek Neuman, "The Nexus between Czech Non-State Actors and Domestic Foreign Policy Making in the EU Presidency Context", 19(1) *Perspectives* (2011), 5–26.

Through the joint effort of these three actor groups – the MFA represented by
the LPTP, the non-governmental sector, and the Czech moral authorities – the
Czech national preference *qua* the European Union's future human rights and
democratization policy began to take shape. Among others, the Czech bureaucracy was urged (i) to recognize the potential the Czech Republic (and other
Central and Eastern European countries) could play in bringing about democratic change (in the near) abroad; (ii) to restructure its own grant scheme and
to initiate a refurbishment of the European Instrument for Democracy and
Human Rights (EIDHR); (iii) to make use of its upcoming Council Presidency,
increasing the visibility of human rights and democracy promotion; and (iv)
to streamline and strengthen institutional cooperation with and within such
groupings as the Visegrád Four, the EU and its institutions, the OSCE, and the
United Nations.[19] Moreover, the Czech Republic was urged to "support only
activities with a clear democracy assistance component."[20] While the LPTP
outlined the confines of the preference-to-be, the remaining actors filled in
the blanks. Many of the actors' suggestions were specific, ranging from advice
on which countries to target, to how to rank the many human rights in terms
of saliency, and to which democratic principles to promote first. However, the
final Czech national preference was articulated rather broadly. As such, domestically it was decided that the Czech Republic, recognizing the progress the
EU achieved with regard to the promotion of human rights, would pursue the
inclusion of a dedicated democratization dimension to the EU's foreign policy,
which was to be reflected in the European Union's legal framework.

Keeping Prague's bilateral transition policy in mind, the above preference
falls short of expectations. Yet, it speaks to the political pragmatism of the
Czech administration, which realized that jointly pursuing both an enhanced
human rights *and* democratization policy would be too complex. Seeing that
the EU had prioritized the promotion of human rights over democracy, Prague
set out to equalize the two policy strands in the eyes of the remaining Member States. By refraining from defining what the Czech Republic considered to

---

19   Jacek Kucharczyk and Jeff Lovitt (eds.), *Democracy's New Champions: European Democ-*
        racy Assistance after EU Enlargement (Policy Association for an Open Society, Prague,
        2008). Especially, see chapters by Jeff Lovitt and Věra Řiháčková, "Is the EU Ready to Put
        Democracy Assistance at the Heart of European Foreign Policy?"; Jacek Kucharczyk and
        Jeff Lovitt, "New Kids on the Block: Can the Visegrad Four Emerge as Effective Players in
        International Democracy Assistance?"; and Věra Řiháčková, "EU Democracy Assistance
        through Civil Society – Reformed?"
20   Vladimír Bartovic, "Limited Resources, Global Ambitions", in Kucharczyk and Lovitt,
        ibid., 32.

be "democracy", Prague opened up the space to multiple interpretations and thereby broadened the maneuvering space within which EU-wide consensus could be found. Finally, the broad character of the preference testifies to the influence the many domestic actors had on the central administration. Each NGO's interests were often very issue-specific and were not always fully compatible with each other.

3   Agreeing the Impossible? Garnering Support for an EU-Wide Advance on Democracy Promotion[21]

To successfully upload its national preference onto the EU level, the Czech Republic devised three intertwined, yet separate, strategies. The first strategy largely remained outside the EU structures, while the remaining two saw Prague make use of the European Union's institutional web.

The first strategy consisted of leading by example. The MFA continued cooperating with local NGOs when implementing democratization projects abroad. To voice its discontent with the EIDHR's bureaucratic character, the Czech Republic, together with the Netherlands Institute for Multiparty Democracy and several private donors, initiated the establishment of the European Partnership for Democracy (EPD) in 2008. The EPD – created outside official EU structures – was modeled on the American National Endowment for Democracy organization. Its purpose was to facilitate the increased need for financial support for democracy-promoting projects in a less cumbersome way.

The remaining two strategies were pursued from within existing EU structures. Prague pursued a shift in the EU's conceptual understanding of assisting democratic efforts in third countries by introducing – and during its Presidency negotiating – a *European Consensus on Democracy*. Modeled on the *European Consensus on Development* adopted in 2005,[22] the document was to comprehensively define the constitutive elements of democracy, institutionalize active democracy promotion within EU structures, and operationalize this by defining an exhaustive list of policy instruments to be employed.

---

21   This section has been presented at ECPR General Conference (Montreal, 26–29 August 2015).

22   "The European Consensus on Development: Joint Statement by the Council and the Representatives of the Governments of the Member States Meeting within the Council, the European Parliament and the Commission on European Union Development Policy: 'The European Consensus'", Official Journal of the European Union C 46 (2006).

The third and final strategy focused on the European Union's democratization policy *on the ground*. Specifically – and in line with Prague's democratization policy's geographic scope – the intended Eastern Partnership (also negotiated during Prague's Council Presidency[23]) was seen as an appropriate testing ground for the Union's reinvigorated approach to democracy building abroad. Besides its own bilateral efforts to further democratic development in Belarus, Georgia, Moldova, and Ukraine, Prague sought to launch a multilateral dimension on behalf of Brussels. This strategy ultimately found its anchoring in the proposed Civil Society Forum (CSF), which became an inseparable dimension of the Eastern Partnership and was intended to significantly strengthen the civil society in the respective partner countries.

The Czech Republic's uploading efforts primarily consisted of raising awareness and familiarizing the other EU capitals with the dire state of democracy in countries such as Belarus, Ukraine, Russia, and Burma. Rather than emphasizing the normative legitimacy of its preference by solely invoking the non-instrumental *right* to live in a democratic society, Prague also made references to the instrumental goal of enhanced internal security stemming from stable democratic neighbors. Preference uploading then took place along both a governmental and non-governmental track, where the former can further be distinguished into formal and informal norm diffusion.

Turning first to governmental norm diffusion, Prague's efforts in Brussels were coordinated by the Permanent Representation of the Czech Republic to the European Union. This task was by no means an easy one. Horizontal coordination difficulties exist with regard to external democratization both within the Council of the European Union and between the Council and other EU institutions (the Commission first and foremost). Indeed, due to the relevance of democracy to policy areas such as international trade, human rights, and development, Prague's representatives to the many involved working groups faced the challenging task of conveying a united message. This was aggravated to an even greater extent by the fact that the two working groups most concerned – the Working Party on Human Rights (COHOM) and the Working Party on Eastern Europe and Central Asia (COEST) – operate differently. The Czech Republic has a permanent representative to COEST, which meets on a weekly basis, if not more. However, at COHOM meetings – which take place only once a month – Prague is represented by MFA staff from Prague's

---

23   Marek Neuman, "The Czech Republic's EU Accession: A Shift-Producing Variable in the EU's Foreign Policy towards Russia?" in Bruno Arcidiacono, Katrin Milzow, Axel Marion, and Pierre-Étienne Bourneouf (eds.), *Europe Twenty Years after the End of the Cold War: The New Europe, New Europes?* (Peter Lang, Brussels, 2012).

headquarters, most often by the LPTP director him/herself. To remedy for the resulting limited socialization opportunities, Czech representatives to the relevant working groups were instructed to at all times make use of their right to outline Prague's position. This strategy was not always embraced by the other states' representatives, who thought it "unnecessarily" prolonged discussions. While some European partners began to label their Czech counterparts as "activists",[24] following a consistent line served the purpose of increasing Prague's visibility *vis-à-vis* external democratization. In addition, the Czech Republic distributed human rights and democracy reports compiled directly by kindred NGOs from Belarus through Coreu, establishing a precedent in terms of the network's employability.[25] The Czech administration also made use of the more informal venues to diffuse its position *qua* external democratization among its European partners. The most striking of these was Milena Vicenová's (then Czech Ambassador to the EU) invitation to the entire Committee of Permanent Representatives II (COREPER II) to a four-day visit to the Czech Republic. This visit was filled with multiple seminars, workshops, and cinematic screenings all meant to convey the spirit of globally strengthening the protection of human rights and democratic development.[26]

The second non-governmental track of preference diffusion was dominated by DEMAS, closely cooperating with the MFA. This entailed the Czech Republic's Permanent Representation to the EU scheduling meetings between DEMAS representatives and relevant EU officials, during which they highlighted the saliency of adopting a reinvigorated EU-wide approach to democracy promotion in line with the Czech preference.[27] Most importantly, DEMAS, together with the MFA and the European Partnership for Democracy, organized the most visible norm uploading event – the aforementioned 2009 conference "Building Consensus about EU Policies on Democracy Support" in Prague. It was here that the fundamental principles of the Consensus-to-be regarding democracy policy were outlined: (i) ownership; (ii) partnership; (iii) dialogue and inclusiveness; (iv) long-term commitment to democracy support;

---

24   Interview, Ministry of Foreign Affairs (Prague, 2011).

25   Traditionally, Coreu – as the EU's diplomatic communication network – is used only to disseminate official documents of the Member States' ministries.

26   Interview, Permanent Representation of the Czech Republic to the European Union (Brussels, 2010).

27   Moreover, not only did the MFA schedule these meetings, it also reimbursed DEMAS' travel expenses. Found in Senka Neuman Stanivuković and Marek Neuman, "From Preference Formation at Home to Preference Promotion Abroad: The Role of Czech Intrastate Actors", 4(2) *Central European Journal of International & Security Studies* (2010), 8–27, at 3–4.

(v) complementarity of existing policies and instruments; (vi) technical as well as political assistance; and (vii) taking a multiple-track approach.[28]

The question of the extent to which the Czech Republic's uploading efforts were successful still remains. Prague was able to garner support for its national preference among its kindred democratization allies – mainly the Baltic countries, the Netherlands, Poland, Sweden, and the United Kingdom. However, Prague encountered opposition in other EU countries. Particularly vocal were France and Italy, with their concerns grounded in both a debate on whether to first promote democracy or (economic) development and a more fundamental debate on whether or not to promote democracy at all, fearing the CEECs' interest in external democratization was a sign of revived Atlanticism.[29] Despite such disagreements, the EU as a whole did agree on the saliency of supporting democracy promotion in its relations with third countries, thereby establishing grounds for future negotiations. On the one hand, then, the Czech Republic's proposal for a Civil Society Forum received backing in the form of the 2008 EC communication on the Eastern Partnership with two of the proposed thematic platforms taking up the matter of democracy building – *Democracy, good governance and stability* and *Contacts between people*.[30] On the other hand, however, the Czech Republic only secured preliminary support for its *European Consensus on Democracy* proposal in early 2009, at which time Prague and Stockholm (the succeeding EU Council Presidency) agreed they would proceed jointly. After circulating a joint non-paper among the other Member States, the matter was picked up by the European Commission, which then circulated its own concept paper largely based on the Czech-Swedish proposal in July 2009[31] – after the end of Prague's Council Presidency. Disregarding the Commission's support, as of fall 2015, a *European Consensus on Democracy* has yet to be adopted. Consequently, the Czech Republic failed in bringing about a legally binding, comprehensive document that would define what the European Union understands to be "democracy." This not only speaks to the sensitivity of democracy as a policy domain, but also to the importance of securing continuous support for ambitious proposals across several consecutive Council Presidencies. Such support faded as a result of the scepter of the Council

28   "Report", *op. cit.*, note 1, 34–35.

29   Jacek Kucharczyk and Jeff Lovitt, "Re-Energising Europe to Champion Democracy", in Kucharczyk and Lovitt, *op. cit.* note 19.

30   "Communication from the Commission to the European Parliament and the Council: Eastern Partnership" (Commission of the European Communities, Brussels, 2008), 9–12.

31   "Joint Paper – Commission/Council General Secretariat on Democracy Building in EU External Relations" (Council of the European Union, Brussels, 2009).

Presidency being passed from Sweden to Spain in 2010, who was generally less euphoric about external democratization.

Regarding the external democratization agenda, the remainder of the Czech Council Presidency was spent negotiating the details of the one Czech proposal that received sufficient initial support from the other Member States – the Civil Society Forum. Being negotiated together with the proposal for an Eastern Partnership, the CSF had to overcome the same difficulties that shaped the negotiation arena at the beginning of 2009. During this time, the Presidency was faced with bringing the 2008/2009 Gaza War to an end, finding a solution to the 2009 Russia-Ukraine gas dispute, and preventing the erection of protectionist measures by the individual Member States as a response to the global economic crisis. Thus, the more normative aspects of Prague's Presidency program were at first somewhat pushed to the sidelines. Despite this – and having secured the Commission's support on both the Partnership and the Forum – Prague proceeded with negotiating the details of the six Eastern European countries' civil societies' involvement. In COHOM, Prague set out (i) to gain the support of the other twenty-six Member States to launch the Forum together with the Eastern Partnership; (ii) to empower the CSF by structuring it as the Partnership's mirror image; and (iii) to equip the CSF with direct access to the Partnership platform.[32] Prague proposed to structure the Forum along the same four thematic platforms on which the Eastern Partnership was to be built, ensuring comparable agendas at both governmental and non-governmental levels.

Each of the Forum's four thematic platforms were to produce recommendations pertinent to its policy area, present these at annual Civil Society Forum conferences, and then have selected representatives brief and participate in the Partnership platforms and ministerial meetings. To achieve the transposition of these goals into the Forum's founding statute, Prague attempted to strengthen its position within COHOM by pointing out its expertise in the democratization domain in Eastern Europe. COHOM meetings were chaired by LPTP director Dlouhá, and the Czech Republic made use of what Haverland terms "expert strategy."[33] This strategy entailed the mobilization of *content expertise* by the government to increase its leverage in Brussels, which may explain policy making beyond the lowest common denominator. Dlouhá illustrated Prague's long-standing experience with supporting non-governmental organizations in the EU's Eastern neighborhood. As already addressed,

---

32   Neuman, *op. cit.*, note 23, 6.

33   Markus Haverland, "How Leader States Influence EU Policy-Making: Analysing the Expert Strategy", 13(25) *European Integration Online Papers* (2009), 2.

Prague's uploading efforts witnessed the precedent of the MFA using Coreu to disseminate non-governmental organizations' policy outputs among EU Member States. Adding to this, Prague also resorted to extraordinary negotiation tactics by inviting NGO representatives to COHOM meetings. The Czech Presidency provided Belorussian and Burmese representatives of their respective civil society sectors the ability to directly brief the twenty-seven EU members about the state of human rights and democracy in their country. As an MFA official maintains, the rationale behind this precedent was that the Czech Republic thought this indispensable "when we constantly declare our commitment to civil society and most COHOM officials never met a representative of an NGO."[34]

While the Czech Republic's unorthodox methods of establishing its authority within COHOM bore fruit in the form of the other EU Member States signing off on the Forum,[35] the other two aspects Prague proposed caused controversy. Once again the group of Member States prone to push the democratization agenda – Austria, the Baltic and the Nordic states, the Visegrád Four, the Netherlands, and the United Kingdom – jointly promoted the empowerment of the Forum *vis-à-vis* the Eastern Partnership. And once again the Southern European "bloc" turned out to be the stumbling block. Specifically, France voiced its discomfort with the proposition of civil society representatives accessing the Partnership's multilateral platform. The Czechs realized that the French position on the CSF was guided by a fear that if the Forum – and the Eastern Partnership *writ large* – turned out to be a success, the then ailing and French-favored Union for the Mediterranean could see its funding reduced in favor of the ENP's Eastern dimension. Ultimately, despite COHOM discussions being generally open to mutual persuasion based on best practices and best arguments,[36] the final agreement between the two opposing coalitions took the form of a political compromise. While the Forum would be structured along the Partnership's thematic platforms, which it would monitor, its representatives would be able to access the Eastern Partnership only upon invitation and on an ad-hoc basis. Hence, while civil society organizations would perform the role of shadow governments to the individual Eastern Partnership thematic platforms by drafting their recommendations, these would not be

---

34   Neuman, *op. cit.*, note 23, 4.

35   Interview, Permanent Representation of the Czech Republic to the European Union (Brussels, 2010).

36   Interview, Permanent Representation of the Netherlands to the European Union (Brussels, 2011).

disseminated among relevant Partnership delegates through *official* channels. The result significantly limited the potency of the Civil Society Forum as envisaged by Prague.

4   Conclusion

The purpose of this study was twofold. First, it assessed the ability of the Czech Republic – one of the new Member States – to have its domestically formed foreign policy preference *qua* external human rights and democratization policy translated into an EU-wide policy approach. To this end, this contribution centered on one empirical case study, which allows us to conclude the extent of Prague's success or failure to bring about change in the EU's approach. Employing detailed process-tracing, we can see that Prague – recognizing a certain misfit between its own bilateral approach to *transition politics* and the European Union's approach to the very same – thought it only natural to set out to bring the EU's approach in line with its own understanding of how to promote both greater human rights and democracy observance abroad. Consequently, the MFA, which was in charge of formulating the Czech Republic's policy program for its 2009 EU Council Presidency, worked closely with the Czech non-governmental sector to formulate both a general national preference *qua* external human rights and democracy promotion and several more specific strategies that it would pursue in Brussels. It was agreed that Prague would not only continue to unilaterally position itself as a serious democratization actor in order to create potential for establishing best practice at a later point in time, but would also attempt a more conceptual policy shift within the EU as a whole by pressing for the adoption of a *European Consensus on Democracy*. Finally, this was to find operationalization in (among others) the Civil Society Forum that was to become an inseparable part of the Eastern Partnership initiative.

By the time Prague received general support from the remaining EU Member States for pursuing both strategies multilaterally, the time span for negotiating the European Consensus had become too narrow. Therefore, Prague focused on bringing the CSF negotiations to a fruitful conclusion. However, these too fell victim to the general disagreement among the European partners as to just how democracy should be promoted abroad, with the overall outcome reflecting the lowest common denominator. While the Czech national preference *qua* external democratization promotion was ambitious, when reflecting upon its success of translating this into EU-wide policy making, the overall verdict is rather sobering. When read through the prism of legislative history, we have to conclude that Prague failed to negotiate a binding document accepted by all twenty-seven Member States that would have clearly established the meaning of the word "democracy" as held by the European Union. Prague was somewhat more successful in negotiating the establishment of a Civil Society Forum accompanying the Eastern Partnership. Yet, it is now the task of legal scholars to assess the potency of this very forum for furthering the external democratization cause in areas lying outside of the EU's borders by studying its founding statute.

This leads us to conclude on the second aspect of this contribution, namely assessing what the implications of the 2004 EU enlargement to the East have been on the EU's foreign policy making. First, the case study clearly indicates that the Czech Republic was well positioned to pursue its national policy on the supranational level. Only a few years after becoming an EU Member State, the MFA acknowledged the importance of pursuing its policy preferences along both a governmental and a non-governmental track. These findings add to the scholarship claiming that the new Member States, rather than causing a dead-lock in the EU's policy making, have quickly learned to maneuver the complex EU institutional structure. Second, we can also answer the final question raised in the introduction to this contribution – whether some of the "unexpected" consequences of the 2004 EU enlargement should have been "expected" all along. Whereas pre-2004 EU integration scholarship expected the new Member States to bring along their unique perspectives *vis-à-vis* the Russian Federation, it failed to see that the individual new Member States would look for a more specific foreign policy niche within which they could – with more or less success – establish their authority. It is this omission that this contribution to some extent remedies. In the Czech Republic's case, this policy niche consisted of focusing on the EU's external human rights and democratization agenda. By observing Prague's bilateral foreign policy over the last two and a half decades, this cannot come as a surprise.

Bibliography

Bartovic, Vladimír. (2008) "Limited Resources, Global Ambitions", in Kucharczyk, Jacek and Lovitt, Jeff. (eds.), *Democracy's New Champions: European Democracy Assistance after EU Enlargement* (Policy Association for an Open Society, Prague).

Baun, Michael and Marek Dan. (2013) *The New Member States and the European Union: Foreign Policy and Europeanization* (Routledge, Abingdon).

Bílková, Veronika and Matějková, Šárka. (2010) "Šíření Demokracie Jako Národní Zájem? Legitimizace České Transformační Politiky (Democracy Promotion as National Interest? The Legitimazation of Czech Transition Politics)", in Drulák, Petr and Horký Ondřej. (eds.), *Hledání Českých Zájmů: Obchod, Lidská Práva a Mezinárodní Rozvoj* (*In Search of Czech Interests: Trade, Human Rights and International Development*) (Ústav mezinárodních vztahů, Institute of International Relations, Prague).

Boerzel, Tanja. (2003) "Shaping and Taking EU Policies: Member State Responses to Europeanisation", *Queen's Papers on Europeanisation* No. 2, 1–15.

Bulmer, Simon and Burch, Martin. (2000) "Coming to Terms with Europe: Europeanisation, Whitehall and the Challenge of Devolution", *Queen's Papers on Europeanisation* No. 9, 1–27.

Dlouhá, Gabriela and Šnaidauf, Jan. (2011) "Toward a Common Approach to the Global Pro-Democracy Agenda and a Revival of Democracy Promotion in the Arab-Muslim World", *Policy Brief by the MFA of the Czech Republic* (Ministry of Foreign Affairs, Prague), 1–4.

Edwards, Geoffrey. (2006) "The New Member States and the Making of EU Foreign Policy", 11(2) *European Foreign Affairs Review*, 143–162.

Gower, Jackie. (2007) "The European Union's Policy on Russia: Rhetoric or Reality?" in Gower, Jackie and Timmins, Graham. (eds.), *Russia and Europe in the Twenty-First Century: An Uneasy Partnership* (Anthem Press, London).

Gower, Jackie. (2000) "EU-Russian Relations and the Eastern Enlargement: Integration or Isolation?" 1(1) *Perspectives on European Politics and Society*, 75–93.

Haverland, Markus. (2009) "How Leader States Influence EU Policy-Making: Analysing the Expert Strategy", 13(25) *European Integration Online Papers*, 1–19.

Jakobsen, Peter Viggo. (2009) "Small States, Big Influence: The Overlooked Nordic Influence on the Civilian ESDP", 47(1) *Journal of Common Market Studies*, 81–102.

Kucharczyk, Jacek and Lovitt, Jeff. (eds.) (2008) *Democracy's New Champions: European Democracy Assistance after EU Enlargement* (Policy Association for an Open Society, Prague).

Kucharczyk, Jacek and Lovitt, Jeff. (2008) "Re-Energising Europe to Champion Democracy", in Kucharczyk, Jacek and Lovitt, Jeff. (eds.), *Democracy's New Champions: European Democracy Assistance after EU Enlargement* (Policy Association for an Open Society, Prague).

Landman, Todd and Larizza, Marco. (2010) "EU Policy Discourse: Democracy, Governance, and Human Rights" (International Institute for Democracy and Electoral Assistance, Stockholm), 1–52.

Menéndez, Agustín José. (2004) "Human Rights: The European Charter of Fundamental Rights", in Carlsnaes, Walter, Sjursen, Helene, and White, Brian. (eds.), *Contemporary European Foreing Policy* (SAGE, London).

Neuman, Marek. (2015) *Too Small to Make an Impact?: The Czech Republic's Influence on the European Union's Foreign Policy* (Peter Lang, Frankfurt am Main).

Neuman, Marek. (2012) "The Czech Republic's EU Accession: A Shift-Producing Variable in the EU's Foreign Policy Towards Russia?" in Arcidiacono, Bruno, Milzow, Katrin, Marion, Axel, and Bourneuf, Pierre-Étienne. (eds.), *Europe Twenty Years after the End of the Cold War: The New Europe, New Europes?* (Peter Lang, Brussels).

Neuman, Marek. (2011) "The Nexus between Czech Non-State Actors and Domestic Foreign Policy Making in the EU Presidency Context", 19(1) *Perspectives*, 5–26.

Neuman Stanivuković, Senka and Neuman, Marek. (2010) "From Preference Formation at Home to Preference Promotion Abroad: The Role of Czech Intrastate Actors", 4(2) *Central European Journal of International & Security Studies*, 8–27.

Raik, Kristi. (2007) "A Europe Divided by Russia? The New Eastern Member States and the EU's Policy Towards the East", in Gower, Jackie and Timmins, Graham. (eds.), *Russia and Europe in the Twenty-First Century: An Uneasy Partnership* (Anthem Press, London).

Risse, Thomas, Green Cowles, Maria, and Caporaso, James A. (2001) "Europeanization and Domestic Change: Introduction", in Green Cowles, Maria, Caporaso, James A., and Risse, Thomas (eds.), *Transforming Europe: Europeanization and Domestic Change* (Cornell University Press, Ithaca).

Smith, Karen E. (2008) *European Union Foreign Policy in a Changing World*, 2nd edition (Polity Press, Cambridge).

Smith, Karen E. (2005) "The Outsiders: The European Neighbourhood Policy", 81(4) *International Affairs*, 757–773.

Smith, Karen E. (2001) "The EU, Human Rights and Relations with Third Countries: 'Foreign Policy' with and Ethical Dimension?" in Smith, Karen E. and Light, Margot. (eds.), *Ethics and Foreign Policy* (Cambridge University Press, Cambridge).

Tallberg, Jonas. (2003) "The Agenda-Shaping Powers of the EU Council Presidency", 10(1) *Journal of European Public Policy*, 1–19.

Whitman, Richard G. (1999) "The Common Foreign and Security Policy after Enlargement", in Curzon Price, Victoria, Landau, Alice, and Whitman, Richard G. (eds.), *The Enlargement of the European Union: Issues and Strategies* (Routledge, London).

CHAPTER 13

The Forgotten Chapter? Post-accession Development Policy of Central and Eastern Europe

Simon Lightfoot and Balázs Szent-Iványi

Abstract

It is now more than ten years since the states in Central and Eastern Europe (CEE) moved from recipients of development aid to donors of development aid. The chapter shows that in the Czech Republic, Hungary, Poland, Slovakia, and Slovenia there has been an increase in aid levels and the creation of legal and administrative structures for development policy. The states under study have clear priority areas for their bilateral aid, focusing on the Eastern Neighborhood and areas of strategic interest. Overall, the chapter argues that a combination of low EU priority, soft law, and lack of political drivers in the accession states created weak foundations for development policy that have had a long lasting legacy. International recognition of the status of being a donor via membership of the Development Assistance Committee (DAC) for some states does little to mask the weaknesses, and more work needs to be done to provide the policy with firm political foundations.

Keywords

development policy – Eastern Neighborhood – Development Assistance Committee

1 Introduction

It is now over ten years since the states in Central and Eastern Europe (CEE) created their international development policies. This provides an ideal opportunity to review their progress towards meeting both European Union (EU) and international norms in development cooperation. Gaining a better understanding of the driving forces behind international development policies of the CEE countries is relevant not just because it is timely, but also because this is an unprecedented historical experiment. Never before in Europe have so many countries turned from being aid recipients to aid donors in such a

© KONINKLIJKE BRILL NV, LEIDEN, 2018 | DOI 10.1163/9789004352070_015 short period.[1] This chapter explains the way that the Visegrád Four, the Czech Republic, Hungary, Poland and Slovakia (V4), and Slovenia have attempted to take on board the EU's *acquis communautaire* in development policy since their accession. Focusing on the V4 + 1 (V4 and Slovenia) is useful as it allows for a more focused comparison than examining all the new Member States.[2]

As we have argued before,[3] development policy is a shared parallel competence between the EU[4] and Member States, and the EU thus has little possibility to legally influence the individual priorities of the Member States. However, we identified a growing body of recommendations for the bilateral aid policies of the members that exist mainly in the form of Council Conclusions, thereby forming an extensive body of "soft law" instruments that are not binding, "but rest solely on their moral force."[5] They therefore carry no explicit legal obligations for the Member States to transpose them to their domestic legislation or base national policies on them. However, it is worth noting that the EU's development *acquis* was much less developed at time of the accession negotiations between 1999 and 2002 than it is today, and there was little practical guidance on what Member States should implement beyond general principles embodied in the founding Treaties like complementarity or coordination. Development issues also had a very low salience in the accession negotiations; it was not, so to speak, a "deal breaker". We therefore argue that a combination of low EU priority, soft law, and lack of political drivers in the accession states created weak foundations for development policy that has had a long lasting legacy. This chapter explains why development is a low EU priority and how the soft law approach used in development policy reflects sensitivities over EU

---

1   Maurizio Carbone, "Development Policy", in Neill Nugent (ed.), *EU Enlargement* (Palgrave, Basingstoke, 2004), 242–252, at 245.

2   Although we concur with the analysis in this contribution around the challenges faced by the V4 + 1. See Patryk Kugiel, "The Development Cooperation Policies of Visegrad Countries: An Unrealised Potential", *The Polish Quarterly of International Affairs* (2012) No.4, 101–121.

3   See Simon Lightfoot and Balázs Szent-Iványi, "Reluctant Donors? The Europeanization of International Development Policies in the New Member States", 52(6) *Journal of Common Market Studies*, 1257–1272; Balázs Szent-Iványi and Simon Lightfoot, *New Europe's New Development Aid* (Routledge, London, 2015); and Jan Orbie and Simon Lightfoot, "Development Policy", in Ian Manners, Richard Whitman, and Amelia Hadfield (eds.), *The Foreign Policies of European Union Member States: Continuity and Europeanisation* (Routledge, London, 2017). This chapter synthesizes and expands material covered in these publications.

4   We utilize EU throughout the chapter even when it may be legally correct to refer to the European Community.

5   Maurizio Carbone, *The European Union and International Development* (Routledge, London, 2007), 50.

involvement in foreign policy decisions. It shows that generally there are a lack of political drivers, both at EU and national level, yet despite that all five states we examine have (eventually in the case of Hungary) become members of the donor community by joining the DAC.

2   Historical Background

Before we can examine EU influence, it is first worth examining the legacy of Communism. There is sensitivity over the terms used to describe the states from CEE that have joined the EU since 2004.[6] Terms such as "new donors" or "emerging donors" are often used to describe these states.[7] For some states, such as Slovenia, this label is relatively accurate as until the end of the collapse of the Eastern bloc they did not exist as independent states. For the other states, the term is more contentious, as the V4 states all had a long history of providing aid bilaterally or via the Council for Mutual Economic Assistance (CMEA), an economic organization of the Communist countries.[8] These countries also often refer to their pre-1989 experiences as donors. During the period of communist rule, the former Soviet bloc thus provided support to "socialist brother" countries or "friendly regimes" throughout the developing world, with much of that aid characterized by a "strong and strategic orientation, concentrating on political allies and friendly countries which were pursuing socialist goals."[9] Within the CMEA, mutual assistance was officially propagated. As with all government functions, international assistance was controlled by the state and party apparatus, and managed according to ideological dictates and Cold War priorities. Radu argues that Czechoslovakia, Hungary, and Poland, although they had some autonomy over which states received their support, the strategic framework for their policies towards the developing world were "directly subordinated to the long-range goals" of the Soviet Union.[10] Slovenia

6   For an academic overview, see Ondřej Horký and Simon Lightfoot (eds.), *From Aid Recipients to Aid Donors. Development Policies of Central and Eastern European States* (Routledge, London, 2012); and Ondřej Horký-Hlucháň and Simon Lightfoot (eds.), *Development Cooperation of the "New" EU Member States* (Palgrave Macmillan, Basingstoke, 2015).

7   Emma Mawdsley, *From Recipients to Donors: Emerging Powers and the Changing Development Landscape* (Zed Books, London, 2012).

8   Steven Browne, *Foreign Aid in Practice* (Pinter, London, 1980), 227.

9   Carbone, *op. sit.* note 1, 244.

10   Michael Radu, *Eastern Europe and the Third World: East vs. South* (Praeger, New York, 1981).

has a slightly different history being part of Yugoslavia until its independence in 1991.[11]

The overriding focus of domestic and to a large extent EU attention after the collapse of the Eastern bloc in 1989 was on economic and political reform within the CEE states. Poverty rates in the CEE countries soared and as a consequence of this transition period, all CEE states saw their engagement with the developing world and any aid programs dramatically reduced.[12] During the 90s, there were basically no foreign aid policies in CEE countries, except for scholarships to students from developing countries, *ad hoc* payments to international organizations, and, in the case of Hungary or Poland, support to ethnic minorities in neighboring countries.

During the second half of the 1990s, some of the CEE states joined the Organization for Economic Co-operation and Development (OECD), the so-called "club of rich country donors" and this led to an increasing, although rather implicit international pressure towards these countries to take a larger share in aiding poorer countries. This pressure became more explicit when the V4 + 1 states began accession negotiations with the EU. Bilateral development assistance was part of the accession negotiation Chapter 26 on External Relations. The *acquis* in this field implied the need to create institutional and legal structures for development policy. Despite the soft nature of the *acquis* in this area, the accession process encouraged accession countries to launch their official bilateral development policies between 2001 and 2003.

A key issue was that modern development aid practices were considerably different than the experience these countries had form their pre-1989 foreign aid policies.[13] As an official from a V4 + 1 country argued "it is true that development cooperation had already existed in a lot of new member states but in a very different way."[14] Another official talked about "un-learning the old ways as a major priority."[15] The crucial problem according to many observers was

---

11   See, for example, Urška Zrinski and Maja Bučar, "Slovenia: What Options for a Small Donor?" in Ondřej Horký-Hlucháň and Simon Lightfoot (eds.), *op. cit.* note 6, 82–106; and Peteris Timofejevs Henriksson, "Europeanization of Foreign-Aid Policy in Central and East Europe: The Role of EU, External Incentives and Identification in Foreign-Aid Policy Adoption in Latvia and Slovenia 1998–2010", 37(4) *Journal of European Integration* (2015), 433–449.

12   Carbone, *op. sit.* note 5, 47.

13   For an overview of this process and the challenges, see Michael Dauderstadt, "Eastern Enlargement and Development Policy", in Michael Dauderstadt (ed.), *EU Eastern Enlargement and Development Cooperation* (Friedrich-Ebert-Stftung, Bonn, 2002), 5–11.

14   Interview 1.

15   Interview 2.

that the V4 + 1 were novices in the field of modern international development cooperation and needed guidance.[16]

The V4 + 1 states see the transformation into aid donors as important for a variety of interconnected and sometimes contradictory reasons. One reason is that EU membership required some form of aid policy, although there is a view that V4 + 1 states could have met their obligations via multilateral aid rather than creating new bilateral aid policies. However, bilateral aid policies seem important for the V4 + 1 states. There is the sense that states have a moral duty to help others and in the case of some of the V4 + 1 this is more pronounced by the feeling that they need to repay the "help" they were given after the fall of Communism. The return to the international stage is also important as are the very clear links that exist between aid policy and foreign and security policies. Finally, national interest, and, in particular, national economic interest is important as aid policy can have commercial benefits. The inter-connection of all these factors explains the desire of states to engage in foreign aid, but they also show the complexity of the aid system within nations. Adding the EU level adds to the complexity of the policy area, with different parts of the EU bureaucracy playing different roles in different geographical parts of the world. The newly formed European External Action Service is meant to clarify roles in EU external relations, although the jury is still out in relation to its impact on development policy.[17]

3   The Role of the EU in the International Development Policies
       of Member States

According to the Copenhagen Criteria, in order to become an EU member, a country must accept and be able to implement all the EU's rules and policies, known as the *acquis communitaire*. Due to the nature of EU development policy as a shared parallel competence, Member States retain full sovereignty over their development policies, and the EU runs its own development policy, essentially acting as a 29th donor.[18] Nonetheless, in past decades, the EU, and

---

16   Marija Adanja, "New EU Donors", Presentation at public hearing of European Parliament, Committee on Development (Brussels, 30 January 2007).

17   Mark Furness, "Who Controls the European External Action Service? Agent Autonomy in EU External Policy", 18 *European Foreign Affairs Review* (2013), 103–126; and Michael Smith, "Foreign Policy and Development in the Post-Lisbon European Union", 26(3) *Cambridge Review of International Affairs* (2013), 519–535.

18   Morton Broberg, "What is the Direction for the EU's Development Cooperation after Lisbon?: A Legal Examination", 16(4) *European Foreign Affairs Review* (2011), 539–557; and

especially the Commission, has clearly increased its role in influencing the bilateral development policies of its members, mainly citing the need to coordinate Member States activities with the view of increasing efficiency. The Treaty of Maastricht, by introducing qualitative requirements for both EU-level and Member State development policies with the concepts of complementarily, coherence, and coordination (the so-called 3C's), gave an implicit role for the Commission in acting as a coordinator.[19]

In the past decade, a large body of *acquis* emerged that applies to Member State development policies. In 2002 the European Council reaffirmed that Member States should increase their aid spending to 0.7% of their gross national incomes by 2015. The V4 + 1 states were set a different goal of 0.17% by 2010 and 0.33% by 2015.[20] Also, in 2005, a joint statement by the Commission, the Council and the Parliament, entitled the "European Consensus on Development", created a new framework for the EU's common development policy and also laid down many requirements for the individual Member States.[21] The EU encourages Member States to channel larger portions of their aid to least developed countries, especially those in Africa. To facilitate this poverty focus, states should harmonize their activities with each other to encourage aid effectiveness. A key component of harmonization is the need for states to focus their efforts on areas (countries or sectors) in which they have "comparative advantages."[22] These requirements have later been elaborated in more detail in several council conclusions, and the EU also published a Code of Conduct for Member States on the division of labor.[23]

Aspects of development policy can be seen as elements of foreign policy. In this field the EU cannot generally pass binding law on Member State and thus most of the *acquis* relating to this should be seen as soft recommendations.

Jeske van Seters and Henrike Klavert, "EU Development Cooperation after the Lisbon Treaty: People, Institutions and Global Trends", *ECDPM Discussion Paper* (2011) No.123.

19   See Carbone, *op. cit.* note 5.

20   Maja Bucar and Mojmir Mrak, "Challenges of Development Cooperation for EU New Member States", Paper Presented at the ABCDE World Bank Conference (Bled, Slovenia, 17–18 May 2007), available at <http://siteresources.worldbank.org/INTABCDESLO2007/Resources/PAPERABCDEBucarMrak.pdf>.

21   European Consensus, "Joint Declaration by the Council and the Representatives of the Governments of the Member States Meeting within the Council, the European Parliament and the Commission on the Development Policy of the European Union Entitled the European Consensus" (Official Journal C 46 of 24 February 2006).

22   European Commission, "EU Donor Atlas 2006" (DG Development/OECD, Brussels).

23   Council of the European Union, "EU Code of Conduct on Complementarity and Division of Labour in Development Policy" (Council Conclusions 9558/07).

While in the past years the EU has increased its monitoring functions, it lacks the coercive competence to require a given Member State to act in a certain way. There clearly was a window of opportunity during the pre-accession phase to shape policies, but this was weaker for foreign policy than other policy areas.[24] Post-accession compliance is clearly of interest here, but again much of the evidence focuses on policy areas where the EU has a stronger competence to act.[25] As development policy was not a "deal-breaker" during accession negotiations, it offers an interesting case study as to how much influence the EU is able to exert over its Member States after accession.

4   Development Policy since Accession

Aid Targets and Performance

Before we examine this topic in more detail, it is worth first highlighting what form V4 + 1 aid takes. Typically aid spending makes up 0.08–0.15% of their gross national incomes, which is very far from both the target of 0.33% which the EU set for the new members to reach by 2015 and the 0.7% that for example the UK has achieved in 2014. A remarkably high part, around 70–75% of V4 + 1 aid is actually multilateral, and most of this multilateral aid goes to the EU. In contrast, Irish aid is 68% delivered as bilateral aid. Bilateral aid is typically in the form of small stand-alone projects, implemented by domestic non-governmental organizations (NGOs). Project values below 10,000 Euro are not rare. While there is no official data, the overwhelming majority of aid is most likely tied, meaning that aid is linked to procurement from the donor.

Joining the EU in 2004 had a significant impact on the quantity of CEE aid, as these countries began contributing to the community budget, and a portion of these contributions can be reported as aid. Correspondingly, between 2004 and 2006, it is possible to observe a rapid growth in the share of aid/GNI

---

24   Jozef Bátora, "Europeanization of Foreign Policy: Whither Central Europe?", in Zlatko Šabič and Petr Drulák (eds.), *Regional and International Relations of Central Europe* (Palgrave, London, 2012), 220–238; and Elsa Tulmets, *East Central European Foreign Policy Identity in Perspective: Back to Europe and the EU's Neighbourhood* (Palgrave Macmillan, Basingstoke, 2014).

25   See Ulrich Sedelmeier and Rachel Epstein, "Beyond Conditionality: International Institutions in Postcommunist Europe after Enlargement", 15 *Journal of European Public Policy* (2008), 795–805; and Ulrich Sedelmeier, "Is Europeanisation through Conditionality Sustainable?: Lock-in of Institutional Change after EU Accession", 35 *West European Politics* (2012), 20–38.

ratios in the V4 + 1 countries.[26] This growth however stopped after 2006, and the years since then have been characterized by either stagnation and decline or only moderate growth. None of them have set clear timetables to reach the 0.33% target, and the eruption of the global economic crisis in 2008 put additional strains on government budgets. Aid budgets are often set on a yearly basis and therefore vulnerable to cuts due to low domestic interest in foreign aid. Some countries, like the Czech Republic, have managed to keep their aid budgets relatively constant despite the Global Financial Crisis of 2008, and between 2011 and 2012 Poland even increased its aid.[27] Much of this however is due to the fact that most countries recently began contributing to the European Development Fund and the World Bank's International Development Association, further increasing multilateral aid, which allowed governments to cut bilateral aid without a noticeable decrease in overall aid volumes. However, the aid volumes have risen sufficiently for the V4 + 1 states to meet the aid quantity targets for DAC membership. One factor that is important in relation to ODA targets is the extent to which domestic political structures support development aid decision-making.

Institutional Structures and Reforms

The main governmental actor in V4 + 1 states tends to be the Ministry of Foreign Affairs (MFA). However, two models have become evident: MFA as coordinator and MFA as lead ministry. In the former model, a wide range of government organizations (mainly other line ministries) are involved in aid and the MFA is tasked with coordinating their activities (Hungary and Poland). The second model is more centralized, with the MFA controlling much of the funds and assuming responsibility for its implementation (often through an agency subordinated to it). This latter model is used in the Czech Republic and Slovakia, although in Slovakia line ministries retain an important role. Slovenia uses a hybrid of the two models.

The MFA itself is far from being a monolithic structure. The main unit responsible for foreign aid policy making is the Department for Official Development Assistance (ODA), and the Czech and Slovak Republics have also created aid-implementing agencies as semi-autonomous bodies of the MFA.

---

26   Simon Lightfoot, "The Europeanisation of International Development Policy", 62 *Europe-Asia Studies* (2010), 329–350; and Balazs Szent-Iványi, "Aid Allocation of the Emerging Central and Eastern European Donors", 15 *Journal of International Relations and Development* (2012), 65–89.

27   *AidWatch 2013: The Unique Role of European Aid. The Fight Against Global Poverty* (CONCORD, Brussels, 2013).

Hungary and Poland have argued that their aid levels are too low to make an agency practical. The aid agency or ODA department may be a champion of development goals, but it may have a difficult time getting this through in face of opposition from other MFA departments which may prefer to promote the more traditional foreign policy goals of the country.

The other line ministries may also have different interests than development. The Ministry of Finance (MoF) and the Ministry of Economy (MoE) may be especially relevant. The MoF, as the department responsible for preparing the government budget, has an important role in suggesting the amounts allocated to each budget line. The MoE is important because in the V4 + 1 countries it is responsible for external economic relations such as trade development and investment promotion. As aid can be seen as a tool to stimulate exports, especially through the usage of tied aid, the MoEs main interest will be to use aid as much as possible to achieve its own mandate of export promotion and "assist" national companies in gaining access to foreign markets. Other ministries may be mainly interested in promoting their sectors in foreign aid. The Ministry of Agriculture for example may be keener on aid projects focusing on rural development, while the Ministry of Education may prefer giving scholarships to students from developing countries.

Only the Czech Republic has fully adapted the MFA as lead ministry model when it reformed its institutional structure from in 2010. In the Czech case we saw a fragmented line ministry structure centralized in 2010, in part due to advice from the DAC, a forum for policy coordination and experience sharing among donors.[28] Since then the MFA has more or less full responsibility for aid, sharing only some competences with the MoF. It also has a strong implementing agency, a development law accepted in 2010 that makes poverty reduction the central aim of Czech foreign aid, and an operational development strategy for 2010–17.[29]

The institutional structures in the other V4 + 1 states are rather fragmented, with several line ministries being involved and the role of the MFA much weaker. Often, the MFA has difficulties influencing other ministries, which makes it difficult for these countries to formulate and implement a clear cut strategic vision on development aid. An extreme case is that of Hungary, where the MFA is especially weak and is often only able to "acknowledge" what the other line ministries do with their aid budgets. While the country did have an implementing agency up until 2010, this no longer exists. Efforts to establish

28   OECD DAC, *Special Review of the Czech Republic* (OECD, Paris, 2007).

29   Zuzanna Végh, *Lessons from Visegrad Development Cooperation Practices: Recommendations for Hungary* (DEMNET, Budapest, 2013).

a development strategy came to fruition only in 2014, when a strategic document for 2014–2020, was accepted.[30] This was shortly followed by the acceptance of the country's first law on development, and promises have been made
to create an implementing agency.

Slovakia, Slovenia, and Poland are somewhere between the two extremes.[31]
Slovakia also carried out some reforms of its institutional structure by creating a strong implementing agency under the MFA, but it did not go as far as
the Czech Republic as to centralize the aid budget. Thus, line ministries are
still important. Slovakia has also passed a law on international development,
and has an operational development strategy. The Polish aid system has seen
several reforms, but mainly only on the level of the MFA. While one may argue
that the MFA has rather large staff numbers devoted to development and thus
stronger capacities than the other CEE countries, the line ministries also retain
important duties. There is no separate implementing agency, but the country
did pass a law on development in 2012.[32] Slovenian aid has undergone reforms
that align its bureaucratic structures with a more standard model, although
the existence of the implementation centers is unique to Slovenia.[33] In terms
of creating strategic and legal frameworks for foreign aid policy, the V4 + 1
states have generally done rather well, and all have made poverty reduction
a goal to some extent, at least on the legal/strategic level. Laws in Poland and
the Czech and Slovak Republics[34] provide a framework in a sense that they detail the main goals and priorities of development cooperation and mainly deal
with setting down the responsibilities of actors in system. The Hungarian law
mainly focuses on operational and organizational aspects. All the V4 + 1 states
have operational strategies[35] that operationalize the principles embodied in
the laws, and specify modalities of support, target countries, priority sectors

---

30   Balazs Szent-Iványi, "*Hungary's New IDC Strategy*", 6(17/18) *Volumen* (2013), 5–6.

31   OECD DAC, *Special Review of Poland* (OECD, Paris, 2010); and OECD DAC, *Special Review of
      the Slovak Republic* (OECD, Paris, 2011).

32   Ela Drążkiewicz-Grodzicka, "From Recipient to Donor: The Case of Polish Developmental
      Cooperation", 72(1) *Human Organization* (2013), 65–75.

33   Zrinski and Bučar, *op. cit.* note 11; and Timofejevs Henriksson, *op. cit.* note 11.

34   Act 151/2010 on Development Cooperation and Humanitarian Aid, and Amending Related
      Laws (Czech Republic) No legal framework in Hungary; Development cooperation act of
      16 September 2011, amended on 11 October 2013 (Poland) Act No. 617/2007 Coll. on Official
      Development Assistance (Slovakia).

35   The Development Cooperation Strategy of the Czech Republic, 2010–2017; Framework
      strategy for Hungary's International Development Cooperation, 2014–2020; Multiannual
      Development Cooperation Programme 2012–2015; Medium-Term Strategy for Official De-
      velopment Assistance, 2009–2013.

and other issues on the medium term. The key seems to be consolidating these reforms and ensuring development policy remains visible within both the MFA and the government as a whole.

The role of the parliaments and ministries other than the Ministry of Foreign Affairs must be studied in more depth. The role of parties and public opinion are also crucial, as is the role played by NGOS. Political parties are starting to engage with international issues within a domestic context, but aid is still a marginal topic. "There are no votes in foreign policy" seems to be the adage here. Public opinion is relatively favorable towards "helping others" but there is a need to engage in further development education projects. Within all five states, the development constituency was historically weaker than in most EU-15 states. The NGO community is mainly funded by their respective MFAs and how to manage this relationship is a challenge in many states. An antagonistic relationship between NGOs and the MFA can actually set back the policy, whilst a more critical friend relationship can help advance the policy area. Within the V4 + 1 it is clear that the NGO community and the aid department within the MFA have developed a mature working relationship, which has helped support bilateral aid policy, especially during the economic crisis.

Aid Allocation

The V4 + 1 donors concentrate most of their aid to the following three groups of recipients:

· The broad Neighborhood, i.e. countries in the Western Balkans and the former Soviet Union.[36]
· Partner countries "inherited" from the Communist period: These are countries with which development partnerships already existed before the transition, and include Yemen, Ethiopia, Vietnam, Mongolia, Cambodia, Angola, Mozambique, or Laos. Formerly (or in some cases even at present), these countries all had socialist-oriented political systems, or for other reasons hoped to gain (development or military) assistance from the Soviet bloc.
· Iraq and Afghanistan have also received substantial amounts as a result of the international obligations V4 + 1 countries have as NATO members and their close ties to the United States. These are however likely to decrease as the international community decreases its level of commitment to these two countries.

---

36   See Tulmets, *op. cit.* note 24.

The V4 + 1 states have a small number of projects in Sub-Saharan Africa and Latin America. For example, in 2012–13, the Czech Republic gave 30% of its bilateral aid to countries in Europe and the former Soviet Union. Former Communist era partners such as Ethiopia and Mongolia also still present in the top ten, although the main recipient of aid was Afghanistan. In case of Hungary, these three groups have similar role, with 42%, 21%, and 4% respectively.[37] The large role of the neighborhood points to the fact that aid allocation thus seems to be heavily driven by foreign policy considerations.[38] Concentrating most of their aid in the neighborhood seems to be in-line with foreign policy considerations like the need for regional stability, the promotion of business interests, or supporting their ethnic minorities living. The CEE countries argue that they have comparative advantages in their neighborhood compared to other donors. They have a shared past, and as many of these countries are coping with reforming their economies and adapting EU rules, the experience of the CEE countries can be useful in this process. Another argument is that the costs of being present in regions like Africa are difficult to justify with low bilateral aid levels.[39] The majority of the recipients of CEE aid therefore belong to the category of lower middle-income countries. However, the focus on the neighborhood fits with the expertise of the V4 + 1 and other CEE donors, especially in terms of transition experience and perhaps is the most efficient use of limited resources.[40] How far this transition experience translates beyond specific European contexts will be important to observe in the coming years, especially in light of Russian activity in the Ukraine and its neighborhood.[41]

---

37   One must also take into consideration that 21% of Czech and 26% of Hungarian bilateral aid did not even actually leave the country and represents expenses like refugee costs, scholarships, development education, and administrative costs.

38   Michael Baun and Dan Marek (eds.), *The New Member States and the European Union: Foreign Policy and Europeanization* (Routledge, Abingdon, 2013).

39   Balazs Szent-Iványi, "Hungarian International Development Cooperation: Context, Stakeholders and Performance", 13(1) *Perspectives on European Politics and Society* (2012), 50–65.

40   See "Harnessing the transition experience in EU's external relations: From policy to implementation", Non-paper by the Czech Republic, Estonia, Hungary, Latvia, Lithuania, Romania, Slovak Republic, and Slovenia, available at <http://www.mzv.cz/file/591175/non_paper_on_the_transition_experience.pdf>.

41   Benedetta Berti, Kristina Mikulova, and Nicu Popescu, *Democratization in EU Foreign Policy: New Member States as Drivers of Democracy Promotion* (Routledge, London, 2015); and Paulina Pospieszna, *Democracy Assistance from the Third Wave: Polish Engagement in Belarus and Ukraine* (University of Pittsburg Press, Pittsburg, 2014).

5   Conclusion

The V4 + 1 donors seem to behave in a similar fashion to the donors that the literature has labeled 'egoistic', at least when it comes to their aid allocation.[42] The five countries mainly support recipients towards which they have political, security, and economic interests, as countries in the Western Balkans and the CIS region. The reduction of global poverty is clearly not a major consideration. While this observed aid allocation is in line with the political and economic interests of the four donor countries, the question arises how much it is due to strategic decisions. It is plausible for example that the V4 + 1 only choose recipients from their neighborhood for reasons of convenience. Providing large scale foreign aid to the least developed countries, especially in Sub-Saharan Africa or other far away developing regions would be much more costly, and the experience of the four (now five) emerging donors in those areas is also much less. A further explanation may be that the four donors have some kind of perceived or actual comparative advantage compared to other donors in the Western Balkan and CIS regions.

International pressure, especially from the EU, was crucial in re-creating CEE aid policies. However, that pressure could be classified as light touch. Post-accession compliance relies more on socialization strategies than overt pressure.[43] The following remark by a senior MFA official illustrates this well: "Don't have any illusions. If the EU didn't require us to do development policy, we wouldn't be doing it. The returns are just too small." Part of the problem is that although the V4 + 1 states classify as high-income countries, socially they are still adjusting to the new status as donors. Neither civil society nor political elites see aid as a salient issue. One can therefore label them the CEE countries as "premature donors."[44] Having said that, all the countries that this chapter discusses, have become members of the donors club, the OECD DAC.[45] This may usher in a new era of aid donorship as DAC membership places requirements onto its members, not least the requirement to undergo regular peer review. DAC membership confers a status onto its members that they are now part of the donor club. Whether that club can survive the challenge of the

---

42   Lightfoot and Szent-Iványi, *op. cit.* note 3.

43   *Ibid.*

44   Balazs Szent-Iványi and András Tétényi, "The East-Central European New Donors: Mapping Capacity Building and Remaining Challenges", 25(6) *Journal of International Development* (2013), 819–831.

45   It is worth noting that Hungary only joined in December 2016, whilst the other states all joined in 2013.

donors from outside, such as China, India, Brazil, and even Turkey is going to be a major challenge for the DAC in the post-2015 aid environment. The role played by the V4 + 1 states in both the DAC and the EU in terms of shaping agendas will never be central, but as recent events have shown in relation to Ukraine, V4 + 1 experience properly harnessed can be important in specific contexts and with support of the larger EU states.

Bibliography

Bátora, Jozef. (2012) "Europeanization of Foreign Policy: Whither Central Europe?", in Šabič, Zlatko and Drulák, Petr. (eds.), *Regional and International Relations of Central Europe* (Palgrave, London), 220–238.

Baun, Michael and Marek, Dan. (eds.) (2013) *The New Member States and the European Union: Foreign Policy and Europeanization* (Routledge, Abingdon).

Berti, Benedetta, Mikulova, Kristina, and Popescu, Nicu. (2015) *Democratization in EU Foreign Policy: New Member States as Drivers of Democracy Promotion* (Routledge, London).

Broberg, Morton. (2011) "What is the Direction for the EU's Development Cooperation after Lisbon?: A Legal Examination", 16(4) *European Foreign Affairs Review*, 539–557.

Browne, Steven. (1980) *Foreign Aid in Practice* (Pinter, London).

Bucar, Maja and Mrak, Mojmir. (2007) "Challenges of Development Cooperation for EU New Member States", Paper Presented at the ABCDE World Bank Conference (Bled, Slovenia, 17–18 May), available at <http://siteresources.worldbank.org/INTABCDESLO2007/Resources/PAPERABCDEBucarMrak.pdf>.

Carbone, Maurizio. (2007) *The European Union and International Development* (Routledge, London).

Carbone, Maurizio. (2004) "Development Policy", in Nugent, Neill. (ed.), *EU Enlargement* (Palgrave, Basingstoke), 242–252.

Dauderstadt, Michael. (2002) "Eastern Enlargement and Development Policy", in Dauderstadt, Michael. (ed.), *EU Eastern Enlargement and Development Cooperation* (Friedrich-Ebert-Stftung, Bonn), 5–11.

Drążkiewicz-Grodzicka, Ela. (2013) "From Recipient to Donor: The Case of Polish Developmental Cooperation", 72(1) *Human Organization*, 65–75.

Furness, Mark. (2013) "Who Controls the European External Action Service? Agent Autonomy in EU External Policy", 18 *European Foreign Affairs Review*, 103–126.

Horký-Hlucháň, Ondřej and Lightfoot, Simon. (eds.) (2015) *Development Cooperation of the "New" EU Member States* (Palgrave Macmillan, Basingstoke).

Horký, Ondřej and Lightfoot, Simon. (eds.) (2012) *From Aid Recipients to Aid Donors: Development Policies of Central and Eastern European States* (Routledge, London).

Kugiel, Patryk. (2012) "The Development Cooperation Policies of Visegrad Countries: An Unrealised Potential", *The Polish Quarterly of International Affairs* No. 4, 101–121.

Lightfoot, Simon. (2010) "The Europeanisation of International Development Policy", 62 *Europe-Asia Studies*, 329–350.

Lightfoot, Simon and Szent-Iványi, Balázs. (2014) "Reluctant Donors? The Europeanization of International Development Policies in the New Member States", 52(6) *Journal of Common Market Studies*, 1257–1272.

Mawdsley, Emma. (2012) *From Recipients to Donors: Emerging Powers and the Changing Development Landscape* (Zed Books, London).

Orbie, Jan and Lightfoot, Simon. (2017) "Development Policy", in Manners, Ian, Whitman, Richard, and Hadfield, Amelia. (eds.), *The Foreign Policies of European Union Member States: Continuity and Europeanisation* (Routledge, London).

Pospieszna, Paulina. (2014) *Democracy Assistance from the Third Wave: Polish Engagement in Belarus and Ukraine* (University of Pittsburg Press, Pittsburg).

Radu, Michael. (1981) *Eastern Europe and the Third World: East vs. South* (Praeger, New York).

Sedelmeier, Ulrich. (2012) "Is Europeanisation through Conditionality Sustainable?: Lock-in of Institutional Change after EU accession", 35 *West European Politics*, 20–38.

Sedelmeier, Ulrich and Epstein, Rachel. (2008) "Beyond Conditionality: International Institutions in Postcommunist Europe after Enlargement", 15 *Journal of European Public Policy*, 795–805.

van Seters, Jeske and Klavert, Henrike. (2011) "EU Development Cooperation after the Lisbon Treaty: People, Institutions and Global Trends", ECDPM *Discussion Paper* No. 123.

Smith, Michael. (2013) "Foreign Policy and Development in the Post-Lisbon European Union", 26(3) *Cambridge Review of International Affairs*, 519–535.

Szent-Iványi, Balázs. (2012) "Aid Allocation of the Emerging Central and Eastern European Donors", 15 *Journal of International Relations and Development*, 65–89.

Szent-Iványi, Balázs. (2012) "Hungarian International Development Cooperation: Context, Stakeholders and Performance", 13(1) *Perspectives on European Politics and Society*, 50–65.

Szent-Iványi, Balázs and Lightfoot, Simon. (2015) *New Europe's New Development Aid* (Routledge, London).

Szent-Iványi, Balázs and Tétényi, Andras. (2013) "The East-Central European New Donors: Mapping Capacity Building and Remaining Challenges", 25(6) *Journal of International Development*, 819–831.

Timofejevs Henriksson, Peteris. (2015) "Europeanization of Foreign-Aid Policy in Central and East Europe: The Role of EU, External Incentives and Identification in Foreign-Aid Policy Adoption in Latvia and Slovenia 1998–2010", 37(4) *Journal of European Integration*, 433–449.

Tulmets, Elsa. (2014) *East Central European Foreign Policy Identity in Perspective: Back to Europe and the EU's Neighbourhood* (Palgrave Macmillan, Basingstoke).

Végh, Zuzanna. (2013) *Lessons from Visegrad Development Cooperation Practices: Recommendations for Hungary* (DEMNET, Budapest).

Zrinski, Urška and Bučar, Maja. (2015) "Slovenia: What Options for a Small Donor?", in Horký-Hlucháň, Ondrej and Lightfoot, Simon (eds.), *Development Cooperation of the "New" EU Member States* (Palgrave Macmillan, Basingstoke), 82–106.

CHAPTER 14

Slovak Parliament's Involvement in the EU Agenda: Kosovo's Independence and the Policy of Non-recognition

Katarína Lezová

Abstract

As of December 2016, Slovakia remains one of the five EU Member States that has not recognized Kosovo as an independent state. Despite external lobbying and efforts by EU and US officials to bring Slovakia to a "yes" on Kosovo, it has not changed its position.[1] This contribution discusses the law that enabled the Slovak Parliament to shape the official stand of Slovakia. Factors in the domestic political scene had a profound impact on Slovakia's stance towards Kosovo; however, this essay will focus mainly on the initial stage that set the scene for a relatively small and new EU Member State to go against EU political consensus. The law enabled the Slovak Parliament – and the opposition leader in particular – to exercise considerable influence on this foreign policy decision and bind the Slovak Government and the Slovak Ministry of Foreign Affairs (MFA) in particular to a course of action it did not initially support.

Keywords

Slovakia – Kosovo – independence – common foreign policy – parliament

1 Introduction

In February 2007, Martti Ahtisaari, the UN Special Envoy for Kosovo and former Finnish President, submitted his proposal on the final status of Kosovo,

---

1 For information on all arguments presented in the literature and a detailed analysis of all factors contributing to the Slovak non-recognition of Kosovo, see Katarína Lezová, "The Influence of Domestic Political Factors on Foreign Policy Formation in an EU Member State: The Case of Slovakia and the Kosovo Status Process", PhD thesis, Goldsmiths, University of London (2013).

and recommended "supervised independence."[2] One year later, on 17 February 2008, Kosovo unilaterally declared independence from Serbia, a move that was recognized shortly afterwards by the United States, the United Kingdom, France, Germany, and Italy. Since then, many other states, including the majority of the Member States of the European Union, have joined them. However, the independence of Kosovo has not been accepted by Serbia and other major international players such as Russia, India, and China.

International opinion remains divided on the issue and as of 1 March 2017, over nine years after Kosovo declared independence, only 114 out of 193 UN members had recognized Kosovo as an independent state.[3] These differences extend to the EU where five countries – Cyprus, Spain, Romania, Greece, and Slovakia – do not recognize Kosovo's statehood. There are some claims that the five EU members have taken this stance because the issue has an indirect influence on their national security and it is not just a question of their foreign political orientation.[4] It has been argued that the independence of Kosovo "has become a much more complicated story than the West anticipated" and "the EU's role cannot fully develop as long as it remains divided over Kosovo."[5] Despite the argument that the position of the five EU non-recognizers is "one of constructive abstention", in practice, it is still considered "a drag on European leadership."[6] Nevertheless, there have also been official views that these five

---

2   Ahtisaari's mandate was to resolve Kosovo's status after a number of years under the rule of the United Nations Interim Administration Mission in Kosovo (UNMIK), which was established in Kosovo following the 1999 NATO bombing against Serbia. UNMIK was created under Resolution 1244 (1999) in order to oversee Kosovo until its status would be settled. However, the resolution was not specific in giving direct time frames or stating what the final settlement should look like. More importantly, it confirmed the territorial integrity and sovereignty of the then Federal Republic of Yugoslavia. Violent riots in Kosovo in 2004 exposed the urgent need to deal with Kosovo's final status. Between February 2006 and March 2007, Ahtisaari led status talks between Belgrade and Pristina; however, after a year of negotiations no agreement was reached between the parties on the final settlement of the province. For a detailed analysis of the status talks, see James Ker-Lindsay, *Kosovo: The Path to Contested Statehood in the Balkans* (I.B. Tauris, London, 2009).

3   In order to take a seat in the UN, Kosovo needs to secure a recommendation by the UN Security Council and the support of a two-thirds majority of the 193 UN General Assembly members.

4   "Kosovo/EU: Pressure eases on anti-independence five", *Oxford Analytica* (4 January 2010), 1; and Shpend Kursani, "Western Balkans and Europe: Waiting for the Mediterranean breeze from Greece", *Art of the Possible: The Cambridge University Journal of Politics* (2011), available at <http://artofthepossible-cambridge.com/index.php?a=12& title=1297598745.html>.

5   "Kosovo/EU", *ibid.*, 1.

6   Justin Vaïsse *et al.*, "European Foreign Policy Scorecard 2013", *European Council on Foreign Relations* (2013), 68.

EU states provided a "guarantee to Belgrade that EU could keep up some kind of neutrality on the issue."[7]

Unlike the case of Montenegro's independence in 2006, when EU members agreed on a common approach to recognizing Montenegro when it seceded from Serbia, a different approach had been taken to the recognition of Kosovo.[8] On 18 February 2008 the General Affairs and External Relations Council of the EU had agreed that the recognition of Kosovo was a matter for national governments to decide "in accordance with national practice and international law, on their relations with Kosovo."[9] As a result, the EU did not show unity on this issue.

The field of International Law has discussed the topic of recognition in depth, however, in the area of International Relations it has not been analyzed in detail.[10] As Ker-Lindsay notes, legal scholars consider the objective condition of statehood independent of recognition, however, although "recognition does not make a state, it does serve to legitimize the state as a member of the wider international community."[11] When it comes to the recognition of states, it is a country's own decision to judge which territory to recognize as an independent state, and why and when to do so.[12] As a result, there is no official process or mechanism that would oblige a state to recognize a country,

---

7   Senior official, "Serbia/Kosovo: The Brussels Agreements and beyond", Workshop at St Antony's College, University of Oxford, Oxford (29 November 2013).

8   "Kosovo: International Law and Recognition", A Summary of the Chatham House International Law Discussion Group meeting, London (22 April 2008), 4. Notably, as Miroslav Lajčák, the Slovak Minister of Foreign Affairs, commented, "unlike Montenegro, which decided to engage in a difficult dialogue with Serbia before declaring independence and to accept compromises in order to consolidate its independence at a later stage in a relatively comfortable manner, Kosovo's leaders chose the opposite way – a simpler road at the beginning, but with the risk of great complications after the separation." "Self-Determination and Territorial Integrity: Awkward Bed-Fellows", Speech of the Minister of Foreign Affairs of the Slovak Republic Miroslav Lajčák, Chatham House, London (20 April 2009).

9   Council of the European Union, "General Affairs and External Relations: External Relations", 2851st Council Meeting, *Press Release*, (Brussels, 18 February 2008) 6496/08 (Presse 41), 7.

10   See James Ker-Lindsay, "Engagement without Recognition: The Limits of Diplomatic Interaction with Contested States", 91(2) *International Affairs* (2015), 267–285, at 269.

11   *Ibid.*

12   James Ker-Lindsay, *The Foreign Policy of Counter Secession: Preventing the Recognition of Contested States* (Oxford University Press, Oxford, 2012), 7. This is an excellent book that provides first comprehensive account of why parent states prevent recognition of territories that unilaterally seceded. It focuses on the cases of Serbia, Cyprus, and Georgia and their attempts to prevent the recognition of Kosovo, the "Turkish Republic of Northern

and the reasons countries refuse to do so vary.[13] Importantly, there is no global consistency in state practice towards declarations of independence; indeed, as Ker-Lindsay observes "we appear to be moving into a strange new era in which there are states that are recognized as such by some countries but not by others."[14]

2   Slovak Opposition towards Kosovo's Independence

Slovakia has not joined the majority of the EU in the recognition process of Kosovo's independence and has not reconsidered its view to date. On the whole, Slovakia's position towards Kosovo's independence raises significant and wide-ranging questions about the impact of Slovakia's membership of the EU, and on its common foreign policy of the EU. It bears note that less than three years after its accession, Slovakia was advocating a position against the majority of the EU.[15] This was a rather unexpected situation, considering Slovakia used to subscribe to EU consensus and was not used to standing out on major foreign policy questions.[16] It was widely expected that the considerable

---

Cyprus", South Ossetia, and Abchazia respectively. For a section on non-recognition in international politics, see 12–14.

13   Ibid., 12–13.

14   Ibid., 18.

15   A more recent example of Slovak disunity (or non-conformity) with its EU partners occurred in September 2015 when the EU's interior ministers approved a plan on redistributing over 120,000 refugees from Greece and Italy between the 28 EU members based on a quota system. Out of the 28 members, Hungary, the Czech Republic, Romania, and Slovakia were against it and Finland abstained. Based on the plan, Slovakia was required to take 802 refugees. Slovakia's position gained even more attention as gradually it became the only country to hold on to its opposition to the quota system when it was ratified on 23 September 2015 by the EU leaders in Brussels. Another disunity was demonstrated earlier in October 2011, when the Slovak Parliament refused a bailout fund for Greece resulting in the collapse of the Slovak government. Notably, Slovakia was the only country of the 17 Euro-zone states to do so. As an analyst observed, "it seems somewhat unfathomable that a country that has not been a member of EMU [European Monetary Union] for even three years could be the one leading to its unravelling." Helen Pidd, "Slovakia Rejects Multibillion Euro Bailout Fund to Deal with Debt Crisis", The Guardian (12 October 2011).

16   As a Senior European diplomat put it, "Slovakia, up to that point [the passing of the Slovak Parliament's Declaration on Kosovo refusing recognition of Kosovo's statehood without the consent of Belgrade] had pursued a line of being in the EU mainstream. Slovaks continued to be very anxious and nervous about departing from the EU mainstream." Interview with a senior European diplomat (April 2011).

international lobbying – mostly by EU and US diplomats – would bear fruit, though, despite all efforts Bratislava did not change its view.

What made Slovakia's position especially significant was that between 2006 and 2007, it was a non-permanent member of the United Nations Security Council (UNSC). It was in early 2007 that Kosovo's future status received special attention in Slovak politics. Kosovo was high on the agenda of the UNSC and thus Slovakia was directly involved in debates on the subject.[17] At that time, Slovakia's position stood in marked contrast to the position adopted by the four other members of the EU on the UNSC (the UK, France, Italy and Belgium),[18] all of whom were broadly in favor of independence. In this context, Slovakia's position was seen as key to preserving EU unity.[19]

A variety of arguments have been put forward to explain Slovakia's negative stance towards Kosovo's independence. These include, first, the Slovak-Serbian relations: it has been argued that Slovakia's traditionally good relations with Serbia and expression of Slavonic solidarity contributed to its position. Second, regional stability: argument that Kosovo's independence could have destabilizing potential for the region and raise security concerns. Third, respect for international law: it was *claimed* that Kosovo's independence violated International Law (in July 2010, the International Court of Justice ruled otherwise[20]). Fourth, the notion of Kosovo as precedent: argument that Kosovo's

---

17   In a leaked confidential cable from a meeting of the US Ambassador to Finland, Marilyn Ware, with Martti Ahtisaari, sent from the Embassy Helsinki, Ware stated: "Ahtisaari is also directly lobbying EU member states and current or incoming UN SC members. Some (he named South Africa, Spain, Romania, Sweden and Slovakia) have needed more persuading than he would have expected." "Ambassador Ware's Meeting with President Ahtisaari", Embassy Helsinki, reference ID 06Helsinki1252 (8 December 2006), available at <http://wikileaks.ch/cable/2006/12/06helsinki1215.html>. The UNSC discussions on Kosovo's status eventually ended without passing any resolution as it became clear that in the case of a UN vote Russia would use its veto right.

18   In addition to the five permanent UNSC members (China, France, Russia, the UK, and the US), the non-permanent members in 2007 were: Belgium, Congo, Ghana, Indonesia, Italy, Panama, Peru, Qatar, South Africa, and Slovakia.

19   "Slovakia will not discuss status issues during UNSC UNMIK meeting", US mission UN New York, reference ID 07USUN NEWYORK (17 March 2007), available at <http://wikileaks.org/cable/2007/03/07USUN NEWYORK215.html>.

20   "Accordance with International Law of the Unilateral Declaration of Independence in Respect of Kosovo", *Advisory Opinion*, International Court of Justice Reports (2010), available at <http://www.icj-cij.org/docket/files/141/15987.pdf>. The Court ruled that there is no international law which prohibits declaration of independence, however, it did not touch upon the question of independence and state recognition itself.

unilateral declaration of independence might set precedent for other regions. This was also linked to Slovak issues with ethnic Hungarian minority living in Slovakia and its relations with Hungary.[21] However, this paper argues that the most influential factors that impacted the non-recognition were related to domestic politics and the role of political party opposition in Slovakia and more relevantly, the changes in the law that allowed these to be major factors. Together with issues around the ethnic Hungarian minority and Slovak-Hungarian relations they led to the failure of all attempts for a "common" EU foreign policy on Kosovo.[22] Therefore, in this case, the implementation of an EU joint policy on Kosovo did not succeed. Rather than illustrating Slovak domestic party politics at length, this contribution instead examines the law in early 2007 that enabled the then opposition leader, Mikuláš Dzurinda, to initiate a debate in the Slovak Parliament leading to the passing of the Slovak Parliament's Declaration on Kosovo. This declaration effectively allowed the Parliament to influence this foreign political decision resulting in a change of the Slovak Ministry of Foreign Affairs'(MFA) planned course of action towards Kosovo. In other words, it set the scene for what followed and considerably restricted the maneuvering space of the MFA in dealing with the issue of Kosovo's statehood.

3   Slovak Accession to the EU and Passing of the Constitutional Act No. 397/2004

Slovak integration into the EU in 2004 has been considered one of the crucial turning points in foreign policy-making. As Haughton and Malová argue, after the independence of Slovakia in 1993, the MFA was primarily oriented towards integration into "Western clubs" (e.g. the EU, NATO).[23] It can be argued that

---

21   See for instance, Kai-Olaf Lang, "Slowakei: Keine Anerkennung, aber Partnerschaft (Slovakia: No Recognition, but Partnership)", 56 Südosteuropa (2008), 435–440, at 439; and Henry H. Perritt Jr., *The Road to Independence for Kosovo* (Cambridge University Press, Cambridge, 2010).

22   For a discussion of the ethnic Hungarian minority aspect specifically, see Katarína Lezová, "The Notion of Kosovo as a Precedent and the Impact of the Hungarian Minority Issue on Slovakia's Policy towards Kosovo's Independence", 65(5) *Europe-Asia Studies* (2013), 965–991.

23   Tim Haughton and Darina Malová, "Emerging Patterns of EU Membership: Drawing Lessons from Slovakia's First Two Years as a Member State", 27(2) *Politics* (2007), 69–75, at 71–72.

prior to the Slovak accession to the EU, it was about a "one-way transfer of EU rules and norms."[24] Significantly, during this time, Slovak foreign policy towards countries outside the EU reflected foreign policy priorities of the EU.[25] However, after Slovakia became a member of the EU and NATO, "a new agenda was needed."[26] In other words, after the period of probation leading to accession, the new EU members were given space to maneuver.[27] Being an EU member means that a country is "no longer a mere object of EU decisions, but is rather a co-maker and co-author;" as a result, states have opportunities to push for policies that are not necessarily advocated by the EU majority.[28] That said, the flip-side is that the EU's leverage over candidate states is considerable once they become actual members.

Following Slovakia's accession to the EU in 2004, there was a change from "full harmonization" with Common Foreign Security Policy (CFSP) towards attempts to pursue Slovak national interests which, at some points, went against views supported by the EU leaders in foreign policy-making.[29] As an example of pursuing Slovak national interests, Bátora and Pulišová refer to the issue of Kosovo's statehood. These Slovak interests became most obvious "in international situations where there is a tension between, on the one hand, the principles of state sovereignty and territorial integrity and, on the other, the right to self-determination of ethnic groups."[30] Having in mind Czechoslovakia's peaceful disintegration, they further emphasize that Slovakia is a supporter of "orderly division" of countries if preceded by an agreement between all parties involved.[31] Indeed, Slovakia did not oppose Kosovo's independence on the basis of its national interests *per se*. In contrast, for the Slovak MFA, it was in the Slovak interest to support an EU common position towards Kosovo. This was considered crucial particularly in view of its membership in the EU, NATO,

---

24   Vladimír Bilčík and Aneta Világi, "Slovakia and the Limits of European Integration", *Study for the Project "Forum for Europe"*, Slovak Foreign Policy Association (2007), 5.

25   Jozef Bátora and Veronika Pulišová, "Slovakia: Learning to Add Value to EU Foreign Policy", in Michael Baun and Dan Marek (eds.), *The New Member States and the European Union: Foreign Policy and Europeanization* (Routledge, London, 2013), 68–83, at 72.

26   Haughton and Malová, *op. cit.* note 23, 71–72.

27   *Ibid.*, 73.

28   Darina Malová and Tim Haughton, "The Causes and Consequences of Slovakia's stance on further European Integration", European Research Institute, University of Birmingham, *European Research Working Paper Series* (2004) No.3, 19.

29   Bátora and Pulišová, *op. cit.* note 25, 68.

30   *Ibid.*, 76.

31   *Ibid.*

and the UNSC.[32] In this respect a constitutional act regulating the cooperation of the Slovak Parliament and the Government on EU issues enabled the Parliament to influence the foreign policy adopted towards Kosovo.

After its accession to the EU, Slovakia passed the Constitutional Act No. 397/2004 on the cooperation of the National Council of the Slovak Republic and the Government of Slovak Republic in EU affairs. As a result of this law, the Slovak Parliament has the right to pass resolutions which bind the Government and its individuals to concrete foreign policy positions.[33] Under this resolution, the Government is obliged to inform the Parliament about the current EU agenda and the Parliament has the right to approve or change the positions of the Slovak Republic in respect of this agenda.[34] The Constitutional Act No. 397/2004 also defines the relationship between the executive and legislative power in the field of European integration. Among other things, it allows the National Council to *approve* Slovak positions on the drafts of legally binding acts of the EU. Parliament may also approve country views on other EU matters if requested by the Government or members of at least one fifth of the National Council. If MPs approve a draft opinion, a member of the Slovak Government is bound by that opinion in EU institutions.[35]

Despite the relatively strong competencies given to the Parliament in relation to EU matters and its control over government positions, the legislative power rarely interferes with the executive's foreign policy decisions. In general, it is the national executive that takes decisions in respect to foreign policy-making, and the national parliaments have limited authority in these matters.[36]

---

32   This was articulated several times by the Slovak Minister of Foreign Affairs, Ján Kubiš. Národná rada Slovenskej republiky (National Council of the Slovak Republic), 5th day of proceedings, 8th session (27 March 2007) *Spoločná Česko-Slovenská digitálna parlamentná knižnica (Common Czecho-Slovak Digital Parliamentary Library)*, available at <http://www.nrsr.sk/dl/>, 23–26.

33   "Ústavný zákon č. 397/2004 Z. z. o spolupráci Národnej rady Slovenskej republiky a vlády Slovenskej republiky v záležitostiach Európskej únie (Constitutional Law Nr. 397/2004 Coll. about Cooperation of the National Council of the Slovak Republic and the Government of the Slovak Republic in EU Affairs)", *Národná rada Slovenskej republiky (National Council of the Slovak Republic)* (24 June 2004).

34   Vladimír Bartovic, "National Council of the Slovak Republic in the EU Agenda: Giant in Theory, Dwarf in Practice", in David Král and Vladimír Bartovic (eds.), *The Czech and Slovak Parliaments after the Lisbon Treaty* (EUROPEUM Institute for European Policy, Prague, 2010), 47–78, at 55.

35   *op. cit.* note 33, Article 2.

36   Eva Gross, "The Europeanization of National Foreign Policy? The Role of the EU CFSP/ESDP in Crisis Decision-Making in Macedonia and Afghanistan", PhD thesis, London School of Economics (2007), 47. Also Tapio Raunio and Simon Hix, "Backbenchers Learn to Fight

Therefore, as a matter of practice, foreign political questions are largely dealt with by the national governments.

In fact, until the initiation of the Slovak Parliament's draft proposal on Kosovo, MPs relied on the resolution to oblige a member of the government with a specific mandate only once – on the question of EU accession negotiations with Turkey.[37] On 30 November 2004, the Slovak Parliament bound the government members "to enforce in the EU Council negotiations such an approach for the initiation of the negotiations for the Turkish EU membership which would respect inevitability of fulfilling criteria and from which the EU would not be bound to accept Turkey as a member of the EU."[38] As Világi and Bilčík argue, in the case of Turkey, the law was used to express a standpoint of strategic importance which received considerable political, media and public interest.[39]

In general, as the aforementioned authors point out in their study, the Slovak Parliament – including its committees – is active on EU matters only in questions related to internal political discourse or those issues related to key domestic political agendas.[40] In other words, it deals with matters closely linked to political party competition. Notably, Világi and Bilčík suggest that in the case of a long-term minority government, the 2004 law remains a "potentially strong instrument in the hands of political opposition", particularly if it disrupts an existing wider political consensus on a Slovak position in the EU. Similarly, a coalition or main opposition political party with clear ideas about Slovak priorities in the EU has good preconditions to use a relatively strong political position of the Parliament on EU matters.[41] In this respect, the Slovak

---

Back: European Integration and Parliamentary Government", 23(4) *West European Politics* (2000), 142–168, at 154.

37   For a detailed analysis of this law's application in the case of Turkey, see Aneta Világi and Vladimír Bilčík, "Fungovanie a koordinácia domácich inštitúcií SR v legislatívnom procese Európskej únie: stav, možnosti a odporúčania (Functioning and Coordination of the National Institutions in the Slovak Republic in the EU Legislative Process: Current State, Options and Recommendations)" (Research Centre of the Slovak Foreign Policy Association, Bratislava, 2007), particularly 19–20.

38   "Uznesenie Národnej Rady Slovenskej Republiky 1340 z 30. novembra 2004 (Resolution of the National Council of the Slovak Republic 1340 from 30 November 2004)", 1759/2004, *Národná rada Slovenskej republiky (National Council of the Slovak Republic)*.

39   Világi and Bilčík, *op. cit.* note 37, 24.

40   *Ibid.*, 31. This study analyzed parliamentary resolutions passed only until the end of November 2006.

41   *Ibid.*, 36. Although, in 2007 when the Slovak Parliament debated the Slovak position towards Kosovo's independence, Slovakia did not have a minority government, this

Government acts in all external issues; in EU matters however, parliamentary scrutiny can determine the Slovak position. Put differently, the Parliament has a say in the formulation of Slovak EU policy.

In respect to resolving Kosovo's statehood, as far as Slovakia was concerned, it was supporting the Ahtisaari process and a compromise between Belgrade and Pristina. Notably, throughout 2006, the Slovak MFA effectively signalled its commitment to support the Ahtisaari mission that was evidently designed to lead towards Kosovo's independence although the Slovak representatives were concerned about the speed of the process.[42] In any case, the Slovak Minister of Foreign Affairs, Ján Kubiš, saw Kosovo's independence as inevitable[43] but as several incidents confirmed, the government did not appear to be united on this issue.[44] For this reason, Kosovo's independence appeared to be a "suitable topic" for the leader of opposition, Mikuláš Dzurinda, for an attack on

---

description entirely fits the case of the Parliament's declaration on Kosovo, where the opposition leader Dzurinda aimed to use the earlier described competency of Slovak Parliament for political gains.

42   See for instance "Slovakia wants to take it slower on Kosovo", US Embassy in Bratislava, reference ID 06Bratislava360 (5 May 2006), available at <http://wikileaks.org/cable/2006/05/06BRATISLAVA360.html>; "Slovakia agrees on Kosovo status, but concerned with timeline of process", US Embassy Bratislava, reference ID 06Bratislava310 (19 April 2006), available at <http://wikileaks.org/cable/2006/04/06BRATISLAVA310.html>.

43   "O Kosove je rozhodnuté, myslí si Kubiš (It Has been Decided about Kosovo, Kubiš Thinks)", *Pravda* (6 February 2007).

44   For instance, in October 2006 the Serbian Prime Minister, Vojislav Koštunica, visited Bratislava. During his visit, the Slovak Minister of Foreign Affairs, Ján Kubiš, voiced support for Ahtisaari's activities. However, the Slovak Prime Minister, Róbert Fico, expressed support for a Kosovo solution that could be revised in the future if necessary. For his part, President Ivan Gašparovič remarked that Kosovo should remain part of Serbia. "Koštunica hovoril na Slovensku o referende (Koštunica Spoke on Referendum in Slovakia)", *Pravda* (2 October 2006); "Koštunica a Fico sa zhodli: Kosovo musí zostať Srbsku (Koštunica and Fico Agreed: Kosovo Must Remain Serbian)", *SME* (2 October 2006). Another incident that appeared to show the continuing divisions between the MFA and other parts of the government arose in March 2007. This time the catalyst for the disagreement was the visit of Zoran Stanković, the Serbian Minister of Defence, to Bratislava. During a joint press conference, his Slovak counterpart, Fratišek Kašický, stated that "it is not possible to support any degree of Kosovo's independence without the consent of Belgrade. It is not possible to support a development resulting in a national minority, which has its own mother state, claiming to create another state", author's own translation. "Zoran Stanković ocenil postoj Slovenska (Zoran Stankovič Appreciated the Stance of Slovakia)", *Obrana* (2007) No. 4, 20. This stood in stark contrast to the message Kubiš had delivered in Belgrade and Pristina. The MFA's attempt to present a single position on Kosovo had once again been obstructed.

the ruling coalition, arguing that coalition leaders were not dealing with an issue so important for Slovak state interests. Dzurinda took a tactical step and challenged the government by arguing that Kosovo should not be granted independence without Belgrade's consent and that Slovakia should be ready to go against the grain of accepted EU common foreign policy.[45]

Dzurinda's sudden reaction surprised not only international but also domestic partners, particularly in view of his very pro-American orientation in the past. As one Senior European diplomat put it, "no one expected Mr Dzurinda to come up with this, to be the catalyst of this change, because after all it had been Mr Dzurinda who had done pretty much everything the EU had asked of him." However, the observer added, it appeared as though he was looking for something with which to embarrass Prime Minister Fico.[46] As the diplomat explained, Dzurinda had by now been out of "power for about eight-nine months and it was about the time that the main opposition leader did something to cause Fico a headache."[47] Indeed, the question of Kosovo's independence appeared to be a suitable topic to challenge Fico on. However, at the EU level, the Slovak position was a surprise, even more so because the initiator of the debate was SDKÚ-DS (Slovak Democratic and Christian Union-Democratic Party), and notably its leader Dzurinda. Dzurinda was the Prime Minister in the previous two governments (1998–2006) and his politics were very EU- and NATO-oriented. It was during his term of office that Slovakia entered both the EU and NATO in 2004.

As a result of two days of heated debates, on 28 March 2007, Parliament eventually approved the "Declaration of the National Council of the Slovak Republic on the Solution of the Future Status of the Serbian province Kosovo", stating the following:

> The National Council of the Slovak Republic expressing its belief that full and unlimited independence of the province of Kosovo is not in the interest of the stability of the region which was exposed to long years of tragedies and crisis; that not all possibilities of dialogue aimed at

---

45 "Dzurinda: Nezávislé Kosovo proti vôli Srbska by bolo chybou (Dzurinda: Independent Kosovo against the Will of Serbia would be a Mistake)", SITA (8 February 2007). Dzurinda also argued that it would not be the first time that Slovakia would be in the minority. For instance, he noted that he was the only one who insisted on the start of EU negotiations with Croatia.

46 Interview with a Senior European diplomat (April 2011).

47 *Ibid.*

reaching an agreement have been exhausted; that the future status solution of Kosovo should be based on Serbia's legitimate needs as well as on respect for the UN Charter and other international legal standards

expects that the Slovak Government will search for a common solution regarding the future settlement of relations in the Western Balkans in cooperation with other EU member countries, with a clear perspective of integrating the Western Balkan countries into the European Union;

believes that the will of the National Council of the Slovak Republic expressed in this way will contribute to the stabilization of the relations in the region.[48]

This Declaration had a considerable impact on the official Slovak stance. Limited attention has been paid to political parties in parliamentary systems' foreign policy-making and very few studies have looked at the role of parliament in foreign political decisions. This is largely because parliaments do not generally influence the external behavior of states and rarely challenge governments on foreign political issues.[49] Competencies of the Slovak Parliament were also overlooked in the European Defense and Security Assembly report, looking into the role of parliaments in the recognition of Kosovo, which was prepared in December 2008. It stated that, on the basis of Slovak constitution, the Slovak Parliament has no power to recognize or refuse recognition of new states as this is a matter for the Slovak Government to deal with as the key decision-maker on domestic and foreign policy.[50] However, on the basis of the earlier mentioned constitutional law, the Slovak Parliament's competencies

---

48   "Vyhlásenie Národnej rady Slovenskej republiky k riešeniu budúceho štatútu srbskej provincie Kosovo (Declaration of the National Council of the Slovak Republic on the solution of the future status of the Serbian province Kosovo)", No. 309, *Národná rada Slovenskej republiky* (*National Council of the Slovak Republic*) (28 March 2007), available at <http://www.nrsr.sk/default.aspx?sid=nrsr/ dokumenty/vyhlasenia>. Text translated by the author. The Declaration was supported by 123 MPs out of 142 in attendance, with no opposing votes.

49   Baris Kesgin and Juliet Kaarbo, "When and How Parliaments Influence Foreign Policy: The Case of Turkey's Iraq Decision", 11(1) *International Studies Perspectives* (2010), 19–36; and Heiner Hänggi, "The Use of Force under International Auspices: Parliamentary Accountability and 'Democratic Deficits'", in Hans Born and Heiner Hänggi (eds.), *The Double Democratic Deficit* (Ashgate, Aldershot, 2004), 3–18.

50   "The role of parliaments in the recognition of Kosovo", Report submitted on behalf of the Parliamentary and Public Relations Committee by Marco Zacchera, Vice-Chairman

on EU-related matters do give it the means to influence and control Slovakian standpoints on EU associated affairs, and Kosovo was clearly one of them.

4   Conclusion

The Slovak opposition leader's goal of regaining domestic political power, ultimately leading to a parliamentary declaration on Kosovo, considerably limited the maneuvering space of the Slovak MFA in the question of Kosovo's independence. In the end, the parliamentary Declaration led to a change of policy and eventually, non-fulfillment of the Ministry's main intent – remaining with the EU on Kosovo and demonstrating its role as a responsible EU, UNSC, and NATO member.

This shows the importance of political party opposition and its impact on Slovak policy, exposing how an internal political issue ended up having a considerable impact on a key foreign policy decision. As a result, Slovak politicians elevated national interests above EU interests and resisted pressure from EU actors.

Ultimately, the Constitutional Act No. 397/2004 meant that in 2007 MPs were brought into the discussion on Slovak foreign policy towards Kosovo's independence, and to a large extent shaped the final Slovak stance as the Parliament issued instructions to the Minister of Foreign Affairs. Therefore, the fact that "parliaments are able to force governments to uphold a position that denies them room for maneuver in the endgame of negotiations" created, particularly in 2007, a difficult situation for Slovakia as an EU Member State.[51]

Any possible changes of the Slovak position in the near future are rather unlikely. However, the last years in Slovak-Kosovo relations show that it is possible to engage with a territory without recognizing it as a state as such and in fact, the bilateral relations show that Slovakia has, from the Visegrád 4 countries, the liveliest relations with Kosovo.[52] Particularly between 2012 and 2013 the number of visits between representatives of both countries increased significantly. Despite these indicators, it remains to be seen if, and under what conditions, Slovakia re-assesses its position towards Kosovo's statehood.

---

and Rapporteur (Italy, Federated Group),Western European Union Assembly Document, A/2023 (3 December 2008).

51   Hussein Kassim, "The Europeanization of Member State Institutions", in Simon Bulmer and Christian Lequesne (eds.), *The Member States of the European Union* (Oxford University Press, Oxford, 2005), 285–316, at 303.

52   The Visegrád Group includes Czech Republic, Hungary, Poland, and Slovakia.

Bibliography

Bartovic, Vladimír. (2010) "National Council of the Slovak Republic in the EU Agenda: Giant in Theory, Dwarf in Practice", in Král, David and Bartovic, Vladimír. (eds.), *The Czech and Slovak Parliaments after the Lisbon Treaty* (EUROPEUM Institute for European Policy, Prague), 47–78.

Bátora, Jozef and Pulišová, Veronika. (2013) "Slovakia: Learning to Add Value to EU Foreign Policy", in Baun, Michael and Marek, Dan. (eds.), *The New Member States and the European Union: Foreign Policy and Europeanization* (Routledge, London), 68–83.

Bilčík, Vladimír and Világi, Aneta. (2007) "Slovakia and the Limits of European Integration", *Study for the Project "Forum for Europe"*, Slovak Foreign Policy Association.

Gross, Eva. (2007) "The Europeanization of National Foreign Policy? The Role of the EU CFSP/ESDP in Crisis Decision-Making in Macedonia and Afghanistan", PhD thesis, London School of Economics.

Hänggi, Heiner. (2004) "The Use of Force under International Auspices: Parliamentary Accountability and 'Democratic Deficits'", in Born, Hans and Hänggi, Heiner. (eds.), *The Double Democratic Deficit* (Ashgate, Aldershot), 3–18.

Haughton, Tim and Malová, Darina. (2007) "Emerging Patterns of EU Membership: Drawing Lessons from Slovakia's First Two Years as a Member State", 27(2) *Politics*, 69–75.

Kassim, Hussein. (2005) "The Europeanization of Member State Institutions", in Bulmer, Simon and Lequesne, Christian. (eds.), *The Member States of the European Union* (Oxford University Press, Oxford), 285–316.

Ker-Lindsay, James. (2015) "Engagement without Recognition: The Limits of Diplomatic Interaction with Contested States", 91(2) *International Affairs*, 267–285.

Ker-Lindsay, James. (2012) *The Foreign Policy of Counter Secession: Preventing the Recognition of Contested States* (Oxford University Press, Oxford).

Ker-Lindsay, James. (2009) *Kosovo: The Path to Contested Statehood in the Balkans* (I.B. Tauris, London).

Kesgin, Baris and Kaarbo, Juliet. (2010) "When and How Parliaments Influence Foreign Policy: The Case of Turkey's Iraq Decision", 11(1) *International Studies Perspectives*, 19–36.

Kursani, Shpend. (2011) "Western Balkans and Europe: Waiting for the Mediterranean Breeze from Greece", *Art of the Possible: The Cambridge University Journal of Politics*, available at <http://artofthepossible-cambridge.com/index.php?a=12& title= 1297598745.html>.

Lang, Kai-Olaf. (2008) "Slowakei: Keine Anerkennung, aber Partnerschaft (Slovakia: No Recognition, but Partnership)", 56 *Südosteuropa*, 435–440.

Lezová, Katarína. (2013) "The Notion of Kosovo as a Precedent and the Impact of the Hungarian Minority Issue on Slovakia's Policy towards Kosovo's Independence", 65(5) *Europe-Asia Studies*, 965–991.

Lezová, Katarína. (2013) "The Influence of Domestic Political Factors on Foreign Policy Formation in an EU Member State: The Case of Slovakia and the Kosovo Status Process", PhD thesis, Goldsmiths, University of London.

Malová, Darina and Haughton, Tim. (2004) "The Causes and Consequences of Slovakia's stance on further European Integration", European Research Institute, University of Birmingham, *European Research Working Paper Series* No.3.

Perritt, Henry H. Jr. (2010) *The Road to Independence for Kosovo* (Cambridge University Press, Cambridge).

Raunio, Tapio and Hix, Simon. (2000) "Backbenchers Learn to Fight Back: European Integration and Parliamentary Government", 23(4) *West European Politics*, 142–168.

Világi, Aneta and Bilčík, Vladimír. (2007), "Fungovanie a koordinácia domácich inštitúcií SR v legislatívnom procese Európskej únie: stav, možnosti a odporúčania (Functioning and Coordination of the National Institutions in the Slovak Republic in the EU Legislative Process: Current State, Options and Recommendations)" (Research Centre of the Slovak Foreign Policy Association, Bratislava).

PART 5

Russia – Beyond the EU

∴

The European Union and Russia during the Two Waves of Enlargement: New Political and Implementation Rationales on Old Issues

Sandra Fernandes

Abstract

Since 2004, the strategic dimension of the EU's relationship with Moscow has been enhanced. Countries of the former Soviet sphere brought new political dimensions alongside the Union's growing assertion as a global actor. EU post-enlargement ambitions also corresponded to a greater strategic orientation towards its neighborhood, materialized in its European Neighborhood Policy (ENP) and a new mode of relationship with Moscow. Academic literature has been focusing mainly on EU's internal adjustments concerning the impact of the Eastern enlargement on its approaches towards Russia, surrounded by the competing views on how to deal with Moscow. This chapter aims instead at focusing on specific policy outcomes, as compared to the initial stated goals advanced by Brussels at the time of enlargement (i.e. up to circa 2008). We argue that already existing tensions and issues have been sharpened in EU-Russia relations but that main priorities have been pursued, such as trade relations. We also argue that the empowerment of both actors is an additional variable that explains the impact of enlargement on a more difficult relationship with Russia. Considering a key EU document from 2004, we analyze the effects of enlargement on EU policies towards Russia and what (and how) core policies have been implemented in the last ten years prior to the Ukrainian crisis.

Keywords

EU-Russia relations – reciprocity – principled cooperation – trade relations – visa policy

1   Introduction

Commonly termed as "Four Common Spaces",[1] the new *ad hoc* structure of co-operation for European Union (EU) – Russia relations was adopted in 2003. At the time EU-Russian relations needed new impetus beyond the 1997 Partnership and Cooperation Agreement (PCA) in order to adapt to systemic changes and advance relationships in preferred sectors. The creation of the four "common spaces" can be interpreted as a necessity to prevent Russia from being excluded in further cooperative dynamics. Russia is neither a Member State nor a partner in the European Neighborhood Policy (ENP).[2]

Legal steps assured the transition and the continuity of the relations of the then EU27 with Russia, namely the extension of the PCA to the new Member States.[3] In fact, the Eastern enlargement represented a systemic change for the Union in the sense that the inclusion of countries that formerly constituted the Soviet space introduced new political orientations in Brussels, specifically, a new EU strategic orientation towards the Eastern neighborhood.

In February 2004, the Commission published a key document portraying Russia as a necessary strategic partner. The document also suggested a new spirit of cooperation to address the lack of cooperative progress.[4] It proposed an EU pro-active attitude, a frank recognition of the obstacles (namely regarding the gap in values) and a relation beyond political rhetoric. Moreover, it advocated a more direct relationship with less corporate language and the adaptation of the relation to the newly created ENP. This report aimed also at

---

1   The 1997 Partnership and Cooperation Agreement is the legal basis for EU-Russian relations. A new framework of cooperation was established at the St. Petersburg summit in 2003. Since then, Brussels and Moscow have cooperated in four areas (the so-called "common spaces"): a common economic space; a common space of freedom, security and justice; a common space of cooperation in the field of external security; and a common space on research, education and culture.

2   The ENP was launched in 2004 and includes Southern Mediterranean countries and six former Soviet Republics participating in the EU's Eastern Partnership (Armenia, Azerbaijan, Belarus, Georgia, Moldova, and Ukraine). The Eastern Partnership was created in 2009 in the context of the ENP to give new impetus to relations with these countries.

3   "Joint Statement on EU Enlargement and EU-Russia Relations" (Brussels, 27 April 2004), available at <http://europa.eu.int/comm./external_relations/russia/russia_docs/js_elarg_270 404.htm>; "Protocol to the Partnership and Cooperation Agreement" (Brussels, 27 April 2004), available at <http://europa.eu.int/comm./external_relations/russia/Russia _docs/protocol_0404.htm>.

4   European Commission, "Communication from the Commission to the Council and the European Parliament on relations with Russia", COM(2004) 106 (Brussels, 9 February, 2004).

proposing measures to create the above-mentioned Four Common Spaces.[5] With this milestone document in mind, the following questions may be raised: What have been the effects of enlargement on EU policies towards Russia? What (and how have) core policies been implemented in the last ten years?

Available literature has significantly contributed to demonstrate the effects of enlargement.[6] New Member States have brought a more critical view on Russia and have raised the Union's convergence demands expectation from Russian cooperation, as far as political standards are concerned, especially the rule of law and human rights. A main feature is the existence of competing views on how to deal with Moscow that affect EU unity.[7]

Given the above mentioned context, we aim at observing the evolution of specific policy outcomes and implementation issues. Sources include semi-structured interviews conducted in Brussels, official policy documents, and secondary literature. In the first section, we observe the evolution in domains that are of EU interest and in the second section we analyze the changes in policy areas of special Russian interest. These two different categories of policies permit to assess whether new Member States are more obstructive or less obstructive towards Russia depending on the EU policy priorities. We focus on

---

5   In fact, the Commission defended a change of attitude towards Russia in order to abandon an accommodative and appeasing attitude in favor of a posture of equality and the recognition of the obstacles that damaged cooperation. The Commission acknowledged, for instance, doubts "about Russia's commitment and ability to uphold core universal and European values and pursue democratic reforms"; that "there has been insufficient overall progress on substance"; and that the Union should "take up difficult issues with Russia in a clear and forthright manner." *Ibid.*

6   For an analysis of the normative gap between the EU and Russia and the impact of new Member States on policy-making in the political system of the EU, see Tom Casier, "Are the Policies of Russia and the EU in Their Shared Neighbourhood Doomed to Clash?", in Roger Kanet and Maria Raquel Freire (eds.), *Competing for Influence: The EU and Russia in Post-Soviet Eurasia* (Republic of Letters, Dordrecht, 2012); Sandra Fernandes, "The EU Institutional Balance: Assessment of its Impact on the Relationship with Russia", in Teresa Cierco (ed.), *The European Union Neighbourhood: Ten Years into the New Millennium* (Ashgate, Surrey, 2013), 143–172; and Mathias Roth, "Bilateral Disputes between EU Member States and Russia", 319 *CEPS Working Document* (2009).

7   The EU is seen as split between two main approaches. On the one hand, some Member States consider that Russia is a partner that ought to be engaged through a process of "creeping integration" that accommodates with some Russian non-compliance with the established rules. On the other hand, some Member States favor a "soft containment" of Russia that would ultimately isolate Russia from the Union and create hostility that would impeach the tackling of common problems in the neighborhood and globally. Mark Leonard and Nicu Popescu, "A Power Audit of EU-Russia Relations", *ECFR Policy Paper* (2007).

the period of 2006–2008 due to specific disputes between new Member States and Moscow that determined the impossibility of new cooperation agreement negotiations, as it was again the case since the Russian annexation of Crimea in March 2014. We also argue that the empowerment of both actors, and in particular Russia,[8] is an additional variable that explains the impact of enlargement on policies towards Russia. At the bottom line, 2008 appears as a turning point in the deteriorating trend of the relationship, affecting all the policy areas of the framework of cooperation and prompting the Union to advance principles over interests.

2   Policies of Special Interest for the EU

The 2005 roadmaps for the implementation of the four common spaces are indicative of the widening and deepening cooperation agenda.[9] Progress reports evidence that economic and trade objectives (first common space) are enhanced, thus giving other areas a secondary priority.[10] The focus of the relationship on economic issues (including energy) is significantly explained by the socioeconomic position of the two actors. One of the main features was that the EU was the main trading partner of Russia and that Russia ranked third for the Union. Furthermore, energy was shown to be "one of the major issues of the bilateral trade relationship between the two areas."[11] In 2005, the Union imported 32% of oil and 42% of gas from Russia, with sharp differences in EU Member States importations. That same year, Russian GDP growth was 6.4% as compared to 1.7% for the Union.[12] Today, they remain top trade partners with a significant GDP contraction in Russia, below –4%.[13]

---

8   We mean here that the Union has widened and deepened the policy areas under its competences and that Russia has improved its internal and external situation. On the EU, see for instance Herman Lelievelt and Sebastiaan Princen, *The Politics of the European Union* (Cambridge University Press, Cambridge, 2011); and on Russian empowerment, see Roger Kanet (ed.), *Russian Foreign Policy in the 21st Century* (Palgrave MacMillan, 2010).

9   For a description of the scope of EU-Russia cooperation, see the EU External Action Service (EUEAS) website.

10   Progress reports are issued since 2007 and are available at the EUEAS website. Further official and public information concerning the cooperative results is provided in the summits press releases and in the official websites of the EU institutions.

11   Eurostat and Rosstat, *The European Union and Russia. Statistical Comparison 1995–2005* (Eurostat, Statistical Books and Rosstat, 2007), 3.

12   *Ibid.*

13   *Trading Economics* (Trading Economics, 2015).

Trade

Addressing trade barriers has been a core element of EU-Russia cooperation. On the basis of regulatory convergence, Russia's WTO membership was considered an essential step towards the creation of an integrated market between the EU and Russia. To implement the Four Common Spaces, the European Commission and the Russian counterparts began expert discussions labeled as "sectorial dialogues." Four years after enlargement, this dialogue had already covered twenty areas.[14] Non-compliance with the PCA provisions for trade and economic relations emerged as the main concern for the EU in the dialogues.[15]

Given this context, the parties needed to solve several problems. The most important issues were export duties on timber, dual energy pricing, and rail and air fees. A case in point, for instance, was the abolition of Siberian overflight payments, agreed in November 2006. Russian access to the WTO was halted, as was further cooperation in the aviation sector, as long as Moscow stalled at signing and implementing the agreement. Some policies, such as the Russian tariffs for railway freight and transportation and the discrimination between domestic and international destinations, are definitely not in line with the non-discrimination principle. These policies seriously affect trade flows namely for those industries dependent on timber imports that cannot afford export duties and subsequent price increases.

Sanitary and phytosanitary issues also affect negatively EU exports of animal and plant products to Russia. The EU compliance with international standards and the principle of proportionality and scientific justification for the application of this type of requirement prevent further agreement developments. These technical measures are linked to political disputes between Brussels and Moscow and affected, in particular, the negotiations of a new cooperation agreement between 2007 and 2008 (see below the issue of the Polish veto). Protection and enforcement of intellectual property rights is also crucial for the Union. At the end of Putin's second term, a new law restricted foreign investment in strategic sectors,[16] further adding to discrimination practices.

---

14   The dialogues are the following: Transport; Industrial and Enterprise Policy; Regulatory Dialogue on Industrial products; Space; Information Society; Agriculture; Fisheries; Macro-economic Policy; Financial Services; Energy; Procurement; Environment; Trade Facilitation; Intellectual Property Rights; Investment; Inter-regional cooperation; Statistics; Investment; Macroeconomic and Financial Issues; Inter-regional Cooperation.

15   Interviews conducted in EU institutions in 2007 and 2012, and Progress Reports published by the European Commission.

16   President of the Russian Federation, Federal Law No. 57-FZ of 29 April 2008 "Procedures for Foreign Investments in the Business Entities of Strategic Importance for Russian National Defence and State Security" (non-official translation) (Federal Anti-monopoly

Despite a trade increase between the Union and Russia, customs and other border crossing procedures applied by Moscow are considered an obstacle to trade and are perceived as fraud encouraging. As a consequence of undeveloped infrastructure, traffic congestion at the borders has become an increasing reality. A special working group was created in mid-2007 to deal with this issue but the Union has not been satisfied with the Russian efforts to enforce measures to ease the traffic, namely in relation to the reduction of the number of federal agencies operating at the border in order to ease congestion. The problem has recently been improved and although there are queues of several days at the border, they are now originated at the border.[17] Concerning EU business in Russia, the Union is worried with the way Russian authorities issue work permits, namely the lack of predictability and obstacles. Another example of a trade barrier that Brussels would like to see abandoned is the inappropriate procedure for the registration of pharmaceuticals. This issue is discussed in the regulatory dialogue.

Rule of Law, Democracy, Human Rights
An always-present component of the institutionalized framework of EU-Russia cooperation is the reference to common values and principles, they are also applied to ENP and considered by the union as essential for a "genuine EU-RU partnership."[18] These principles and values are: the rule of law; good governance; the respect for human rights, including minority rights; the promotion of good neighborly relations; the principles of market economy and sustainable development.[19] This element of EU-Russia relations, promoted by the Union side, has either been deemed as a normative issue or, more negatively, as a normative gap.[20] We will argue below that the EU's growing dissatisfaction with the political developments in Russia and the path of internal reforms has affected the relationship significantly since enlargement. Although Brussels cannot use the conditionality tool towards Russia (as a way to promote

---

Service of the Russian Federation, 2008), available at <http://www.fas.gov.ru/english/leg islation/20300.shtml>.

17 Interview with an Estonian representative (Brussels, 12 September 2012).

18 European Council, "Conclusions of the Presidency. European Council of Göteborg, 15 and 16 June (SN 200/101VER 1)" (2001), 13.

19 European Commission, "Communication from the Commission to the Council and the European Parliament. Wider Europe – Neighbourhood: A New Framework for Relations with our Eastern and Southern Neighbours", COM (2003) 104 final (Brussels, March 11, 2003).

20 Nathalie Tocci et al., "The European Union as a Normative Foreign Policy Actor", 281 CEPS Working Document (2008).

convergence with EU standards by offering enlargement perspectives),[21] new Member States have raised the Union's critical tone.

The impact of enlargement on EU-Russia relations is especially visible in the European Parliament which as a "whistle blower" has voiced direct and harsh criticism against EU policies towards Moscow and against Putin's rule. The European Parliament has done so through different instruments: resolutions, reports, oral and written questions to the Commission and the Council, direct contact with the deputies of the *Duma* and the Federal Assembly (Delegation work) and by the monitoring of Russian politics (committees work), namely on human rights.[22] Sharp divergences between two MEPs of the 2004–2009 legislature evidence the novel tone that newcomers have brought regarding the EU's stance towards Russia. Italian MEP Chiesa defended pro-Kremlin lines and stressed trade and energy interdependences. Polish MEP Onyszkiewicz demonstrated great concern about Russian evolution and its negative impact on Europe.[23]

The European Commission has maintained a pragmatic stance. While stating rhetorically the principles of the relation towards Russia, the EU pursued progress mainly on energy and WTO membership. For Brussels this would transform Russia into a more transparent and credible partner. This goal by itself is not straightforwardly normative but the purpose is in fact to bind Russia to specific international regimes.

Despite the fact that there have been a lot of statements in that direction, the EU was not really inclined to go beyond these "normative lectures" on Russia, until the Ukrainian crisis started in late 2013. Since the Russian annexation of Crimea, the Union has somehow changed its enduring vision that Russia was a partner despite the existing normative gap. It already constitutes a dramatic sign that high level biannual summits have not convened since early 2014. EU sanctions also make part of this revision.

The EU insistence on the discourse about common principles and shared values, such as human rights and democracy, has provoked an unexpected reaction in Russia. The Kremlin has reasserted the Russian cultural specificity

---

21   On conditionality, see Gergana Noutcheva, Karolina Pomorska, and Giselle Bosse (eds.), *The EU and its Neighbours:Values versus Security in European Foreign Policy* (Manchester University Press, 2013).

22   See the European Parliament's website available at <www.europarl.europa.eu>; European Parliament (2004), (Directorate General For External Policies Of The Union, PE 342.078, 6 July); and European Parliament (2009), (Directorate General For External Policies Of The Union: EUR/SP/CS/EK, 23 July).

23   Speech by Giuletto Chiesa (European Parliament, Brussels, 27 June 2007) and Janusz Onyszkiewicz (European Parliament, Brussels, 27 June 2007).

and its right to have a different interpretation of democracy ("sovereign democracy"). Putin's plans to monitor human rights records of EU Member States,[24] as much as the reciprocation of sanctions against the Union (especially travel bans) since March 2014 underlines the Russian stance.

The Stalemates: 2006–2008 and 2014 Onward

The period comprised between 2006 and 2008 has been marked by the impossibility of launching negotiations on a new cooperation treaty between the Union and Moscow. The main impediments have to be found at internal EU level. Some Member States established a connection between the EU negotiations with Moscow and their bilateral disputes with Russia. Poland was at the forefront of the countries that blocked any negotiations for a new PCA as long as their trade disputes with Moscow were not solved. At the end of Putin's term as formal president of the Russian Federation in 2008, a climax was reached in EU-Russian relations. Besides the more or less enthusiastic recognition of the achievements of the relationship, observers agreed on the need to bring it to a more workable level. As Burghardt underlines, a "fresh restart" that took into account the changes from both sides was needed.[25] Today, a similar blockage is present further explained by Russia's strong bargaining power.

The Commission issued a draft mandate in July 2006 that received a reading from COEST but was not approved at COREPER level[26] since it had already been blocked at COEST working level. Roth acknowledges that the bilateral disputes between Member States and Russia[27] have already existed since the 90's and that they also inform EU relations with other third parties, such as China or Turkey. Nonetheless, Roth underlines that, in the Russian case, they are especially relevant for two reasons. Firstly, EU policies towards Russia are one of the most divisive topics of external relations. Secondly, Moscow has employed these issues to its greatest advantage in various ways.[28] Although Member

---

24   Nikolaus von Twickel, "Putin Says Russia Will Check EU on Rights", *The Moscow Times* (29 October, 2007).

25   Günther Burghardt, "Session II: The Way Ahead: Prospects for EU-Russia Relations", *Conference on EU-Russia Relations: a Trouble Strategic Partnership?* (Palais d'Egmont, Brussels, 27 February, 2008).

26   Interview (Brussels, 27 June 2007). COEST is the working party on Eastern Europe and Central Asia at the General Secretariat of the Council of the European Union. COREPER is the Committee of Permanent Representatives of EU Member States.

27   Roth, *op. cit.* note 6.

28   *Ibid*, 1–9.

States neighboring Russia are more affected by disputes, other Member States are also involved. This is so because of close trade relations that depend on industrial access to the Russian[29] markets.

In 2006, Poland decided to use its veto power over a trade dispute regarding a meat ban with Moscow. Later in 2007, another dispute with Estonia added political difficulties to the making of an agreement on a mandate for the Commission. In 2008, Lithuania joined Poland in vetoing the launching of negotiations. That same year, a change in the Polish executive allowed to overcome the two years bilateral trade dispute with Russia and to lift the veto that Warsaw had placed on the EU-Russian negotiations. On 11 May, the Slovenian Presidency of the EU reached an agreement between Lithuania and the European Commission to overcome its veto. The limbo concerning the launching of negotiations lasted for eighteen months, giving path to the current cycle informed by the difficulties to agree on a new text treaty.

The context created by the 2008 presidential election in Russia contributed also to putting the issue of EU-Russian relations on stand-by, specifically the post-PCA issue. Despite the need to unblock the negotiations, this context also contributed to provoke a cautious "wait and see" attitude from the Union. Germany embodied a Member States' perception that problems were to be managed from patience. The bottom-line was that there was no alternative to engagement with Moscow and that "even a substance-free summit was preferable to no talks and a possible confrontation."[30]

Since the Polish veto in 2006 and the activation of the Four Common Spaces in 2005, cooperation has been stalled. In the limbo period from 2006 to 2008, the EU-Russian relationship depended particularly on the short-term conjuncture. This is because progress of any kind was dependent on the absence of new events that could trigger negative rhetoric. New Member States vetoes contributed to new internal trends at the 2007 Samara summit because the Commission and the Presidency voiced the principle of solidarity among Member States for the first time, providing thus direct support to Poland, Estonia, and Lithuania.[31]

---

29   *Ibid*, 5–6.

30   Jonathan Eyal, "The European Union and Russia: A Halting Relationship", *RUSI Commentary* (21 May 2007), available at <https://rusi.org/commentary/european-union-and-russia-halting-relationship>.

31   "Samara, la Russie et l'Union européenne étalent leurs différends", *Le Monde* (18 May 2007).

The limbo was over when negotiations for a new cooperation agreement were launched in May 2008 and the first round occurred in July 2008. This development was immediately soured by the Russian-Georgian war of August 2008 that drove the EU into an internal crisis concerning the attitude to adopt towards Moscow. Some Member States wished to reconsider cooperation with Russia on the basis of Russia's non-normative behavior, while others favored a more pragmatic approach. After a brief "reflection period" from September to October 2008, the agenda for cooperation refocused on core interests. However, since 2008, EU officials have perceived that Russia engages selectively in the several domains of cooperation, based solely on its own interests disregarding any time pressure.[32] Even before the Ukrainian crisis had burst out, negotiations for a new cooperation agreement were facing a stalemate because Russia insisted on linking trade talks to its own integration projects in Eurasia.[33]

3   Policies of Special Interest For Russia

The previous section analyzed two main EU concerns affecting negotiations and policy implementation, especially in the first common space. Concern with Russian rule of law and the need to settle reciprocity are features of the EU approach previous to the enlargement and which, from 2004 onward, have had a greater impact in cooperation, prompting a more difficult relationship. All EU actors recognize that energy and visa issues are top Russian priorities. This is confirmed by Russian rhetoric and by the fact that the Kremlin has not been willing to meet with the EU at the level of senior officials[34] except for the visa dialogue.[35] We shall see below the rationales in these two policy areas of Russian special interest.[36]

---

32   Interviews conducted in September 2012 at the EEAS, the European Commission, the Council of the EU and Member States representations.

33   Interview at the EEAS and with a Polish representative (Brussels, September 2012).

34   See Fernandes, *op. cit.* note 6 for a detailed analysis of how preferences are shaped and advanced in the political system of the Union towards Russia.

35   Interview at a new Member State permanent representation (Brussels, 12 September 2012).

36   Besides the rationales that sustain that these two policies are of special Russian interest in the relation with the EU, the fact that Moscow does not want to negotiate energy and visa under the new cooperation agreement but as separate issues is also elucidative. This Russian position in the negotiation rounds has been retrieved from interviews with Member States representatives (Brussels, September 2012).

Energy[37]

The energy agenda has been highlighted since 2006 because Russia seeks the recovery of energy revenues and its distribution. Energy is one of the most prominent topics in the first common space related to trade and investment issues. Russia has been the world's largest exporter of gas and the second largest oil exporter, with considerable reserves not only of both hydrocarbons but also of coal. The country has the world's largest natural gas reserves and it is the third largest consumer of energy.[38] In 2000, the parties had already engaged in an energy dialogue. The ratification of the 1994 Energy Charter (ECT) by the Russian Federation has been a recurrent issue between the two parties. The Charter and related documents regulate energy relations based on free access to energy markets; free transit of energy products; and free flow of investment capital in energy. Putin, as prime minister, definitely closed the issue of ratification when foreign governments were notified that Russia would not join the Charter.[39] The main consequence of this development was that there is no mutual access to energy markets and that Gazprom retains its monopoly, namely regarding natural gas pipelines from Central Asia to the European Union. The parties disagree on the necessity to adopt a new treaty.

As a consequence of the deterioration of energy relations since the first gas crisis of 2006 that disrupted gas deliveries towards Europe, the parties agreed to create an early-warning mechanism to prevent energy disruptions. The above mentioned law on strategic sectors also negatively affects foreign investment in production and infrastructure in Russia. Given the close interrelations between the EU and Russia in the energy sector, Brussels is strategically interested in improving energy trade conditions. This includes guarantees of supplies, operational infrastructures, principles of transparency, reciprocal access to markets, diversification, and energy efficiency. In the case of oil supplies, disruptions have affected particularly Lithuania and Latvia since mid-2006 (Druzhba pipeline). Reciprocal need is one of the recurring mottoes in the Russian demands, namely in the energy dialogue. It refers not only to equal access but also to exploitation deals. Energy has also been highlighted since 2006 because Russia seeks to recoup the revenues from energy production and distribution, which were partly managed by foreign companies.

---

37   This subsection draws its argument from Sandra Fernandes, "Russia and Transforming Security Relations in Europe: A Mix of Strategic and Normative Rationales", *e-cadernos ces* (2013) No.19.

38   EIA, "Russia. Background" (May 2008), available at <http://www.eia.doe.gov/cabs/Russia/Background.html>.

39   RIA Novosti, "Russia says 'no' to Energy Charter, urges new agreement", *RIA Novosti* (22 May 2009).

Besides the Russian non-application of the ECT, the fact that the EU has no integrated policy on energy adds a break on its management of the issue, as opposed to bilateral relations of Member States with Moscow. Pipelines routes intersect political dependencies: the EU as much as Russia wants more autonomy in relation to the transit countries. Both parties have preferred, then, to explore alternatives in friendly countries (diversification) and bilateral agreements have been undermining the prospects for a coherent and integrated energy policy at the EU level. France, Germany, and Italy have signed agreements with Gazprom that involve, for instance, two new pipelines ("Nordstream" and "Southstream") and opened distribution market for Gazprom in exchange of guaranteed supplies, with the support of new Member States such as Bulgaria, Slovenia and Croatia.[40] The aim is to create direct connections with the final consumers in Western Europe and, therefore, avoiding the transit countries in Central Europe.[41]

As Delcour and Verluise emphasize, Brussels and Moscow have taken divergent approaches since 2006.[42] The Union pursues the goal of a market-ruled and transparent energy sector, whereas Russia seeks to protect a strategic sector for the development of the Federation. Individually, some Member States have preferred to secure their supply levels and to downgrade relations between Russia and the European Commission to mere technical issues, thus, supporting Russia's goals. To face this situation, the EU needs to find at the same time alternative suppliers and alternative pipeline routes that bypass Russian territory and also agree on a common policy. The difficulty to materialize these combined needs is illustrated by a Polish MEP's sharp criticism towards Italy and the *Southstream*.[43]

Visa Liberalization

Visa regimes are negotiated under the second space of cooperation dealing with "Freedom, Security and Justice." It was considered a growing area of cooperation with a shared goal towards a visa free area, until the suspension of the

---

40   CASE, "The Economic Aspects of the Energy Sector in the CIS Countries", 327 CASE Economic Papers (2008); Steven Eke, "Russia Signs Gas Pipeline Deals", BBC (15 May 2009); and Government of the Republic of Croatia, News and Announcements (2 February 2010), available at <http://www.vlada.hr/en/naslovnica/novosti_i_najave/2010/ozujak/hrvatska_i_rusija_potpisale_sporazum_o_plinovodu_juznom_toku>.

41   Jean-Sylvestre Mongrenier, *La Russie menace-t-elle l'Occident?* (Choiseul, Paris, 2009), 142–143.

42   Laure Delcour and Pierre Verluise, "Regards croisés sur les relations Union européenne-Russie: la dépendance énergétique", 12 *Actualités de la Russie et de la CEI* (2009).

43   Jacek Saryusz-Wolski, "CEPS Lunchtime Meeting" (Brussels, 28 November 2007).

talks as an EU sanction after Russia annexed Crimea in March 2014. This domain of cooperation aimed at tackling terrorism, illegal migration and cross-border crime (which includes trafficking in human beings and drugs).

Visa liberalization arose in July 2007 in the context of the visa dialogue and, since December 2011, cooperation occurs under the agreement entitled "the Common steps towards visa free short-term travel of Russian and EU citizens" (European Commission 2013). Facilitation is monitored by the Joint EU-Russia Committee. This independent body lists technical issues arising from both sides during implementation. Similarly, the Joint Readmission Committee monitors the implementation of the Readmission Agreement of 2007.[44]

The Union has been complaining particularly about the registration procedures on the Russian side, which are considered very complicated and are therefore creating travel obstacles. Similarly to the trade domain, non-reciprocity in the application of the agreements is a concern for Brussels.[45] Additionally, some Member States required bilateral implementation protocols for readmission, which have delayed the proper application of the agreement with all the EU Member States.

Contrary to the Russian will to move faster to the negotiations phase of a concrete visa-free regime, the Union is committed to follow the procedure of dialogue, organized in four blocks. These sections are: document security, including biometrics; illegal migration, including readmission; public order and security; external relations. Progresses in the visa dialogue are, thus, dependent on developments in the implementation of the visa facilitation and readmission agreements.

There is a widespread understanding that Moscow is pushing more insistently on liberalization, and concomitantly complaining that Brussels is too demanding and responsible for slow progress. In that sense, a Russian official, Andrey Klimov, referred to the need to transform parliamentary dialogue into a real "laboratory", as opposed to a "talking-shop."[46] He gave the specific example of Russia's preferred choice of visa free regime. Klimov stressed that the Russian population is becoming more suspicious, namely since the EU 2004

---

44   The agreements are available at the website of EEAS, available at <http://eeas.europa.eu/
      delegations/russia/eu_russia/fields_cooperation/visas_readmission/index_en.htm>.

45   Besides the general understanding of "reciprocity" as a core principle of the visa dialogue,
      the Commission has introduced a reciprocity mechanism to ensure that EU citizens
      receive equal treatment in third countries. In 2001, a Council Regulation identified the
      nationals needing a visa, and those who don't, to cross the EU borders (Council of the
      European Union, 2001). This constitutes the core of the EU common visa policy.

46   Speech by Andrey Klimov (European Parliament, Brussels, 24 June 2008).

enlargement because Russian citizens lost the possibility of traveling freely to the Baltic States and Cyprus. These declarations reveal the distance that sets the two parties apart. On the one hand, the EU's will to have a principled relationship that respects, namely, the *acquis* of the Union, such as enlargement, and the UN charter, and, on the other hand, the Russian view about the observance of these provisions. The issue of human rights, democracy and the rule of law is also addressed in the second common space, where the European Commission acknowledges that "some gap exists between declarations and expressions of intent and reality on the ground."[47]

The EU's lack of trust has, consequently, emerged as an obstacle in the implementation phase. The perception that Moscow uses the visa policy politically has entrenched these rules of the game, as the 2007 elections illustrate. The Russians used the pretext of visa procedures to create obstacles to the external monitoring of the ballots by the Office for Democratic Institutions and Human Rights (ODIHR). They argued that the observers requested their visas on a short notice. Nevertheless, Russia maintained its invitation towards the mission but, in practice, it was invalidated by the failure to deliver visas. Previously, the Russian executive had insisted on a sharp cut of the number of observers from 400 to 70.

4   Conclusion

Post-enlargement EU-Russia relations have been marked by two major political crises. First, the limbo period from 2006–2008 shed light on new Member States capacities to impact on a more cautious EU attitude towards Russia that should not be driven solely by strategic interest (mainly trade and investment). Second, the Ukrainian crisis which started in 2013 and the Russian annexation of Crimea in early 2014 overcame some of the Member States division on how to deal with Russia and shed an unequivocal light on the need to consider, beyond rhetoric, the normative gap between the parties.

In policies of special EU interest, the issue of reciprocity in the implementation process appears as a core concern for Brussels. This is especially noticeable in the new Member States stance regarding the observance of common values and principles such as the rule of law, democracy and human rights. Reciprocity also affects trade relations in the sense that the Union expects a more predictable and stable relation in this domain. Additionally, trade dispute

---

47   European Commission (March 2008), 8, available at <http://ec.europa.eu/external_rela-
         tions/russia/russia_docs/commonspaces_prog_report2007.pdf>.

between new Member States and Russia have escalated to rather political level, postponing the negotiations for a new EU-Russia cooperation agreement from 2006 to 2008. Internally, there is no straightforward process in which a Member State's problem with Russia can become an EU problem, even if internal solidarity has been enhanced in EU discourses since 2007.

In policies of special Russian interest, energy has gained greater visibility since the gas crisis of 2006. EU-Russian energy competition is primarily related to, on the one hand, the search for alternatives routes and suppliers, and, on the other hand, on the Russian will to strengthen Gazprom monopoly. In this domain, new Member States have contributed to highlight the need for an integrated energy policy at the Union level and to a direct critic towards the Member States that seal bilateral deals with Gazprom. In the visa agenda, there is a shared interest in negotiating a visa free regime on both sides. Brussels and some Member States are worried about the rule of law in Russia and due procedures despite the importance of the visa dialogue to secure the EU borders, whereas Moscow is somehow frustrated by slow progress in this area of dialogue. This policy area is currently suspended as a response to Russian annexation of Crimea.[48]

Looking back at ten years of enlargement and its impact on the implementation of policies in EU-Russia relations, the analysis has evidenced that key features of the Commission report of 2004 have been enacted by the new Member States, especially the Baltic States and Poland. Although new Member States have contributed to greater tensions in EU-Russia relations, the issues that have arisen since enlargement correspond to problems that were identified back to February 2004. The EU has in fact adopted a more critical tone towards Russia and addressed implementation issues more straightforwardly in an expanding agenda of cooperation. The global political context of EU-Russian relations was not conducive to progress in visa liberalization talks, given the standstill in the negotiations for a new partnership agreement (initiated in July 2008) and growing concerns over human rights in Russia and normative convergence. On its side, Russia appears to have lost interest in a bilateral agreement, owing in particular to progress achieved in the Eurasian integration process led by Moscow. Any progress on EU-Russia agenda should, therefore, be further analyzed taking the current Ukrainian crisis and the Eurasian project into consideration.

---

48   On the visa dialogue, see Laure Delcour and Sandra Fernandes, "Visa Liberalization Processes in the EU's Eastern Neighbourhood: Understanding Policy Outcomes", *Cambridge Review of International Affairs* (2016), 1–20.

Bibliography

CASE. (2008) "The Economic Aspects of the Energy Sector in the CIS Countries", 327 *Centre for Social and Economic Research (CASE) Economic Papers*.

Casier, Tom. (2012) "Are the Policies of Russia and the EU in Their Shared Neighbourhood Doomed to Clash?", in Kanet, Roger and Raquel Freire, Maria. (eds.), *Competing for Influence: The EU and Russia in Post-Soviet Eurasia* (Republic of Letters, Dordrecht).

Delcour, Laure and Fernandes, Sandra. (2016) "Visa Liberalization Processes in the EU's Eastern Neighbourhood: Understanding Policy Outcomes", *Cambridge Review of International Affairs*, 1–20.

Delcour, Laure and Verluise, Pierre. (2009) "Regards croisés sur les relations Union européenne-Russie: la dépendance énergétique", 12 *Actualités de la Russie et de la CEI*.

Fernandes, Sandra. (2013) "The EU Institutional Balance: Assessment of its Impact on the Relationship with Russia", in Cierco, Teresa. (ed.), *The European Union Neighbourhood: Ten Years into the New Millennium* (Ashgate, Surrey), 143–172.

Fernandes, Sandra. (2013) "Russia and Transforming Security Relations in Europe: A Mix of Strategic and Normative Rationales", *e-cadernos ces* No. 19.

Kanet, Roger. (ed.) (2010) *Russian Foreign Policy in the 21st Century* (Palgrave MacMillan).

Lelievelt, Herman and Princen, Sebastiaan. (2011) *The Politics of the European Union* (Cambridge University Press, Cambridge).

Leonard, Mark and Popescu, Nicu. (2007) "A Power Audit of EU-Russia Relations", *ECFR Policy Paper*.

Mongrenier, Jean-Sylvestre. (2009) *La Russie menace-t-elle l'Occident?* (Choiseul, Paris).

Noutcheva, Gergana, Pomorska, Karolina, and Bosse, Giselle. (eds.) (2013) *The EU and its Neighbours:Values versus Security in European Foreign Policy* (Manchester University Press).

Roth, Mathias. (2009) "Bilateral Disputes between EU Member States and Russia", 319 *CEPS Working Document*.

Tocci, Nathalie *et al.* (2008), "The European Union as a Normative Foreign Policy Actor", 281 *CEPS Working Document*.

CHAPTER 16

EU-Russia Cooperation on Energy Efficiency: An Unexpected Benefit of Regional Interdependence between Russia and the CEE Member States?

Olga Khrushcheva

Abstract

In October 2012, the European Union (EU) adopted Directive 2012/27/EU on energy efficiency. The Directive proposes a common framework of measures to promote energy efficiency and to ensure that the EU meets its 20% target on energy efficiency by 2020. Prior to the liberalization of markets, the years of the communist influence shaped the economic structure of the Central and Eastern European (CEE) states, and the logic of planned economy did not promote energy efficiency. As a result, the energy intensity of the post-communist states was roughly 2.5 times of that of Western Europe. On the road to EU membership, the CEE states demonstrated significant improvement in energy efficiency even prior to the 2012 Directive. Beyond CEE, Russia had comparable problems in improving energy efficiency, and Russia's economy is still rather wasteful. This chapter thus aims to investigate if there is a potential for strengthening the cooperation between Russia and the EU on energy efficiency, and what role the CEE Member States may play in EU-Russia energy efficiency cooperation.

Keywords

energy efficiency – EU-Russia energy relations – energy security – regional cooperation

1 Introduction

The EU-Russia energy relations are widely discussed in the literature,[1] but many analyses tend to focus on the securitization of such relations, caused

---

1 Caroline Kuzemko, Andrei Belyi, Andreas Goldthau, and Michael F. Keating (eds.), *Dynamics of Energy Governance in Europe and Russia* (Palgrave Macmillan, 2012); and Tom Casier,

by the high level of interdependence and clash of interests between Russia and the EU Member States. Currently, the EU imports about half of its energy requirements, and this is estimated to increase up to 80% by 2030.[2] The EU imports 38% of its gas requirements and 33% of oil from Russia.[3] Against this background, it is often argued that the Eastern enlargement brought additional problems to the EU-Russia energy relations.[4] However, there are significant variations in import-dependency and attitude to Russia among the Southeast European, Baltic, and Central European states. Bulgaria and Romania, for example, are less import-dependent as compared to the EU average (22% and 40% respectively), and less reliant on Russian supplies.[5] On the other hand, the Baltic and Central European states import on average more than 50% of their energy consumption.[6] Slovakia is the most import-dependent country out of the group, and relies on external energy supplies for 63% of its energy requirements.[7] The most notable exception in the group is Estonia, with import-dependence of only 13%.[8] Nonetheless, former members of the Eastern bloc rely heavily on Russian oil and gas supplies, and therefore, are concerned about security of supply.[9] In 2004, after the first wave of the Eastern enlargements, Gazprom was the only natural gas supplier to Estonia, Latvia, Lithuania, and Slovakia,[10] and the enlargement increased Russia's share of European energy market, changing the political context of EU-Russia relations.

      "The Rise of Energy to the Top of the EU-Russia Agenda: From Interdependence to Dependence", 16(3) *Geopolitics* (2011), 536–552.

2   Filipos Proedrou, *EU Energy Security in the Gas Sector* (Ashgate, Farnham, 2012), 57.

3   European Energy Security Strategy (2014), available at <http://ec.europa.eu/energy/doc/20140528_energy_security_communication.pdf>.

4   See e.g. Fraser Cameron, "The Politics of EU-Russia Energy Relations", *OGEL Collection, Euroconfidential* (EU-Russia Centre, Brussels, 2010), 25–38; Marek Neuman, "EU-Russian Energy Relations after 2004/2007 EU Enlargement: An EU Perspective", 18(3) *Journal of Contemporary European Studies* (2010), 341–360.

5   "European Economy – Member States' Energy Dependence: An Indicator-Based Assessment", *Occasional Papers* (April 2013) No. 145, available at <http://ec.europa.eu/economy_finance/publications/occasional_paper/2013/pdf/ocp145_en.pdf>, 83.

6   *Ibid.*

7   *Ibid.*, 245.

8   *Ibid.*, 107.

9   Jeffrey Mankoff, "Relationship with the EU", in Stephen Wegren (ed.), *Return to Putin's Russia: Past Imperfect, Future Uncertain* (Rowman & Littlefield, Plymouth, 2013), 282.

10   Diana Urge-Vorsatz, Gergana Miladinova, and Laszlo Paizs, "Energy in Transition: From the Iron Curtain to the European Union", 34(15) *Energy Policy* (2005), 2279–2297, at 2280.

In fact, prior to the 2004 enlargement, only four of the new Member States (Bulgaria, Latvia, Estonia, and Lithuania) were interested in maintaining relations with both the West and Russia, according to an Eurobarometer survey.[11] The remaining seven did not see Russia as an important political partner, to say the least.

Some of the new Member States are too familiar with the consequences of supply interruptions.[12] Many CEE states view Russia as a threat to their security and promote a more assertive EU policy towards Russia.[13] That is why the academic literature mainly focused on the negative consequences of the Eastern enlargement on EU-Russia energy relations (e.g. Polish veto of the new Partnership and Cooperation Agreement with Russia in 2007).[14] The unfolding Ukrainian crisis led to the worst escalation of EU-Russia relations since the Cold War. The EU Member States imposed sanctions on Russia, and put on hold many joint initiatives.[15] This chapter argues that after 2004/2007 enlargements the overall state of EU-Russia energy relations worsened due to high levels of import-dependence on Russian energy supplies and existing political tensions. EU-Russia energy relations are securitized and fossil fuel orientated, and in the short term it is unlikely to change.[16] However, in less politicized areas of EU-Russia energy relations (such as cooperation on energy

---

11   Central and Eastern Eurobarometer, "Public Opinion and the European Union" (March 1996), available at <http://www.ab.gov.tr/files/ardb/evt/1_avrupa_birligi/1_6_raporlar/1_4 _eurobarometers/central_and_eastern_eurobarometer._public_opinion_and_the _european_union_19_countries_survey_march_1996.pdf>.

12   Keith Smith, *Russian Energy Politics in the Baltics, Poland, and Ukraine* (CSIS Press, Washington DC, 2004).

13   Proedrou, *op. cit.* note 2, 91.

14   The academic literature mainly focuses on the consequences of Russian-Ukrainian gas transit conflicts in 2006 and 2009, e.g. the negative reaction of Poland on the Russian-German agreements on the Nord Stream pipeline. See Olga Khrushcheva, "The Creation of an Energy Security Society as the Way to Decrease Securitization Levels between the EU and Russia in Energy Trade", 7(2) *Journal of Contemporary European Research* (2011), 216–230.

15   Council Regulation (EU) No 833/2014 of 31 July 2014 Concerning Restrictive Measures in View of Russia's Actions Destabilising the Situation in Ukraine (July 2014), available at <http://eur-lex.europa.eu/legal-content/EN/TXT/PDF/?uri=CELEX:32014R0833&from= EN>.

16   Olga Khrushcheva and Tomas Maltby, "Evolutions and Revolutions in EU-Russia Energy Relations", in Claire Dupont and Sebastian Oberthur (eds.), *Decarbonization in the European Union* (Palgrave Macmillan, Houndmills, 2015).

efficiency), close regional ties between Russian and CEE energy sectors can potentially contribute to long-term normalization of EU-Russia energy relations.
This chapter looks at the current progress in developing energy efficiency in
the EU, and analyses the potential for closer EU-Russia cooperation on energy
efficiency.

2   The EU Legislation on Energy Efficiency

Since the mid-2000s, the speed of EU transition to the low-carbon economy
quickened significantly. The de-carbonisation agenda has become an integral
part of the EU energy policy development. For instance, Article 176A of the
Lisbon Treaty states that the EU shall aim to "promote energy efficiency and
energy saving and the development of new and renewable forms of energy."[17]
Energy efficiency is important for the development and functioning of the internal energy market.[18] De-carbonization agenda (including energy efficiency)
is seen not only as a way to tackle climate change, but also as "a remedy against
an increasing global energy demand, and as a way to ensure the security of energy supply."[19] According to Jones et al., "if the EU only continues the energy
efficiency policies already announced, one can expect that in 2050 EU will need
about 10% more energy than it uses today."[20] In 2009, the EU set the target of
improving energy efficiency by 20% by 2020.[21] The target is increased to 27%
by 2030.[22] The target is non-binding, but the Member States are expected to set
national energy efficiency targets. For instance, the Energy Services Directive
(2006/32/EC) requires Member States to set an overall national energy saving
target of 9% by 2016.[23] In 2012, the EU adopted a Directive on energy efficiency.

---

17   Treaty of Lisbon Amending the Treaty on European Union and the Treaty Establishing
      the European Community, signed at Lisbon (13 December 2007), *Official Journal of the
      European Union*, 2007/C 306/01, available at <http://eur-lex.europa.eu/JOHtml.do?uri=OJ
      :C:2007:306:SOM:EN:HTML>.
18   *Ibid.*
19   Mats Nilsson, "Red Light for Green Paper: The EU Policy on Energy Efficiency", 35(1) *En-
      ergy Policy* (2007), 540–547, at 541.
20   Christopher Jones and Jean-Michel Glachant, "Toward a Zero-Carbon Energy Policy in
      Europe: Defining a Viable Solution", 23(3) *The Electricity Journal* (2010), 15–25, at 17.
21   2020 Climate and Energy Package (2009), available at <http://ec.europa.eu/clima/
      policies/strategies/2020/index_en.htm>.
22   2030 Climate and Energy Goals for a Competitive, Secure and Low-carbon EU Economy
      (22 Jan 2014), available at <http://europa.eu/rapid/press-release_IP-14-54_en.htm>.
23   Directive 2006/32/EC of the European Parliament and of the Council of 5 April 2006 on
      Energy End-use Efficiency and Energy Services and Repealing Council Directive 93/76/

The aim of Directive 2012/27/EU is to establish a framework of measures to promote more efficient energy usage in the EU to support the Member States in reaching the 2020 20% energy efficiency target.[24] The Directive also obliges Member States to set indicative national energy efficiency targets, and to develop National Energy Efficiency Action Plans (NEEAP), and, as from 2013, Member States should report on the progress achieved to the European Commission.[25] The deadline for transposition of the Directive 2012/27/EU into national law was 5 June 2014.[26] Only 5 Member States (Cyprus, Denmark, Sweden, Italy, and Malta) completed transposition by the set deadline.[27] The EU also set energy efficiency standards for buildings and a broad range of energy-using products. For example, the Energy Performance of Buildings Directive (2010/31/EU) requires Member States to adopt energy performance standards for new buildings.[28] Furthermore the Ecodesign Directive (2009/125/EC) and the Energy Labeling Directive (2010/30/EU) introduce minimum energy efficiency standards and compulsory energy efficiency labels for a number of energy-using products.[29]

As of November 2015, all 28 Member States adopted the NEEAPs and submitted first three progress reports to the European Commission.[30] Different Member

---

EEC (2006), available at <http://eur-lex.europa.eu/legal-content/EN/TXT/HTML/?uri=U RISERV:l27057&from=EN>.

24 Directive 2012/27/EU of the European Parliament and of the Council of 25 October 2012 on Energy Efficiency, Amending Directives 2009/125/EC and 2010/20/EU and Repealing Directives 2004/8/EC and 2006/32/EC (October 2012), available at <http://eur-lex.europa .eu/LexUriServ/LexUriServ.do?uri=OJ:L:2012:315:0001:0056:EN:PDF>.

25 *Ibid.*

26 *Ibid.*

27 Communication from the Commission to the European Parliament and the Council, COM (2014)520, Energy Efficiency and its Contribution to Energy Security and the 2030 Framework for Climate and Energy Policy, available at <https://ec.europa.eu/energy/sites/ener/ files/documents/2014_eec_communication_adopted_0.pdf>.

28 Directive 2010/31/EU of the European Parliament and of the Council of 19 May 2010 on the Energy Performance of Buildings (May 2010), available at <http://eur-lex.europa.eu/ LexUriServ/LexUriServ.do?uri=OJ:L:2010:153:0013:0035:EN:PDF>.

29 Directive 2009/125/EC of the European Parliament and of the Council of 21 October 2009 Establishing a Framework for the Setting of Eco-design Requirements for Energy-related Products (October 2009), available at <http://eur-lex.europa.eu/legal-content/ EN/TXT/PDF/?uri=CELEX:32009L0125&from=EN>; and Directive 2010/30/EU of the European Parliament and of the Council of 19 May 2010 on the Indication by Labelling and Standard Product Information of the Consumption of Energy and Other Resources by Energy Related Products (May 2010), available at <http://eur-lex.europa.eu/LexUriServ/ LexUriServ.do?uri=OJ:L:2010:153:0001:0012:en:PDF>.

30 National Energy Efficiency Action Plans and Annual Reports from 2013–2015 are available at <https://ec.europa.eu/energy/en/topics/energy-efficiency/energy-efficiency-directive/ national-energy-efficiency-action-plans>.

States have different internal barriers and circumstances (financial, political, or economic) which will necessarily spill over and result in different rates of change. Slower progress in improving energy efficiency may prevent the EU from achieving the 2020 targets. Recent estimates suggest that the EU will achieve energy savings of 18–19% by 2020.[31] To illustrate this point better, it is important to consider energy intensity, the term used to assess the energy efficiency of a country's economy. It is expressed as units of energy per unit of GDP, and a number of factors are taken into consideration (the economic structure of a country, the climate, the standard of living).[32] The lower the energy intensity figure is, the higher the economy's energy efficiency.[33] Graph 16.1 demonstrates how energy efficiency of EU Member States improved as compared to 2003.

As compared to the EU-15, the energy intensity of the CEE Member States is high. In this group, Bulgaria has the highest energy intensity of 610.6 kg of oil equivalent required to produce a unit of GDP, and Croatia has the lowest energy intensity of 219.5.[34] In comparison, the energy intensity of the EU-15 is

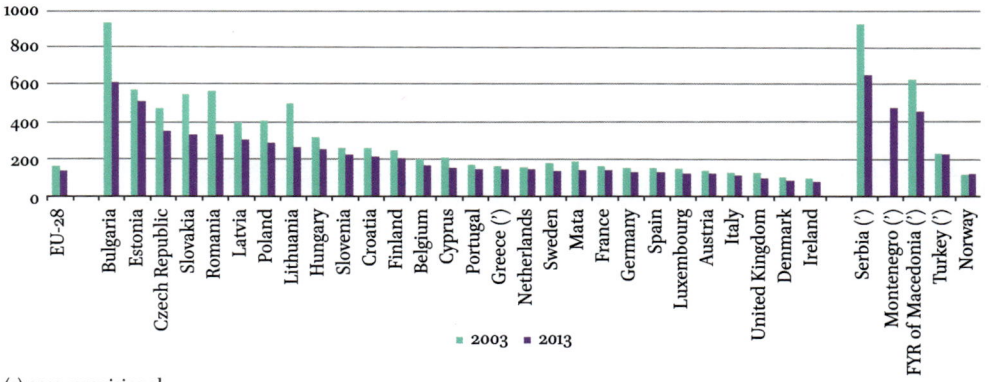

(1) 2013: provisional.
(2) 2013: estimate.
(3) 2012 instead of 2013, 2003: not available.
(4) 2010 instead of 2013.
Source: Eurostat (online data code: tsdec360)

GRAPH 16.1   *Energy efficiency of EU member states.*
SOURCE: EUROSTAT, ENERGY INTENSITY OF THE ECONOMY, 2003 AND 2013
(IN KG OF OIL EQUIVALENT PER UNIT OF GDP)

31   COM (2014)520, *op. cit.* note 27, 4.

32   "Key Figures on the Enlargement Countries", 2013 Edition, available at <http://epp.euro-stat.ec.europa.eu/cache/ITY_OFFPUB/KS-GO-13-001/EN/KS-GO-13-001-EN.pdf>.

33   *Ibid.*

34   "Eurostat: Energy Intensity of the Economy, Gross Inland Consumption of Energy Divided by GDP", available at <http://ec.europa.eu/eurostat/tgm/table.do?tab=table&init=1&lang uage=en&pcode=tsdec360&plugin=1>.

ranging between 82.4 (Ireland) and 205.9 (Finland).[35] However, it is important to put these figures into perspective. Countries in the Post-Soviet region had one of the least efficient economies because of the nature of the planned economies: "to facilitate industrial production and social welfare, central planners kept energy prices well below cost-recovery levels."[36] As a result, in 1990s, the energy intensity of the CEE was significantly higher as compared to the EU-15. All 11 CEE states share some similar characteristics: regulated energy prices for domestic consumers, dependence on Russian energy supplies, and relatively high share of solid fuels in the energy mix.[37] There are, of course, some regional variations between them. For instance, energy prices for end-users in Estonia, Poland, and Slovenia are the lowest in the group, and are way below the EU average.[38] Poland and Bulgaria enjoy relatively low levels of import-dependence, but the share of solid fuels (including coal) in energy mix is higher as compared to the EU-15.[39] Thus, the compliance with the EU energy efficiency regulations is harder for CEE than for the EU-15. The key challenges are: transposition of EU legislation and financing energy efficiency projects. The majority of the post-communist states shares these problems.

To comply with the EU legislation, the CEE states had to adopt national energy policies to the EU standards. This transition was not easy, and the CEE states had to rely on the knowledge transfer and the technical assistance from the EU. Furthermore, transposition of the EU legislation on energy efficiency is costly. According to the European Commission, Member States will incur the average annual cost of around EUR 2 billion to achieve energy efficiency targets.[40] For instance, Member States need to fund ongoing renewal of energy infrastructure. The building sector has the biggest energy saving potential – around 40% of residential buildings were built before 1960.[41] Thus, to tap into this potential, Member States need to invest into renovation of the existing residential buildings. The Directive 2012/27/EU identifies different funding sources available to support energy efficiency projects, including the structural and cohesion funds.[42] For example, "in the 2007–2013 cohesion policy programmes for sustainable energy investments amounts to about EUR 9.4 billion, of which

35   Ibid.
36   Fan Zhang, "The Energy Transition of the Transition Economies: An Empirical Analysis", 40 Energy Economies (2013), 679–686, at 680.
37   "European Economy", op. cit, note 5.
38   Ibid.
39   Ibid.
40   COM (2014)520, op. cit. note 27, 11.
41   Ibid.
42   Directive 2012/27/EU, op. cit. note 24.

approximately EUR 5.1 billion targeted at improving energy efficiency."[43] The EU budget for 2014–2020 allocates at least EUR 38 billion for "low carbon economy investments under the European Structural and Investment Funds."[44] Among other programs financing energy efficiency in the EU are Horizon 2020, the Joint European Support for Sustainable Investment in City Areas (JESSICA), and the Intelligent Energy-Europe (IEE). The JESSICA initiative offered Member States the possibility "to invest some of their structural funds allocations in [...] public-private partnerships and other projects included in integrated plans for sustainable urban development."[45] The IEE provides help to private businesses willing to invest in energy sustainability.[46] The table (16.1) below demonstrates the funding allocation on energy efficiency and environmental protection in CEE from the Cohesion Funds 2007–2013.

Despite the initial problems, the CEE states achieved remarkable progress in improving the energy efficiency of their economies. In 1989–2002 (even prior to the 2004 enlargement), some of the CEE Member States demonstrated a significant decrease in energy intensity: Poland achieved an improvement of around 46% while the Czech Republic demonstrated an improvement of 15% by 2002.[47] Technical and financial assistance from the EU allowed the CEE states to improve the energy efficiency even further. Table 16.2 below illustrates this point.

All new Member States reduced the energy intensity of their economies after joining the EU. This success is based on the combination of the following

TABLE 16.1   *Cohesion funds 2007–2013 on energy efficiency in CEE*

Country	Funding allocation and description
Bulgaria	EUR 2.8 billion (42% of fund allocations) has been allocated to support environment, risk prevention and energy projects
Czech Republic	EUR 1 billion has been allocated to support energy efficiency and renewable energy
Estonia	EUR 1.2 billion has been allocated to protect and improve the environment

43   Financing Energy Efficiency, available at <http://ec.europa.eu/energy/efficiency/financ ing/financing_en.htm>.

44   COM (2014)520, *op. cit.* note 27, 13.

45   *Ibid.*

46   Maria de Garca Garvalho, "EU Energy and Climate Change Strategy", 40(1) *Energy* (2012), 19–22, at 21.

47   Urge-Vorsatz, *op. cit.* note 10, 2288.

Country	Funding allocation and description
Latvia	EUR 1 billion has been allocated to improve the environment, including 73 energy efficient houses construction
Lithuania	EUR 437 million has been allocated to promote the use of renewable energy and improve energy efficiency
Poland	EUR 2.2 billion (or 3.4% of total fund allocations) has been invested in energy efficiency projects
Romania	EUR 604 million has been allocated to projects on energy efficiency and renewable energy
Slovenia	EUR 160 million (4% of fund allocations) was targeted at the use of renewable energy sources and energy efficiency projects
Slovakia	EUR 169 million has been invested into energy efficiency and renewable energies

SOURCE: EUROPEAN COMMISSION, FINANCING ENERGY EFFICIENCY

TABLE 16.2 *Energy Intensity of the CEE Member States (before and after Accession)*

Country	2004	2007	2013
Estonia	550.8	–	512.7
Czech Republic	465.7	–	353.8
Slovakia	512.7	–	337.2
Latvia	382.2	–	310.6
Poland	387.1	–	294.7
Lithuania	474.4	–	266.4
Hungary	306.6	–	256.6
Slovenia	259.2	–	225.8
Bulgaria	–	759.9	610.6
Romania	–	441.5	334.7
Croatia	–	–	219.5

SOURCE: EUROSTAT, ENERGY INTENSITY OF THE ECONOMY (KG OF OIL EQUIVALENT PER UNIT OF GDP)

measures: integration of EU-wide legislation, adjustment of the energy tariffs closer to the price of supply, integration of energy efficiency regulations into the national legislation, development of the energy efficiency targets and standards, and the allocation of the budget to support the implementation of these goals. The experience of the CEE states could be applicable to promotion of energy efficiency in Russia. After the collapse of the Soviet Union and the Eastern bloc, the energy intensity of both Russian and the CEE economies was high compared to the West. In 1990, the Soviet Union's energy intensity was 70% higher as compared to the United States.[48] According to Russian National Program on Energy Savings and Energy Efficiency until 2020, the energy intensity of the Russian economy decreased annually by 5% between 2000 and 2008.[49] Nonetheless, in 2013, energy efficiency of the Russian economy remained one of the lowest in the world.[50] Stuggins *et al.* argue that applying the experience of the CEE countries to other states in the region (including Russia) could facilitate the development of energy efficiency in these countries as well.[51] The next section evaluates the potential for EU-Russia cooperation on energy efficiency.

3   EU-Russia Cooperation on Energy Efficiency

Both the EU and Russia see cooperation on energy efficiency as mutually beneficial.[52] For the EU it promises potential economic benefits, such as technology transfer, maintaining good relations with one of major energy suppliers, and ensuring the security of supply. For Russia, it gives an opportunity to reduce domestic energy consumption. Natural gas consumption increased in Russia from 12 to 15 trillion cubic feet in 1997–2012.[53] Thus, Russia needs to improve energy efficiency to ensure export volumes of natural gas. Furthermore, cooperation on energy efficiency is less politicized and securitized in contrast

---

48   Zhang, *op. cit.* note 36, 680.

49   State National Program of the Russian Federaion on Energy Savings and Improvement of Energy Efficiency until 2020 (27 December 2010), available at <http://www.consultant.ru/document/cons_doc_LAW_142439/?frame=1>.

50   OECD Economic Surveys, Russian Federation 2013, OECD (January 2014), 22.

51   Gary Stuggins, Alexander Sharaboroff, and Yadviga Semikolenova, *Energy Efficiency Learned from Success Stories* (World Bank Publications, 2013), available at <https://openknowledge.worldbank.org/handle/10986/12236>.

52   Andrei Belyi and Ksenia Petrichenko, "Energy Efficiency Regimes: Possibilities and Limits of Best-Practice Transfer between Europe and Russia", in Kuzemko *et al.* (eds.), *op. cit.* note 1, 110; "Roadmap on EU-Russia Energy Cooperation until 2050" (March 2013), available at <https://ec.europa.eu/energy/sites/ener/files/documents/2013_03_eu_russia_roadmap_2050_signed.pdf>.

53   Sergey Paltsev, "Scenarios for Russia's Natural Gas Exports to 2050", 42 *Energy Economics* (2014), 262–270, at 265.

to trade in fossil fuels.[54] Russia faces similar challenges in improving energy efficiency as the rest of the post-communist states: subsidized domestic energy consumption, aging infrastructure, inconsistency of legal framework, and the lack of state funding.

Potential for Technology Transfer

The EU is interested in investing into the modernization of Russian energy sector to ensure the long-term security of energy supply.[55] There are a number of mechanisms allowing the EU to invest in energy efficiency projects in Russia, e.g. the market based mechanisms of the Kyoto Protocol (the Joint Implementation projects). Russia has 97 registered Joint Implementation projects, and 30 of them are energy efficiency focused projects with EU Member States (predominantly with the UK, Finland, and the Netherlands).[56] However, the implementation progress is slow due to inconsistent Russian FDI legislation, and the unpredictability of Russian political context.[57]

Institutionalization of EU-Russia Cooperation on Energy Efficiency

Legislative weaknesses slow down the implementation of energy efficiency projects. In 2009, the Russian Government adopted the Federal Law N261 on energy saving and improvement of energy efficiency. The law sets the target of improving energy efficiency of the Russian economy by 40% by 2020.[58] In the last 5 years, further 12 laws were revised and amended to comply with the 261 law.[59] Despite these developments, the law has been criticized for "incompleteness, prioritizing administrative methods and lacking long-term financial

---

54 Tatiana Romanova, "Legal Approximation in Energy: A New Approach for the European Union and Russia", in Kuzemko *et al.* (eds.), *op. cit.* note 1, 33.

55 Maria Garbuzova and Reinhard Madlener, "Towards an Efficient and Low Carbon Economy Post-2012: Opportunities and Barriers for Foreign Companies in the Russian Energy Market", 17(4) *Mitigation and Adaptation Strategies for Global Change* (2012), 387–413, at 397.

56 UNEP JI Projects (2015), available at <http://cdmpipeline.org/publications/JiPipeline.xlsx>.

57 Garbuzova and Madlener, *op. cit.* note 55, 408.

58 Federal Law N261-FZ from 23 November 2009, "On Energy Saving, Increasing Energy Efficiency and on Amending Legislative Acts of the Russian Federation", available at <http://www.rg.ru/2009/11/27/energo-dok.html>.

59 "List of the Major Legal and Regulatory Acts on Energy Saving and Energy Efficiency" (2015), available at <http://rosenergo.gov.ru/regulations_and_methodologies/normativnie_akti_v_oblasti_energosberezheniya>.

capital."[60] Experts argue that the minimum of 150 amendments need to be adopted to make implementation of energy efficiency regulations possible.[61] The Central and Eastern European states had to adopt and bring into force the laws, regulations and administrative provisions necessary to comply with the EU regulations. The EU membership influenced legislative change in CEE. In the case of Russia, the development of the legal framework depends on the political will of the Russian government.

The EU has a limited ability to influence this process due to the lack of a legally binding international framework regulating EU-Russia energy relations. This is especially the case since Russia withdrew from the Energy Charter Treaty.[62] Nonetheless, the externalization of energy efficiency cooperation is possible through the greater institutionalization of EU-Russia energy relations. When talking about the institutionalization of energy efficiency cooperation, it is important to mention EU-Russia energy dialogue, EU-Russia Modernization Partnership, Northern Dimension, and a number of international frameworks such as International Partnership for Energy Efficiency Cooperation (IPEEC). All of these institutions promote energy efficiency and support implementation of joint energy efficiency projects. The importance of energy efficiency has been mentioned as early as 1997 within the discussion on the Partnership and Cooperation Agreement.[63] However, in the late 1990s such cooperation existed mainly "on paper", and "the real cooperation was lagging behind because there were too few practical projects."[64] The EU-Russia Energy Dialogue is one of the main institutions promoting the energy efficiency cooperation, with one of the thematic groups devoted specifically to energy efficiency.[65] The group meets biannually to discuss the EU-Russia cooperation and to set common goals, including: "the change of information on legislative and regulatory frameworks; to share experience and knowledge on projects in the field of energy efficiency, energy savings, gas flaring and renewable energy

---

60   Alexander Gusev, "Energy Efficiency Policy in Russia: Scope for EU-Russia Cooperation" (2013), available at <http://www.isn.ethz.ch/Digital-Library/Publications/Detail/?eng=en&ots627=0c54e363-1e9c-bele-2c24-a6a8c7060233&id=165063>, 2.

61   *Ibid.*

62   Sergey Lavrov, "State of the Union Russia-EU: Prospects for Partnership in the Changing World", 51 *Journal of Common Market Studies Annual Review* (2013), 6–12, at 6.

63   Gusev, *op. cit.* note 60, 1.

64   Vadim Kononenko, "Forever a Pilot? Assessing the Policy Dialogue and Project-based Cooperation in Energy Efficiency between the EU and Russia", *The Finnish Institute of International Affairs Working Paper* (2011) No. 73, 13.

65   *Ibid.*, 18.

sources; to implement joint projects of common interests."[66] In 2006, an EU-Russia Energy Efficiency Initiative was established to promote dialogue and cooperation on legal and policy related issues. In 2010, a Common Spaces Facility project on energy efficiency was set up to provide financial assistance for projects on de-carburization.[67] The Ukrainian crisis slowed down the development of EU-Russia relations (including energy relations), many joint initiatives are suspended and sanctions have been adopted.[68]

Bilateral Cooperation on Energy Efficiency

The Roadmap on the EU-Russia energy cooperation until 2050 emphasizes the importance of "mutual learning and exchange of best practice" between Russia and the EU Member States.[69] As well as "adjustment of appropriate federal and regional legislation"[70] in Russia. The Russian government also encourages the exchange of best practice on implementation of energy efficiency. On the bilateral level, Russia signed the memorandums of understanding with a number of the European Member States, including Germany, Finland, France, Italy, Netherlands, Denmark, and Great Britain. The experience of the Central and Eastern European states in 1990–2015 provide a good case for knowledge transfer. Leonard and Popescu suggest that Bulgaria, Slovakia, and Hungary can become especially important in future EU-Russia energy relations: "Russia is Bulgaria's second most important trade partner. Hungary and Slovakia have close energy partnership with Russia."[71] The Ministry of Economic Development underlines the importance of the inter-company links and joint investment strategies to strengthen cooperation with the CEE on energy efficiency.[72] In the recent years, the representatives of governments and energy companies of Russia and the CEE held a number of conferences on energy, and energy efficiency. For instance, the conference on energy cooperation between Russia and Romania held in June 2011 payed special attention to knowledge

---

66   *Ibid.*

67   Romanova, *op. cit.* note 54, 32.

68   Marc Leonard and Nicu Popescu, "A Power Audit of EU-Russia Relations", European Council on Foreign Relations (November 2007), available at <http://ecfr.eu/content/entry/eu_russia_relations/>.

69   Roadmap, *op. cit.*, note 52, 26.

70   *Ibid.*, 25.

71   Leonard and Popescu, *op. cit.* note 68.

72   "Economicheskoe sotrudnichestvo so stranami Evropy (Economic Cooperation with the European States)", Ministry of Economic Development of the Russian Federation, available at <http://www.economy.gov.ru/minec/activity/sections/foreignEconomicActivity/coop eration/economicEurope>.

exchange on energy efficiency and energy savings.[73] In January 2011, the agreement on the importance of cooperation on energy efficiency had been reached by Hungary and Russia.[74] In September 2011, the Czech Republic and Russia also discussed the benefits of cooperation on energy efficiency within the overall logic of bilateral energy relations.[75] Despite the increased communication between Russia and the CEE on energy efficiency in the recent years, the practical cooperation is rather limited. The actual bilateral and multilateral projects are necessary to drive the cooperation further. In the current political context, any significant progress in EU-Russia energy efficiency cooperation on state level is unlikely. However, in the long term existing bilateral ties and the inter-company links can help to overcome some of the existing tensions.

The Role of Private Sector

Germany and Finland are leading Russian partners on energy saving and energy efficiency cooperation.[76] For instance, the German Energy Agency co-initiated the establishment of the German-Russian Energy Agency (RUDEA) in 2008 (the German Energy Agency owned 40% of the company, while Russia had the remaining 60%).[77] RUDEA contributed the initial EUR 4 million in funds to support the energy efficiency projects mainly through the transfer of German technology to the Russian economy. "German" projects were mainly implemented in Yekaterinburg and the Yekaterinburg oblast.[78] The RUDEA was closed in March 2013; in his final statement the representative of the RUDEA said that during the years of its existence, the agency "opened the door for German companies, wishing to invest in development of energy efficient technology in Russia."[79] Finland and Russia set up the Finnish-Russian

---

73   "Russia and Romania are developing energy cooperation" (14 June 2011), Ministry of Energy of the Russian Federation, available at <http://www.minenergo.gov.ru/press/min_news/7905.html>.

74   "Russia and Hungary are Implementing Cooperation in Buildings, Energy Efficiency and Energy Savings", available at <http://www.energy2020.ru/international_experience/cooperation_between_russia_and_foreign_countries/news159.php>.

75   "Russia and the Czech Republic are Promoting Energy Cooperation" (19 September 2011), available at <http://www.energy2020.ru/international_experience/cooperation_between-russia-and-foreign-countries/news1733.php>.

76   "International Cooperation on Energy Efficiency", available at <http://minenergo.gov.ru/activity/energoeffektivnost/foreign/>.

77   Kononenko, op. cit. note 64, 22.

78   Ibid., 23.

79   "Rossiisko-Nemetskoe energeticheskoe agenstvo RUDEA budet zakryto (Russian-German Energy Agency will be Closed Down)" (March 2013), available at <http://www.smartgrid.ru/novosti/v-rossii/rossiysko-nemeckoe-energeticheskoe-agentstvo-rudea-budet-zakryto/>.

energy club in 2010, which also aims to promote energy efficiency projects in Russia.[80]

In the case of energy efficiency cooperation, the existing interdependence of the CEE states and Russian energy sectors can become an advantage. Following the logic of the externalization some of the regional factors, such as the high levels of dependence on Russian energy supplies and inter-connectedness of the energy systems, create not only energy security risks, but also an opportunity for the CEE states to look into developing and implementing energy efficiency projects together with the Russian partners. The links are already established among the non-state actors in CEE. The Baltic region is especially active in promoting EU-Russia cooperation on sustainability and energy efficiency. Since the 1970s, Russia has exported energy resources to the neighboring states including CEE: "this way firm links prevail between Russia, and Baltic States, Finland, Germany and Poland."[81] Tatiana Romanova provides two examples of such links between companies: Baltic Gas and Baltrel. Baltic Gas is an association of 15 gas companies working on development of an integral natural gas; Baltrel was established in 1998 by 16 electricity companies from Belarus, Denmark, Estonia, Latvia, Lithuania, Norway, Poland, Russia, and Sweden.[82] Baltrel has underlined the importance of energy efficiency as early as 2004.[83] Another example worth mentioning is the Bergen Declaration on a sustainable energy supply around the Baltic which was signed by the Nordic Prime Ministers in 1997. In 1999, the Baltic Sea Region Energy Cooperation (BASREC) has been set to promote the energy cooperation further within more permanent regional forum. BASREC brings together 11 countries: Russia, Germany, Poland, Estonia, Latvia, Lithuania, Sweden, Denmark, Finland, Iceland, Norway, and the European Commission.[84] The decisions were made at the ministerial meetings held on demand (at least once every three years). The daily work of BASREC is carried out through the system of rotating presidencies. A country holding a

---

80   Kononenko, *op. cit.* note 64, 21.

81   Tatiana Romanova, "Energy Dialogue from Strategic Partnership to the Regional Level of the Northern Dimension", in Pami Aalto (ed.), *The EU-Russia Energy Dialogue: Europe's Future Energy Security* (Ashgate, 2008), 77.

82   *Ibid.*, 80.

83   *Consequences of Emissions Trading and Different Allocation Methods to the Functioning of the Power Market*, Final Report of the Emissions Trading Task Force of Baltrel presented in Baltrel Committee Meeting, Riga (4 November 2004).

84   Adrian Gheorge *et al.* "An Energy Security Strategy for Romania: Promoting Energy Efficiency and Renewable Energy Sources", in Adrian Gheorge and Liviu Muresan (eds.), *Energy Security: International and Local Issues, Theoretical Perspectives, and Critical Energy Infrastructure* (Springer, 2011), 403.

presidency is responsible for financing the presidency.[85] During Russian presidency, the energy efficiency has been defined as a priority in energy cooperation in the Baltic region.[86] The Baltic States and Russia are also engaged in the information sharing projects, such as the Baltic Chain Project (Clearing House and Information Network) which focuses on the small-scale energy projects in Estonia, Latvia, Lithuania, Poland, and Russia.[87] The information network allows the participating states to access data on energy efficiency projects in the region.[88] However, successful implementation of energy efficiency initiatives depends on the political will and commitment both in Russia and the EU. Considering the escalation of political tensions in the region, following the Ukrainian crisis and Russian involvement in the Syrian conflict, any significant de-securitization in EU-Russia energy relations in the near future is unlikely. In the long-term, there is an undeniable potential for the cooperation on energy efficiency between Russia and the CEE states. The existing bilateral and inter-company ties could and should be used to broaden EU-Russia cooperation on energy efficiency.

4   Conclusion

The energy sectors of former members of the Eastern bloc are closely interconnected. The Central and Eastern European states are dependent on Russian energy supplies, because the energy infrastructure is often inherited from the Soviet past. In the 1990s, some of the Central European states suffered from the interruptions of Russian supplies.[89] Furthermore, some of the Central European states traditionally see Russia as a threat to their security. The 2004/2007 enlargements changed the context of the EU-Russia energy relations. The Union's dependence on Russian energy supply increased, and the nature of this dependence changed. In the mid-2000s, the EU-Russia energy relations took a turn to increased securitization and politicization. This chapter looks at development of energy efficiency in the EU, and evaluates the

---

85   "About BASREC", available at <http://basrec.net/about-basrec/>.

86   The Russian Presidency of the Council of the Baltic Sea States, Ministry of Foreign Affairs of the Russian Federation (July 2012-June 2013), available at <http://www.cbss-russia.ru/ sbgm_eng.pdf>.

87   Lena Kempmann *et al.*, "Framework Conditions for the Promotion of Energy Efficiency in the Russian Federation", in *Promoting Energy Efficiency, Country Report, The Russian Federation, Energy Series*, No 25, (Geneva, EE21 Project Office, 2005), 63.

88   *Ibid.*

89   Smith, *op.* cit. note 12.

potential for closer cooperation between Russia and the EU on energy efficiency. The analysis of the European and Russian legislation demonstrated that energy efficiency plays an important role in the energy strategies of both the EU and Russia. For the EU, it is one of the ways to reduce dependence on oil and gas (and especially from the external exports); and in case of Russia, the decrease in the energy intensity of the economy can reduce the domestic energy consumption and save energy for export needs.

The Member States which joined the Union in 2004 and 2007 had to integrate a big body of the European legislation into national policies, pushing them for major market reforms. There are some problems in achieving full energy saving potential, including the market failures, funding and investment issues. Despite these problems, new Member States managed to improve the energy efficiency of their economies, and reduces the gap between the EU-15 and new Member States. The implementation of energy efficiency regulations is problematic in Russia as well, due to the nature of the decision-making process, the limitations of the existing legislation, the lack of information, and funding opportunities. These problems – as well as the problems of CEE – are largely rooted in the communist past. Russia has a great potential in decreasing the energy intensity of its economy and is open to cooperation with the EU Member States on technology and knowledge transfer.[90] The experience of the new EU Member States can be especially valuable for Russia, since all of the post-communist states had to overcome similar challenges during transition from the planned economy. Recently, Russia signed a number of memorandums of understanding with different European states on development of energy efficiency. Unfortunately, practical cooperation is rather limited. The cooperation is driven by the existing inter-company links, and the strongest links exist between Russia, the Baltic States, Poland, Finland, and Germany. In the long term, such cooperation based on the mutually beneficial aspect of energy relations might lead to the gradual de-securitization of EU-Russia energy relations.

Bibliography

Belyi, Andrei and Petrichenko, Ksenia. (2012) "Energy Efficiency Regimes: Possibilities and Limits of Best-Practice Transfer between Europe and Russia", in Kuzemko, Caroline, Belyi, Andrei, Goldthau, Andreas, and Keating, Michael F. (eds.), *Dynamics of Energy Governance in Europe and Russia* (Palgrave Macmillan).

---

90   Gusev, *op. cit.* note 60, 8.

Cameron, Fraser. (2010) "The Politics of EU-Russia Energy Relations", *OGEL Collection, Euroconfidential* (EU-Russia Centre, Brussels), 25–38.

Casier, Tom. (2011) "The Rise of Energy to the Top of the EU-Russia Agenda: From Inter-dependence to Dependence", 16(3) *Geopolitics*, 536–552.

Jones, Christopher and Glachant, Jean-Michel. (2010) "Toward a Zero-Carbon Energy Policy in Europe: Defining a Viable Solution", 23(3) *The Electricity Journal*, 15–25.

Garbuzova, Maria and Madlener, Reinhard. (2012) "Towards an Efficient and Low Carbon Economy Post-2012: Opportunities and Barriers for Foreign Companies in the Russian Energy Market", 17(4) *Mitigation and Adaptation Strategies for Global Change*, 387–413.

Garvalho, Maria de Garca. (2012) "EU Energy and Climate Change Strategy", 40(10) *Energy*, 19–22.

Gheorge, Adrian. *et al.* (2011) "An Energy Security Strategy for Romania: Promoting En-ergy Efficiency and Renewable Energy Sources", in Gheorge, Adrian and Muresan, Liviu. (eds.), *Energy Security: International and Local Issues, Theoretical Perspectives, and Critical Energy Infrastructure* (Springer).

Khrushcheva, Olga. (2011) "The Creation of an Energy Security Society as the Way to Decrease Securitization Levels between the EU and Russia in Energy Trade", 7(2) *Journal of Contemporary European Research*, 216–230.

Khrushcheva, Olga and Maltby, Tomas. (2015) "Evolutions and Revolutions in EU-Russia Energy Relations", in Dupont, Claire and Oberthur, Sebastian. (eds.), *Decarboniza-tion in the European Union* (Palgrave Macmillan, Houndmills).

Kononenko, Vadim. (2011) "Forever a Pilot? Assessing the Policy Dialogue and Project-based Cooperation in Energy Efficiency between the EU and Russia", *The Finnish Institute of International Affairs Working Paper* No. 73.

Kuzemko, Caroline, Belyi, Andrei, Goldthau, Andreas, and Keating, Michael F. (eds.) (2012) *Dynamics of Energy Governance in Europe and Russia* (Palgrave Macmillan).

Lavrov, Sergey. (2013) "State of the Union Russia-EU: Prospects for Partnership in the Changing World", 51 *Journal of Common Market Studies Annual Review*, 6–12.

Mankoff, Jeffrey. (2013) "Relationship with the EU", in Wegren, Stephen. (ed.), *Return to Putin's Russia: Past Imperfect, Future Uncertain* (Rowman & Littlefield, Plymouth).

Neuman, Marek. (2010) "EU-Russian Energy Relations after 2004/2007 EU Enlarge-ment: An EU Perspective", 18(3) *Journal of Contemporary European Studies*, 341–360.

Nilsson, Mats. (2007) "Red Light for Green Paper: The EU Policy on Energy Efficiency", 35(1) *Energy Policy*, 540–547.

Paltsev, Sergey. (2014) "Scenarios for Russia's Natural Gas Exports to 2050", 42 *Energy Economics*, 262–270.

Proedrou, Filipos. (2012) *EU Energy Security in the Gas Sector* (Ashgate, Farnham).

Romanova, Tatiana. (2012) "Legal Approximation in Energy: A New Approach for the European Union and Russia", in Kuzemko, Caroline, Belyi, Andrei, Goldthau,

Andreas, and Keating, Michael F. (eds.), *Dynamics of Energy Governance in Europe and Russia* (Palgrave Macmillan).

Romanova, Tatiana. (2008) "Energy Dialogue from Strategic Partnership to the Regional Level of the Northern Dimension", in Aalto, Pami. (ed.), *The EU-Russia Energy Dialogue: Europe's Future Energy Security* (Ashgate).

Smith, Keith. (2004) *Russian Energy Politics in the Baltics, Poland, and Ukraine* (CSIS Press, Washington DC).

Stuggins, Gary, Sharaboroff, Alexander, and Semikolenova, Yadviga. (2013) *Energy Efficiency Learned from Success Stories,* (World Bank Publications), available at <https://openknowledge.worldbank.org/handle/10986/12236>.

Urge-Vorsatz, Diana, Miladinova, Gergana, and Paizs, Laszlo. (2005) "Energy in Transition: From the Iron Curtain to the European Union", 34(15) *Energy Policy*, 2279–2297.

Zhang, Fan. (2013) "The Energy Transition of the Transition Economies: An Empirical Analysis", 40 *Energy Economics*, 679–686.

CHAPTER 17

The European Union's Influence over Media Discourse on Renewable Energy Sources in Russia

Marianna Poberezhskaya

Abstract

This chapter looks at how renewable energy discourse in Russian media has been influenced by the prolonged and intricate EU-Russia energy relationship that was substantially intensified after the EU's Eastern enlargement of 2004. Through the analysis of news articles published by the Internet news agency *RIA Novosti* over 10 years (2004–2013), it has been concluded that in publications referring to renewable energy sources (RES), the frame of "Europeanization" occupies one third of the studied material. Whenever the EU enters the discussion, renewable energy sources are discussed as a solution in combating environmental degradation, a cause for cooperation, or another way to provide energy security. It is argued that, among other factors, the EU plays a positive role in the popularization of RES in Russian media discourse.

Keywords

Russia – media discourse – renewable energy sources – energy security – frame analysis

1   Introduction

On 22 March 2013, the "Roadmap of EU-Russia Energy Cooperation until 2050"[1] was signed in Moscow. The first paragraph of the document emphasizes the mutual importance that Russia and the European Union (EU) represent for each other with regards to their energy security.[2] The Roadmap became a logical continuation of Russia and the EU's significant energy interdependency

---

1   "Roadmap EU-Russia Energy Cooperation until 2050" (2013), available at <http://ec.europa
    .eu/energy/international/russia/doc/2013_03_eu_russia_roadmap_2050_signed.pdf>.
2   *Ibid.*, 3.

and relations which have lasted for several decades.[3] One could state that these relations intensified following the EU's Eastern enlargement in 2004.[4] This was influenced by the accession of countries significantly dependent on Russian fossil fuels. For instance, 36% of the EU's total gas imports came from Russia at the time of the Roadmap,[5] whilst in Poland 62% of its overall gas supply comes from Russia and in the Baltic states this figure reaches up to 100% during the first five years of their accession to the EU.[6] It could be argued that after the 2004 accession, the continuous energy dependency has also influenced the EU's interest in the development of renewable energy sources (RES) in Russia.

Indeed, in the Roadmap, one out of seven sections is solely devoted to RES, which states that EU-Russia cooperation in the renewable sector will benefit both sides. Russia will be able to use the EU's experience for advancing the national legislature in this area as well as receive access to the latest technologies and knowledge in the field. The EU will gain access to a new market for these products and services. Furthermore, since more Russian energy will be available for export, "the availability of Russian [RES], and [...] 'green energy', could contribute to reducing costs for energy, including electricity in the EU."[7]

The Roadmap does not directly commit Russia to any legal steps[8] with regards to improvements in energy efficiency. However, it could be argued that from a normative perspective this agreement forces Russia to accept some EU norms or positions; for instance, the perception of RES as an energy source of the future. Interestingly, the Roadmap states that one of the barriers hindering

---

3   Debra Johnson, "Russia-EU Energy Links", in Debra Johnson and Paul Robinson (eds.), *Perspectives on EU-Russia Relations* (Routledge, Oxon, 2005), 164–182.

4   Surely, the ongoing conflict in Ukraine followed by the EU's economic sanctions against Russia challenged the very nature of the EU-Russia cooperation schemes. Nevertheless, the analytical framework presented in this chapter remains relevant in addition to the legal arrangements which the EU and Russia continue to observe. See the introductory chapter to this volume by Tom Hashimoto and Michael Rhimes.

5   European Commission, "EU-Russia Energy Relations" (2013), available at <http://ec.europa .eu/energy/international/russia/russia_en.htm>.

6   Indra Overland and Heidi Kjarnet, *Russian Renewable Energy: The Potential for International Cooperation* (Ashgate, Surrey, 2009).

7   "Roadmap", *op. cit.* note 1, 22.

8   Russian environmental law as well as the role of law in Russia's environmental policy present an interesting and fascinating area of research, starting with the detention of Greenpeace activists (who tried to prevent the exploitation of the Arctic by Russian companies) and finishing with a high profile case of Khimkinskiy forest (which has resulted in a series of law suits). However, it is very difficult to determine the influence of EU politics over Russian environmental legal activism. A more substantial study is required.

the development of RES in Russia is the "information barrier" which includes a disparity in the levels of general public awareness of the benefits of renewable energy.

Through the application of frame analysis, this chapter explores how EU-Russian energy relations after the 2004 Eastern enlargement have influenced the discourse on RES in Russian mass media. As further demonstrated, one third of the studied news articles dedicated to RES were dominated by EU-related frames. This led to the development of an argument detailing the EU's positive contribution in stimulating the popularization of RES in Russian media space. This can be considered one of the "unexpected results" (or "spillover effects"[9]) of the EU's Eastern expansion and its growing dependency on Russia's energy resources.

The chapter proceeds by contextualizing Russian and EU approaches to the development of RES, a theoretical and methodological discussion, and the presentation of the analyzed data. It concludes with an analytical discussion on the EU's role in framing Russian media discourse on RES.

2   Context

The Russian economy, with its heavy reliance on fossil fuel extraction, produces one of the greatest amount of greenhouse gas (GHG) emissions per unit of GDP in the world. In fact, the carbon intensity of Russia's economy exceeds European countries by 3.8 times[10] and the world average by 2.3 times.[11] This has led to two negative outcomes. Firstly, over-relying on one type of export good has made Russia's "monocultural" economy very vulnerable[12] to changes in global economic climate and fossil fuel market. Secondly, it has made Russia one of the most heavily polluting countries in the world.[13] Both problems could be alleviated through the development of Russian RES which can diversify its energy market and at the same time unlock the country's vast potential for

9   See Carsten Stroby-Jensen, "Neofunctionalist Theories and the Development of European Social and Labour Market Policy", 38(1) *Journal of Common Market Studies* (2000), 71–92.

10   Renat Perelet, Sergey Pegov, and Mikhail Yulkin, "Climate Change: Russia Country Paper", *Human Development Report 2007/2008* (2007), 10.

11   Vyacheslav Kulagin, "Energy Efficiency and Development of Renewables: Russia's Approach", 46 *Russian Analytical Digest* (2008), 2–8, at 2.

12   Sergey Aleksashenko, "Russia's Economic Agenda", 88(1) *International Affairs* (2012), 31–48, at 43.

13   CRS, "Greenhouse Gas Emissions: Perspectives on the Top 20 Emitters and Developed versus Developing Nations", Report for Congress: RL32721 (2008).

economic de-carbonization,[14] benefiting both Russia's economic development and global GHG reduction goals. Russia falls far behind the majority of both developed and developing countries in utilizing renewable energy despite its capacity.[15] For example, all regions in Russia can develop and utilize at least one form of renewable energy, such that it "corresponds to about 30 percent of the country's actual total primary energy supply."[16]

In Russia's 2020 Energy Strategy,[17] RES is seen as a way to ensure energy supplies in regions with "decentralized energy supply systems" (such as the far north of Siberia), or in regions where the centralized energy supplying system does exist but the region experiences "a deficit of energy." An IEA report on Russia's RES states that even though Russia is one of the greatest exporters of fossil fuels in the world, the distribution of the fossil fuels within the country is not equal.[18] This causes energy poor regions to import fossil fuels from those that have such resources in excess. For example, the Arkhangelsk region has to import coal and oil for its industrial needs from other regions in Russia.[19]

Development of RES in Russia is also seen as a solution to environmental problems.[20] Based on the calculations of the technical and economic potential of RES in Russia, Overland and Kjarnet[21] state that RES development could help Russia to pledge much tougher GHG reduction commitments without any economic sacrifice. The reduction of GHG is also important in terms of the EU's environmental interests and EU-Russia relations. For instance, the EU became the key actor negotiating with Russia on signing the Kyoto Protocol. Arguably, the main reason for Russia's eventual ratification of the Protocol in 2004 was

14   A.T. Bagirov and Georgiy Safonov, *Energobezopasnost' i Klimat: Global'nye Vyzovy dlia Rossii (Energy Security and Climate: Global Challenge for Russia)* (Teis, Moscow, 2010); and Overland and Kjarnet, *op. cit.* note 6.

15   Overland and Kjarnet, *op. cit.* note 6, 7; and V.P. Shuiskii, S.S. Alabyan, A.V. Komissarov, and O.V. Morozenkova, "The Global Markets of Renewable Energy Sources and the National Interests of Russia", 21(3) *Studies on Russian Economic Development* (2010), 318–327.

16   International Energy Agency, *Renewables in Russia: From Opportunity to Reality* (OECD/IEA, Paris, 2003), 9.

17   Ministry of Energy of the Russian Federation, "The Summary of the Energy Strategy of Russia for the Period of up to 2020" (2003), available at <http://ec.europa.eu/energy/russia/events/doc/2003_strategy_2020_en.pdf>.

18   International Energy Agency, *op. cit.* note 16, 10; and O.S. Popel', "Vozobnovliaemye Istochniki Energii v Regionakh Rossiyskoy Federatsii: Problemy i Perspecktivy (Renewable Energy Sources in the Regions of Russian Federation: Problems and Prospects)", 5(18) *Energosvet* (2011), 1–7.

19   Barbara Buchner and Silvia Dall'Olio, "Russia and the Kyoto Protocol: The Long Road to Ratification", 12(2) *Transition Studies Review* (2005), 349–382, at 363.

20   Ministry of Energy of the Russian Federation, *op. cit.* note 17.

21   Overland and Kjarnet, *op. cit.* note 6, 5.

the EU's encouragement, by offering Russia various compromises and benefits from signing the agreement.[22]

Besides international climate change mitigation policy, the EU's interest in developing Russian RES concerns the problem of the EU's own level of GHG emissions. Boute and Willems highlight the fact that the "Directive 2009/28/EC on Renewable Energy makes it possible for member states to achieve their targets by importing electricity produced from [RES] from non-EU countries."[23] Thus, EU Member States can contribute towards developing RES in Russia, and in the instances when electricity produced by these energy sources will be consumed by EU states, it can count towards their national strategies for GHG emissions reductions. Overland and Kjarnet's[24] database on all existing international renewable energy projects in Russia demonstrates that the majority (more than 45 projects) are supported by the EU or individual EU Member States (predominately Finland and Sweden).

Overall, in the last decade we can observe an increasing interest in developing RES in Russia. The Russian Energy Strategy aims to increase the share of RES by up to 4.5% by 2020, and this initiative was also supported by the acceptance of a Presidential Decree, the government resolution, as well as the Federal Law on energy efficiency.[25] As has been suggested, one of the possible reasons for Russia's growing interest in RES is the external influence of the EU, where the energy cooperation between Russia and the EU leads to the unexpected outcomes of promoting a more sustainable energy strategy in Russia. These "unexpected outcomes" can be explained through the "spillover" effect.

---

22   Stavros Afionis and Ioannis Chatzopoulos, "Russia's Role in UNFCCC Negotiations Since the Exit of the United States in 2001", 10(1) *International Environmental Agreements-Politics Law and Economics* (2010), 45–63; Liliana Andonova, "The Climate Regime and Domestic Politics: the Case of Russia", 21(4) *Cambridge Review of International Affairs* (2008), 483–504; and Laura Henry and Vladimir Douhovnikoff, "Environmental Issues in Russia", 33 *Annual Review of Environment and Resources* (2008), 437–460.

23   Anatole Boute and Patrick Willems, "RUSTEC: Greening Europe's Energy Supply by Developing Russia's Renewable Energy Potential", 51 *Energy Policy* (2012), 618–629, at 618; see also International Finance Corporation, *Renewable Energy Policy in Russia: Waking the Green Giant* (International Finance Corporation, Washington, 2011).

24   Overland and Kjarnet, *op. cit.* note 6.

25   President of the Russian Federation, "On Some Measures to Improve Energy and Environmental Performance of the Russian Economy", Decree No.889 (4 June 2008); Government of the Russian Federation, Resolution no. 1-r "[O]n the Main Directions for the State Policy to Improve the Energy Efficiency of the Electricity Sector on the Basis of Renewable Energy Sources for the Period up to 2020" (8 January 2009); and Government of the Russian Federation, Federal Law N261-FZ "On Energy Saving and Energy Efficiency" (23 November 2009).

3   Theoretical Approach

The "spillover" effect is a key concept in one of the grand theories aiming to explain the peculiarities of European integration: Neo-Functionalism. This theory, originally introduced by Ernst Haas,[26] suggests that regional integration should be understood in a more complex and broader sense, considering all the processes happening amongst various interest groups and non-state actors. The nature of some of these processes can be described through the concept of "spillover", which refers to a situation when a political step requires a series of additional steps in order to achieve the original goal, therefore, involving in the process more and more political spheres and actors.[27] Stroby-Jensen[28] notes that the "spillover processes" are usually divided into ones which are caused by some technicalities ("functional spillover") and the ones which have a more "political nature" ("political spillover").[29] "Functional spillover" suggests that "projects of integration engender new problems which, in turn, can only be solved by further integration"[30] in a related area. The classic example of the "functional spillover" is the creation of the European Coal and Steel Community, which led to the coordination of EU Member States' energy markets, currency exchange rates and so on.[31] The "political spillover" concerns ideas, interests and ideologies of the interested parties rather than economic or technical necessities: "actors who have an interest in a political initiative in one area support other actors who have an interest in different areas and *vice versa.*"[32]

---

26   Ernst Haas, *The Uniting of Europe: Political, Social and Economic Forces, 1950–1957* (Stanford University Press, Stanford, 1958).

27   Stroby-Jensen, *op. cit.* note 9, 74.

28   *Ibid.*, 74.

29   See also Neil Nugent, *The Government and Politics of the European Union*, 7th edition (Palgrave Macmillan, Basingstoke, 2010).

30   Jeppe Tranholm-Mikkelsen (1991), cited in Catherine Macmillan, "The Application of Neofunctionalism to the Enlargement Process: the Case of Turkey", 47(4) *Journal of Common Market Studies* (2009), 789–809, at 791; and Lisbet Hooghe and Gary Marks, "The Neofunctionalists were (Almost) Right: Politicisation and European Integration", 55 *Constitutional Web Papers* (2005), available at <https://www.wiso.uni-hamburg.de/fileadmin/sowi/politik/governance/ConWeb_Papers/conweb5-2005.pdf>.

31   Mark Pollack, "Theorising EU Policy-Making", in Helen Wallace, Mark Pollack, and Alasdair Young (eds.), *Policy-Making in the European Union* (Oxford University Press, Oxford, 2010), 15–44.

32   Stroby-Jensen, *op. cit.* note 9, 74.

Whilst the concept of "spillover" is usually utilized in order to explain the integration processes happening inside the EU,[33] and in some cases processes connected with the EU's prospective members (enlargement process),[34] in this chapter the idea of "spillover" will be applied to the EU's external relations. It has been hypothesized that EU influence over media discourse on Russian RES is the result of the "spillover effect" of the EU's increasing dependence on Russia's energy market. Hence, even though EU-Russian energy relations have traditionally been discussed with regards to gas trade, it is argued here that EU influence has not been restricted to the development of hydrocarbon trade with Russia. Rather, it also concerns Russia's domestic development of RES, or in this case, with the framing of media discourse on RES in Russia.

4   Methodological Considerations

This study is based on an analysis of news articles published by the Russian international news agency *RIA Novosti*. The information agencies lead the hierarchy of information sources in Russia.[35] *RIA Novosti*, being one of the largest agencies in Russia, informs a wide variety of societal groups (e.g. national and foreign mass media, the presidential administration, Russian central and regional governments, NGOs, business organizations, and ordinary people).[36] The analyzed data was accessed through the *RIA Novosti* website, the search being restricted by the keywords "renewable energy sources" (vozobnovliaemye istochniki energii) and the time-frame 2004–2013. Overall, the search generated 957 news items. The data was narrowed down to a research sample of 100 news articles (by the random selection of 10 news articles from each year).

In order to identify whether there is any EU influence over Russian discourse on RES, this chapter applies the frame analysis to the news on RES published by *RIA Novosti*. "Framing" suggests a representation of the reality, which allows us to underline or undermine certain aspects of it in the (media) text.[37] The methodological approach of frame analysis enables us to read the hidden

---

33   Arne Niemann, *Explaining Decisions in the European Union* (Cambridge University Press, Cambridge, 2006).

34   Macmillan, *op. cit.* note 30.

35   Olessia Koltsova, *News Media and Power in Russia* (Routledge, Oxon, 2006).

36   "O RIA Novosti (About RIA Novosti)", *RIA Novosti* (2012), available at <http://eco.ria.ru/>.

37   Entman (1993), cited in Rens Vliegenthart and Liesbet van Zoonen "Power to the Frame: Bringing Sociology back to Frame Analysis", 26(2) *European Journal of Communication* (2011), 101–115, at 105.

messages ("metamessages")[38] within the text and to unravel how this particular perception of reality was formed. Guo *et al.* state that frame analysis is "particularly useful [in] transnational comparative media research", for instance, in the identification of "which force – globalization or domestication – has more influence on news media's framing of a given issue."[39]

Similarly, this study of media coverage of RES in Russia looks at the influence of three processes, i.e. "Europeanization", "Domestication", and "Internationalization", and each news item was analyzed according to the dominant frames categorized into these three processes. The frame "Europeanization" refers to EU RES or how the EU influences the growth of RES around the world and in Russia. The news articles which were collated under the frame "Domestication" look at RES only from the position of Russia without any references to a foreign actor. Lastly, the frame "Internationalization" is represented by articles bringing in third countries/actors (not Russia or the EU) into the discussion of RES. To identify the central theme in each article, the presence and role of "social players and/or sources"[40] was also studied. Sources were grouped within three categories: "EU", "Domestic", and "International", corresponding to the three frames, contributing to a more precise identification of the dominant (or "central") frame within the studied texts. Further on, within the primary frame "Europeanization", four subsidiary frames were identified: "Energy cooperation", "Environment", "Energy security", and "Economic development" (Figure 17.1).

This algorithm will allow us to test the hypothesis that the EU-Russia energy cooperation after the EU's Eastern enlargement led to a number of unintended "spillover" effects such as the growing influence of the EU over Russian media discourse on RES. The methodology applied in this research study is inspired by Gamson and Modigliani's "media package" approach which sees media texts as a "set of interpretive packages" with the "internal structure" based on "a central organizing idea, or frame."[41] This central idea is often transmitted through linguistic tools such as "metaphor or other symbolic device" used by journalists.[42]

---

38   Deborah Tannen, "Introduction", in Deborah Tannen (ed.), *Framing in Discourse* (Oxford University Press, New York, 1993), 3–13.

39   Lei Guo, Avery Holton, and Sun Ho Jeong, "Transnational Comparative Framing: A Model for an Emerging Framing Approach", 6 *International Journal of Communication* (2012), 1918–1941, at 1919.

40   *Ibid.*

41   William Gamson and Andre Modigliani, "Media Discourse and Public Opinion on Nuclear Power: A Constructionist Approach", 95(1) *American Journal of Sociology* (1989), 1–37, at 3.

42   *Ibid.*

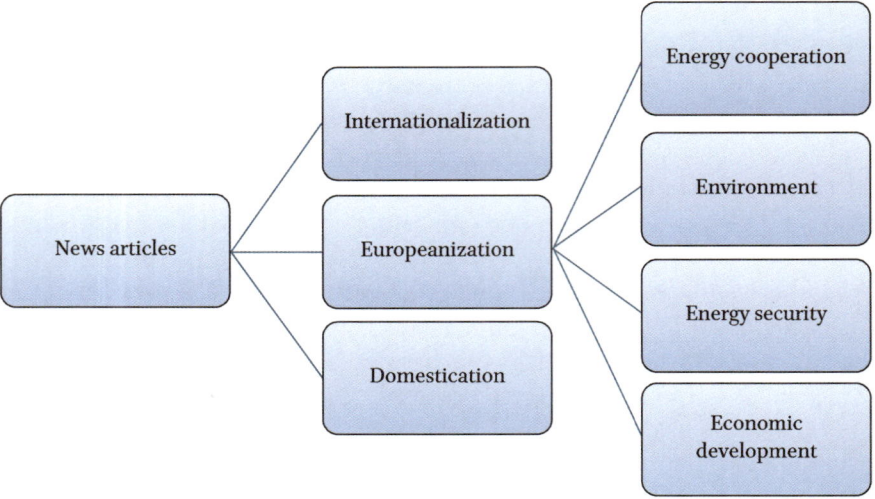

FIGURE 17.1   *Algorithm of frame detection.*

Frames can change and evolve over time due to "structural conditions change",[43] and therefore, the analysis of the way frames have developed in the Russian news illustrates the progression of the EU's role in influencing media discourse.

The single central frame is recognized for one news item (a unit of analysis). However, the same unit can contain multiple subsidiary frames. This frame analysis is text-based, the coding is conducted manually, whilst the frames are determined both deductively and inductively.[44] The deductive approach suggests finding particular frames in the texts, whilst the inductive approach (which is used to define subsidiary frames) suggests "reconstruct[ing] [frames] from clues in news or interview texts",[45] making the frame analysis tailored to this particular study.

---

43   Gaye Tuchman, "Qualitative Methods in the Study of News", in Klaus Jensen and Nicholas Jankowski (eds.), *A Handbook of Qualitative Methodologies for Mass Communication Research* (Routledge, London, 1991), 79–92, at 89; and Petr Kratochvil, Petra Cibulkova, and Michal Benik, "The EU as a 'Framing Actor': Reflections on Media Debates about EU Foreign Policy", 49(2) *Journal of Common Market Studies* (2011), 391–412, at 394.

44   Jorg Matthes, "What's in a Frame? A Content Analysis of Media Framing Studies in the World's Leading Communication Journals", 86(2) *Journalism and Mass Communication Quarterly* (2009), 349–367.

45   Vliegenthart and van Zoonen, *op. cit.* note 37, 106.

5   Analysis

As the analysis demonstrates, a slight majority of the analyzed news items (37%) belongs to the frame "Domestication" (Figure 17.2). In the majority of those cases, RES were only mentioned among other energy sources which all together contribute to Russia's energy security. The articles that did discuss RES concentrated on Russia's great national geographical and technological capabilities. For example, the discussion of "one in the world" orthogonal turbines[46] or Russia's great natural resources which allow it to produce sustainable energy almost in any geographical region.[47] Interestingly, throughout various news items united within this frame, RES are frequently mentioned as a solution to fight "energy poverty"[48] by helping energy poor countries gain access to resources. At the same time, in a few articles, RES are described as a danger to Russia's economic well-being – their development can serve to weaken Russia's position in the international energy market which is supported by

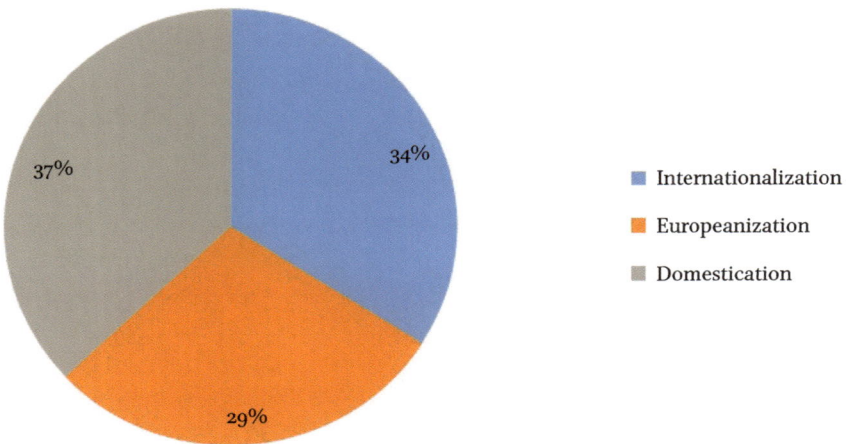

FIGURE 17.2   *Central frames within the analyzed texts.*

---

46   "Posle Desiatiletnego Prostoua v Murmanskoy Oblasti Vvedena v Ekspluatatsiyu Edinstvennaia v Rossii Prilivnaia Elektrostantsiia (After Ten-Year Stoppage the Only Tidal Power Station in Russia was Commissioned in Murmansk Oblast)", *RIA Novosti* (21 December 2004), available at <http://ria.ru/economy/20041221/766492.html#ixzz2SiNgbHvC>.

47   "Medvedev Podpisal Postanovlenie o Stimulirovanii Ispol'zovaniia VIE (Medvedev Signed the Resolution Promoting the RES)", *RIA Novosti* (28 May 2013), available at <http://ria.ru/science/20130528/939904963.html#ixzz2Wq6UfieL>.

48   "Rossiia Gotovit Pozitsii k Sammitu 'Bol'shoy Vos'merki' (Russia is Preparing its Positions for the G-8 Summit)", *RIA Novosti* (4 June 2007), available at <http://ria.ru/analytics/20070604/66629919.html#ixzz2SoOpmNOG>.

the state's fossil fuel industry.[49] The prioritization of state economic welfare over its sustainable development is not new to Russia. Since the time of the Soviet Union, Russia has continuously sacrificed its environmental protection towards economic stabilization and growth.[50] The former special adviser to President Boris Yeltsin on environmental and public health affairs, Alexey Yablokov, argues that Russia's natural resources are abused by the government in order to achieve a certain level of economic development.[51] This statement corresponds with the issues discussed above relating to Russia's dependency on its resources and its reluctant behavior during the international environmental negotiations,[52] which all arguably contributes to the perception of RES as an economic issue rather than an environmental one. Therefore, these factors make them vulnerable to any changes in Russia's economic situation. For instance, economic sanctions imposed by the EU as a result of Russia's involvement in the Ukrainian military conflict, could postpone any environmentally-oriented policy. In this case, RES will be considered only if they bring clear economic benefits.

The second popular frame "Internationalization" (34%) united news items which discussed RES in relation to countries outside of the EU. The prevailing theme in this group is RES as another item of international cooperation through exchange of technologies and experiences in this field,[53] as well as an acknowledgment of global energy interdependence and the fragile nature of global energy security.[54] Within this frame, RES were largely discussed as

---

49   "Al'ternativnaia Energetika Mozhet Oslabit' Pozitsii Rossii na Energorunke (Alternative Energy Might Weaken Russia's Position on the Energy Market)", *RIA Novosti* (16 October 2008), available at <http://ria.ru/economy/20081016/153275297.html#ixzz2SoZRdUAG>.

50   Henry and Douhovnikoff, *op. cit.* note 22; Laura Henry, "Between Transnationalism and State Power: the Development of Russia's Post-Soviet Environmental Movement", 19(5) *Environmental Politics* (2010), 756–781; and Boris Porfiriev, "Environmental Policy in Russia: Economic, Legal and Organisational Issues", 21(2) *Environmental Management* (1997), 147–157.

51   Alexey Yablokov, "The Environment and Politics in Russia", 79 *Russian Analytical Digest* (2010), 2–4, at 3.

52   Marianna Poberezhskaya, *Communicating Climate Change in Russia: State and Propaganda* (Routledge, Abingdon, 2016).

53   "SHOS Namerena Dobivat'sia Ravnopravnogo Mirovogo Finansovogo Poriadka (SCO Intends to Seek Fair Global Financial Order)", *RIA Novosti* (16 June 2009), available at <http://ria.ru/economy/20090616/174529403.html#ixzz2Sok59kaT>.

54   "V Belorussii k 2020 Godu Planiruetsia Sokratit' Ezhegodnoe Potreblenie Gaza s 18,4 do 16,9 mlrd kubometrov (Belarus Plans to Cut Annual Gas Consumption from 18.4 to 16.9 bln Cubic Meters)", *RIA Novosti* (18 August 2004), available at <http://ria.ru/economy/20040818/657280.html#ixzz2SiTkaHSJ>.

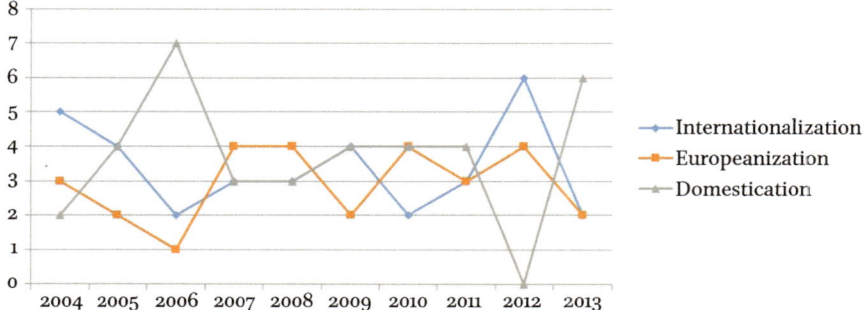

FIGURE 17.3   *Development of the central frames over time.*

a solution to the world's environmental problems, especially, climate change. However, the most frequent and adequate discussion of RES within environmental discourse is presented within the frame of "Europeanization."

As the data shows, the frame "Europeanization" is slightly less popular than the other two. Nevertheless, it does not fall too far behind with 29% of news items included in this category. As Figure 17.3 demonstrates, this frame had a slight increase after the first few years (within the studied time-frame). Overall, it has stayed quite stable, occupying just under one third of the studied articles.

As has been mentioned before, four subsidiary frames were identified here: "Energy cooperation", "Energy security", "Economic Development", and "Environment" (Figure 17.4). The first three subsidiary frames have been discussed and briefly described with regards to the other two primary frames of "Domestication" and "Internationalization." In the case of "Europeanization", the concepts of "Energy cooperation", "Energy security", and "Economic development" were discussed in a similar way to the frames "Domestication" and "Internationalization." For example, the issue of energy security is discussed within the context of EU Member States' vulnerability and their dependency on imported hydrocarbons, and RES capacity to provide a safety net: "we intend to develop our own energy sources in the UK. It will protect us from the shocking measures from the past."[55] The subsidiary frame "Energy cooperation" stresses the EU's willingness and capabilities to cooperate with the rest of the world and particularly with Russia. Cooperation has for instance taken the

---

55   "Samaia Bol'shaia v Mire 'Vetrianaia Ferma' Zarabotala v Velikobritanii (World's Largest Wind Farm Begins to Function in the UK)", *RIA Novosti* (23 September 2010), available at <http://ria.ru/eco/20100923/278618770.html#ixzz2UhVT2lG>.

■ Energy cooperation ■ Environment ■ Energy security ■ Economic development

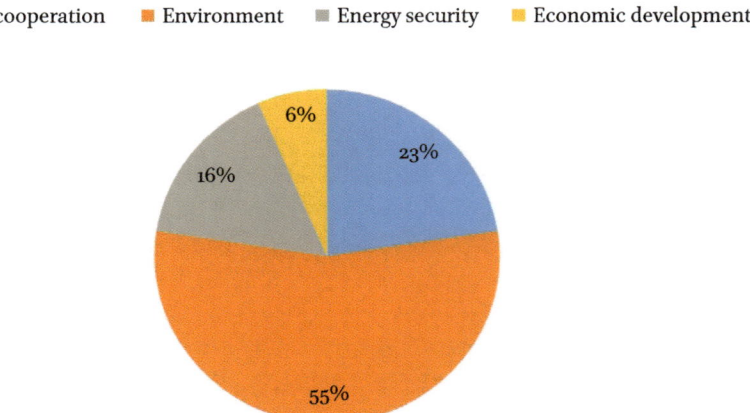

FIGURE 17.4   *Share of the subsidiary frames within the central frame "Europeanization".*

form of investments in the Russian renewable energy sector under the European Neighborhood Partnership Instrument (ENPI) policy[56] or within the framework of European energy forum.[57] The "Economic development" subsidiary
frame can be illustrated by the EU's consideration of the economic aspects of
RES development, which have to be environmentally and financially sound.[58]
Otherwise, the EU Member States should not over-rely on RES since it might
weaken their energy security and bring economic loses.[59] This idea is particularly interesting considering that the EU's energy insecurity is to a great extent
influenced by its reliance on Russia's fossil fuels.

The majority of the news articles within the "Europeanization" frame (55%)
belongs to the subsidiary frame "Environment" in which RES are often accompanied by the adjectives "clean", "environmentally friendly", "economi-
cal", and "sustainable." The EU is presented as a leader in developing RES with

---

56   "Vetropark v Nenetskom AO Budet Sozdan pri Podderzhke Programmy Kolarctic (Wind
      Park in Nenetsk AO will be Built with the Support of the Kolarctic Program)", *RIA Novosti*
      (29 December 2012), available at <http://ria.ru/economy/20121229/916717221.html#ixzz2
      Wpqm7igu>.

57   "V Rime Otkrulsia Energeticheskiy Forum (Energy Forum Opens in Rome)", *RIA Novosti* (26
      April 2004), available at <http://ria.ru/economy/20040426/577361.html#ixzz2SiLi4iBs>.

58   "V Shotlandii Razrabotchiki Prilivnykh Energotekhnologiy Poluchat Premiyu (In Scot-
      land, Developers of Tidal Energy Technologies Receive Award)", *RIA Novosti* (3 December
      2008), available at <http://ria.ru/eco/20081203/156401146.html#ixzz2SoYkoFMg>.

59   "Pol'sha i Chekhiia Namereny Prodvigat' Ideyu Ispol'zovaniia Atomnoy Energii (Poland
      and the Czech Republic Intend to Promote the Idea of Nuclear Power Usage)", *RIA Novosti*
      (16 July 2011), available at <http://ria.ru/eco/20110716/402439774.html#ixzz2VAqCGLdu>.

"the largest share of the investments in RES."[60] A number of articles also discussed some interesting examples about the use or promotion of RES in EU Member States. For example, the British "eco-mosque" which uses energy only produced by RES;[61] Spain's decision to invest EUR 2.5 billion in the renewable energy sector;[62] or Greenpeace's success in achieving a ban on building a new nuclear power station in the UK and popularizing the development of RES.[63]

RES are often discussed as one of the main tools in fighting climate change. Consequently, RES featured in numerous discussions of EU climate change mitigation policy and its "infamous" 20-20-20 strategy aiming to cut EU "polluting emissions by 20 percent by 2020 and increase the share of RES by 20 percent."[64] Notably, the EU's carbon reduction strategy and a goal to achieve a low carbon society by 2050 heavily depend on the development of renewable energy.[65] In addition to the environmental benefits, this change in energy supply should improve EU energy security, decrease energy costs inside EU Member States and will "create new business opportunities" and have "positive impact on employment and GDP growth."[66]

Belyi and Overland in their exploration of Russian and western narratives on RES, argue that "Russia sees sustainable development as an additional

---

60   "Kuliki dlia Anglii i Roditeli dlia Belogo Medvedia (Sandpipers for the UK and Parents for a Polar Bear)", *RIA Novosti* (18 November 2011), available at <http://weekend.ria.ru/resume/20111118/492036878.html#ixzz2VAporvHX>.

61   "V Manchestere Poiavilas 'Ekologichnaia' Mechet' ('Environmental' Mosque Opens in Manchester)", *RIA Novosti* (9 July 2008), available at <http://ria.ru/eco/20080709/113634422 .html#ixzz2Sobi2SrD>.

62   "V Ispanii Vveden Nalog na Pokupku 'Griaznukh' Mashin (Spain Introduces a Tax on Buying 'Dirty' Cars)", *RIA Novosti* (3 August 2007), available at <http://ria.ru/society/20070803/70245882.html#ixzz2SoOZE4jA>.

63   "Greenpeace Dobilsia Peresmotra Britaniey Resheniia o Stroitel'stve Novykh AES (Greenpeace Encourages the UK to Reconsider Decisions on Building New Nuclear Power Stations)", *RIA Novosti* (15 February 2007), available at <http://ria.ru/world/20070215/60782858 .html#ixzz2SoQq42AJ>.

64   "Sammit ES: Dvoynoy Uspekh Shvedskogo Predsedatel'stva (EU Summit: Double Success of Swedish Presidency)", *RIA Novosti* (30 October 2009), available at <http://ria.ru/world/20091030/191355689.html#ixzz2SoiPNUoW>; and "Vesenniy Sammit ES Otkryvaetsia v Bryussele (EU Spring Summit Starts in Brussels)", *RIA Novosti* (8 March 2007), available at <http://ria.ru/politics/20070308/61717804.html#ixzz2SoQaYLLy>.

65   European Commission, "A Roadmap for Moving to a Competitive Low Carbon Economy in 2050", COM (2011) 112 (Commission of the European Communities, Brussels, 2011).

66   European Commission, "Renewable Energy Road Map. Renewable Energies in the 21st Century: Building a More Sustainable Future", COM (2006) 848 (Commission of the European Communities, Brussels, 2007).

opportunity to export more oil and gas, whereas most of the energy-importing states are targeting more ambitious objectives related to climate change."[67] Kulagin shares the same position and argues that "the threat of global warming does not drive Russian policies. Rather, the main impetus for enhancing energy efficiency is to meet rising energy demands at home and maintain, or even increase, export volumes."[68] Indeed, considering Russia's concerns with the "economic cost" of RES development, the EU's strong reliance on increasing the share of sustainable energy sources contrasts as one of the steps in fighting environmental degradation. In Russia, RES discourse is shaped by the "resource-oriented" nature of its economy. However, the EU brings the environmental aspects of RES development into the Russian media discourse. Arguably, it is EU environmental leadership that has the most influence over RES discourse in Russian media where alternative energy sources are pictured as the necessary attribute of the future sustainable society and economy.

The use of RES in Russia is still handicapped despite Russia's potential to develop its renewable energy sector. Shuiskii *et al.* note that the reasons for such a reluctant attitude towards the development of RES are the relative cheapness of energy available from hydrocarbons, the imperfect legal framework, as well as "a lack of data on resources, technologies, and possibilities of RES."[69] Simultaneously, the authors note that this pessimistic situation has started to change. Non-conventional technologies have become more economically competitive due to modifications in ecological requirements for the power stations working on hydrocarbons (getting stricter), as well as the government's increasing interest and willingness to stimulate the development of the renewable energy market in Russia (through the acceptance of necessary laws and decrees).

In addition to these internal changes, some authors argue that the development of Russia's energy efficiency in general and RES in particular, could also be improved from outside by the demonstration of the EU's "good model."[70] Goldthau states that "since existing instruments such as the Dialogue provide no direct lever, the EU has only indirect means to influence changes in domestic Russian policies" such as "encouraging" and "convincing" the Russian government of the benefits of a more sustainable policy.[71] Kratochvil *et al.*

---

67   Andrei Belyi and Indra Overland, "New Narratives on Russian Renewable Energy Policy", *Revue de l'Energie* (2010) No.594, 99–105, at 104.

68   Kulagin, *op. cit.* note 11, 2.

69   Shuiskii *et al. op. cit.* note 15, 326.

70   Peter Richards, "European Practices Offer a Good Model for Russia", 46 *Russian Analytical Digest* (2008), 12–14.

71   Andreas Goldthau, "Improving Russian Energy Efficiency: Next Steps", 46 *Russian Analytical Digest* (2008), 9–11.

support the same idea by claiming that the EU behaves as "an attractive actor" by possessing the "ability to radiate its norms to the outside environment, even though this normative transformation may not be the result of an intentional action of the Union, but rather an unforeseen consequence of its existence."[72] Russia is considered to be quite resistant to EU norms influence.[73] Yet, as this analysis demonstrates, at least in media coverage of RES, the EU can indeed act as a "good model" by demonstrating how RES can serve as a foundation for the state's future environmental policy, energy efficiency, and growing economy.

6   Conclusion

By the use of frame analysis this chapter has explored whether or not we can observe the influence of EU-Russian energy relations since the Eastern enlargement of 2004 over the Russian media discourse on RES. It has been demonstrated that there is a strong presence of the EU in Russian RES media discourse where almost one third of the published material from the studied sample referred to the Union. Furthermore, the majority of the articles in this category discuss RES with regards to EU environmental leadership, the "good" practices of the development of renewables in EU Member States or as another item in international cooperation and in particular energy cooperation between the EU and Russia. The research conducted here does not allow us to confirm the degree to which the EU exercises its power over Russian renewable energy policy. However, it can be said that EU policy on RES and its cooperation with Russia in this field does have significant influence over the media coverage of renewable energy. Hence, the EU does contribute to the popularization of RES in Russia which helps to deal with another problem of Russian RES – the reluctant public attitude or lack of awareness of the issue.[74] This outcome became an "unexpected result" or a "spillover effect" of EU-Russia political relations, and in particular, their intricate and (in some cases) very ambiguous energy policies. Such ambiguity often creates tensions between Russia and the EU's Eastern Member States that are heavily reliant on Russian energy supplies.

---

72   Kratochvil *et al., op. cit.* note 43, 395.

73   Petr Kratochvil, "The Discursive Resistance to EU-Enticement: The Russian Elite and (the Lack of) Europeanization", 60(3) *Europe-Asia Studies* (2008), 397–422.

74   Kseniia Vakhrusheva, "Renewable Energy Globally and in Russia in 2010: When will Russia Commit to Green Energy Possibilities?" (2011), available at <http://bellona.org/news/renewable-energy/2011-01-renewable-energy-globally-and-in-russia-in-2010-when-will-russia-commit-to-green-energy-possibilities>.

Oleg Yanitsky argues that with regards to the Russian environmental policy the "exacerbation of the sometimes difficult relations between Russia and the EU always pushes environmental issues to the sidelines", whilst Russia is in great need of "a strategic dialogue with Europe."[75] These conclusions could also be applied to the development of RES in Russia. Though they are already present in EU-Russia energy dialogue, Russian renewables would significantly benefit from a more active and straightforward cooperative policy between these two political actors, at least through even greater coverage of the EU's positive practices in media discourse.

Bibliography

Afionis, Stavros and Chatzopoulos, Ioannis. (2010) "Russia's Role in UNFCCC Negotiations Since the Exit of the United States in 2001", 10(1) *International Environmental Agreements-Politics Law and Economics*, 45–63.

Aleksashenko, Sergey. (2012) "Russia's Economic Agenda", 88(1) *International Affairs*, 31–48.

Andonova, Liliana. (2008) "The Climate Regime and Domestic Politics: the Case of Russia", 21(4) *Cambridge Review of International Affairs*, 483–504.

Bagirov, A.T. and Safonov, Georgiy. (2010) *Energobezopasnost' i Klimat: Global'nye Vyzovy dlia Rossii (Energy Security and Climate: Global Challenge for Russia)* (Teis, Moscow).

Belyi, Andrei and Overland, Indra. (2010) "New Narratives on Russian Renewable Energy Policy", *Revue de l'Energie* No. 594, 99–105.

Boute, Anatole and Willems, Patrick. (2012) "RUSTEC: Greening Europe's Energy Supply by Developing Russia's Renewable Energy Potential", 51 *Energy Policy*, 618–629.

Buchner, Barbara and Dall'Olio, Silvia. (2005) "Russia and the Kyoto Protocol: The Long Road to Ratification", 12(2) *Transition Studies Review*, 349–382.

Gamson, William and Modigliani, Andre. (1989) "Media Discourse and Public Opinion on Nuclear Power: A Constructionist Approach", 95(1) *American Journal of Sociology*, 1–37.

Goldthau, Andreas. (2008) "Improving Russian Energy Efficiency: Next Steps", 46 *Russian Analytical Digest*, 9–11.

Guo, Lei, Holton, Avery, and Jeong, Sun Ho. (2012) "Transnational Comparative Framing: A Model for an Emerging Framing Approach", 6 *International Journal of Communication*, 1918–1941.

---

75   Oleg Yanitsky, "The Shift of Environmental Debates in Russia", 57(6) *Current Sociology* (2009), 747–766, at 764.

Haas, Ernst. (1958) *The Uniting of Europe: Political, Social and Economic Forces, 1950–1957* (Stanford University Press, Stanford).

Henry, Laura. (2010) "Between Transnationalism and State Power: the Development of Russia's Post-Soviet Environmental Movement", 19(5) *Environmental Politics*, 756–781.

Henry, Laura and Douhovnikoff, Vladimir. (2008) "Environmental Issues in Russia", 33 *Annual Review of Environment and Resources*, 437–460.

Hooghe, Lisbet and Marks, Gary. (2005) "The Neofunctionalists were (Almost) Right: Politicisation and European Integration", 55 *Constitutional Web Papers*, available at <https://www.wiso.uni-hamburg.de/fileadmin/sowi/politik/governance/ConWeb _Papers/conweb5-2005.pdf>.

Johnson, Debra. (2005) "Russia-EU Energy Links", in Johnson, Debra and Robinson, Paul. (eds.), *Perspectives on EU-Russia Relations* (Routledge, Oxon), 164–182.

Koltsova, Olessia. (2006) *News Media and Power in Russia* (Routledge, Oxon).

Kratochvil, Petr. (2008) "The Discursive Resistance to EU-Enticement: The Russian Elite and (the Lack of) Europeanization", 60(3) *Europe-Asia Studies*, 397–422.

Kratochvil, Petr, Cibulkova, Petra, and Benik, Michal. (2011) "The EU as a 'Framing Actor': Reflections on Media Debates about EU Foreign Policy", 49(2) *Journal of Common Market Studies*, 391–412.

Kulagin, Vyacheslav. (2008) "Energy Efficiency and Development of Renewables: Russia's Approach", 46 *Russian Analytical Digest*, 2–8.

Macmillan, Catherine. (2009) "The Application of Neofunctionalism to the Enlargement Process: the Case of Turkey", 47(4) *Journal of Common Market Studies*, 789–809.

Matthes, Jorg. (2009) "What's in a Frame? A Content Analysis of Media Framing Studies in the World's Leading Communication Journals", 86(2) *Journalism and Mass Communication Quarterly*, 349–367.

Niemann, Arne. (2006) *Explaining Decisions in the European Union* (Cambridge University Press, Cambridge).

Nugent, Neil. (2010) *The Government and Politics of the European Union*, 7th edition (Palgrave Macmillan, Basingstoke).

Overland, Indra and Kjarnet, Heidi. (2009) *Russian Renewable Energy: The Potential for International Cooperation* (Ashgate, Surrey).

Perelet, Renat, Pegov, Sergey, and Yulkin, Mikhail. (2007) "Climate Change: Russia Country Paper", *Human Development Report 2007/2008*.

Poberezhskaya, Marianna. (2016) *Communicating Climate Change in Russia: State and Propaganda* (Routledge, Abingdon).

Pollack, Mark. (2010) "Theorising EU Policy-Making", in Wallace, Hellen, Pollack, Mark, and Young, Alasdair. (eds.), *A Policy-Making in the European Union*, (Oxford University Press, Oxford), 15–44.

Popel', O.S. (2011) "Vozobnovliaemye Istochniki Energii v Regionakh Rossiyskoy Federatsii: Problemy i Perspecktivy (Renewable Energy Sources in the Regions of the Russian Federation: Problems and Prospects)", 5(18) *Energosvet*, 1–7.

Porfiriev, Boris. (1997) "Environmental Policy in Russia: Economic, Legal and Organisational Issues", 21(2) *Environmental Management*, 147–157.

Richards, Peter. (2008) "European Practices Offer a Good Model for Russia", 46 *Russian Analytical Digest*, 12–14.

Shuiskii, V.P., Alabyan, S.S., Komissarov, A.V., and Morozenkova, O.V. (2010) "The Global Markets of Renewable Energy Sources and the National Interests of Russia", 21(3) *Studies on Russian Economic Development*, 318–327.

Stroby-Jensen, Carsten. (2000) "Neofunctionalist Theories and the Development of European Social and Labour Market Policy", 38(1) *Journal of Common Market Studies*, 71–92.

Tannen, Deborah. (1993) "Introduction", in Tannen, Deborah. (ed.), *Framing in Discourse* (Oxford University Press, New York), 3–13.

Tuchman, Gaye. (1991) "Qualitative Methods in the Study of News", in Jensen, Klaus and Jankowski, Nicholas. (eds.), *A Handbook of Qualitative Methodologies for Mass Communication Research* (Routledge, London), 79–92.

Vakhrusheva, Kseniia. (2011) "Renewable Energy Globally and in Russia in 2010: When will Russia Commit to Green Energy Possibilities?", available at <http://bellona .org/news/renewable-energy/2011-01-renewable-energy-globally-and-in-russia-in -2010-when-will-russia-commit-to-green-energy-possibilities>.

Vliegenthart, Rens and van Zoonen, Liesbet. (2011) "Power to the Frame: Bringing Sociology back to Frame Analysis", 26(2) *European Journal of Communication*, 101–115.

Yablokov, Alexey. (2010) "The Environment and Politics in Russia", 79 *Russian Analytical Digest*, 2–4.

Yanitsky, Oleg. (2009) "The Shift of Environmental Debates in Russia", 57(6) *Current Sociology*, 747–766.

Index

This index lists items which can be found in a cross-chapter manner, supplementing the keywords presented at the beginning of each chapter. Obvious and overly frequent items in this volume, such as 'Eastern enlargement', 'Europeanization', and 'European Commission', are omitted from the list in order to optimize the usefulness of the index.